Neil Simon on Screen

Neil Simon on Screen

*Adaptations and Original
Scripts for Film
and Television*

PETER SHELLEY

McFarland & Company, Inc., Publishers
Jefferson, North Carolina

Acknowledgments

I offer thanks for their assistance and encouragement
in the writing of this book to Barry Lowe, Catherine Alfred,
Chris Lewis, Kath Perry, Stewart South, and
Lauren Branstetter and the Purple Rose Theatre Company.

LIBRARY OF CONGRESS CATALOGUING-IN-PUBLICATION DATA

Shelley, Peter, 1962–
Neil Simon on screen : adaptations and original scripts for film and
television / Peter Shelley.
p.   cm
Includes bibliographical references and index.

ISBN 978-0-7864-7198-0 (softcover : acid free paper) ∞
ISBN 978-1-4766-1752-7 (ebook)

1. Simon, Neil—Film adaptations.   I. Title.

PS3537.I663Z787 2015   812'.54—dc23   2014050109

BRITISH LIBRARY CATALOGUING DATA ARE AVAILABLE

On the cover: Biltmore Theatre on West 47th Street. Playwright Neil Simon and
director Mike Nichols of *Barefoot in the Park* (1963–1967 Broadway) (Photofest)

Printed in the United States of America

*McFarland & Company, Inc., Publishers
Box 611, Jefferson, North Carolina 28640
www.mcfarlandpub.com*

Table of Contents

❖ Part Three: Television Specials and Adaptations

Preface

I haven't seen many of Neil Simon's plays on stage. I think the first of only three experiences was seeing *Last of the Red Hot Lovers* as a schoolboy, taken by a progressive teacher. The subject of a married man having a mid-life crisis was not something I could relate to, and my strongest memory of the night was the sound of the lapping water during the performance underneath the harbor-side theatre. But I think I must have taken away something else because, as a boy, I began to read Simon's plays. The second production I saw was *Brighton Beach Memoirs* on Broadway during a trip to New York. As a young man of twenty I was considering becoming an actor, so my reaction to seeing Matthew Broderick in the play was, "I could play that part." By the time I came to see the third production, *Chapter Two*, my idea of becoming an actor had been replaced by a greater interest in playwriting. Reading Simon's plays had been part of what I saw as my education in the field, and the wit and rhythms of his dialogue helped me with my own attempts at writing comedy. However, when I saw the movie versions of some of Simon's plays, I was fascinated by the differences between the film and stage productions. In *Chapter Two*, for example, I was impressed by how much better the telephone scenes worked in film than on stage and when acted by the bigger stars (James Caan and Marsha Mason) the film presented. I could understand why Simon wanted his plays filmed, for permanency, since theatre life is so transient, but I could also see the difficulty in the translation. Even as a playwright who appreciates dialogue, I could see how some filmed plays arrived dead on the screen. That's what made me interested in studying the adaptation of Simon plays for film and television, and also his original screenplays and teleplays.

Previous studies of Simon have not dealt much with his film adaptations. In her 1979 book, Edythe M. McGovern makes no reference to them, preferring to write on the earlier plays, up to *Chapter Two*. In his 1983 book, Robert K. Johnson also writes mainly on the plays and only sometimes on the screenplays. There is even less mention of film in Gary Konas' 1997 *Neil Simon: A Casebook* and Susan Koprince's 2002 *Understanding Neil Simon*. The best coverage is perhaps in Jerry Robert's 2003 *The Great American Playwrights on the Screen*, although Simon only gets twelve pages and these are devoted to capsule reviews.

This book, then, is an attempt to provide a study of Simon's work for television and film, as well as of the adaptations of his plays made by others. However, it cannot be considered a complete study because, regrettably, there are some titles I could not access. The biggest regret is the television special *The Trouble with People*, because it is just not available. However, I gathered as much information as possible about it, including the synopsis described in the *New York Times* review. My other big regret is that the screenplay for *Bogart Slept Here*, the film of which was never made, is also not commercially available. Two more absent titles are the French made-for-TV movie of *Rumors* (1992) and the Spanish made-for-TV movie of *They're Playing Our Song*, neither of which is available. Readers may be surprised by the omission of *The Lonely Guy* (1984). This is because although Simon is given screen credit for the adaptation of the book *The Lonely Guy's Book of Life* by Bruce Jay Friedman, the screenplay credit is given to Ed Weinberger and Stan Daniels. This makes it impossible to measure the extent of Simon's contribution. The 1970 to 1975 television series *The Odd Couple* is also not included, since Simon was not associated with it. Additionally, some of Simon's work has not to date been adapted for film and television (see appendix).

For my introduction I have described Simon's writing origins and his work prior to changing from a writer for television to a writer for the theatre. The writer's two memoirs, *Rewrites* and *The Play Goes On*, contain a wealth of biographical material and I have used them, together with other sources, to provide background information on several of the titles discussed.

I have divided the book into three sections: adaptations for film, original screenplays, and television work. The adaptations are by Simon of his plays, with four exceptions. Three of these are adaptions of Simon plays by other screenwriters: *Come Blow Your Horn; Sweet Charity*, for which Simon wrote the Broadway book; and *Star Spangled Girl*. The fourth is an adaptation by Simon of Bruce Jay Friedman's short story for *The Heartbreak Kid*. For each of Simon's films and television projects I have created a separate chapter.

My descriptions of content, critical evaluation and assessment are based on personal viewing of each of the available titles. I have also commented on the source material's adaptation, including what of significance has been cut or moved and what has been added. I have included new, noteworthy (generally funny) lines and new scenes that have a narrative impact or consequence. I describe the "opening up" of the material (generally if the original play was limited to interior settings) and list significant new narrative locations. I also highlight interesting material from the source, including funny lines retained, and make observations on narrative and characterization. I give my opinion on direction and acting performances. I also supply any behind-the-scenes information I can, and give Simon's view of the end product if known.

Titles of films are recorded as presented on screen. An example is *The Out of Towners*, which is often written as *The Out-of-Towners*; even Simon himself refers to it as the latter in his memoir *Rewrites*. When the title is prefaced by "Neil Simon's" the hyphens have been dropped. Each chapter has a cast and crew filmography taken from the actual film. I have advised of any alternative titles that movies are known by. An example is *The Marrying Man*, which is also known as *Too Hot to Handle*. Listings are supplemented by information from the Internet Movie Database, the Turner Classic Movies Web site, and the Internet Theatre Database. The chapters also provide a plot synopsis, the titles of any songs, the filming dates of the production, any location sites, the release or screening date, any publicity taglines, a summary of period and contemporary reviews, details of any Academy Awards or nominations, information about remakes and sequels, and the VHS or DVD availability. The release dates are those for the United States. I have also provided relevant stills where possible.

I hope my study of the film and television work of Neil Simon is as satisfying for my readers as it was for me, and that my book encourages others to seek out and find all that I have found, and more.

Introduction

According to his first memoir, *Rewrites*, Neil Simon's first writing was done around 1942 when he was fifteen years old and still at high school. His older brother Danny had a job as the assistant manager of the boys' clothing department at Abraham and Straus in Brooklyn. The store hired freelance producer/director Ernest Gluckman to put on the annual employees' show with original sketches and songs, which mostly dealt with the life of working in a department store. Danny introduced himself to Gluckman and read him some comic monologues that he and Neil had written. Liking the material and Danny's comic ability, Gluckman hired Danny as an actor and both the Simon brothers to write comedy sketches for the show. They spent two months writing the sketches at nights and on weekends. The work so exhausted Simon that he would sleep through his classes, and as a result he failed an English literature class. On the opening night the audience laughed and gave the actor a standing ovation, so Simon considered the sketches a success. However, he was aware that the material had been designed to amuse the lower-level employees at the expense of the store executives and floor managers.

Around 1946 the Simon brothers landed an audition with CBS radio producer Goodman Ace. The assignment was to write a sketch in which an usherette at Loew's Pitkin Theater reviewed a Joan Crawford movie. They were hired and wrote for radio comics Robert Q. Lewis, Jan Murray, and Phil Foster. They were also introduced to Beckman and Pransky, who booked acts into the many hotels in the Catskill Mountains, a popular holiday destination close to New York City. This allowed the brothers to meet the young, up-and-coming comics of the time, and the older comics who were on their way down, and led to them writing stand-up material for both. The brothers were established as a writing team.

Simon and Danny wrote monologues and special material for stand-up comics such as Buddy Hackett, Phil Silvers, Victor Borge, Milton Berle, Red Buttons, Dick Shawn, Jack E. Leonard, Joey Adams, and many others. They got their first jobs in television on November 24, 1948, on Phil Silver's thirty-minute comedy special *The Arrow Show*. Next was the family game-show *Beat the Clock*, although when they worked specifically on this show is unknown. In 1951 they worked on *The Tallulah Bankhead Show* and in 1952, *The Jackie Gleason Show*. In his *Playboy* interview Simon says that he hated this experience, since he felt Gleason had little respect for writers. The same year the brothers are said to have also worked on *The Red Buttons Show*, though writer Larry Gelbart reports that the Simons replaced him on that show in its second season, in 1953. In his *Playboy* interview Simon said that working on the Buttons show was "no thrill." The year 1952 also saw the brothers join the entertainment staff at Camp Tamiment, located in the Pocono Mountains of Pennsylvania. The shows they wrote for Tamiment were performed live and ran for an hour and a half. These variety shows were presented each weekend of the ten-week summer.

The Tamiment producer, Max Liebman, also hired the Simon brothers for the NBC television variety show *Your Show of Shows*, which Liebman had created for the comic team of Sid Caesar and Imogene Coca. The series ran for four seasons, from January 25, 1950, to June 5, 1954, and was filmed at the International Theatre in New York. Some sources claim that Neil Simon wrote for *Your Shows of Shows* from 1952 to 1954. Others say that he and Danny joined the show near the end of the fourth season in 1954. In his 2006 Kennedy Center Mark Twain Prize for American Humor speech, Carl Reiner claimed that he met Simon in 1951, and that that was the year Simon came to work on the show. In his book *Caesar's Hours*, Sid Caesar writes that the Simons were originally hired for a six-week engagement when Groucho Marx was due to be a guest star on the show. For some reason Marx did not turn up for the appearance, and the Simons were kept on the writing team.

Sources also differ about which writers worked on the shows. In his book Sid Caesar states that the writers were Mel Brooks, Lucille Kallen, and Mel Tolkin, that Joe Stein was brought in for the last two seasons of the show, and that Max Liebman, Caesar and Carl Reiner also contributed to the writing. In his *Playboy* interview Simon said that Liebman was more an editor than a writer. Other sources claim that Caesar's brother David also wrote for the show, although Caesar writes that he was brought in only for the follow-up show, *Caesar's Hour.*

The writers had been selected to provide an amalgamation of talent. Some were good at witticisms, some at physical comedy; others were more erudite. Being a writer on the show was the highest paid job that a television comic writer could get at the time and one every comic aspired to have. Simon said that the writers were highly competitive in a fun way, like children in a family trying to get the attention of Daddy, aka Caesar. They all wanted to be Sid's favorite.

Your Show of Shows performed thirty-nine ninety-minute shows a year. The series' dream run ended when Imogene Coca left for her own show, though her decision to leave was no doubt influenced by her knowledge of the show's steadily declining ratings. Some felt that the Broadway-style revue and satirical comedy of the show was initially appreciated by viewers from affluent urban homes, the only people who could afford to own a television set then. However, as television spread to middle-class Americans, they failed to connect with the show, accounting for the falling ratings. It is thought that middle-class Americans preferred material such as *The Lawrence Welk Show*, which also featured musical numbers and skits and ran for twenty-seven seasons from 1955 to 1982.

Your Show of Shows won the Emmy Award for Best Variety Show in 1952 and 1953, and was nominated for the same award in 1951 and 1954. In 1954, Caesar was nominated for Best Male Star of a Regular Series, Coca was nominated for Best Female Star of a Regular Series, and Carl Reiner was nominated for Best Series Supporting Actor.

There is one sketch that can be identified as having been solely written by the Simon brothers on *Your Show of Shows*. It was called "The Clock" and was broadcast on September 25, 1953. This episode appeared in the compilation of ten sketches entitled *10 from Your Show of Shows*, which was released theatrically in 1973. In the DVD *The Sid Caesar Collection: The 50th Anniversary*, Carl Reiner reports that it was Caesar who came up with the idea of doing a sketch about miniature figures in a clock in the Bavarian town of Bauerhof. Simon says that at the time, he and Danny had been employed to replace Lucille Kallen, who had fallen pregnant. Their workplace was an office on a landing on the staircase of the building. Simon described them as being kept in the hallway, outside the writers' room. The brothers were given the assignment, which helped boost their standing and eventually resulted in them being allowed into the writers' room.

Danny reports that it was his idea that something should go wrong with the clock in the sketch, which has Caesar, Imogene Coca, Carl Reiner and Howard Morris playing mechanical figures who help to strike the clock on the hour. With the aid of a narrator, music and sound effects, the seven-minute sketch first establishes how on the hour the four figures appear and walk in jerky, staccato movement. They congregate in the center of the face of the clock, where there is an anvil on a stand. As Caesar and Reiner strike the anvil with mallets, and Howard Morris blows a wind bellow, Coca ladles water from a pail and then pours into on the anvil. It is the men's striking that announces the hour. The first two hourly strikes goes to plan. However, the third hour's mishap is prefigured by the hands of the clock moving bumpily to the hour position. This time Coca's figure throws the water into Caesar's figure's face, while the other three figures behave as usual. The narrator acknowledges the problem by announcing that the clock must be prepared. The fourth-hour strike has Coca's movement slowed down but again she throws water into Caesar's face.

The narrator tells us that the clock is still not perfect and that a new main spring is given to it. This results in the fifth-hour strike, when the movement of the figures is now accelerated. Coca's figure continues to throw water into Caesar's figure's face, repeatedly, faster than she had done before. The humor comes from the matching of Caesar's striking the anvil and Coca's throwing water into his face. The camera then shakes to indicate that the clock has totally malfunctioned, and the figures stop moving.

The sketch employs a running gag, a technique Simon later used extensively in his plays and screenplays. It also demonstrates the fact that, like drama, comedy requires conflict. The faulty behavior of the clock figures, despite their still allowing the hour to be struck, shows the conflict of seemingly aggressive behavior. The Caesar figure does not retaliate; perhaps this is partly because the figure is not human and therefore is incapable of reacting to the phenomena. Equally, Coca's figure's behavior cannot be classified as intentional aggression, since it is accidental. However, despite this setup, the humor perhaps originates from Caesar being expected to react to having water thrown in his face, although he never does. There is also humor from the choice of music, sound effects, and the silly, mechanical movements of the actors. Additionally, there is a punch line at the end when the narrator asks, "Anybody wanna buy a ten tonne clock?"

Two other sketches that the Simons are said to have written were described and performed by Carl Reiner at the 1996 Writer's Guild Reunion. The first was known as a magician spot. Reiner played a magician who placed a handkerchief over his hand, which had one extended finger. When he removed the handkerchief he revealed that the extended finger had disappeared. In reality all the magician had done was retract the finger into a fist. The slight humor of the spot came from Sid Caesar as the witness to the trick and his naïve wonder in not being able to understand where the finger had gone. The handkerchief bit can be seen as the beginning of the sketch "The Professor on Magic," which aired on September 29, 1951. The bit was continued when Caesar tried to imitate the trick and broke his finger as he attempted to make his finger disappear under the handkerchief.

The second was a spy sketch. Reiner played a spymaster giving instructions to a spy, played by Caesar. He was to carry a cumbersome diamond in a brown paper bag. The diamond was the size of a doorknob. Reiner told Caesar that when he went to Istanbul a man would come up to him and say, "Give me the diamond." However, Reiner told Caesar not to give it to him because, he said, the man asked everybody for their diamonds. Reiner adds that a beautiful blonde woman wearing a tight-fitting satin dress and two long earrings would also go up to Caesar and say to him, "Give me the diamond." Caesar was to give her the diamond. Reiner then told Caesar, "That woman will be me." Caesar asked if it would be Reiner in disguise, and Reiner answered, "No. I'm in disguise now."

The brothers were also credited as writing sketches, and Danny as directing, for a Broadway review entitled *Catch a Star!* The show ran from September 6 to 24, 1955, at the Plymouth Theatre. They also contributed a sketch called "Madame Interpreter" to another Broadway revue, *New Faces of 1956,* which had a lengthy run from June 14 to December 22, 1956, at the Ethel Barrymore Theatre. These productions were presumably long in gestation, since it is said that by 1954 the Simons had broken up as a writing team. Some sources claim this happened in 1956, though in his memoir, *Rewrites,* Simon writes it was 1954.

There had been a perception of imbalance in the brother's professional relationship. The feeling was that Neil was a tagalong, a way for Danny to pick up a second salary. As the dominant and more vocal brother, Danny was assumed to be the more gifted and valuable one. In his 1993 *Inside the Comedy Mind* interview with Alan King, Neil claimed that he was nearly fired when they worked for Phil Silvers because it was thought that he didn't contribute anything. His problem stemmed from shyness. In the 2006 Kennedy Center Mark Twain Award show Carl Reiner spoke of Neil in the *Your Show of Shows* writer's room, saying that he had "the voice of a turtle" and that if he told Reiner a proposed joke, Reiner would repeat it for the room. Reiner claimed that he would preface the joke with "Neil's got it," which he said became a catchphrase in the room. In the King interview Neil said he whispered the jokes to Reiner because he was afraid that the other writers would say they were no good. In the *Biography* episode on Neil, Mel Brooks claimed that Danny also received and voiced his brother's jokes. Brooks also commented that Neil's behavior was atypical for a comedy writer, and he would later reference Neil's reputation as a shy whisperer in his film *My Favourite Year* (1982), which was inspired by his experience of working with Sid Caesar. The character Herb Lee only whispers, until the climax of the narrative, when he speaks out loud.

However, even if Neil was soft-voiced and shy, he still knew what he wanted. He had to end the writing partnership with Danny because he needed his own singular voice. In the *Inside the Comedy Mind* interview, Neil commented that their writing partnership ultimately became too hard because it got in the way of the work, a sentiment also expressed in his later play *Broadway Bound*. It wasn't just that they were siblings. It was more that Danny had a paternal attitude towards his brother. However, despite the brothers' separation as a working team, Neil said everything he knew about comedy he had learned from Danny. This is a claim that Woody Allen has also made about Danny's influence on his own writing. In the *Biography* episode, Neil said he felt tremendous guilt at what he saw as his abandoning Danny. Danny says that although he soon got the job as the head writer on *The Red Buttons Show*, for a long time afterwards he felt lost without his brother.

A differing perception of the brothers' abilities is suggested by the fact that, in 1950, Danny wrote for the *Colgate Comedy Hour* without Neil. Danny was also credited as a writer on *Your Show of Shows* from 1950, before Neil was. Danny wrote solo for *The Imogene Coca Show* in 1954, and some sources also claim that he wrote for *Caesar's Hour* from 1956. He continued to write specifically for television until the early 1980s, while Neil stopped doing so in the late 1950s. Danny also went to Hollywood to become a television director, and directed episodes of television comedy in the 1970s. Like his brother, Danny also wanted to write plays. His sixty-minute play *Trouble-in-Law* was produced on April 8, 1959, on television's *The United States Steel Hour*, but it did not receive good reviews. In addition Danny taught the craft of comedy writing at colleges and universities around the United States and Canada, as well as in London and at several locations in Europe. He also established a private school in Los Angeles.

Producer Max Liebman used Neil but not Danny as one of the adaptation-writing team for a series of live television musical "spectaculars" that were broadcast from 1954 to 1959. These were *Satin and Spurs* (1954), *Best Foot Forward* (1954), *Babes in Toyland* (1954), *A Connecticut Yankee* (1955), *The Chocolate Solider* (1955), *The Merry Widow* (1955), *The Desert Song* (1955), *The Great Waltz* (1955), *The Adventures of Marco Polo* (1956), and *Heidi* (1959). Liebman also used the same writers for the comedy variety special *Promenade* (1955), while for *Dearest Enemy* (1955) Simon got sole credit for the adaptation of the Herbert Fields book of the musical by Richard Rodgers and Lorenz Hart. In the 2006 Kennedy Center Mark Twain Award show, a clip was shown from an undated *Sunday Spectacular Max Liebman Presents* show. The sketch featured in the clip was written by Neil. In it Bert Lahr plays C.H. Kraus, a manufacturer of ladies' garments. Kraus has his secretary, played by Tammy Grimes, running all over Manhattan delivering messages. Tony Randall appears to show Kraus the new telephone system for delivering messages. Grimes dials a client and passes the telephone to Kraus. Although she had been able to hear the client, Kraus cannot, and he tells her to run up to Yonkers and tells Mr. Wilson to talk louder. Lahr then says to the audience as a punchline, "Maybe if he screams I can hear him." Neil is also credited as one of the writers on a short-lived comedy series entitled *Stanley*, which ran from September 24, 1956, to March 11, 1957. The stars of the series were Buddy Hackett and Carol Burnett.

Simon went back to writing for Sid Caesar on *Caesar's Hour* from 1956 to 1957, although there are no sketches that are known to have been written solely by him. The new show was Sid Caesar's follow-up after Imogene Coca decided to leave *Your Show of Shows.* The other writers that stayed on from *Your Show of Shows* were Mel Tolkin, Joe Stein, and Mel Brooks. The new writers brought in for the show were Tony Webster, Aaron Ruben, Phil Sharp, Charles Andrews, Sheldon Keller, Larry Gelbart, Selma Diamond, Mike Stewart, Gary Belkin and Caesar's brother David. Woody Allen is said by some to have joined *Caesar's Hour* in its last year. However, he actually only worked with Caesar on some specials that were made after the show had ended. *Caesar's Hour* had a one-hour running time, and originally it was devised to follow a single story. However, the format was soon changed to sketches, as on *Your Show of Shows,* although some of them ran as long as thirty minutes or more. The show ran for three seasons from September 27, 1954, to May 25, 1957. Nanette Fabray was brought in to replace Imogene Coca for regular female roles.

Caesar's Hour and those associated with it won several Emmy Awards: the show, for Best Series in 1957; Nanette Fabray, for Best Supporting Actress in 1956 and 1957; Caesar, for Best Continuing Performance by a Comedian in a Series in 1957; Carl Reiner, for Best Supporting Actor in 1957 and 1958; and Pat Carroll, for Best Supporting Actress in 1957. The writing team, including Neil, was nominated for Best Comedy Writing for all three years but did not win. Simon may have been awarded an Emmy in 1959 for his contributions to both *Caesar's Hour* and *Your Show of Shows,* although accounts vary.

In the spring of 1957, Neil's agent offered him an opportunity to work with Jerry Lewis on his hour-long *The Jerry Lewis Show.* The show was to be produced and directed by Ernest Glucksman. Neil had previously co-written a television special for Lewis with Mel Tolkin. Since Tolkin was now not available, Lewis asked Simon if he could do this one alone. The job would be in California, which was one of the drawbacks, although Danny had since moved there and now lived in "the Valley." The other drawback was that Neil would have to work with Lewis, whom he described as a "wild, uninhibited lunatic." However, needing the money, he took the job. One sketch he wrote involved Lewis as an inspector from the Department of Safety, looking over a factory for danger areas. The idea was that he walked in wearing an ill-fitting suit and a "Jewish Inspector Clouseau" look on his face, and within seconds he was twisted, mangled, pressed, stomped, and stretched by every machine and moving part he came in touch with. A second sketch also required physical humor, and although Simon couldn't recall the particulars in his memoir, *Rewrites,* he does remember that the end had Lewis falling into a vat of hot oatmeal. Lewis liked what Simon had written for him, but since filming was not to take place for another five weeks, the writer decided to use the time to start the play that he always wanted to write.

By this time, Simon was aged thirty and was frustrated by writing for television. Although he was earning around $1,600 a week, he felt a need to grow as a writer. He didn't want to be working for television for the rest of his life. His agent at William Morris told him it was difficult to get him a film job because all his credits were in television. Simon dreamed of writing for the stage, but he was afraid, especially since two of his television-writer friends had had their plays flop on Broadway, each closing after only three performances. However, on October 15, 1957, he typed the title page of his first play, calling it *One Shoe Off.* This title would be changed twice, first to *The Mating Game,* and then to *Come Blow Your Horn.* In his 2006 Mark Twain Award acceptance

Some of the writing staff on *Caesar's Hour* (circa mid-fifties): from left, front row: Gary Belkin, Sheldon Keller, Neil Simon, Michael Stewart, Mel Tolkin, Mel Brooks and Larry Gelbart (Photofest).

speech Simon said that he had originally called the play *Joan, Ellen, Nancy, and Chips, Who Died*, since he had based it on the members of his family. He says he changed it to *Come Blow Your Horn* after finding the phrase in a children's nursery book.

After the Lewis show was filmed and aired, Simon returned to New York and continued work on the play. It would take him two and half years to write and rewrite, and he completed twenty-seven drafts. During this time he continued to write for television to support his family. He returned to Sid Caesar to write for Caesar's short-lived, thirty-minute, new series, *Sid Caesar Invites You* in 1958. He next joined the writing teams on *The Phil Silvers Show*, aka the *Sgt. Bilko Show*, in 1958 and 1959, and *The Gary Moore Show* in 1959 and 1960. The *Biography* episode says that Simon also wrote for *The Red Buttons Show* at this time, though this cannot be confirmed.

Simon said of Phil Silvers that he had a "facile, sharp-tongued wit." He also said that the scripts written for his show were ten or twelve pages longer than for other comics because Silvers spoke so fast. The episodes that Neil Simon is credited for on *The Phil Silvers Show* are as follows. In season 3 they are "Bilko Presents Kay Kendall," broadcast January 17, 1958, "Bilko's Vacation," broadcast May 23, 1958, and "Bilko's Prize Poodle," broadcast June 6, 1958. In season 4 they are "Gold Fever," broadcast

September 23, 1958, "Bilko the Potato Sack King," broadcast October 15, 1958, "Bilko's Big Woman Hunt," broadcast November 5, 1958, "Bilko and the Medium," broadcast December 22, 1958, "Viva Bilko," broadcast February 11, 1958, "Bilko's Sharpshooter," broadcast February 25, 1959, "Warrant Officer Paparelli," broadcast March 25, 1959, "Bilko's Godson," broadcast April 3, 1959, "Bilko in Outer Space," broadcast June 5, 1959, and "The Weekend Colonel," broadcast June 17, 1959. For all these episodes except one Simon is credited as co-writer with Terry Ryan, the exception being "Bilko vs. Covington," which was broadcast October 22, 1958, and for which Arnie Rosen is also credited. Simon may have been awarded an Emmy in 1959 for his contribution to the series, but this cannot be confirmed. What can be confirmed is that Terry Ryan and Arnie Rosen were awarded the Best Comedy Writing Emmy as part of the team in 1958.

Two sketches can be identified as having been written by Simon for *The Gary Moore Show.* In the 2006 Kennedy Center Mark Twain Prize show, a clip is shown of a Simon sketch that features Carol Burnett and Durward Kirby. She plays a secretary who is called in to take dictation on the ten major points in safety. The running gag of the sketch is how Kirby keeps hurting Burnett out of carelessness. He burns her with a cigarette he stubs out on her hand after she moves the ashtray to him. He knocks her out of her chair with a pointer. He stands on her hand. The sketch is funny because of Burnett's physical comedy, and there are two good lines. After she has been pushed out of the chair, Kirby slaps her face as if to bring her out of unconsciousness and asks her if she is all right. She tells him, "It's the slapping that hurts." When he tries to help her up he tells her he can't get her up, and Burnett says, "Try getting off my hand."

In the 2007 American Masters documentary on Burnett, *A Woman of Character,* she introduces part of the 1959 sketch "Playhouse 90 Seconds." Burnett says it was the first time that she was asked to perform a stunt. In the sketch Burnett and Kirby play Jack and Jill. Jack is in hospital and Jill visits him, asking, "Why'd you have to go up the hill?" The end of the sketch has Jill jumping out the window of the hospital room, after she tells the attending doctor, "I'll just go tumbling after." Moore later became one of the investors in the production of *Come Blow Your Horn.*

The play's development faltered as potential producers and directors came and went. At one point Preston Sturges was interested in directing. His career in Hollywood had ended and he was attempting to go back to Broadway, where he had started. However, after repeatedly failing to get Sturges on the telephone, Simon got the news that he had died of a heart attack. In March 1960 Simon was offered a job as part of the writing staff of a new variety show in California. The money was more than he had ever been offered before. He also had an opportunity to have his play trialed in New York in summer stock. Simon chose his future with the play. There were disappointing audience reactions, more rewrites, director and actor replacements, and an audience member having a heart attack during an out-of-town tryout, but the production eventually came to Broadway. Reviews for the show were mostly good and an early closing was avoided with the help of Noel Coward and Hollywood agent Irving "Swifty" Lazar, who were quoted in the *New York Post*'s Leonard Lyons column as saying that the play was the funniest in New York. It ran for almost two years, and while it was not a big enough hit to justify Simon's taking the chance of leaving television permanently, he left anyway. When Paramount Pictures made a film offer for the play and asked Simon to write the screenplay, he turned them down. He wanted to continue to work in the theatre, not to go to Hollywood. However, he would later write both film and television adaptations of his plays.

Simon went on to have twenty-five original plays and five musicals performed on Broadway. No other American playwright has been as prolific. He won multiple Tony Awards, the Pulitzer Prize for Drama, the Mark Twain Prize for Humor, and a Kennedy Center Honor for Lifetime Achievement. He also owned and operated his own theatre on Broadway for around fifteen years, and the Alvin Theatre was renamed the Neil Simon Theatre in 1983 in his honor. Most of Simon's plays were adapted for film or television. He also wrote original screenplays and specials for television. Neil Simon's name as a successful writer stayed in the public consciousness for the next five decades and remains there today.

PART ONE

Film Adaptations

Come Blow Your Horn (1963)

Paramount Pictures/Essex Productions/Tandem Enterprises.

CREW: Bud Yorkin (Director/Producer), Norman Lear (Producer/Screenplay from the play by Neil Simon), Howard W. Koch (Executive Producer), William H. Daniels (Photography), Frank P. Keller (Editor), Nelson Riddle (Music), Hal Pereira and Roland Anderson (Art Direction), Sam Comer and James Payne (Set Decoration), Edith Head (Costumes), Hickey Freeman (Tony Bill's Suits and Sportswear), After Six Formals (Tony Bill's Formal Clothes), Wembley (Tony Bill's Neckwear), Jack Baker (Choreography), John Carter, Jay Sebring (Hair for Frank Sinatra and Tony Bill), Christine Widmeyer (Hair for Barbara Rush), Gene Shacove (Hair for Jill St. John), Frederic Jones (Hair for Phyllis McGuire), Wally Westmore (Makeup), Howard A. Anderson Co. (Titles). Filmed at Paramount Studios, Los Angeles, California. Color, 112 minutes.

CAST: Frank Sinatra (Alan Baker), Lee J. Cobb (Harry R. Baker), Molly Picon (Mrs. Sophie Baker), Barbara Rush (Connie), Jill St. John (Peggy John), Dan Blocker (Mr. Eckman), Phyllis McGuire (Mrs. Eckman), Tony Bill (Buddy Baker). Uncredited: Phil Arnold (Clothing Store Tailor), R.G. Brown, June Ericson, Carole Evern, Frank Gardner, Shelby Grant, Harvey Johnson, Norman Lear, Lisa Seagram, Elizabeth Thompson (Party Guests), Mary Grace Canfield (Mildred Looking for JFK at Party), Warren Cathcart (Willie the Dry Cleaner), James Cavanaugh (Shoe Salesman), George Davis (Hansom Cab Driver), Vinnie De Carlo (Maxie the Bookie), Herbie Faye (Waiter), Charlotte Fletcher (Manicurist), Frank Hagney, John Indrisano, Hollis Morrison (Taxi Drivers), Dean Martin (the Bum), Jack Nestle (Hampshire House Desk Clerk), Joyce Nizzari (Snow Eskanazi), Eddie Quillan (Elevator Boy), Greta Randall (Tall Girl), George Sawaya, Al Silvani (Bell-Hop), Grady Sutton (Clothing Store Manager), Romo Vincent (Rudy the Barber), Carole Wells (Eunice), Fred Zendar.

SONGS: "Come Blow Your Horn" (lyrics by Sammy Cahn, music by James Van Heusen), Frank Sinatra.

SYNOPSIS: Twenty-one-year-old Buddy Baker leaves the home of his parents, Harry and Sophie, in Yonkers, New York. He moves into the Manhattan apartment of his thirty-nine-year-old brother, Alan, who makes over Buddy into his own image. Alan's girlfriend, Connie, does not like how he sees other women. When he refuses to marry

15

her, she ends their relationship. Alan comes to disapprove of Buddy's new lifestyle and agrees to marry Connie. The married couple tell Buddy the news, as the Baker parents are visiting the apartment. The new extended family all go out to brunch to celebrate.

NOTES: Neil Simon did not do the play's adaptation, and it is interesting to see what screenwriter Norman Lear cuts and what he adds. The screenplay presents the subjects of family and Jewishness and explores the theme of traditional and radical behavior. Simon has admitted to the autobiographical nature of the family presented, with Simon seen as Buddy the aspiring writer and his older brother Danny presented as the womanizing Alan. The latter characterizations are idealized as movie stars for the film version, as will also occur with *Barefoot in the Park*.

The source play is "opened up" with the locations of the Yonkers house, Mrs. Eckman's hotel, a restaurant, a bar, cars, a hansom cab, and the street. The theatrical devices of farce, where unexpected characters arrive with bad timing and others pretend to be someone they are not, comic set pieces and running gags are used. Farce is used for the first appearance of Mrs. Eckman, Mr. Eckman at the foyer of the hotel where Mrs. Eckman is staying, and Alan's appearance at the hotel. There is a repeated gag of the sound of a falling chandelier as a result of Harry's slamming a door in anger. The first time it is used is when Harry exits Alan's apartment, and we hear a chandelier rattle and fall. This pays off Buddy's earlier comment about how at home, Harry's door slamming had caused the chandelier in the foyer to fall down. The gag is repeated later when Harry leaves the apartment a second time and an unseen chandelier is heard to crash.

That Buddy is a Simon-substitute writer is apparent from some lines kept from the play. Harry comments on the letter Buddy wrote him being the only writing he has seen from his son: "Letters you write beautifully. I don't know who's going to buy them but they're terrific." Harry will also make further cracks at Buddy as a writer when he refers to him as Tennessee Williams, when he tells Buddy to write what he wants to say to him in a play, and when he refers to Buddy as the Pulitzer Prize winner.

Lear's new opening scene has some obvious and unfunny attempts at humor, but it also has some genuine wit. Sophie tells Buddy when she is cooking stuffed peppers, "I can't leave the stove. I'm trapped here like an animal." Sophie complains of a back ache and comments, "Khrushchev should have such a back ache." She chides Harry for leaving his newspapers on the dining room table, and he tells her, "They're clean. I had them boiled." She also suggests Harry eat to get over his complaints about Alan, to which Harry responds, "Eat. Some solution. They're looking for you at the United Nations." Lear adds a scene with lines that come from the play, using Harry and Sophie three months after Harry last saw his sons. When he comes home, Sophie asks, "Harry? Is that you?" When we hear the door slam, which has become an action that Harry has repeatedly performed, she adds, "That's you." His apparent refusal to speak to his wife for three months soon ends when Sophie reminds Harry that the day is their forty-third anniversary. Sophie tells him, "I wish you all the happiness in the world," and he replies, "I wish you what you wish me." This leads Sophie to ask, "What did I do that you should say such a thing?"

A new scene in the restaurant has Alan ordering a steak that he holds onto the black eye that the punch from Mr. Eckman has caused. Another addition pays off the steak when the bum outside the restaurant, played in a cameo by Dean Martin, asks for help. The bum tells Alan that he hasn't eaten in two days, and Alan gives him the steak. Martin's saying to the camera, "Why didn't I tell him what I really wanted?" is an even more self-conscious moment than the montage of Sinatra singing the title song. Another new scene has Alan and Connie in the hansom cab, where she asks him why he sees other women. His telling her that he has made sacrifices while seeing Connie for six months implies that he sees the other women to have the sex that he is not having with her.

The scene in which Sophie answers successive telephones in Alan's apartment is a set piece that Lear slightly varies from Simon's play. Director Bud Yorkin adds the business of Sophie hanging up the first telephone when she looks for a pencil to take a message with. This allows for the caller, Mrs. Eckman, to ring again, but on a second telephone, and Lear gives Sophie an additional fifth call to answer. Alan's having multiple telephones with the same line within close proximity to each other is a contrivance that we can let pass. Mrs. Eckman's calling on the second telephone also allows Yorkin to add a silent joke. Sophie gestures to the first phone, where Mrs. Eckman had called before, as if she is still on that line. The sequence retains the idea that Sophie unwittingly gives out confidential information to the wrong person. Additionally there is a running joke of her saying, "No, I'm not kidding," in response to the presumed dis- belief that Alan's mother is answering his telephone. Lear also keeps Simon's payoff line when Alan calls and Sophie says to him, "Did anyone call? The whole world called." Yorkin keeps Simon's payoff, a visual gag. After the repeated business of Sophie not being able to find a pencil, we see Buddy find lots of them in a container with a lift-up lid.

Some of Simon's retained lines are occasionally funny. Buddy gives Sophie a glass of water and asks if she feels better. She tells him, "When did I ever feel better?" Buddy leaves to get Sophie a taxi and she tells him, "Don't rush." Then, aware that he has left the apartment, she says to herself, "Who am I talking to?"

Changes from the play include the name Peggy Evans being changed to Peggy John and Alan's Hollywood friend at the ski resort coming from Paramount and not MGM, presumably since Paramount is the film's producer. In the play the producer was named Oscar Mandheim. In the film he is called Paul Macintosh, perhaps in an effort to angli- cize the character. A line that Connie says to Alan may have been lost because of Sinatra being cast. Alan asks her if she thinks he is good looking, and she tells him, "Oh, god no. You've got just enough things wrong with your face to make you very attractive." The Meltzer account that Alan has lost and tries to win back is changed to a Neiman Marcus account and the salesperson changed to a woman, Mrs. Eckman. The film's sex change of Meltzer to Mrs. Eckman gives Alan one more female love interest to juggle.

The play's conclusion is also different from the film. In the play Connie appears to tell Alan that she is leaving to go to Europe for a job as Miss Automatic Toaster for the Electrical Appliance Dealers of America. Alan asks her not to go and tells her, "I have flung." This recalls his earlier line to her, "I didn't actually start my bachelor fling until late in life. And to tell the truth, I don't know if I'm flung out yet." Alan proposes to Connie, and the play ends with Aunt Gussie at the front door. She is a character repeat- edly spoken of by Harry, although her appearance provides no real plot payoff. The film has Alan present Connie as his wife although we don't see him propose, and introduces the new idea that Buddy is taking over the apartment lease from Julia Merrit. This confirms Buddy's final transformation into Alan's swinger persona, as Buddy repeats a line that we had earlier heard Alan say to Connie on the telephone: "Don't you know you could get arrested for having such a sexy voice?" Aunt Gussie is not in the film.

The Bakers' being Jewish allows them to be presented as stereotypes. The gesture we see Harry use of pinching Alan on the cheek is also used by Alan to Buddy. It may be seen as a European form of intimacy but also is one that signifies an older man's feeling for a younger man. This gesture will be repeated for the film's conclusion, when Harry pinches Alan's cheek to suggest that he has forgiven him now that Alan is a married man. The Bakers' being Jewish also presents them as an oppressive environment that the sons wish to escape from. The opening scene shows how the parents bicker, and this is despite their being unaware that Buddy has left the home.

The play's central theme of radicalism of behavior is demonstrated in Alan's change of Buddy, which recalls the story of Pygmalion in having a guileless character remade into a supposed sophisticate. The Pygmalion motif is referenced in the play, where Alan calls Buddy a Frankenstein, but this is a line not kept for the film. Buddy is shown to be ripe for change since he is infantilized by his parents. Despite the idealized way that his parents see him, Buddy begins as a weak character because he cannot face his father with the idea of wanting to leave home. He writes him a letter instead. Even after Harry reads Buddy's letter, Buddy tell his father that he wants his blessing to live with Alan. Harry's control over Buddy gets a payoff when the six-month trial period Harry suggests is revealed to mean six more months of living with his parents.

Front: Molly Picon and Lee J. Cobb; back: Frank Sinatra and Tony Bill, in a lobby card for *Come Blow Your Horn* (1963).

The comparison made between Buddy and Alan is that Alan has been corrupted and is a "bum." Harry refers to Buddy as a bum after he read's Buddy letter that tells him he wants to move away from home. Buddy is also considered a bum because he doesn't want to work for his father, like Alan. Alan has an apparently weak work ethic because he is more interested in chasing women, but he is also a bum because he is not married at thirty-nine years of age. Alan's womanizing is evident from his juggling the affections of three women—Peggy, Connie and Mrs. Eckman. The film's conclusion also reveals that Alan has been kept by another woman, Julia Merrit, who is not seen in the narrative. His bachelor sexual free-dom is presented in two sly jokes. When Peggy tells him she can't imagine why the pro-ducer from Paramount would want to travel a long way to meet her, Alan looks at her derriere in tight pants to show the reason. When Harry is about to leave Alan's apart-ment, Alan tells him he was just getting ready to go to bed. Harry opens the door and Peggy is there, returning as prearranged for a tryst with Alan. The party sequence has another suggested sex joke in regards to the strip scrabble. We see that a woman has removed five garments for the word "build"; later Alan looks as we hear that she must now remove seven more items for "thyroid."

Alan's relationship with Peggy presents her as dumb and whorish. When Buddy suggests that she could call to check up on the Paramount producers being legitimate, Alan tells him, "She doesn't know how to dial." Peggy being perceived as whorish is implied by her admission that she is "not totally inexperienced." Although she uses this line in reference to her acting experience, Buddy's response, "Alan told me," gives her line a more sexual connotation. In contrast to the easygoing Peggy, Connie is presented as a more traditional woman and somewhat aggressive in her stance, which is perhaps the reason Alan is afraid to commit to her. Connie gives Alan the ultimatum of marrying her or having an affair, which is presumably code for sex. However, her telling him that she is in love with him tells us which option she prefers. This is proven true when Alan chooses the affair and Connie initially refuses the option. Later Connie comes to Alan's apartment with her suitcase to suggest that she will accept the affair after all. It is then that he tells her that he loves her but he cannot immediately marry her as she desires. She then tells him that their relationship is over and she leaves. This suggests that Con-nie may think she can be happy just having an affair with Alan, but then realizes that it is not enough to satisfy her emotionally.

Alan seems to be independent, however his independence is ambiguous. After Buddy learns that Alan has broken up with Connie, Buddy comments that Alan needs her. Alan tells Buddy, "I don't need anybody." Interestingly, this is not Simon's line, but Lear's. However, Alan will change his mind about needing Connie, after his fight with Buddy at the party. The fight is revealing because it has Buddy telling Alan, "You don't belong here. I'm just starting my fling. You're flung." Buddy's comment draws the dis-tinction between the ages of the two brothers, and perhaps it is a sign of Alan's maturity that leads him to now agree to marry Connie. The film's conclusion also comments on Alan's former state of independence. It reveals that he has won the Copeland account that Harry had long desired, which shows that Alan still wants to work for his father. Additionally, the reveal that Alan has been leasing his apartment from Julia Merrit pres-ents him as being less independent than imagined.

The influence on Buddy of Alan shows first in his changes to his younger brother's exterior. He changes his wardrobe so that Buddy appears more hip than their traditional and "square" parents. Alan encourages Buddy to walk against traffic lights and through cars in traffic, and at one point Alan leads Buddy to walk through the doors of a taxi. Alan also has Buddy drink martinis rather than the scotch and ginger ale he previously preferred. Buddy being drunk gives him the courage to have a date with Peggy, although Peggy's being an implied prostitute makes the "date" easier. For Alan to arrange the date presents him as pimping, and it is worse since he lies to Peggy about whom she is to meet, telling her that Buddy is the Paramount producer. He somehow makes her complicit in her own humiliation due to her wanting to be discovered.

The plot point of Buddy's initial declining of the date because he wants to watch a television program on the United Nations is paid off when we see how Buddy succumbs to Peggy's advances as they watch television together. Buddy's smoking on the date also seems to imitate Alan, although we never see Alan smoke in the film. Buddy's coughing as he smokes suggests that he is unused to the behavior, one that we see him soon abandon. Buddy's initial fear of Peggy suggests that he is a virgin. However, there is dubious humor from seeing a sexually aggressive woman coming on to a fearful, virginal younger man. Why Buddy is afraid of Peggy is an interesting question, but it is easily answered when he succumbs to her advances. When she asks him, "Is there anything you would like me to do?" the pause that Yorkin gives Buddy implies that Peggy is offering sexual favors. This point is furthered when she offers to "massage his think muscle." Yorkin has Peggy rest Buddy's head on her chest as she massages his head, and her comment, "I know how to get that tenseness right out of you," implies that they are to have sex. Yorkin shows their feet as they watch television, and Buddy's feet fall one by one onto Peggy's feet, after we have seen her kiss him, implying Buddy's acquiescence to Peggy's advances. Yorkin then shows a cannon firing on the television screen, to suggest an orgasm.

The implied seduction by Peggy allows Buddy to initiate his further change, in which Buddy uses Alan's drycleaner, his bookmaker, his barber, manicurist and shoeshiner. Buddy soon transforms into a copy of Alan, and worse, does it better than Alan. This is evident when Buddy has a date with the Tall Girl, a woman Alan does not know. Buddy also lies to copy Alan's behavior, since we see him lie many times. Buddy's superseding Alan is highlighted at the party, during which the excesses of behavior are disapproved of by Alan. He calls Buddy a "bum" and Buddy accuses Alan of acting like his father. The use of "bum" also gets a twist when Sophie refers to herself as one to Harry after she moves into the apartment.

Harry's oppressive demands on his sons and his easy disapproval climax in the film when we see that Sophie has left him. The importance of her connection to her sons is expressed by her seeming choice of them over her husband. However, even after the family is seemingly reconciled over Alan's marriage to Connie, the narrative ends with a question. We see a portrait of the five Bakers, recalling the family portrait of the Bakers in the opening credits, only now Connie is added. However, Yorkin implies that the conclusive image is not a resolution of the conflicts by putting a question mark after his "The End" title. This idea of unresolved conflict is prefigured by Buddy's not immediately joining his family to celebrate the marriage. Rather he is on the telephone with Julia Merrit to secure his place in the apartment.

The film's stage origins are often evident from the filmic choices made. Bud Yorkin does not use any close-ups, so that the long shots recall a filmed stage show, and scenes have a long running time, which also makes them seen more like a play. Yorkin uses intercutting to break up this perception. Examples are intercuts between the scene between Peggy and Buddy, with first Alan at Mrs. Eckman's Hampshire House hotel room, and then Alan and Connie at the restaurant and later in the hansom cab. Yorkin also intercuts the long scene between Buddy and Peggy that includes Harry's arrival, with the scenes between Alan and Connie. The set of Alan's apartment where most of the action takes place also reads as a stage, although here it is enormous and also populated with artwork. The size and trimmings may seem like a Hollywood contrivance, but this very point is raised in the narrative, since Alan is revealed to be a kept man.

Yorkin uses some visual gags. He scores a laugh from Alan's tumble into the lift after he is punched by Mr. Eckman, with Alan on the floor and a raised finger seen as he tells the lift operator, "Down please." He repeats the cinematic conceit of having the camera inside a refrigerator that is opened so we get the point of view of the contents. The first time this is done, he lets the screen go black as the door is closed, before the door is opened again. Mrs. Eckman crushes Alan's foot under her shoe as he lies to her about breaking their date. Connie arrives in a second lift just as Mrs. Eckman leaves in the first. Alan steals a taxi from another man outside the apartment building by throwing coins on the ground so that the man thinks that they are *his.* The man's stopping to retrieve the coins allows Alan and Buddy to take the taxi. After Harry leaves the apartment building in the rain in a taxi, Connie arrives in her car. Yorkin has Alan kiss Mrs. Eckman and see Mr. Eckman as he continues to kiss as a repeat of the scene in the lift when Alan kissed Peggy and looked out into the hallway, still kissing her, when the lift doors open.

Yorkin's use of score is sometimes intrusive, and the sequence of Sinatra singing the title song comes across as contextually odd. This is because it is the only musical sequence in the film and the only time that fast motion is employed. There are other odd choices. The party scene has a moment when we see Buddy kissing Eunice; she appears to be participating in the kiss, but then she slaps him. Yorkin scores an unintentional laugh when he makes the party go quiet after Alan slaps Buddy. There is odd spotlighting for the interior of the hansom cab that Alan and Connie ride in and also for the interior of her car when they later have a conversation.

None of the Broadway cast repeated their roles for the film, which is a shame because the film performances are uneven. As Buddy, Tony Bill over-gesticulates as if he is signaling to the back row, but at least he doesn't yell as Lee J. Cobb does as Harry. Although Cobb's yelling may have narrative context, it still reads as being overblown and theatrical. Thankfully, in the leading role of Alan, Frank Sinatra uses a light touch and gives a realistic and funny performance, even doing an impersonation of JFK in the party scene. He occasionally mugs, for example when he pretends to Mr. Eckman that he wears contact lenses. Sinatra also yells in anger towards Buddy, although this is presumably done to imitate Lee J. Cobb once Alan becomes disapproving of his brother.

In his memoir, *Rewrites,* Simon says that he was not pleased with the film, which he considered to have been turned into a vehicle for Sinatra. Simon describes the film as a "ring-a-ding-ding pseudo-hip Hollywood comedy that had more glitz than wit."

Maureen Stapleton had been offered the role of Sophie Baker. She turned it down because she did not want to play the mother of Sinatra, since in real life she was ten years younger than he was. The actress would go on to appear in the film version of Simon's play *Plaza Suite.* Lee J. Cobb presumably did not have this same fear, since he played Sinatra's father while only four years older than Sinatra.

In *His Way: The Unauthorized Biography of Frank Sinatra,* author Kitty Kelley says that Phyllis McGuire was cast as Mrs. Eckman by Sinatra because she was the girlfriend of gangster Sam Giancana. Kelley also says that Giancana often visited the set. She also claims that Sinatra tried to cast Tommy Sands, the husband of his daughter Nancy, in the film in an unknown part. Since Sands knew that the producers and director did not want him, he turned down the opportunity. In Tony Bill's autobiography, *Movie Speak: How to Talk Like You Belong on a Film Set,* he tells the story of how Sinatra was cast in the film. Sinatra was said to be the biggest star in the world at the time, and Bud Yorkin and Norman Lear were a fledgling director and producer team. To get Sinatra to read the script they are said to have delivered a comfortable leather armchair, a reading lamp, and a bottle of Jack Daniels with the script. Since the star had a great sense of humor and an appreciation for audacity, this tactic helped to score his commitment.

In her book on Simon, *A Critical Study,* Edythe asserts that Harry's being a wax fruit manufacturer is a metaphor for his character's rigidity. She also points out that for Alan to give Buddy Peggy as a gift prefigures the hooker given as a gift to Marvin by his brother Harry in *California Suite.* In the book, *Hollywood in the Sixties,* John Baxter writes of a moment that does not appear in the film. Baxter describes Buddy after the party unrolling a collapsible bed to find a befuddle guest inside, with trombone, and also finding another guest with a half-gallon of tomato juice under his arm pulling back a blind and recoiling with a hoarse cry of agony from the light.

RELEASE: June 5, 1963, with the taglines, "Based on Neil Simon's Smash Broadway Comedy," "I tell ya, chum ... laughs it is!" "Twice as Frank as he ever was in one of his all time swingers! The crackling comedy that had the world busting with laughter!" and "Little boy blue ... come blow your horn ... there's chicks in the penthouse from sunset till morn!!" One of the posters features Sinatra seated on a pillow, holding a horn in his mouth. He is surrounded by Barbara Rush, Phyllis McGuire and Jill St. John. Since the women are all touching him, his blowing into a horn in reaction to their attention has an apparent sexual connotation.

REVIEWS: Mixed reaction from *Variety,* Daniel O'Brien in his book *The Frank Sinatra Film Guide* and John Douglas Eames in *The Paramount Story.* In the *New York Times* Bosley Crowther wrote that the filmmakers and Sinatra had really butchered the play in the garish screen version. He complained of its "dullness, lack of pace in the direction and clumsy performances."

AWARDS: Academy Award nomination for Best Art Direction/Set Decoration.

REMAKE: The film was remade as a German made-for-TV movie in 1970.

DVD: DVD and Blu-ray released by Olive Films on March 27, 2012.

Barefoot in the Park (1967)

Paramount Pictures/Hal Wallis Production/Nancy Enterprises.

CREW: Gene Saks (Director), Hal B. Wallis (Producer), Paul Nathan (Associate Producer), Joseph H. Hazen (uncredited Executive Producer), Neil Simon (Screenplay, based on his play/uncredited Associate Producer), Joseph LaShelle (Photography), William Lyon (Editor), Neal Hefti (Music), Hal Pereira and Walter Tyler (Art Direction), Robert Benton and Arthur Krams (Set Decoration), Edith Head (Costumes), Wally Westmore (Makeup), Nellie Manley (Hair), Paul K. Lerpac (Special Photographic Effects). Color, 101 minutes. Filmed from November 1966 to January 1967 in New York.

CAST: Robert Redford (Paul Bratter), Jane Fonda (Corie Bratter), Charles Boyer (Victor Velasco), Mildred Natwick (Ethel Banks), Herbert Edelman (Harry Pepper), Mabel Albertson (Aunt Harriet), Fritz Feld (Kishama, Restaurant Proprietor), James F. Stone (Delivery Man), Frank (Ted Hartley). Uncredited: Billie Bird (Drunken Neighbor), Paul E. Burns (Bum in Park), John Indrisano (Policeman with Drunk), Doris Roberts (Hotel Maid).

SONGS: "Barefoot in the Park" (music by Neal Hefti, lyrics by Johnny Mercer), opening and end credits; "Shama Shama," band at the Four Winds Restaurant, with Jane Fonda and Robert Redford.

SYNOPSIS: After honeymooning in the Plaza Hotel, newlyweds Paul and Corie Bratter move into a five-floor walk-up apartment at 49 West 10th Street in New York. Paul is twenty-six and a lawyer and Corie is to be a housewife. Corie arranges for the couple and her mother, Ethel Banks, to have dinner with their upstairs neighbor, Victor Velasco, at the Four Winds restaurant on Staten Island. The night is a disaster, and Corie is so disappointed with Paul that she asks for a divorce. Having caught a cold, Paul gets drunk and goes barefoot in the Washington Square Park. Corie finds him and the couple go home to reconcile.

NOTES: Unlike for *Come Blow Your Horn*, Simon did the screenplay adaptation of his own play. The film's themes reflect those of *Come Blow Your Horn*—the importance of family and marriage, and conservatism versus a radical lifestyle. It also presents a female protagonist as opposed to the male protagonists of *Come Blow Your Horn*. The autobiographical element is Simon having used the beginning of his first marriage for the married couple here, with the beautiful Jane Fonda and Robert Redford presented as idealized versions of the Simons.

Simon "opens up" the play by adding locations such as the street for the horse-drawn carriage ride under the opening credits, the Plaza Hotel, the bus stop on the street near the apartment, the ferry ride to Staten Island, the car drive to the Four Winds restaurant, the interior of the restaurant, the scene on the stoop when Ethel tumbles down the stairs, Central Park, and the climax on the rooftop of the apartment building. We also see the ladder that leads to Victor's apartment, which is spoken of but not seen in the play.

Simon uses two running gags: uncollected newspapers being left by the bellboy outside the Bratters' honeymoon suite over five days, and the apartment as a five-flight walk-up and people out of breath when they get to the top. The first gag is commented on by a hotel a maid who says to the bus boy, "Forget it. They're never coming out." The implication is that the couple have spent five days having sex, although they could be doing other things in their room. The latter gag is added to with the furniture delivery from Bloomingdale's and Ethel's surprise visit. The wheeze of the delivery man gets a laugh in his inability to speak, and Corie's line after he leaves, retained from the play, is a nice button. She tells Harry, "That's a shame giving a job like that to an old man."

Theatrical devices are also employed, such as characters speaking to themselves, and farce. The most farcical moment is visual and retained from the play, in the way Paul carries Ethel back into the apartment after their dinner at the restaurant and the climb up the five stair flights. Another farcical touch is that Paul knocks over a collection of tuna cans in the hallway. This knocking-over gag is also repeated for Ethel to do the

Mixed reactions to news of a blind date. From left: Victor Velasco (Charles Boyer), Ethel Banks (Mildred Natwick), Corie Bratter (Jane Fonda) and Paul Bratter (Robert Redford) in a still for *Barefoot in the Park* (1967).

same unintentionally, with her apology adding humor to the moment. A change Simon makes presents the moment when Paul exits to go to the park and Ethel enters more theatrical; in the play Paul has a brief exchange with Ethel before he leaves. However, there are other retained moments from the play that work. These are Paul's advance to get a drink being interpreted by Harry as a threat and Harry retreating in fear, and Ethel flipping a peanut back and forward in her hands before popping it into her mouth in the bar scene with Corie.

The screenplay provides some new scenes, and characters, such as Frank and Harriet, that are only spoken of in the play but shown here. Other new scenes have funny elements. Corie is in the bedroom measuring for the bed and says, "The bed is six feet long and the room is five and half feet and I'm in big trouble." Harriet is seen in her car with Ethel outside the apartment. Harriet comments that Corie as a young bride is probably dying for her advice, and Ethel replies, "Not Corie. She gives her own advice." Paul witnesses a drunken neighbor meeting a policeman at her door. The woman states, "Drunk again. I'll take care of him," and pulls the policeman into her apartment. This defies the assumption that it is the drunk in plain clothes who lives with the woman, and the moment helps to pay off Paul's later speech to Corie about the "weirdos" that live in the building. Ethel answers Corie's telephone call to confirm their dinner, giving Ethel a laugh line in her thrice-repeated, "At two o'clock in the morning." There is also a funny new scene in which Ethel falls down the stairs on the stoop due to slipping on ice, and a new scene in a bar with Ethel and Corie in which Ethel is shown to be drinking ouzo and now able to pop a peanut into her mouth the way she was unable to do previously with the knichi.

Simon also adds three new scenes without dialogue: on the ferry, where Victor and Corie play with the telescope; at the bus stop, where we see Paul alight; and Harry being frightened by the telephone ringing as soon as he has fixed it. The film ends with two new moments, as first a crowd in the street, and then Ethel and Victor, react to Paul and Corie's kissing on the rooftop.

The funny word "schlurp" is retained from the play and is used as the suggestion Corie makes to Harry Pepper as to how to drink some water from a tap when she has no glass. There are also funny retained lines. Harry hears that the delivery man with Corie's furniture have arrived downstairs, and he says, "I don't want to see this." Of course this refers to the anticipated anguish of the men climbing the five flights, carrying furniture. Corie tells Paul that the stoop doesn't count as another flight to be climbed, and he replies, "It may look like a stoop but it climbs like a flight." He tells Ethel that to sleep in the bed in their small bedroom, "We have to turn in unison." Corie accuses him of being a watcher and he replies, "It was a little bit harder to watch what you did than it was for you to do what I was watching." Corie tells Paul that she is going to get a dog, and he says to himself, "He'll take one look at those stairs and go right for her throat." Ethel sees Corie vigorously shaking a boxed present, and when Corie asks what it is, Ethel tells her, "I think it's a broken clock." When Corie asks whether the coffee pot comes with directions, Ethel tells her, "If I'd known about this kitchen it would have come with hot coffee." Corie tells her mother about her time at the Plaza Hotel and asks, "Do you know what happened to me?" to which Ethel replies, "I promised myself I wouldn't ask." Ethel panics when she has to climb up the ladder to get to Victor's apartment and tells Corie, "You should have told me about this. I would have gone into training." When Ethel is not able to get out of the floor-pillow in Victor's apartment without Paul's help, she says, "It won't let go of me." Ethel, wearing Victor's robe, asks him where her clothes are and he produces a cleaning ticket, to which she says, "I'm sure I wore more than that." That the dinner at the Four Winds restaurant makes all those who have eaten it unable to make a fist is another funny idea.

Simon's changes to lines from the play include the comment made when Paul catches Victor giving Corie a boost to turn on the radiator. In the play Victor says to Corie, "I thought you said he works during the day," while in the film, Corie tells Paul, "We were just warming up the apartment," which gives the moment a more overt sexual connotation. The addition of the park scene provides a major change from the play, in which Paul returns drunk to the apartment. In the screenplay Corie goes looking for him and Paul is first heard laughing before he is seen by her. The scene has Paul demonstrate his drunkenness by stating that he doesn't need a coat, a payoff of his earlier need to wear gloves. He also is shown to be barefoot, dancing and jumping over a bench. A nice touch is that Corie picks up Paul's shoes and he has them on again when the couple arrive back in the apartment.

The narrative here differentiates between the conservative Paul and the radical Corie. That Paul is a lawyer cements his conservatism, although Corie's role as housewife also gives her a semblance of conservatism. Presumably a case of opposites attracting, it is the couple's differences in attitude that create the conflict that eventually threatens to end their relationship. The conclusion sees each approximate a little of the other's behavior to come together again. Paul shows Corie that he can walk barefoot in the park, and she is both afraid of and thankful for this.

Paul's conservatism is also highlighted in his criticisms of the state of the apartment on the night they move in. It is also telling that he calls Victor a "nut" and also an "old nut." Paul is seemingly presented as a coward when he sends Corie out to investigate the noise they hear, which is revealed to be Victor breaking into the apartment. Later, Corie also call him a coward for not wanting to talk to her about their marriage crisis. The idea of Paul's weakness in not investigating the noise is somewhat lessened by how seemingly harmless Victor is shown to be, both as burglar and as a sexual threat to Corie. However, there is an underlying dishonesty about Victor, who has been locked out of his apartment for not paying rent for four months, although he describes himself as a "thoroughly nice fellow." The narrative explores this perception by later seeming to put Ethel at risk, and Victor's impulsiveness is paralleled with Corie's, as Paul's conservatism is paralleled with Ethel's. Both couples appear to be mismatched but ultimately are revealed to be compatible. The conservatism of Paul is also seen in his nibbling the knichi, in his insistence on wearing gloves when Victor doesn't wear a coat to go to Staten Island, in his not joining in when Corie and Victor play with the telescope on the ferry, in his embarrassed reaction to Mushka's belly dance, and in his refusal to dance with Corie at the restaurant.

Corie's radicalism is expressed in what can be viewed as inappropriate social behavior. She kisses Paul in public and tells him that if the honeymoon doesn't work that they should kill each other rather than divorce. She is emotional and somewhat clingy, so that Paul has to pry his hand from her grip in order to sign the hotel register. Her emotional and physical neediness for Paul is continued with the idea that she meets him at the bus stop because she can't wait for him to climb the stairs to get home. Corie grabs Paul in a crowed elevator and embarrasses him when they get out by announcing, "Mr. Adams, I hope you realize I'm only fifteen years old," justifying herself by saying that the other people in the hotel are "stuffy." She further embarrasses Paul when she appears in the hallway wearing only a pajama top when he attempts to leave for work, threatening to take that off unless he gives her a real goodbye kiss. In a second crowded elevator gag she pretends to be a prostitute, saying to Paul, "Thank you, Mr. Dooley. Next time you're in New York just call me up." Corie's sexual voracity is demonstrated when she shows Paul a black lace nightgown that she plans to wear for him and when she becomes hurt when Paul becomes preoccupied with his first law case. She does a Cambodian fertility dance to get his attention but even then she tells him, "I'm trying to get you all hot and bothered and you're summing up for the jury. Our whole marriage is over." For Corie to jump to this impatient conclusion prefigures their later argument that leads her to want a divorce.

A fear of conservatism by Corie is demonstrated in her concern that Ethel will not approve of the apartment. Corie tells Paul that her mother "has a different set of values.

She's practical. Not young like us." This concern is extended to Corie's asking Paul to lie about the amount the couple pay in rent. Ethel's acceptance of Corie is demonstrated in the scene when she makes a surprise visit to the apartment. While Ethel expresses some small disapproval, she also defends Corie, who says, "What is it they say in Harpers Bazar? It won't take shape until the bride's personality becomes clearly defined." In response Ethel comments, "I don't know. I think it's you right now." This comment, however, will get a later payoff when Ethel sees how Corie decorates the apartment and calls it "magnificent." Corie's concern for her mother's lack of a love life is demonstrated when she lies about the dinner with Victor to entrap Ethel, although she can't understand Ethel's "panic" over the prospect.

The close relationship between Corie and her mother is apparent from the fact that she kept her mother on the telephone for two hours. Corie's upset when she finds that Ethel has spent the night in Victor's apartment is a mixed message, given she had deliberately set up her mother as a match for Victor and that, after the couple had left together, she told Paul that she was grateful to have something about her mother to worry about. However, Corie doesn't believe Ethel when she tells her that nothing happened with Victor, after Ethel loses her clothes. Perhaps because of her experience, Ethel is shown to be more tolerant of people, since she is not angry at Victor, and her advice to Corie about Paul is to "give up a little bit of you for him." Ethel's further comment, "Don't make everything a game. Just late at night in that little room upstairs," suggests that she believes that Corie can still retain her sexuality even if she has to exchange some of her radicalism for conservatism.

Ethel is initially presented to be as conservative as Paul, although her surprise visit to the apartment suggests impulsivity. This is spelled out in lines dropped from the play in which Ethel tells Corie, "You're so impulsive. You jump first. Paul is like me. He looks first"; to which Corie replies, "He doesn't look. He stares. That's the trouble with both of you." Ethel and Paul are also aligned in their mutual exhaustion after the trek to Staten Island, and juxtaposed with the energy of Victor and Corie. It is perhaps Ethel's refusal to take Victor's offered hand on the stoop that allows her to tumble down the stairs when she slips on the ice, but Ethel scores points for going off with Victor, and the payoff is that she is able to sleep in his apartment without her board under her bed. His comment that she is a "good sport" suggests that he may have no romantic interest in her, but the narrative ends with them going out together for another dinner.

Paul's response to the arranged date between Ethel and Victor is the narrative's major conflict. The clash of represented conservatism and radicalism, where Corie says that he is a watcher and she is a doer, will lead to the couple contemplating a divorce. Paul leaves Corie to go barefoot in the park when he is drunk as a sign of an attempt at being "ridiculous," even though he is only drunk from the alcohol he takes for his cold. The narrative has a shift in power when Paul tells Corie that he wants her to move out and also when he makes a sexual advance towards her that she is afraid of. This is a seeming switching of attitudes where Paul is now the radical and Corie is the conservative. Corie's fear of this new Paul is perhaps a fear of her own radicalism, and his stance causes her to become passive in response to his demands. However, his apparent new power is soon diminished when he becomes incapable of getting down from the roof without her help.

Of the Broadway cast, only Robert Redford, Mildred Natwick and Herb Edelman we retained for the film. The naturalistic performance of the actors is a tribute to director Gene Saks, though he errs with the timed entrance of Ethel into the apartment for the dinner with Victor since it appears too theatrical. He uses the evocative sound of Corie's echoed voice calling out to the visitors to suggest the distance from the ground floor. However, the climactic fight between Corie and Paul lacks emotional resonance, highlighted in her crying, which Jane Fonda makes more comic than real. Again, Paul and Corie's scene on the rooftop doesn't convince us that either character is in any real physical danger; the scene is weakened by the obvious use of rear projection to convey the building's height.

Jane Fonda's casting as Corie results from her having greater film box office appeal than Elizabeth Ashley, who played the part on stage. Fonda adds an interesting combination of sex kitten, tomboy petulance, and childlike innocence to the role. Fonda is also funny in her timing, and her physicality with Redford expresses Corie's clinging attraction to him. This is paid off in Redford's breathlessness in climbing the stairs when being held back by her, when Fonda appears to make an improvised exclamation "Bfff" and Redford laughs in reaction to it. Natwick makes Ethel likeable, funny and touching. She covers her disapproval of the empty apartment with polite disdain, and still makes occasional amusing asides such as "No bathtub" or "Very attractive." She is funny when repeating Ethel's behavior from the play of nervous over-laughing in the dinner scene, and in her first attempt to flip the knichi from one hand to another and pop it into her mouth. Boyer is equally likeable as Victor, diluting the potential sexual threat he could pose to Corie.

The role of Corie was said to have been offered first to Natalie Wood, who declined because she wanted time off from making movies. Also considered for the part were Sandra Dee, Geraldine Chaplin, Yvette Mimieux, Tuesday Weld, Sue Lyon, and Nancy Sinatra. Marlo Thomas, who had played the part in London in 1965, wanted to do the film but was not considered.

Simon writes in *Rewrites* that Mike Nichols had not wanted to repeat his Broadway direction of the play for the screen. Simon said that Saks' approach to the film was a little stage-bound, which made it often static, but that the actors were brilliant. The screenwriter found Redford and Fonda "magical" together and Natwick "superb." Simon said that producer Hal Wallis seemed more concerned with making the film under budget than with making it as good as it could be. He gives an example of one day when Wallis had the set changed so that the crew was ready for the next shot. Saks was unaware of what had been done, since, after three takes of a scene, he had left to confer with the actors. When Saks returned and questioned Wallis about what had been done, he was told that he had to speak up to avoid the situation reoccurring.

A still exists of a deleted scene that shows Paul standing behind a desk on the telephone. He is presumably in his law office and receiving a call from Corie. The man also in the room sitting at the desk in the still is unidentified.

RELEASE: May 25, 1967, with the taglines "Broadway's barest, rarest, unsquarest love play," "Break the rules! Rock the boat! Make love! Fall over laughing!!!" and "The barest rarest unsquarest love play that ever left Broadway to find happiness on the big wide color screen!"

REVIEWS: Acclaimed by John Douglas Eames in *The Paramount Story,* and by *Variety,* who said it was "one howl of a picture" and that Gene Saks makes a "sock debut." Mixed reaction from Bosley Crowther in the *New York Times,* Pauline Kael in *5001 Nights at the Movies* and John Baxter in *Hollywood in the Sixties.*

AWARDS: Mildred Natwick was nominated for the Best Supporting Actress Academy Award.

DVD: Released by Paramount on December 21, 1999.

REMAKES: Remade as a television series, with black actors, which only ran for twelve episodes and one season in 1970. A made-for-TV movie was also broadcast in 1981 with Richard Thomas playing Paul, Beth Armstrong as Corie, Hans Conried as Victor Velasco, and Barbara Barrie as Ethel Banks. Shot for HBO Films, this was a version of the stage play filmed in a theatre with a live audience. The play was also filmed for the French television series *Au theatre ce soir* and broadcast on January 15, 1982. Season 1, episode 14, of the television series *Love American Style,* entitled "Love and the Good Deal," broadcast on November 14, 1969, was credited as "suggested by" a play by Neil Simon, namely *Barefoot in the Park.* The teleplay was written by Gary Marshall and Jerry Belson and the episode was directed by Jerry Paris. The twenty-minute episode saw the characters of Paul and Corie Bratter repeated, as well as Harry Pepper, here known as Harry Dorfman, Victor Velasco and Ethel Banks, though she is only referred to by Corie as Mother. Starring as Paul was Redford-lookalike Phillip Clark, Skye Aubrey as Corie, Frank Campanella as Harry, Hans Conreid as Victor, and Jane Wyatt as Ethel. Repeated is the running gag of breathless visitors to the Bratter apartment, the small size of their bedroom, and the hallway ladder and trapdoor entrance to Victor's apartment. The episode's plot had the couple buying a custom-made bed from a New Jersey factory wholesaler, which turns out to be noisy and uncomfortable. The problem is solved after Paul hurts his back and is taken to hospital, where he discovers that a hospital bed is the perfect size for the Bratter's bedroom.

The Odd Couple (1968)
Paramount Pictures/Howard W. Koch Production.

CREW: Gene Saks (Director), Howard W. Koch (Producer), Neil Simon (Screenplay based on his play), Robert B. Hauser (Photography), Frank Bracht (Editor), Neal Hefti (Music), Hal Pereira and Walter Tyler (Art Direction), Robert Benton and Ray Moyer (Set Decoration), Wally Westmore (Makeup), Nellie Manley (Hair), Jack Bear (Costumes), John Anderson (Men's Wardrobe), Paul K. Lerpae (Special Photographic Effects). Color, 100 minutes. Filmed in New York including Shea Stadium in Flushing Meadows Park, Queens.

CAST: Jack Lemmon (Felix Ungar), Walter Matthau (Oscar Madison), John Fiedler (Vinnie), Herbert Edelman (Murray), David Sheiner (Roy), Larry Haines (Speed), Monica Evans (Cecily Pigeon), Carole Shelley (Gwendolyn Pigeon), Iris Adrian (Waitress). Uncredited: Matty Alou (Himself), Bill Baldwin (Sports Announcer), Al Barlick (Home Plate Umpire), John C. Becher (Hotel Clerk), Ted Beniades (Bartender), Billie Bird (Chambermaid), Patricia D. Bohannon (Bowler), Ken Boyer (Himself), Heywood Hale Broun (Himself, Sportswriter), Jerry Buchek (Himself), Roberto Clemente (Himself),

Tommy Davis (Himself), Augie Donatelli (First Base Umpire), Jack Fisher (Himself), Ann Graeff (Scrubwoman), Bud Harrelson (Himself), Cleon Jones (Himself), Ed Kranepool (Himself), Vernon Law (Himself), Jack Lightcap (Public Address Announcer), Bill Mazeroski (Himself), Joe Palma (Butcher), Angelique Pettyjohn (Go-Go Dancer), Harry Spear (Janitor), Ralph Stantley (Cop), Maury Wills (Himself).

SONGS: "Rule Britannia" (music by Thomas Augustine Arne, words by James Thomson), Walter Matthau.

SYNOPSIS: In New York, television news writer Felix Ungar has broken up with his wife Frances after twelve years of marriage. After an unsuccessful attempt to kill himself he comes to the apartment of his friend sportswriter Oscar Madison. Oscar is divorced from his wife, Blanche. The two men regularly play poker at Oscar's house with their friends. Oscar offers to let Felix move in with him although both state that they are impossible to live with. After three weeks, Oscar arranges for a double date with his British secretary neighbors, the Pigeon sisters. The date is a disaster and Oscar tells Felix to move out. Felix moves in with the sisters and Oscar invites him to join the next poker game night.

NOTES: For his screen adaptation, Simon provided new scenes. The screenplay presents the subject of male bonding, friends as family and the theme of incompatible partners. *Come Blow Your Horn* presented a form of male bonding between two brothers, but here it is demonstrated between two non-related friends. As opposed to Simon's previous two screenplays, this one does not present family as being a support system, since both protagonists are divorced and essentially without family. The conflict of incompatible characters was also demonstrated in *Come Blow Your Horn* in the opposing moral values of the family and their sons, and in *Barefoot in the Park* in the diametrically opposed attitudes to life that the married couple and the older couple seemed to possess.

The play is "opened up" with locations in the street as well as the Hotel Flanders, the Metropole Café, a luncheonette, Grant's Tomb, a baseball stadium, a bus, a telephone booth, a bowling alley, a pool hall, a pinball machine parlor, a bar, and the market where Felix shops for food. The foyer, elevator and rooftop of the apartment building are also utilized. Simon also adds some new moments of farce. When Felix first leaves the poker room to go into the kitchen, the men watch him to express their greater concern over him than over playing the game. They quickly turn back when he returns. This moment prefigures the action retained from the play when Oscar quickly closes the window after Felix has commented on the "pretty view" and asks whether it is twelve floors up. The men also watch Felix as he goes to the "john," follow him to wait outside the door, and then run back to the poker table when they hear that he is coming out. Another farcical touch is how Felix is revealed to be crushed behind Oscar's bedroom door, which Murray forces open when we think that Felix has jumped from one of the two shown open windows. The reveal is made with the sound of Felix moaning, "My back."

The new opening with Felix at the Hotel Flanders comes from dialogue in the play in which Felix tells Oscar that he went to an unnamed hotel. For the screenplay Simon adds more detail. We guess that Felix wants to commit suicide when he asks for a higher room after he is given room 307. After he is then given room 914 he says goodbye to the maid in the hallway rather than good night. His agenda is continued when he see him placing his wallet and watch in an envelope that we see is addressed to "My wife and beloved children." The room being dark because Felix hasn't turned the lights on adds to the foreboding, which is undercut by the comic touch of Felix's being unable to remove his wedding ring from his finger and also by the score which sounds comic. His attempt to open the stuck window hurts his back, stopping him from the suicide attempt. Felix's later look at the river makes us think that he will jump into it, but he chooses to go to Oscar's apartment instead.

In the scene at the Metropole Café, Felix's mild reaction to the go-go dancer confirms the idea of Felix as heterosexual, something already proven since he has a wife and children. The scene gets a narrative payoff when Felix hurts his neck by swigging the scotch he buys. A later scene of Felix banging against the elevator door outside Oscar's apartment adds to his established physical pain. There is also a minor joke where the barman wears an earpiece and mouths the words to Felix, "What will you have?" since he cannot be heard over the noise of the live band. The scene at the baseball stadium also has a narrative payoff. Since Oscar takes the telephone call from Felix he misses seeing a triple play. The scene also shows Oscar at work, although it is noteworthy that Simon does not show Felix at work as a television news writer. However, the fact of his marriage disruption may provide a context for his not working.

The new luncheonette scene is perhaps the most famous of the film; in it Felix makes moose noises to clear his head, although this action comes from the play. Simon also adds a joke concerning the air conditioning in the locale. Felix tells Oscar that he had an air conditioner in the bedroom but that he never let Frances turn it on in summer, because of his allergy to it. In response, Oscar says, "Oh, she must be crazy about that." A new scene shows Oscar and Felix in the apartment building foyer silently catching the elevator and then Oscar slamming the apartment door in Felix's face when Oscar goes inside. Felix says nothing to Oscar in response, and he will continue this silence during the following tantrum by Oscar.

The tantrum scene is a set piece retained from the play. Simon changes the play's action from Oscar being in the bedroom as Felix vacuums the living room to both men being in the living room and Oscar pulling out the vacuum cleaner plug from the power outlet. Simon loses the sequence of Oscar dropping a cigar wrapper and a match onto the floor and smoking the cigar, Felix dropping the cigar wrapper and the match into Oscar's hat, and Oscar taking the wrapper and putting it into an ashtray and then dumping the contents of the ashtray onto the floor. For the film Simon adds Oscar tilting a wall painting, throwing flowers from a case onto the floor, and wiping his shoed feet on the curtains. Simon also loses the moment in the play where Felix teases Oscar with the smell from his plate of linguini, which then justifies Oscar's spraying the aerosol spray around Felix and onto his food plate. The screenwriter adds the moment when Oscar stands on the vacuum cleaner plug as Felix is retrieving it, and then Oscar stepping off so that Felix pulls it and falls back in the kitchen. Simon also adds Felix's turning off the television that Oscar is watching before Felix sits down to eat his meal. Oscar's spraying of the aerosol on Felix's plate after he has sprayed around him is also made more explicit.

There is another new moment when the two men stand on either side of a woman at the elevator who holds two dogs in her arms. When they growl at Oscar he tells her,

"Those dogs should be on a leash," which seems more like a Felix response. A scene with Oscar and his friends driving in Murray's police car, looking for Felix, is also new for the screenplay. Simon adds a moment where another police car stops by the car and Murray tells the cop, "Off duty arrest. Caught them gambling." This comment references the fact that friends had come to Oscar's apartment to play poker and that poker is gambling. Simon also changes the fact of Felix of staying with the Pigeon sisters from being requested in the play to already having been decided in the screenplay. It is interesting that Simon should have thought that bringing the sisters back in the third act of the play should have been such an inspired idea, since apart from giving Felix a safe landing after Oscar's eviction of him, it doesn't really get a payoff. There is the suggestion that he will aggravate the sisters as much as he did Oscar; however, both play and film end before this is demonstrated.

Funny moments and lines retained from the play include Oscar's line on the telephone to his son Bruce about how the boy has drawn a stamp on a letter, and Oscar's line about the perceived danger of Felix being in the kid's bathroom: "The worst he could do is brush his teeth to death." A funny retained exchange occurs when Frances calls and speaks to Oscar. Felix tells him, "I'm not here. You haven't heard from me. You don't know where I've been. You didn't see me. I didn't call and I'm not here. I'm not here." In response, Oscar tells Frances, "Yes, he's here." Another retained funny line is this of Oscar's: "Getting a clear picture on Channel Two is not my idea of whoopee." Felix calls Oscar a "dumb ignoramus" for naming a ladle a spoon, and Oscar's line on his entrance with the cocktails, "Is everybody happy?" is a cliché that gets a laugh from the fact that he says it before he sees that Felix and the Pigeon sisters are all crying. Oscar gets another funny line in response to Felix's telling him that he cried in front of two women. Oscar replies, "And they loved it. I'm thinking of getting hysterical." Simon also makes

Felix Ungar (Jack Lemmon, left) looks unhappy in an elevator with Oscar Madison (Walter Matthau), in a still for *The Odd Couple* (1968).

reference to Oscar's earlier assumption as to why Felix was looking at Oscar's living room window. Oscar opens the window before he leaves to go to the Pigeon sisters' apartment and tells Felix, "It's twelve floors, not eleven." Simon retains the funny line in Oscar's reference to Felix's leaving little notes on his pillow that say "F.U." He says, "It took me three hours to figure out that F.U. was Felix Ungar." Of course the F.U. is also known to stand for a common expletive, which is presumably the joke. Felix tells Oscar, "In other words, you're throwing me out," and he replies, "Not in other words. Those are the perfect words." Oscar also has a funny line after Felix tells him, "Let it be on your head," over Oscar evicting Felix. Oscar says, "What the hell is that, the Curse of the Cat People?"

Simon's changes to the play include Speed's line to Murray concerning his shuffling the deck in the poker game. In the play Speed says, "Tell me, Mr. Maverick, is this your first time on the riverboat?" In the film Speed's line is, "Excuse me, sir, but aren't you the one they call the Cincinnati Kid?" Simon changes the action from the play when Oscar only strides down the hallway, "glaringly maniacally," after Felix has mentioned the floor of Oscar's bathroom being wet. For the screenplay Simon has Oscar tell Felix, "I'm gonna kill you," and run after him. Simon also loses the moment in the play when Oscar produces Felix's suitcase and throws kitchen utensils in it.

The notion of certain behaviors demonstrating homosexual traits is toyed with in the narrative. Felix's fussiness and his becoming a "wife" for Oscar after he moves in can be interpreted as such. Equally, Oscar's use of words like "pussycat," "darling," "honey" and "sweetheart" might also make us wonder about Oscar. Both men are married, but separated, so that the scene in which Oscar gives Felix a massage for the nerve spasm in his neck has a potential subtext. But we never really believe that the men are homosexual. Felix's behavior is more obsessive-compulsive than gender-defining, and Oscar's language reads more as the affectation of a heterosexual man who is not threatened by being perceived as being homosexual. Perhaps to overcome the affectation, which Felix does not use, the narrative goes to lengths to defend Oscar's heterosexuality. His sexual preference is confirmed in his advance towards the waitress at the luncheonette, his eyeing women at the bowling alley, and it being his idea to have a date with the Pigeon sisters. Oscar and Felix are called "playboys" by Vinnie and this implies that they are both heterosexual and sexually available.

It is interesting that Oscar is initially reluctant to meet with both Pigeon sisters alone once Felix refuses to join him in their apartment, which would seem to be a womanizer's dream. Oscar tells Felix he wants fun, but it is noteworthy that Oscar needs Felix to have fun with him. This explains the double date with the Pigeon sisters. We can interpret Oscar's wanting Felix along as his continued concern for his friend, although Oscar says that his chances with one of the sisters will be better if Felix is occupied. Felix agrees to the double date with the Pigeon sisters, although his preoccupation with cooking the dinner suggests that romance is not his priority. He tells Oscar that he feels guilty about seeing any other women because he is recently separated, and that he is only doing the date for Oscar. The Pigeon sisters being initially presented as giggling bimbos justifies Felix's lack of interest in them, although their later empathy with Felix, which results in crying, gives them redemptive depth. The fact that Oscar fails to bed either one of them, because they spend their time with him asking about

Felix, also shows that they are not the sexual pushovers that Oscar predicts. Oscar is good at seductive chatter, but Felix is uncomfortable being alone with the sisters. This failure of Felix may come from his admitted disinterest in the women as dates, although he is more comfortable when he tells them about his family. He is better at being friends than a seducer, which makes them comfortable enough to later ask him to move in with them after Oscar has thrown Felix out.

The massage that Oscar gives Felix also demonstrates Oscar's feeling of friendship, which is evident from the fact that he invites Felix to move in with him. Oscar rationalizes the offer by telling Felix that he can't stand living alone; Simon drops a line from the play in which Oscar tells Felix that he loves him. However, it is the men living together that ironically is counterproductive, since it creates a strain on their friendship. It also antagonizes his other friends, since we see at the second poker game how Felix's demands make the other players flee.

A difference that is demonstrated between the two men is that Felix gets no pleasure from throwing the tea cup against the wall of the living room, as Oscar suggests. We assume that the action is one that Oscar would enjoy doing, as evidenced by his later throwing a plate of linguini against the wall of the kitchen. But throwing the tea cup only makes Felix feel worse, because the effort hurts his arm. Oscar's throwing of the linguini also works for Oscar because it deprives Felix of a meal; because it makes a mess, which Oscar knows will disturb Felix, and also because Felix knows that Oscar will not clean the mess. The latter plot point is actually a brilliant narrative stroke in providing the believable excess of Oscar's slovenliness, and since we don't see Felix clean up the mess we might assume that the linguini stays there.

Oscar's antagonism toward Felix doesn't really emerge until what was the third act in the play. Before that he feels irritation. The end of what was the play's second act has Oscar opening the window of the living room to suggest that he wants Felix to jump from it, although Oscar had only made the assumption that this was what Felix wanted to do previously. The balance that Simon attempts to create between the two men's behavioral idiosyncrasies is that Felix will express that he is as irritated by Oscar as Oscar is by Felix. However, perversely, Felix is able to accept Oscar more than his friend accepts him, and this is revealed in Felix's telling-off of Oscar. Before Felix can tell Oscar that he finds him "one of the biggest slobs in the world, unreliable, undependable, and irresponsible," he will also tell him that he has been wonderful to him. Oscar, on the other hand, is drawn to violence in his inability to accept Felix and expresses this with physical threats and by running after Felix before asking him to leave. Simon modifies Oscar's assumed threat to Felix by having Felix not being afraid to go into Oscar's room to talk to him. The threat is also modified in Oscar's response; he is prepared to talk to Felix, and Oscar says that the "topper" of the things that aggravate him about Felix is the result of the date. Oscar's anger also transitions to crying when he "tells off" Felix and says that the aggravation is going to make him have a nervous breakdown. However, the "topper" gets topped when Felix warns Oscar about walking on the paper in his wet-floored bathroom, which causes Oscar to chase after him.

That Oscar asks Felix to come back after telling him to leave suggests that he feels concerned that Felix may commit suicide. This is implied by Felix's line, "Let it be on your head." The fact that Felix seeks refuge with the Pigeon sisters shows that he is not as friendless as he believed he was in the beginning of the narrative. Simon ups the issue of Oscar's concern for Felix by having Oscar and his friends drive around in Murray's police car, looking for him. The men being back in Oscar's apartment and pretending not to be concerned about Felix when he returns is a repeat of their pretense when Felix first came to the apartment for the poker game. However, as in the play, this pretense is undercut when Gwendolyn is at the door and not Felix. Oscar's guilt over evicting Felix can be lessened when he learns that Felix has moved in with the Pigeon sisters, and his desire to keep Felix as a friend is indicated by reminding him to join the others for the next poker game night. The narrative also suggests that perhaps Felix has influenced Oscar's behavior, since the telephone call Oscar has with Blanche shows that he has been able to save money to pay her alimony checks. There is also the implication that Felix has also influenced Oscar's future behavior when the screenplay ends, as the play does, when Oscar tells the other poker players to watch their cigarette butts.

A minor plot point that is repeated from a line in *Come Blow Your Horn* is Felix repeatedly asking someone to eat over a plate. He first asks this of Vinnie in regards to the sandwich Felix has made for him, and then later asks it of Oscar in the kitchen when Oscar takes a piece of cake to eat. The point seems to underline Felix as a neatnik who doesn't want crumbs on the floor, the way the mother requested the same of her son does in *Come Blow Your Horn*. However, it also suggests that the person asking is being condescending.

Director Gene Saks' casting has Walter Matthau, John Fiedler, Monica Evans and Carole Shelley repeat their roles from the Broadway production. Saks opens the film with a view of Times Square and the surrounding hotels before transitioning to the Hotel Flanders to show how it is a low-market establishment by comparison. This idea is reinforced by the hotel clerk eating at his desk, the room costing Felix five dollars, the lift being out of order, the maid in the hallway smoking, and the window in Felix's room being unable to be opened. Saks cuts from the bowling ball rolling toward the pins in the bowling alley to balls scattered on a pool table in the pool hall. He then transitions to the Oscar and Felix playing a pinball machine and then being in a bar to talk about dating the Pigeon sisters.

Saks repeats the action from the play when Felix meets the Pigeon sisters. As he steps up to the landing he comes nose to nose with Oscar. The play describes how Felix then steps aside to usher the girls down into the room. However, the screenplay has Felix slink behind the girls before all four people move down into the room. Another action repeated from the play is Felix's lighting of Gwendolyn's cigarette; he takes the cigarette back since it is caught in the lighter. However, Saks adds to the moment when Felix lights a second cigarette for her: she quickly pulls it back after it is lit to avoid the same thing happening. A moment that is perhaps not in the play is that Saks has the Pigeon sisters lean on Felix when they are all crying. This ironically shows how Felix obtains physical contact from them before Oscar, who never does in the narrative. Saks also changes the moment in the play when Oscar offers Gwendolyn her drink. In the play he gives up, since she is too busy crying to accept it, and he puts it back on the serving tray. He then drinks his own drink. For the film Oscar drinks her drink after she refuses it.

Neither Oscar's slovenliness nor Felix's neatness is presented as being excessive, which dilutes some of the narrative humor. That Oscar throws the linguini against the wall with the idea that he would leave it there suggests an excess that is not confirmed. We don't see the linguini being cleaned up, but neither do we see it on the wall again, so there is an ambiguity about the issue. Perhaps at the time of the stage play and the film it was funnier to see men behave the way the characters do. This is particularly important in relation to Felix who could be read as behaving like a traditional woman or an effeminate or homosexual man. However, this point is modified because Jack Lemmon plays Felix with understatement, so that he is more realistic than comic. The real problem with the film is one of tone, since neither of the men's behavior or their antagonism seems funny. Oscar's physical threat is especially unfunny despite Simon's modification of it, and also when Oscar runs through the apartment after Felix. One can appreciate Simon's gift for writing argumentative banter, but sometimes it reads as more intellectual wordplay than as having emotional resonance.

Jack Lemmon makes the noises Felix produces funny. These include his reaction to Oscar's massage, and his clearing his ears in the luncheonette scene. The latter gets more laughs from the reaction of the other people in the restaurant. Felix clears his ears in the play; the action is described in the stage directions as humming then bellowing like a moose, although in the play Felix only makes these noises in front of Oscar. Later in the screenplay Oscar will describe the sound as "moose calls." Matthau is funny when Oscar gives a massage and runs his hand over Felix's back and head, and in his freeze with his back to the camera after Felix mistakenly calls him "Frances." This moment has been retained from the play, described in the stage directions as Oscar "stops dead." Oscar has another frozen moment that is not from the play where he reacts to Felix, asking him why he didn't call to tell him that he would be late for the dinner date with the Pigeon sisters. In the play the stage directions only describe Oscar's reaction as a pause. Matthau is also funny in Oscar's anger at Felix, when the actor deadpans, and also when he uses a pronounced New York accent as in the way he says "irony" and "choice" and "curse." Equally, he has a good reaction to Felix's heated thanks, and moves his head around amusingly when Oscar asks, "Have I just been told off? I think I may have missed it." Matthau also makes Oscar's crying funny when he tells off Felix and he expresses feeling after Oscar asks Felix to come back after he has evicted him.

Producer Howard W. Koch used the West End Avenue apartment he had lived in as a boy as the model for Oscar's apartment. In the Centennial Collection audio commentary, it is reported that Koch originally wanted Frank Sinatra to play Felix and Jackie Gleason to play Oscar. However, Matthau changed the producer's mind. It probably also helped that the actor had just won the Best Supporting Actor Academy Award for *The Fortune Cookie* (1966), in which he co-starred with Jack Lemmon. The commentary also mentions that Billy Wilder was originally attached to direct the film. In the Centennial Collection DVD featurette "Inside The Odd Couple," Robert Evans speaks about why Wilder lost the directing job. The former head of Paramount Pictures claims that Lemmon and Matthau "doublecrossed" Wilder by their own casting. This was particularly because Lemmon demanded a one-million-dollar pay check and the small budget could not accommodate the two actors and Wilder's salary. The featurette also reports that there was a three-week rehearsal period before shooting began.

In another featurette, "Memories from the Set," it is reported that Matthau had broken his left arm in a bicycle accident a week before shooting was to begin. The actor's arm was in a cast, so the production rearranged the shooting schedule so that the second part of the film was shot first. This was done because Matthau had less required of his arm in these scenes. Gene Saks reports that the actor's condition helped to create the business in the film where Oscar holds sandwiches under his left armpit as he checks his cards in the first poker scene.

RELEASE: May 2, 1968, with the taglines "Jack Lemmon and Walter Matthau are The Odd Couple ... say no more," "Jack Lemmon and Walter Matthau are The Odd Couple," "Even More Funny on the Screen ... Than It Was as a Broadway and City-to-City Stage Smash!" and "Wives? Ever wondered how he'd get along without you? Husbands? Ever long for those good old bachelor days?"

REVIEWS: Critically acclaimed by *Variety*, Renata Adler in the *New York Times*, John Douglas Eames in *The Paramount Story*, and Robert K. Johnson. Given a mixed reaction by Roger Ebert in the *Chicago Sun-Times* and John Baxter in *Hollywood in the Sixties*. In *Going Steady*, Pauline Kael commented on the film's "technical ineptitude and visual ugliness."

AWARDS: Nominated for Best Adapted Screenplay Academy Award and Best Editing.

DVD: Released by Paramount on December 12, 2000. The Centennial Collection edition was released by Paramount on March 24, 2009.

REMAKE: Famously made into a TV series that starred Tony Randall as Felix and Jack Klugman as Oscar. In his *Playboy* interview, Simon commented that he found Klugman and Randall "perfect" in it. The series ran for five seasons, from 1970 to 1975. Monica Evans and Carole Shelley appeared as the Pigeon sisters in four episodes. Also remade as *The Oddball Couple*, which was a 1975 family cartoon comedy that featured as roommates the neatnik cat Spiffy and the slovenly dog Fleabag, a West German TV series that only ran for one season in 1980, *The New Odd Couple*, which was an African-American remake that only had eighteen episodes for one season from 1982 to 1983, a French made-for-TV movie in 1990, Spanish made-for-TV movies in 1995 and 1999, and a German made-for-TV movie in 2004.

SEQUEL: *The Odd Couple II* (1998), directed by Howard Deutch, with Jack Lemmon and Walter Matthau reprising their roles.

Sweet Charity (1969) (aka *Sweet Charity: The Adventures of a Girl Who Wanted to Be Loved*)

Universal Pictures.

CREW: Bob Fosse (Director and Choreographer), Robert Arthur (Producer), Peter Stone (Screenplay, based upon the screenplay "Nights of Cabiria" by Federico Felini, Tullio Pinelli and Ennio Flaiano), Robert Surtees (Photography), Stuart Gilmore (Editor), Cy Coleman (Music), Dorothy Fields (Lyrics), Alexander Golitzen and George C. Webb (Art Directors), Jack D. Moore (Set Decorator), Edith Head (Costumes), Bud Westmore (Makeup), Larry Germain (Hair), Sydney Guilaroff (Miss MacLaine's Hair), Howard A. Anderson Co. (Title Design). Color, 152 minutes. Filmed at Universal Studios and on location in New York in Central Park, on Wall Street and at Yankee Stadium.

CAST: Shirley MacLaine (Charity Hope Valentine), John McMartin (Oscar Lindquist), Chita Rivera (Nickie), Paula Kelly (Helene), Stubby Kaye (Herman), Barbara Bouchet (Ursula), Ricardo Montalban (Vittorio Vitale), Sammy Davis, Jr. (Big Daddy), Suzanne Charny (Pony-tailed Head Dancer in Pompeii Club), Alan Hewitt (Nicholsby), Dante D'Paulo (Charlie), Bud Vest, Ben Vereen, Lee Roy Reams, Al Lanti, John Wheeler (Dancers), Leon Bing (Model). Uncredited: Leon Alton, Marie Bahruth, Toni Basil, Larry Billman, Carol Birner, Herman Boden, Donald Bradburn, Chelsea Brown, Ray Chabeau, Cheryl Christiansen, Linda Clifford, Dick Colacino, Bryan Da Silva, Marguerite DeLain, Kathryn Doby, Jimmy Fields, Lynn Fields, Ben Gooding, Ellen Halpin, Carlton Johnson, Kirk Kirksey, Richard Korthaze, Jennifer Laws, Lance LeGault, Trish Mahoney, Lynn McMurrey, Gloria Mills, Ted Monson, April Nevins, Maris O'Neill, Walter Painter, Louise Quick, Frank Radcliffe, Ed Robinson, Sandy Rovetta, Charlene Ryan, Dom Salinaro, Juleste Salve, Victoria Scruton, Patrick Spohn, Kristoffer Tabori, Bob Thompson, Jr., Jerry Trent, Tifni Twitchell, Renata Vaselle, Bonnie G. West, Lorene Yarnell Jansson, Kay York, Adele Yoshioka (Dancers), Richard Angarola (Maitre d'), Henry Beckman, Jeff Burton (Policemen), Charles Brewer (Young Man on Bridge), Lonnie Burr (Willie), Ceil Cabot (Married Woman), Dee Carroll (Woman on Tandem), Kathleen Cody (Blonde Flower Girl), Bud Cort (Flower Child), John Craig, John Frayer, Paul Shipton, Walter Stratton (Patrons at Dance Hall), Alfred Dennis (Waiter at "Chile Hacienda"), Dave Gold (Panhandler), Bick Goss (Drummer Boy), Bill Harrison, Buddy Hart (Baseball Players), Chuck Harrod, Jerry Mann (Singers), Sharon Harvey (Young Woman on Bridge), Tom Hatten (Man in Tandem), Nolan Leary (Manfred), Diki Lerner (Man with Dog on Bridge), Buddy Lewis (Appliance Salesman), Judith Lowry (Old Lady on Park Bench), Joseph Mell (Man on Bridge), Jackie Mitchell, Carroll Roebke (Models), Geraldine O'Brien (Lady on Bridge), Alma Platt (Lady with Hat on Bridge), Maudie Prickett (Nurse on Bridge), Norman Stevans (Concession), Chet Stratton (Waiter), Robert Terry (Doorman), Roger Til (Greeter at "Pompeii Club").

SONGS: "My Personal Property," Shirley MacLaine; "Big Spender," girls at Dance Hall; "Rich Man's Frug," orchestra at the Pompeii Club; "If My Friends Could See Me Now," Shirley Maclaine; "There's Gotta Be Something Better than This," Shirley MacLaine, Chita Rivera and Paula Kelly; "It's a Nice Face," Shirley MacLaine; "The Rhythm of Life," Sammy Davis, Jr. and church congregation; "Sweet Charity," John McMartin; "I'm a Brass Band," Shirley MacLaine and boy dancers; "I Love to Cry at Weddings," Stubby Kaye and crowd at Dance Hall; "Where Am I Going?" Shirley MacLaine.

SYNOPSIS: Charity has been a dance hall hostess in New York's Fan-Dango Ballroom for eight years. She is pushed into Central Park Lake and robbed of her purse by her fiancé Charlie. She meets Italian movie star Vittorio Vitale in the street and he takes her to the Pompeii Club. He then takes her home for supper and gives her mementos. Charity yearns to change her life but fails in getting a job at an employment agency. She meets life insurance actuary Oscar Lindquist when they are trapped together in a stalled elevator. They date for two weeks. When Charity tells Oscar the truth about herself he proposes. However, he changes his mind and abandons her at the marriage license bureau. Charity is comforted by flower children in Central Park and leaves the park to continue her life.

NOTES: The screenplay adaptation of the Broadway show with book by Simon was not done by him but rather by Peter Stone. Stone cut some of the play's songs and dialogue and supporting characters, opened up the play by adding locations, and created scenes and dialogue of his own. The film's subject repeats some of the narrative concerns from previous Simon films. The importance of family is presented by Charity's friendship with the girls at the Fan-Dango Club, in lieu of Charity having blood family. That the three girls also live together is a further sign of their bond. Charity's desire to marry Oscar shows her need to belong to another form of family as a wife. The division between convention and radicalism is explored through Charity's being a dance hall hostess and also in the odd-couple matching of her and Oscar as a more conventional man. His ultimate rejection of her will be based on his inability to accept Charity's past, which he sees as unconventional. The character of Charity is only Simon's second female protagonist after Corie Bratter from *Barefoot in the Park*.

Simon based his book on the main plot points of the Federico Fellini film *Le notti di Cabiria*, aka *Nights of Cabiria* (1957). In that film Giulietta Masina's Cabiria is a tough Roman streetwalker who behaves more aggressively than Charity. This is evidenced by her general attitude and her attacking another prostitute who makes fun of her. Cabiria as an aging prostitute is also an issue that was not carried over into the book or screenplay, and there are other minor plot points that have been changed. Cabiria's near-drowning after being pushed into a river by Giorgio is more serious, but a funny moment occurs when she enters the main room of the Piccadilly Club and gets caught in a curtain. Another difference is the fact of Cabiria being short in stature, which is highlighted when she and Alberto Lazzaril dance together. Alberto plays Beethoven in his house and hides Cabiria in his bathroom, where there is also a puppy. The Viva Maria mass that Cabiria attends can be likened to the "Rhythm of Life" church ceremony, and there is a flower connection. The magician at the music hall gives Cabiria a headdress of flowers, and when he sees her picking flowers in her hypnotized state he tells her, "Picking flowers indicates a gentle soul." Oscar Donofrio also brings Cabiria flowers on their date, but he does not grow them. There is an ambiguity about whether Oscar marries Cabiria, and while he reveals that he only wants the money she obtained from selling her house as a dowry, he does not express a disapproval of her life as a prostitute. Also, Oscar does not push her over the cliff and into the lake for the climactic scene. However, the scene does have a darker tone, since Cabiria asks Oscar to kill her. The last scene has young couples and musicians around Cabiria as she walks on the road on the side of woods after Oscar has run away from her, and the "Good evening" that a girl says to her prefigures the screenplay's flower children. Another observation is the way Cabiria dances the mambo and the way the two black dancers in the Piccadilly nightclub dance. These would seem to have inspired some of director Bob Fosse's choreography.

For *Sweet Charity*'s screenplay Peter Stone adds new locations, which include the streets of New York, the Careers Unlimited employment agency and the office of Mr. Nicholsby, a museum, a train station, telephone booths, Wall Street, Lincoln Center, Yankee Stadium, and the marriage license bureau. The rooftop of the Fan-Dango dance hall is also seen. The new scene with Nicholsby has three good moments. After Charity has repeated "No" to questions about her office skills, she says "No" to his "Um" in anticipation. When she tells him, "I must be able to do something. Everybody knows how to do something," he replies, "I used to think so." The topper is when Nicholsby assumes that she has been sent to him as a gag from the boys in the office. Charity is wise enough to realize that the best response is to go along with his assumption, although it also implies her own humiliation in being a joke to him.

In the new rooftop scene between Charity, Nickie and Helene, Charity says about Oscar, "Who needs him. I don't need anybody and if I needed anybody it sure wouldn't be him." In reply, Helene says, "She's nuts about him." After Charity says that she plans to tell Oscar the truth about herself, Nickie comments, "You are an extremely honest, open and stupid broad." The location of Oscar's rejection of Charity being the marriage license bureau rather than Central Park provides a new moment. Oscar points out a sign to Charity that reads, "Please do not throw any rice in the halls or on the stairs." He rationalizes his disapproval of Charity's breaking the rule because of his work in life insurance, and tells her that accidents in public buildings are common. Stone also has the couple witness another leaving the Bureau who are just married, and it is perhaps that fact that the bride and groom are both fat grotesques that makes Oscar look at them in distaste. It is Charity's sprinkling the couple with rice and then Oscar that makes him point out her action being illegal.

Stone adds some slapstick, such as Oscar tripping over his suitcase and perching on the shelf in the elevator scene, and Charity taking lots of napkins from the dispenser to cry into at Barney's Chile Hacinenda. This latter scene also has comedy from Oscar and Charity sitting back to back, exchanging seats and again sitting back to back, and the slapstick moment after Oscar asks Charity to give him her hand when they first miss each other's offered hand on the shoulder and then at the waist. Another new scene has a comic payoff, when Oscar and Charity are in aligned telephone bones, he tells her how her likes her innocence, and the scene ends with Charity leaving her booth and Oscar finding another woman in it. Stone provides the character trait of Oscar growing his own flowers and giving Charity a bunch when he meets her in the park. The idea of Oscar meeting her at the park bridge comes from an ignorance of what has happened to Charity there previously and is a nice payoff for Charity.

Funny lines retained from the play include Charity's line when she is held upside down after she is rescued from the lake and says, "Oh, my God. I'm in Australia." Another is when the a cop asks Charity what her lost shoe looks like and, indicating the other shoe, she tells him, "Like this one!" There is a witty line when Oscar tells Charity that he was in group analysis for being painfully shy, but "never had the nerve to bring it up." Also retained is the funny but sad exchange when Oscar tells her, "I would destroy you," and she replies, "That's ok. I'm not doing much now anyway." There is another laugh when Vittorio asks Charity, "Are you busy tonight?" She thinks he is asking the doorman and says to him, "He wants to know if you're busy tonight." Also kept is an exchange between Charity and Vittorio when he brings her the cane; her responses go from "I couldn't" to "Oh really, I can't" to "I'll take it," after his "I insist."

Stone's changes from the play include Vittorio Vidal becoming Vittorio Vitale. Of the songs, Stone cuts "Charity's Soliloquy," the reprise of "If My Friends Could See Me Now" after Charity leaves Vittorio's house, Vittorio's "Too Many Tomorrows," and Nickie and Helene's "Baby, Dream Your Dream." He replaces Charity's opening song, "You

Should See Yourself," with "My Personal Property," and "I'm the Bravest Individual," the song that Charity and Oscar sing together in the elevator, with Charity's "It's a Nice Face." Cut is a funny line of Charity's that relates to her not letting Charlie speak. In the play she tells him she knew what he was going to say and, after projecting lines of praise, Charity says, "Oh brother, you sure know how to talk to a girl." Another change is the moment before Charity and Vittorio dance. In the play Charity faints before they can start, and in the film she steps on his foot, which stops them dancing, a narrative improvement. Fosse adds to the impact of the dance with the reaction of the dancers around them and the use of music to create a build-up that is then dashed.

The ending of the play is also changed. Stone cuts Oscar's pushing Charity into the Central Park lake as Charlie had done, and the appearance of the Good Fairy. Instead he has Charity go alone to the park's bridge, detach the "Almost Married" sign from her suitcase, throw it into the lake, and then be approached by the flower children the next day. The alternative ending for the film has Oscar trip over Charity's suitcase on the bridge, which causes him to fall into the lake. Stone also adds some revealing dialogue. Oscar tells Charity, "I get upset when I'm with you and I suffocate to death when I'm not. Then it occurred to me. I'm the small closed-in place in here suffocating inside myself." Charity replies, "I could have told you that." When Oscar asks her why she didn't, she says, "I didn't think of it till you just said it." Oscar prefigures his second marriage proposal by telling Charity, "You're the only breath of fresh air I've ever had," and Stone reprises the "somebody loves me" line from Charity's song "I'm a Brass Band" before the couple leave the bridge together.

The world of exploitation and indifference presented here is embodied by the phony blind man that Charity gives money to. Her good nature can be perceived in her being willing to give the man money although she sees that he is a fraud. Charity's nature also makes her delusional in thinking the best of Charlie after he has pushed her into the lake, before she comes to accept the truth. Her delusions continue in the way she describes her evening with Vittorio to the girls at the dance hall. She lies about them dancing together and also about how he offered to have his car drive her home. Charity doesn't technically lie to Oscar about working in a bank, but lets him believe that she does. Fosse plays the noise of a train in the station to blot out Charity's excuse as to why she doesn't want to meet Oscar outside the bank. Since he cannot hear her lie, Oscar's suggestion that they meet at the bridge saves her

Charity Hope Valentine (Shirley MacLaine) in a portrait for *Sweet Charity* (1969).

exposure. Charity also lies to him about living in Brooklyn, and she lies to Nickie and Helene about telling Oscar about her job. Oscar by comparison shows affection to her when he kisses her hand at the train station, since he is too shy to kiss her on the mouth. It helps that Fosse stages this moment with the characters standing either side of a fence so that they would find it awkward to kiss on the mouth.

The silent Charlie who wears sunglasses is presented as an obvious exploiter so we know he will abuse Charity. Vittorio also wears sunglasses, but he is contrasted with Charlie because he shows Charity some kindness after his initial coldness. He gives her the mementos of an autographed photograph, a top hat, and a cane. He also kisses her with thanks for the time they have together, although revealingly he kisses her on the forehead. When Vittorio takes Charity to his house there is not the suggestion that he does so because he desires her, although Charity expresses a hope that he does. Even her desire for him is based on his being a movie star rather than a romantic man. When Vittorio hides Charity from Ursula in the closet he gives her the mementos as well as something to eat, and later the cold beer she has asked for when he returns to hang something. The narrative saves Ursula from appearing to be a total bimbo when she decides against looking in the closet where Charity hides. Vittorio's telling Ursula that the closet is where the girl is hiding is a risk that pays off, for both himself and Charity. However, Ursula is presumably not as great a fan of Vittorio's movies as Charity is, since she doesn't seem to recognize his movie line, "Without love, life has no purpose." His repeating the line as a make-out line to Ursula also shows Vittorio to be shameless, particularly when he knows Charity to be in the closet and she is presumably able to hear him.

The issue of whether Charity is a prostitute having sex with the customers of the Fan-Dango is never made explicit in the screenplay. It is implied by actions such as Vittorio's offering her money when she leaves his apartment, and her shame to Oscar. The gum that Charity chews at Vittorio's house demonstrates her social status to be lower class; some of the other girls at the dance hall also chew gum in the party scene at the Fan-Dango. Charity tells Nicholsby at the Careers Unlimited employment agency that she only has a public school education. Her class matches her ignorance of the Brahms that Vittorio plays in his house, her mispronunciation of Monica Monicelli, and her use of the phrase "up yours." However, the gum gets a narrative payoff when she reattaches the knob that had detached from the bannister when she arrived. While Nickie and Helene at the Fan-Dango don't chew gum like Charity, their small ambitions mark them as being similar to her. In "There's Gotta Be Something Better than This," Nickie dreams of being a receptionist and Helene a hatcheck girl. In comparison, Charity cannot name a profession, although only she of the three girls is prepared to try to get a conventional job.

Charity also appears to be a social radical, with her red hair and the theatrical makeup that she wears in the street as well as in the dance hall. When she goes to the employment agency her idea of dressing more conservatively is to wear a polka-dot patterned blouse and plain sweater over her simple sleeveless black dress and red beads, although she still wears big spangle earrings. Charity also attempts to dress more conservatively for her dates with Oscar, wearing a plain white blouse under her black dress and tan coat, but still the spangly big earrings. For her next date with Oscar, Charity wears the white blouse with a black and white tie and the same earrings. In the Barney's Chile Hacienda scene we see Oscar wearing a bland, tan coat that resembles Charity's. Charity's clothes get a payoff through her wearing her black dress sleeveless at the party at the dancehall where Oscar sees her arm tattoo, and in the blue flowered dress she wears to the marriage license bureau. This dress is accompanied by a flower in her hair, which matches the dress pattern; this is another tribute to Oscar's love of flowers and will be paid off at the end with the flower children, who give her a flower. Fosse also delays the reveal of the flowered dress by having Charity initially wearing her tan coat over it. However, she continues to wear the same spangly big earrings.

Nickie and Helene in their apartment with Charity are shown to dress conservatively, which emphasizes the fact that the clothes they wear at the Fan-Dango are work clothes. This behavior differentiates them from Charity, who is seen to wear her Fan-Dango outfit outside of work. Nickie and Helene also dress more conservatively at the party at the Fan-Dango for Charity's farewell, as more evidence that they are not working. The way that Charity dresses for the dance hall is ironic; both her dress and her being pushed into the lake in Central Park get her attention that she doesn't want. She expresses her objection to the attention she receives from the crowd in the park after she is rescued. Those in the park who ignore her cries for help as she drowns in the water indicate the callousness and indifference of people, while the two cyclists who save her demonstrate that not everyone is so selfish.

The people at the Pompeii Club represent another form of radicalism in comparison to Charity. They are rich and stylized eccentric celebrities who keep a cheetah in a cage and drink champagne. Vittorio is also a radical in one way as a movie star, but his wealth implies that he is also a conservative. This latter point may explain why he is not romantically attracted to Charity and finds the more conventional Ursula more appealing. The hippie congregation of the "Rhythm of Life" church also appear radical when compared to Charity and Oscar, and more hippies will be seen as flower children at the film's end. It is ironic that the children should appear radical compared to Charity, although her again wearing the tan coat over her black dress presents her in the conventional garb that she had attempted for Oscar.

Oscar initially appears kinder than Charlie and Vittorio in the way he holds the elevator doors open for her. Equally, Charity's eventual concern for Oscar in the elevator shows her good nature, even though fate will be cruel in giving her a romantic interest who will ultimately disappoint her. Charity's need for love has her willing to return to Central Park to meet Oscar, after the trauma of being pushed off the bridge, even though she doesn't agree to meet him. This makes her decision to leave when she sees Oscar less cruel, a feeling that is also leavened by the fact of Oscar's seeing her before she leaves the park. For Charity to leave the telephone booth when Oscar is speaking to her, however, reads as cruel, since she flees when she is ashamed that Oscar thinks her innocent. Oscar's rejection of Charity by refusing to marry her is his ultimate cruelty, although he does stop her from humiliating herself further when she practically begs to marry him. The narrative slowly changes Charity's reaction to Oscar's change of mind from trying to talk him around by being reasonable to becoming pathetic in wanting someone who does not want her. Even Charity's return to the Central Park bridge seems to be masochistic, as it is the scene of her prior rejection and humiliation by

Charlie. However, it will be staying in the park that allows her to be rejuvenated by acts of kindness of the flower children. They do not try to persuade her to join them but rather only give her a flower and wish her love.

The film's chosen ending does not allow us to know what happens to Oscar, whereas the alternative ending did. In it he finds his claustrophobia has returned and he cannot breathe in his apartment, which is shown to be populated with flowers. His finding Charity in Central Park comes out of accident rather than intention, although after he finds her he realizes his mistake in leaving her and asks to marry her again. Charity jumps into the lake after Oscar, despite us knowing from the first bridge scene that she cannot swim; this is extreme evidence of her generosity in light of Oscar's rejection. When he tells her that he doesn't know how long he will be able to stay with her, it is a realistic admission of his ambiguous feelings towards her and not the ultra-romantic conclusion we might expect. However, Charity's acceptance of this condition shows her overwhelming need, highlighted by her reprise of the line "Somebody loves me" from the song "I'm a Brass Band." Oscar's ambiguity is reflected in the end title, "And she lived hopefully ever after."

Fosse uses freeze-frames, color tinting, strobe lighting, zooms, out-of-focus and soft-focus effects, point-of-view camerawork, a flash pan, slow motion, and superimpositions. He also employs the devices of dialogue of one scene over an image of another, stills for some transitions, and some interesting editing. Charity talking to herself in voice-over is device that is repeatedly used and can be viewed as a variation on her singing to herself. Oscar will also be shown to talk to himself in the film's alternate ending, although not in voice-over.

The presentation of the musical numbers by Fosse alternates between songs performed to the camera and those performed in the context of a show. The latter device, where he often has action in the foreground incorporated into the dance, can upstage the performance. This is disappointing, since it pulls focus away from the spectacular choreography. He also features odd framing in the numbers, as when there is a close-up of Charity's eyes as she speaks but the rest of her is blocked by the shoulder of Vittorio, and when Oscar is lying on the floor of the elevator, blocking the close-up of Charity during "It's a Nice Face."

For "If My Friends Could See Me Now," Fosse pays off the narrative point of Vittorio's giving Charity a top hat by using the way it pops up, beginning with a montage of Charity popping the hat. The number progresses so that Charity dims the lights of Vittorio's room before a spotlight appears and Fosse transitions her to a stage with a chandelier. When the song is over, she transitions back when Vittorio raises the lights again. The repeated use of light flares into the camera is paid off by Fosse in the use of car headlights in "The Rhythm of Life," which opens with a group of car headlights and closes with the headlights turned off and a policeman's torch shone into the camera. It is ironic that this song became the most recognizable from the score, since it is the weakest because its sound is generic. Fosse doesn't help matters by making the coverage of the song too long and the accompanying dancing forgettable.

Of the Broadway cast only John McMartin and the dancers Suzanne Charney, Kathryn Doby, Lee Roy Reams, Charlene Ryan and John Wheeler were kept for the film. Gwen Verdon was not asked to repeat her Broadway performance, despite the fact that at one time she was considered being cast with Jack Lemmon as Oscar to ensure a box office name. In his book *City of Dreams: The Making and Remaking of Universal Pictures,* Bernard F. Dick reports that Ross Hunter wanted to produce the film with Verdon, but he was outvoted by the studio. Verdon was generous enough to be the uncredited coach for Shirley MacLaine's performance for the film. However, the memory of Verdon hangs uneasily over MacLaine who can be read as a poor copy. While Verdon does not have a great singing voice, it is serviceable.

MacLaine's likeability and sensitivity compensates somewhat for *her* weak singing voice, which underwhelms some of the songs Charity sings. An example of this is "Where Am I Going?" in which MacLaine's vocal is bad. One can accept MacLaine's voice as it is since Charity is not meant to be a professional singer, only a professional dancer. Additionally, it adds to the vulnerability of the character. However, when we hear Chita Rivera and Paula Kelly singing "There's Gotta Be Something Better than This," we can hear what a difference a good voice makes. Sammy Davis, Jr., singing "The Rhythm of Life," also shows the difference of a good vocalist. John McMartin's vocal for "Sweet Charity" demonstrates a serviceable voice, though oddly it is presented doubly, presumably to strengthen the sound. MacLaine's dancing is better than her singing. Rivera and Kelly may be better dancers, but one's eye is drawn to MacLaine when the three are together in "There's Gotta Be Something Better than This." This explains why MacLaine is a movie star and the two others are not. MacLaine also supplies tears in the scene at Barney's Chile Hacienda and appears unflatteringly with mascara running down her face. She is also touchingly pathetic when Charity tries to talk Oscar out of not wanting to marry her. Fosse also ends the film on a close-up of MacLaine.

McMartin is very funny when expressing Oscar's panic in the elevator, especially in his slapstick moves such as tripping over his suitcase and perching on the wall shelf. He also manages to make Oscar appear troubled but not hateful in his rejection of Charity. The film's ending is moving because of Cy Coleman's score; he uses the same beautiful piece of music that he does when Charity leaves the dancehall and before she meets Vittorio.

In the DVD featurette *From Stage to Screen—a Director's Dilemma,* Fosse talks about MacLaine. He says, "That face gave me many moments of confidence. Every time I look at her I see a circus, a circus of gaiety, hope, kindness, hurt, bewilderment. I knew if we could get some of these qualities we'd be ok." In the documentary, MacLaine comments on Charity's "incessant optimism" despite the fact that she is written as a victim: "The pathos of her is that she sees joy regardless of the mud she's thrown in." In her Hollywood memoir, *My Lucky Stars,* MacLaine advises that for the entire shoot she had an infected root canal but did not tell anyone so as to not hold up filming. There is a rumor that MacLaine had an uncredited dance double named Michelle Graham. However, it is not as obvious as, say, the dance doubles used for Jennifer Beals in *Flashdance* (1983).

In his book *All His Jazz: The Life and Death of Bob Fosse,* Martin Gottfried reported that the Central Park bridge scene in the film was actually filmed on a bridge in California. He also says that the alternative ending was shot at the Universal's request because they found the original too downbeat. Gottfried says that studio cut fifteen minutes out of the film, although he doesn't say what was cut. The *Turner Classic Movies* page on the film advises that several scenes were changed for the television version. The montage between the dance hall dressing room scene and the sidewalk scene where Charity sees Vittorio was cut; the "Rhythm of Life" and "I'm a Brass Band" numbers were shortened; "I Love to Cry at Weddings" faded out and ended as Charity and Oscar leave the dance hall; the scene in the phone booth and the conclusion of "Where Am I Going?" was cut, as was the overture, intermission and exit music.

In his *Turner Classic Movies* article, Frank Miller reports that it was MacLaine who helped get the film green-lighted after Universal had been looking to do a musical following the success of musicals such as Warner Bros.' *My Fair Lady* (1964) and 20th Century–Fox's *The Sound of Music* (1965). MacLaine insisted that Fosse be hired as a payback for his hiring her for the stage show *The Pajama Game.* Miller also reports that Ross Hunter was removed as producer because Fosse disagreed with the style that the film should use, Fosse wanting a gritty style and Hunter a more glamorous approach.

RELEASE: Premiered February 14, 1969, in Boston, Massachusetts. Premiered March 29, 1969, in Los Angeles and April 1, 1969, in New York. The taglines included "Hey Big Spender !" "Spend a Wonderful Time with 'Sweet Charity'" "The Musical Excitement of the 70's," "Love is what it's all about!" and "The Musical Motion Picture of the 70's!"

REVIEWS: Lauded by *Variety* and John Baxter in *Hollywood in the Sixties.* Lambasted by Vincent Canby in the *New York Times,* Clive Hirshhorn in *The Universal Story* and *The Hollywood Musical,* and Pauline Kael in *5001 Nights at the Movies.* Kael does comment that "it had some of the best dancing in American musicals of the period."

AWARDS: Nominated for Best Art Direction—Set Decoration, Best Costume Design and Best Score Academy Awards.

DVD: Released by Universal Studios on March 4, 2003. The DVD features the film's alternative ending and the featurettes *From Stage to Screen—a Director's Dilemma* and *The Art of Exaggeration: Designs for Sweet Charity by Edith Head.* The alternative ending shows Oscar in his apartment not being able to breathe, even after he opens a window. He goes to Central Park and sees Charity sitting on the bridge. Thinking she is going to jump in to commit suicide, he runs to her but trips over her suitcase and falls in the lake. Charity jumps in after him. Oscar asks her to marry him and they get out of the lake and walk away from the bridge.

Plaza Suite (1971)

Paramount Pictures/Howard W. Koch Production.

CREW: Arthur Hiller (Director), Howard W. Koch (Producer), Neil Simon (Screenplay), Jack Marta (Photography), Frank Bracht (Editor), Maurice Jarre (Music), Arthur Lonergan (Production Design), Reg Allen (Set Decorator), Gary Morris (Makeup), Joan Phillips (Hair), Jack Bear (Costumes), After Six (Men's Formal Wear), Don Record (Titles). Color, 114 minutes. Filmed at Paramount Studios and on location in the Plaza Hotel, New York.

CAST: Walter Matthau (Sam Nash/Jesse Kiplinger/Roy Hubley), Maureen Stapleton (Karen Nash), Barbara Harris (Muriel Tate), Lee Grant (Norma Hubley), Louise Sorel (Miss Jean McCormack), Jose Ocasio (Room Service Waiter), Dan Ferrone (Bellboy), Thomas Carey (Borden Eisler), Jenny Sullivan (Mimsey Hubley), Augusta Dabney (Mrs. Eisler), Alan North (Mr. Walter Eisler). Uncredited: Frank Albanese (Parking Lot Attendant), Raina Barrett (Girl in Lobby), Jack Beers (Man in Hotel), James Bryson (Ernie the Doorman), Jordan Charney (Jesse's Aide), Gordon B. Clarke (Hotel Manager), Alan DeWitt, Michael Irving (Men in Lobby), Kay Elliot (Chambermaid), Joseph Ferrari (Maitre d'), Joan Gordon, Kelly McCormick, Vicky Ruane (Wedding Guests), Peter Gumeny (Doorman), Nancy Harewood (Attractive Woman), Michael H. Ingram, Kurt Vladek (Desk Clerks), Jack Knight (Young Man), Maurice Marks, Robert Melendez, Jon Richards (Waiters), Gabor Morea (Elevator Operator), Florence Wallach (Woman in Lobby), Frank Wayne (Band Leader), Allister Whitman (Minister).

SONGS: "Tangerine" (Johnny Mercer and Victor Schertzinger), Maureen Stapleton.

SYNOPSIS: Forty-seven-year-old Karen Nash books room 719 at New York's Plaza Hotel for herself and her fifty-one-year-old husband Sam for their twenty-third wedding anniversary. Sam reveals that he is having an affair with his secretary, Miss McCormack. Hollywood producer Jesse Kiplinger invites his old girlfriend of fifteen years, New Jersey housewife Muriel Tate, to visit him in room 719 the next day. Jesse overcomes Muriel's objections and seduces her. The following day, room 719 has Roy and Norma Hubley, whose twenty-one-year-old daughter Mimsey is to be married in the hotel's Baroque Room. However, Mimsey locks herself in the bathroom and refuses to come out. When the lawyer groom Borden is called for her, he speaks to Mimsey and she comes out and the wedding takes place.

NOTES: Simon's screen adaptation of his play continues his focus on the subject of marriage and family and the theme of conservative versus radical behavior. He also explores the topics of aging and the emptiness of success, showing two male characters having middle-age crises, marital infidelity, and the generation gap. Unlike the later *California Suite*, in which Simon intercuts narrative between four stories, here he maintains the source play's structure of three consecutive stories. The third story is slightly different, however, since its narrative is intercut with other action. While the stories can be generally classified as a drama, a comedy and a farce, the first story successfully includes comedy within the drama. The screenplay is notable for Simon's use of profanity, some of which comes from the play, and some of which is added. This appears to be a precedent for the writer and perhaps a nod to the new permissiveness of cinema of the time. Simon also uses the word "faggot" in the screenplay, which can be read as unnecessarily homophobic, even when its use is slightly leavened by the reference being to a lesbian and not a gay man and the word is spoken by an embittered abandoned husband.

The play is "opened up" with scenes of Karen introduced walking and shopping in the city, the street outside the hotel, Muriel driving in her car over the bridge from New Jersey, and the car park. In the first story Karen throws a paper airplane out her room window, whereas in the play it was only thrown across the room. We then see what Karen sees—a young couple kissing as they sit on a bench. We are also shown the hotel foyer, the front desk, the elevator, the hallway, the Baroque Room, and ledges, as well as the rooms where most of the action takes place. In the second story Simon adds a scene of synchronicity outside the Plaza, where Jesse's car arrives after Karen walks by.

The screenwriter repeats synchronicity for the beginning of the third story as Jesse leaves the hotel in his car and is passed by wedding guests entering the lobby.

Simon employs the theatrical device of having characters speak to themselves, and running gags that include the idea that the hotel provides anchovies even when you don't order them, Muriel's paranoia about being seen at the hotel, and Mimsey's refusal to come out of the bathroom.

Some new scenes have narrative payoffs. The scene of Jesse's dialogue with his aide includes asking him if he has a good-looking sister or a pretty girlfriend "willing to sacrifice herself for your future." Jesse's subsequent advance on the girl in the street defines him as a womanizer and prefigures his seduction of Muriel. The scene of her leaving her car with the parking attendant has her repeat the line she had said to herself in the car, "One quick drink then I'm going," to the attendant when he asks her how long she will be. Muriel's behavior at the hotel desk also presents her self-consciousness as she initially moves away when a couple appear behind her. In the third story Simon adds scenes in the Baroque Room, where Roy has encounters with the band leader, a waiter, and the man who has made the matchbooks and napkins. The scenes between Roy and Norma are also in counterpoint to small conversations in the room between the Eislers, the priest telling Mr. Eisler that he has another appointment to attend soon, and a silent scene of the wedding guests waiting. The end of the third act occurs in the street outside the hotel, where we see Mimsey and Borden ride a motorbike away and Roy and Norma watch. It is also the location where Roy delivers the play's last line, that Mimsey was better off in the bathroom. Norma wears a white fur piece over her dress that we had not seen her grab before she and Roy and Mimsey left the hotel room for the wedding, though this is a plot point than can rationalized given the passage of time presented.

The new scenes also have new funny lines. Sam calls Karen from the foyer, and she asks him if he remembers room 719. After she hangs up she says, "He doesn't remember." The point of Karen giving Sam a lipstick when she can't find a pencil is topped by Karen's line, "You want to go round again?" after she has told him twice that she doesn't have a pencil. Karen has lines to herself that express her perception that she has handled moments badly. These indicate her desired intention for the evening, and include "Shut up, Karen. Keep your stupid mouth shut" and "You blew it again." The screenplay adds the moment where Sam asks Karen if she has anything to read to occupy herself as he works. She reads a passage from the Bible and says, "I read it." There is a funny exchange after Jesse kisses Muriel, which makes reference to them being on the seventh floor of the hotel. Muriel asks, "Suppose someone saw us through a window?" to which Jesse replies, "Who? A couple of pigeons?" Jesse tells Muriel, "I've got a three hundred and sixty degree bed and one hundred and eighty degrees of it are empty."

Another funny moment is when a woman named Bess calls out, "My God, what are you doing here?" as Muriel waits at the elevator. Muriel replies, "Nothing!" and then we see that Bess is speaking to a man also at the elevator, and that neither he nor Bess appear to hear Muriel's response. In the third story, Norma has a new line before she answers the Eislers on the telephone: "They'll know I'm lying. They'll hear the panic in my voice." Roy has a new line when he asks Norma after breaking the chair against the

Top left: Jesse Kiplinger (Walter Matthau) and Muriel Tate (Barbara Harris); top right: Sam Nash (Matthau) and Karen Nash (Maureen Stapleton); bottom: Norma Hubley (Lee Grant) and Roy Hubley (Matthau), in a composite still for *Plaza Suite* (1971).

bathroom door, "Do you know what that chair is gonna cost me? About as much as that door is gonna cost me." Before Mr. Eisler telephones the Hubleys, Mrs. Eisler asks, "Maybe her zipper broke?" Mr. Eisler replies, "For twenty minutes?" Roy has a funny line to his daughter after his coat is ripped and before he exits the window: "I'm coming after you, Mimsey. I'm coming after you with my one good arm." Norma also has a new moment after she looks out the window for Roy and her hat gets wet from the rain. This leads to her looking in the mirror and crying before Roy reappears at the door.

Funny lines retained from the play include Karen's telling Sam that she wants him to put his eye drops in because "it's the only time lately you look at me," and telling Sam, "You'll be the youngest one in the cemetery," after he says that he refuses to accept being older. Another is Karen's line in answer to Sam's telling her that he could get tickets for a show, as he has to work. He asks, "Something you'd like to see?" and Karen replies, "What you and Miss McCormack will be doing later." Sam tells Karen that he doesn't even remember how the affair got started and she replies, "Think, it'll come back to you." Sam describes the affair as "cheating, sneaking, sordid," and Karen comments, "If it helps you to romanticize it, Sam." When Karen won't lash out further at Sam to give him satisfaction, she tells him, "You're adorable. Eat your heart out." Karen also tells him that she knows he'll come back because he forgot to take his eye drops. This line pays off the earlier business of Karen attempting to put them into Sam's eyes. Roy tells Norma, "Well how long do you think we can keep this a secret? As soon as that boy down there says I do and there's nobody standing next to him, they're going to suspect something." Norma tells Roy, "That's right. Tell a woman who's having a heart attack that her daughter jumped out the window." After Roy complains that it is "me, me, me" that has to explain Mimsey's delay in appearing for the wedding, he tells Norma to answer the telephone. She asks him, "What happened to me, me, me?" Norma tells Roy, "Don't you wave your broken arm at me!" Norma comments over Mimsey's toilet paper note, "Did she have to write it on this kind of paper?" After Roy comes out of the bathroom and he telephones for Borden in the Baroque Room, Norma comments on his not telling her what Mimsey has told him. Norma says, "It's so bad words can't form in your mouth?"

In one change from the play's first story, Simon cuts the small joke about Jean's name only being revealed during Sam's confession. This allowed Karen in the play to ask who is Jean and to say, "For a minute I thought there were two of them." Simon also cuts the imitation Karen does of Jean after Karen is told of the affair. From the play's second act, Simon cuts Muriel's telling Jesse not to look at her because she has been stuck in the Holland Tunnel for two hours. He changes the play's line to, "It's been fifteen years and I haven't had my hair done," which adds to the repeated reminders Muriel makes about her hair appointment and provides context for her messy hair. The movie person Jesse is to meet later in the hotel gets a new payoff when Jesse asks Muriel if she wants to stay to meet Lee Marvin. She replies, "I think I'm past the age when I get excited by meeting a movie star," saying this is something her fourteen-year-old daughter would do. However, clearly Muriel *is* excited by the prospect. The secret Jesse reveals of his third wife is also new. Simon misdirects us by having Jesse ask Muriel, "Do you know a famous movie star with the initials A.W.?" and then has Jesse say that the lover was that star's wife. "He married a faggot."

For the third story, the screenplay adds Roy on the ledge and the pigeons that obstruct him, as well as his finding that the bathroom window is locked. Another addition is Norma tearing the lapels of Roy's coat, which pays off her earlier ripping the back of the coat. The main cut from the play is the action of Mimsey that comes before she slips the toilet paper note under the door. Roy suggests that she knock on the door to indicate whether she wants to marry Borden, and a joke comes from the interpretation of the number of knocks Mimsey does. The note is also different in the play and the screenplay. The play makes more of Mimsey's preference to speak to Roy before the note is received, as Norma tells Roy that she thinks what is wrong with Mimsey is something she can't discuss with him. Norma asks Mimsey if she wants her to come in to talk to her daughter. Mimsey's note then reads as "I would rather talk to Daddy." The screenplay has the note reading "I would like to talk to Daddy," and although Simon keeps Norma's later comments about how she thought she and Mimsey were friends, the rejection seems less stinging.

Sam and Karen as a married couple are presented as family. Sam's middle-age crisis has him having an affair with his secretary to demonstrate a move away from convention. Jesse is a single, middle-aged man attempting to have an affair with a married woman, who is presented as more radical than Sam in costume and attitude. While Sam too is a philanderer, his approach seems less overt than Jesse's. Jesse is also presented as more radical than Muriel since he is a Hollywood producer and she a New Jersey housewife. Muriel's being currently married and Jesse's having been married three times unsuccessfully, and the couple's willingness to have an extramarital affair, presents a more cynical view of marriage and family. The third story's study of the generation gap is represented by Mimsey's locking herself in the bathroom on her wedding day because she wants something better than the kind of marriage her parents have. The story comments on the lack of communication in families since it is only Mimsey's husband-to-be, and not her parents, that can convince her to come out. The radicalism of Mimsey and Borden is also demonstrated by their leaving the wedding on a motorbike rather than a traditional limousine, and Mimsey's wedding dress being shortened for the ride. This gets a last comment from Roy, who says that she was better off in the bathroom.

In the first story, Karen's effusive talking to the hotel staff presents her as a naive out-of-towner, and this quality is echoed in the play's first act being entitled "Visitor from Mamaroneck." Sam comments on Karen's behavior when he asks her why she speaks to the waiter as if she has known him for twenty years. Sam's reticence shows he is more sophisticated. Karen's good cheer is also contrasted with Sam's narcissism, his affair being another sign of the same. Sam can also be read as being a spoil-sport in the way he corrects Karen's notions of it being the couple's anniversary and that they are in the same room they had on their honeymoon. Sam's rejection of Karen's affection also suggests his guilt over the affair he is having as much as his physical disinterest in his wife. Karen guesses that Sam is having the affair before he admits to it, and his initial denial adds to his duplicity. There is a moment after the discussion of Sam not being flabby when it appears that he is going to tell Karen something, before he changes his mind. If he was going to tell Karen about the affair, this moment suggests his remorse and a consideration of his wife's rejection. This moment will be paid off later after he admits to the affair. It is noteworthy that Jean is said to be divorced. This makes her involvement in the affair seem less of a manipulation, as she is a more experienced woman. The screenplay still leaves the conclusion of the first act ambiguous, despite Simon's adding a scene in which Karen leaves the hotel alone. This doesn't necessarily mean that Sam has left her, since we had been shown that she arrived alone as well.

In the second story, Jesse is another out-of-towner, although he is more sophisticated than the Nashes. By contrast, it is Muriel as the New Yorker who seems to be more naïve than he. Her culpability in the affair is explored. She presents as a ditz in the way she keeps saying a different time for her hair appointment. However, this can be given context by her mixture of fear and desire about meeting Jesse. Her recall of the details of their previous date shows how important he was to her, although she tries to pretend otherwise. This is apparent from her reaction to Jesse's touching her. Muriel's self-consciousness also comes from her status in relation to Jesse, whom she perceives as being more successful than her. Another factor contributing to Muriel's behavior is her drinking. However, her suddenly kissing Jesse as she talks about her husband Larry suggests that there is something not satisfying in the marriage. Muriel's eventual seduction by Jesse comes from his catering to her star worship, although her being drunk may also be responsible for her becoming pliant.

The play entitled the third act "Visitor from Forest Hills," although the screenplay does not state where the Hubleys are from. The idea of them as out-of-towners continues the idea from the first two stories, with the Hubleys are presented as unsophisticated. The third story also continues the schadenfreude that had colored Simon's screenplay for *The Out of Towners*. This is because the Hubleys endure a succession of bad fortune that is apparently meant to be funny.

Director Arthur Hiller uses a melancholy score for the first story, a more jovial one for the second, and a less apparent one for the third. He manages to make the first story seem less stage-bound, and is aided by the sensitive performances of Matthau and Stapleton. The second story reads as more stagey since it is one extended conversation between two people, whereas there were interruptions in the first story's exchange. The third story's actions and performances manage to overcome the stage origins of the material.

In the first story, Hiller has the camera initially on Karen's back for Sam's confession of the affair and then moves it around to her front for us to see Stapleton's reaction. In the second story, Hiller is perhaps too close on Matthau as Jesse, presenting him as a grotesque, and the director has an odd moment after Muriel closes Jesse's hotel room door. The camera stays in the hallway and we hear Jesse and Muriel speaking. Hiller has a shot of Jesse running his hands over Muriel's knees before the camera moves up to the couple's faces for the suggestion that Jesse slips his hand under Muriel's dress. The director has the couple slide down behind the couch when Jesse kisses Muriel, so that they are both out of view. Hiller also shows the couple in a long shot for their talk in the hallway as the camera stays at the open door watching them. He brings back music for the ending, when Jesse moves Muriel into the bedroom to indicate that Jesse's seduction is now successful, and pans away from the couple to show a painting on the wall of a semi-naked couple.

For the transition in the third story, Hiller shows wedding guests entering the hotel and passing a sign of the various event rooms. He zooms in on the notice of the Baroque Room, which is hosting the Hubley-Eisler wedding. Hiller then zooms out on a flower stand in the Baroque Room and pans over to a shot of Mr. and Mrs. Eisler. The couple are seen in close-up in the background of the shot as wedding guests stand in the foreground, out of focus. Hiller then cuts to Roy as he argues with the band leader. There is a continuity question over Roy's broken arm, since after it is broken, Matthau's gesturing seems not to take that into consideration. Hiller has the camera behind the backs of Roy and Norma when they sit on the bed to talk about doing their best, and has Roy break the chair into the camera as if it is the bathroom door. The director cuts to the silent guests in the Baroque Room after this violence, and then back to the door, which is shown to be dented. Hiller allows Roy and Norma a slow reaction to her ripping his rented coat as he tries to climb out the window. Hiller also ends the third story with a surprise. We see a limousine in the foreground on the street outside the hotel, and a crowd around Mimsey and Borden. When the crowd moves we see the couple drive away on a motorbike. Hiller also has the lead actors perform theatrical bows to the camera for the end credits.

The director only uses Maureen Stapleton and Jose Ocasio from the original Broadway cast, with Stapleton repeating only one of three roles she played. Simon said in his *Playboy* interview that he didn't want Walter Matthau to appear in all three stories of the film. He only wanted him to be in the last one, since Simon believed that audiences would get tired of seeing the same actor. However, Matthau told Paramount that he wouldn't do the film unless he could do all three stories. Simon tried to suggest then that three other actors be hired, but he lost the argument. However, the writer maintains that he was right, since he finds the actor was really only good in the third story. Simon is quoted in the article on *Turner Classic Movies* that Peter Sellers might have been better able to play the three roles. Another source claims that Sellers was at one time proposed for the film, but only in one role. In 1969 Paramount announced that the movie's three stories would star George C. Scott and Maureen Stapleton, Peter Sellers and Barbra Streisand, and Walter Matthau and Lucille Ball.

Pauline Kael in her book *Reeling* and Vincent Canby in his review of the film in the *New York Times* both state that Matthau wears wigs in his three roles. As Sam Nash, Matthau wears a black moustache and has black hair, which gives him a sinister look. This matches the duplicity that the character has. Matthau makes Sam funny in the way he yells when Karen stabs him with the eye dropper, and brings pathos to Sam's yearning to start his life over again. However, the actor cannot make Sam sympathetic. For the second story, Matthau has no moustache and his hair with bangs is honey-blonde. He uses a more pronounced New York intonation and he makes Jesse's lechery funny. Matthau's glance at Muriel, before he tells her that his mother sent him the newspaper article about her, tells us that he is lying. The actor looks into the camera in response to Muriel's asking Jesse if he went to the Academy Awards. As Roy, Matthau's hair is grey and is off his forehead. In the third story the actor gives a broad performance to match the farcical tone, and his anger is funny. He also uses his pronounced New York accent, and acts like Frankenstein's monster when Roy reappears at the hotel room door after having been on the window ledge. Matthau also provides pathos in Roy's speech about how he cried on his pillow the night before the wedding and is realistic when he tells Norma that Mimsey does not want to become like them.

Maureen Stapleton brings likeability to Karen as well as humor. She also suggests Karen's Jewishness with intonation and gestures. Stapleton makes Karen running to answer the two telephones funny, as well as running to get Sam a pencil. Stapleton is also funny in the way she poses sexily when Karen asks how she looks for a forty-seven-year-old woman, a moment retained from the play, and when she imitates Sam's body not moving after he is undressed at night. She uses a circle sign with three fingers to underscore Karen's reminding Sam that he is fifty-one. Stapleton retains the play's gesture of Karen's snapping her fingers when she tells Sam that she chooses for him to stop seeing Jean, and also the comic collapse onto the couch after Sam tells Karen not to blame Jean for the affair. Stapleton's anger is almost operatic and nearly threatens to overwhelm the material. However, this problem is leavened by Simon's interspersing comedy with the drama. Stapleton also supplies vulnerability to Karen, mixing fear with her pride and anger at the prospect of Sam leaving. In contrast with Stapleton, Barbara Harris underplays Muriel, which gives subtlety to her laugh lines. As Norma, Lee Grant is as likeable as Stapleton and Harris, and supplies vulnerability. This is perhaps easy since of the three women, Grant is the smallest when coupled with Matthau. Grant gives a fake laugh to Norma's line about Mimsey being a very lucky girl, and is funny when using a sugary voice to cover her panic. Grant scores a laugh that comes from the play when Norma gestures to the heavens as she says, "I should have invited your cousin Lillie. She wished this on me, I know it." She also cries, although there are no apparent tears.

In Gordon Gow's article on Hiller for *Films and Filming,* the director comments on the casting of the three actresses in the leading roles of the three stories. He says that he couldn't find an actress who could play all the three parts on screen. Hiller says he had started out with the idea of casting three different actors to play the male leading roles, which then determined the need for three different actresses. However, the actors he spoke to all wanted full star payment although each of them would only be doing one-third of the film. This would have tripled the budget, although Hiller could see their point of view. They would have been paid for their names and not their screen time.

The director says that Stapleton could not have pulled off playing Muriel on film, because she was a younger woman, despite being a remarkable actress. He said that Stapleton as Karen made the sadness of the realization of the end of her marriage "so true and real."

In his *Playgirl* interview Simon said that his brother Danny was a part of the inspiration for the character of Jesse. Simon also said that he doesn't like the movie at all, and that he blames himself for some of it. He said he should have opened up the film more so that not all the stories took place in the same suite and more of the hotel and New York could have been used.

RELEASE: May 12, 1971, with the taglines "Book into Neil Simon's Hotel Suite for the time of your life" and "Plaza Suite. Through its portals pass the world's most mixed up mortals."

REVIEWS: Praised by *Variety,* John Douglas Eames in *The Paramount Story,* and Gordon Gow in his article on Arthur Hiller in *Films and Filming.* Lambasted by Vincent Canby in the *New York Times,* Jerry Roberts in his book, *The Great American Play-*

wrights on the Screen, and Robert K. Johnson, who commented that the roles of Sam and Jesse were "beyond the range of Matthau as a performer."

DVD: Released by Paramount on November 25, 2003.

REMAKES: Two subsequent versions of the play have filmed. In 1982 one was filmed for HBO cable television and starred Lee Grant and Jerry Orbach in the three leading roles in all three acts. It was directed by Harvey Medlinsky and filmed before a live audience. On December 3, 1987, a made-for-television version was aired that was directed by Roger Beatty and Kenny Solms. Carol Burnett played all three leading female parts and the male leading roles were taken by Hal Holbrook, Dabney Coleman, and Richard Crenna. In his review in the *New York Times,* John J. O'Connor noted that the play's dialogue had been updated throughout, with trendy references to such current icons as Dr. Ruth, Cybill Shepherd and Bruce Willis. Part of the play was produced for Greek television in 2007 as part of the television series "To kokkino domatio."

Star Spangled Girl (1971)

Paramount Pictures/Howard W. Koch Production.

CREW: Jerry Paris (Director), Howard W. Koch (Producer), Arnold Margolin and Jim Parker (Screenplay, based on the play by Neil Simon), Sam Leavitt (Photography), Frank Bracht (Editor), Charles Fox (Music), Lawrence G. Paull (Production Design), Reg Allen (Set Decoration), Lee Harmon (Makeup), Joan Phillips (Hair), Wayne Fitzgerald (Titles). Color, 93 minutes. Filmed at Paramount Studios and on location in Los Angeles.

CAST: Sandy Duncan (Amelia "Amy" Cooper), Tony Roberts (Andy Hobart), Todd Susman (Norman Cornell), Elizabeth Allen (Mrs. MacKaninee), Artie Lewis (Mr. Karlson), Helen Kleeb (Receptionist, YWCA), Allen Yung (Hip Woo), Harry Northup (Cowboy on Bus), Gordon Bosserman, Jim Connors (Karlson Boys Lem and Roy), Peter Hobbs (Man in Car). Uncredited: Alan Paige, Sally Yarnell (Neighbors), Betty Palivoda (Checker in Market), Victor Paul, Charlie Picerni (Policemen).

SONGS: "Girl" (music by Charles Fox, lyrics by Norman Gimbel), Davy Jones; "The Battle Hymn of the Republic" (music by William Steffe, lyrics by Julia Ward Howe), Sandy Duncan.

SYNOPSIS: Olympic swimmer Amy Cooper comes from Florida to Los Angeles and moves into a bungalow at the Hampshire Court with her white cat Buster. Another bungalow houses the office of the underground protest newspaper *Nitty Gritty,* which is written by Norman Cornell and edited and managed by Andy Hobart. Norman is physically attracted to Amy and his stalking her leads her to get fired from her job as a swimming instructor at the YWCA. Andy hires her for the newspaper as a secretary. Amy discovers that she is attracted to Andy but, as he does not feel the same for her, she decides to go back to Florida. Norman decides to move out but then stays, no longer interested in Amy. Andy realizes that he does feel attracted to Amy and goes after her.

NOTES: This is another screenplay that Simon did not adapt from his own play. Screenwriters Arnold Margolin and Jim Parker cut some of Simon's play and added their own lines. Like the play, the film explores Simon's subject of friendship as family, and the theme of radical and conservative behavior. This difference gets a spin with the

Tony Roberts (left), Sandy Duncan and Todd Susman in a still for *Star Spangled Girl* (1971).

idea that Norman's interest in Amy is an unhealthy obsession from physical attraction. The narrative also presents Amy as an out-of-towner, although here the town is Los Angeles and not New York. Additionally there is some suggestion of homophobia, following on from the "faggot" line in *Plaza Suite.*

The play is "opened up" with the new locations of a Greyhound bus that is used for the beginning and the end of the narrative, the street, Hip Woo's Chinese Laundry, a supermarket, and the YMCA. The exterior of the Hampshire Court bungalows and Mrs. MacKaninee's office are also shown. Some of these locations have a narrative payoff. Amy has a conversation with a cowboy on the bus, who is styled to recall Jon Voight from *Midnight Cowboy* (1969), and who tells her he is from New York. Andy and Mrs. MacKaninee are seen riding a motorbike in the street, water ski and surf at a beach, and fly a light plane. This action is repeated for the end of the film when Norman skydives with Amy. Amy on the bus to the YWCA sees the street signs that Norman paints for her that read "Norman is fond of Amy," "Norman is very fond of Amy," "Norman is crazy about Amy," and "I'm getting to you."

The YMCA scene operates as a set piece and shows Norman delivering the duck in the box to Amy, and the swimming pool and showers where the duck appears. We also see the three policemen at the YMCA, one slipping on the floor of the shower room, and all of them falling into the pool. Interestingly, the screenplay does not show the police finding Norman at the YWCA or them taking him away in the patrol car. The scene also does not include the actions described in the play of the gym teacher hanging from the basketball hoop in reaction to the duck and the duck chasing a seventy-three-year-old arts and crafts teacher off the pool's diving board.

The fight scene between Andy and Norman includes Norman's new line, "Is it your intention to weaken me with laughter?" at the sight of Andy's fighting pose. Another addition is the gay-panic Norman has in reaction to Andy's kissing him and telling him that he loves him after Norman says he is through with Amy and will now get back to work. Even though there it is apparent that Andy is being friendly and not making an advance, Norman's reaction suggests he fears otherwise. He tells Andy, "I'm through with her. Not with girls. Leave me alone." There is another moment that is retained from the play that is given a gay-panic resonance. Norman thinks that the hand put on his shoulder as he types is Amy's and he kisses it. Then he retreats when he sees that the hand belongs to Andy. Again, Andy is only expressing gratitude that Norman is working, although Andy responds with a presumably different idea.

There are some funny new lines. The man in the car who initially refuses to buy a copy of *Nitty Gritty* from Andy tells him repeatedly to "take your hands off the car." When Andy tells the man that the paper includes an article about a love-in, the man tells him, "Give me a copy and then take your hands off the car." Andy tells Norman that his job is keeping him alive but not happy, and Norman replies, "If I'm not happy, I don't write well. If I don't write well, we don't eat well. If we don't eat well, I'm not happy." Norman threatens to chew off his paw if Andy doesn't release him from the handcuffs. Andy replies, "Please, not while I'm eating," since he eats a tiny kumquat sandwich.

Some of Simon's funny lines from the play are retained. Norman gets the idea to give Amy flowers every day and then wonders that the gesture is not big enough. Andy comments, "How about trees?" Norman tells Andy that he can't work under coercion and Andy replies, "How about savage beatings?" To reference Norman's attention to Amy, Andy tells him, "I'd had just about as much of King Kong and Fay Wray as I can take." Amy shines a lamp on her face to show Andy her nervous tension hives. When she asks him if he knows what causes her to get hives, Andy replies, "Holding a lamp to your face?" Andy says to Amy, "Will you stop kicking me? I have very thin socks." Andy tells Norman about his being sunburned: "The only time I had a shadow was when a bird flew over me. You can see his outline on my back." When Amy comes to confront Norman about his causing her to be fired, Andy tells her, "He's out there eating his heart out." She replies, "Well tell him not to bother cos I'm going to get a big dog to do it for him." Amy offers her hand after she agrees to work for him, and he asks if he is supposed to shake it. She tells him, "You're supposed to put eighty-five dollars in it." After Amy has been licking stamps, she asks Andy, "Can my tongue rest? The well has dried up." Andy asks Amy how she can explain being engaged and attracted to another man. She tells him, "Very simple explanation. I can't explain it." Andy asks what about her fiancée, and she replies, "He can't explain it either." Another funny exchange occurs after Andy asks Norman if he has ever lied to him in the eight years he has known him. Norman replies, "Yes, I've known you for nine years." At Andy's sit-in Norman tells Andy that his answer to passive resistance is "active kicking."

The play's locale of San Francisco is changed to Los Angeles, and the accommodations are changed from apartments to bungalows. Sophie Rauschmeyer is now Amy, her fiancé changed from First Lieutenant Marine Burt Fenneman to a member of the UCLA swim team, and her origin is changed from Hunnicut to Cypress Gardens, Florida. The man that Andy and Norman owe printing money is changed from Mr. Franklyn to Mr. Karlson. The newspaper that was *Fallout* is now *Nitty Gritty*, the article title of "Twenty-Seven Ways to Burn a Wet Draft Card" is now a recipe for twenty-seven ways to cook a draft card served for six, and lost is the article entitled "Is LBJ on LSD?" The song sung by Amy to distract Andy is changed from "Yankee Doodle" to "The Battle Hymn of the Republic," and the use of the latter song for the play's end is cut for the film.

Andy says he buys groceries in the play, but he steals them in the film. The plot point of Norman's stealing clothes from the apartment building roof is changed to Andy buying laundry as new clothes. Andy tells Amy that they only borrow other people's laundry and steal food to stay alive. The play has Norman buy a bottle of champagne for the party Andy suggests they have, but the film makes it muscatel. Interestingly, in the play Norman suggests getting muscatel, but Andy tells him to get champagne. Andy produces the handcuffs seemingly from nowhere, whereas in the play they come from the pool table, and the screenplay has Norman handcuffed to the living room railing, whereas in the play it is to a steampipe.

The adaptation loses the play's plot points of Norman's leaving Hershey bars in the girl's mailbox, tying a bottle of eau de cologne to her cat's tail, and watching her through a telescope. Norman's awareness of Amy's presence now comes from his smelling her scent and the end of his interest comes when he can no longer smell her approach. The screenwriters dilute the connection between the kind of girl Norman wants and how Amy supposedly fits his desire. This is more apparent in the play, where he spoke of wanting a "beautiful, gorgeous blonde." In the film Norman tells Andy that the girl he wants is "nice-looking" with a good sense of humor and nice legs, and loves pizza and cherry Cokes. However, Amy does not seem to match these specifics.

The screenplay also changes the play's ending in which Amy returned before Andy had a chance to go after her. In the play she says that she had intended to get the bus but that she forgot the fare. Now she leaves on another Greyhound bus for Florida and Andy follows her on a motorbike. Andy initially goes in the opposite direction from the bus and then turns around to follow it, so that his intention is clear. However, his being unable to stop the motorbike reads as a failed attempt at humor, equally as silly as Norman's being seen skydiving with Mrs. MacKaninee. The screenplay also changes the idea that the newspaper edition would be finished. This is something that happens in the play, but the film's destruction of Norman's typewriter and his skydiving with Mrs. MacKaninee suggest otherwise.

Amy is presented as a radical in the way she has her head out of the Greyhound bus window when it comes into the city. However, the narrative will show that she is more conservative than Norman. Under the opening credits director Jerry Paris has pictures of Amy with a psychedelic pattern that features stars, recalling those on the American flag. This idea supports the notion from the film's title, that Amy is an all–American girl. Amy's being an Olympic swimmer adds to this idea, and her coming from Florida and her accent also allude to her being unsophisticated.

The fact that Andy dresses in disguise as a hippie to sell *Nitty Gritty* in the street alludes to his real conservative nature, since he appears more conservative when he goes to Hip Woo's and the supermarket and when he returns home. However, his drinking milk at the supermarket and filling the empty carton with pickles, raisins and nuts is radical behavior, since Andy only pays for the milk. He will later admit to this behavior as theft, rationalized by him and Norman being poor. However, the idea of poverty becomes questionable when we see that Norman buys delicacies for a basket to give to Amy. Andy is also presented as being radical in his dating Mrs. MacKaninee to save rent money, since the dates include riding a motorbike, water skiing, surfing, and flying a light plane.

Norman smells Amy before he sees her, and this idea of his attraction being to her scent is continued in the narrative. It is paid off when Amy realizes that she is attracted to Andy's smell and again at the conclusion when his noticing Amy's lingering smell in his house confirms that he is attracted to her. The characters of Amy and Norman are initially aligned by the fact of the both of them talking too much, although Norman is struck dumb when he is first faced by Amy and then reduced to baby talk when he wants to speak to her. He can only speak normally to her after he has overcome his physical attraction to her. Norman is different from both Andy and Amy since his interest in her is shown to be an obsession. When Amy and Andy come to feel the same attraction, they do not become as possessed as Norman. Thankfully, he is aware that his behavior is abnormal, though that doesn't seem to help him control it. It supposedly gets context from Norman's being infatuated with Amy. While perhaps this was acceptable as a convention of a period romantic comedy, a modern reading of the film provides a darker psychological undertone.

Amy is presented as generous when she gives Norman a warning to leave her alone rather than going straight to the police to have him arrested for "invasion of privacy." She also warns that her fiancé may beat Norman up. However, her hitting Norman after the warnings shows that she is not afraid to get violent. This strike can be somewhat leavened since at the time he advances towards her and tries to touch her. Amy also demonstrates her superior physical strength when she overpowers Andy and holds his arm behind his back. In reaction to Norman's advances, Amy's hair falls out and she gets hives from nervous tension. These conditions undermine the supposed charm of his attention. Amy does eventually call the police about Norman, although we don't see them until they come to the YWCA. Even then we don't see Norman arrested and only hear from him that it has happened. Amy's willingness to work for Andy and Norman, after Norman's appearance at the YWCA gets her fired, shows that she is not afraid of Norman and that she is willing to smile for Norman if that will control him. However, we see that Andy is wrong in thinking that just a smile will satisfy Norman. Having her around makes Norman even more interested in Amy, and Norman fails in keeping Andy away from her since Andy is seen to be occupied with Miss MacKaninee. Amy threatens to press charges after Norman bites her earlobe, though she doesn't do it. This is perhaps because her realization that she is attracted to Andy sidetracks her.

The idea that Amy is attracted to Andy is introduced with romantic convention. She deliberately makes noise in the office when he has asked her not to, with her aggravation given context by the fact that Andy has not paid her what he has promised.

Despite Norman's pursuit of Amy appearing to be pathological, Andy's condescension towards her reads as more intellectually cruel. Norman may only want to sleep with Amy, but he doesn't think her stupid, as Andy does. Amy's being dressed in tight sweaters and cut-off shorts may seem to confirm Andy's idea of her as a bimbo, but it also has context from her being an athlete. Andy's slow reaction to Amy's confession of her attraction to him shows that he is not the physical opportunist that Norman is. Andy's hesitation in kissing Amy also comes from the fact that she is engaged to another man, something that didn't stop Norman. Amy must make an advance toward Andy and even humiliate herself by asking him to touch her, to get him to respond. He only kisses her because she says that she wants to feel repulsed by him. However, the kiss only makes her more interested in Andy and she tells him, "I liked it. We're in big trouble." Norman then walks in on Amy and Andy when they are kissing for the second time; another convention for the romantic triangle presented. The fact that both Norman and Amy want to move away from the residential court shows the affection they both have for Andy. Norman's feeling of betrayal has a familial connotation if we view them as partners, since Norman needs Andy to motivate him to write and Andy needs Norman's writing.

Andy wants Norman to stay so that the current issue of the newspaper can be finished, more than Andy fears losing a friend. Andy is even prepared to fight Norman to keep him for the work; however, this bluff is soon exposed when both men injure each other in their first blows. Neither are shown to be superior fighters, which emasculates both characters. However, Andy is shown to be the more deceitful man when he handcuffs Norman to the railing. Amy tells Norman that she forgives him for his attention towards her because she now understands the feeling of physical attraction that she has for Andy. While Amy reports that she has broken her engagement to her fiancé, he is still supposedly due to come and beat up Andy. It is Amy's leaving that seemingly makes Andy unlock Norman's handcuffs because he has lost interest in the newspaper. This defeat of Andy makes Norman want to stay and help his friend. Andy even encourages Norman to go after Amy while Norman finishes the work. This shows a new generosity of spirit in Norman and is a confirmation that he is no longer attracted to Amy. However, the narrative denies us an immediate happy ending for Amy and Andy when he loses control of the motorbike before she can get off the bus to go back with him. In another touch of emasculation, Andy doesn't know how to stop the motorbike because he says he has never driven one before; we have only seen him previously behind Mrs. MacKaninee on the bike. Despite his apparent reluctance to skydive, Norman's being with Mrs. MacKaninee suggests that he has used her money to pay off the Karlsons and has become her new lover. This suggests Norman's own form of character growth and a new female interest in his life.

Jerry Paris uses a freeze frame when Norman jumps in the air, and repeats the device of having the camera stay in one position while other activity is suggested. Examples are when the camera is on Mrs. MacKaninee's "manager" sign as we hear Andy talking to her, with music also heard suggesting that they dance; and when Norman goes to Amy's bungalow to mope and the camera stays on the screen door. We hear dialogue and the sound of a breaking lamp, and Norman apologizing by stating, "That was an accident." The camera stays on the doorway to the kitchen of Andy's bungalow as we hear that Amy breaks dishes, and when Andy tells her that her apron is slipping and the sound we hear suggests that she hits him with a frypan. This camera position is repeated once again when Norman claims to help Amy get the vacuum cleaner, we hear her scream and a crash, and Norman tells Andy that he bit her earlobe. There is a comic shot from behind of Norman and Amy lying on the ground as they have their heads in bushes looking for Buster, and Paris attempts to provide farce when Norman goes to the YWCA with the duck and when we see Andy and Mrs. MacKaninee upside down in the light plane. Paris conceals the moment when Andy strikes Norman on the head with the ukulele. He only shows us Andy holding the instrument to strike, then we hear a crash and the next time we see Norman he has a bandage on his head. However, the sound of the tape recording becoming distorted after we see Andy's intention to strike also suggests that Andy has struck the machine instead. Since Norman uses the machine again for another telephone ruse to Mr. Karlson, this tells us that the machine is still operational. The cries of Buster when Norman spills paint on him are more disturbing than funny, and the scenes where Norman and then three policemen enter the YWCA are grimly unfunny. Equally perplexing is why the women scream at the sight of a duck. Paris protects the nudity of the women in the shower by showing only their legs when the duck and the policeman who slips onto the floor are present.

Paris' treatment is most successful in the scene between Andy and Amy when she realizes that she is attracted to him. This is because Sandy Duncan and Tony Roberts make the banter work better than Todd Susman and Roberts, whose encounters with theatrical rapid-fire delivery read more as blather. It is also aided by the sensitive way Paris handles Duncan and Roberts in their reactions to each other. The climactic reunion of Amy and Andy, before the narrative has Andy lose control of the motorbike and ride away from her, also works. The score helps to provide the sentiment and romance in the moment of reunion, even if their attraction is diminished by the idea of its only being physical. Military-style music is used as Amy goes Norman's bungalow to confront him after she is fired, and also briefly when Andy decides to go after Amy's bus when she has decided to leave town. Paris presents the Karlson sons in the background and on either side of Norman, who is in the foreground typing when they appear; and as Mr. Karlson is immediately behind Norman, he is initially unseen. The director cuts from Norman's scream for Mrs. MacKaninee after the typewriter is broken in half to the harmonica in the score as Andy pursues Amy. The score uses a full orchestra for emotional impact in the climax, and repeats the opening song, "Girl," for the end.

As Amy, Sandy Duncan is funny when using the appeasing smile Amy has agreed to give Norman when she works for *Nitty Gritty*, when she flutters her eyes at Andy in fake flirtation, and she shows hurt in reaction to Andy's insults to her. Tony Roberts makes Andy the more masculine of the two men and presents the character's combination of arrogance and sensitivity. As Norman, Todd Susman's performance is problematic, mainly because it is so broad. He also does not always look at Andy when he is supposed to be speaking to him, which creates the impression that he is talking to himself, which he does on other occasions. Norman is described in the play's stage directions as "an incorrigible adolescent" when he is not writing. In the screenplay the description by Andy is "impulsive, repulsive, incorrigible and irrepressible"; in the play it is "impulsive, compulsive, irrepressible and incorrigible." While this fits Susman, his childlike and sexless presence undermines any romantic appeal Norman might have had. When Norman advances on his knees to Amy when she tells him to leave her alone as she retreats to the door, he is childishly pathetic. In the scene where he enters the YWCA, it appears that the women scream in reaction more to the duck he brings than to the fact of his being male. Susman is better when he calms down after Norman has lost interest in Amy and when he says goodbye to Andy, since both scenes are played more realistically.

Britt Ekland, Ali MacGraw, Cybill Shepherd, and Goldie Hawn were offered the role of Amy but turned it down. The April 1967 *Hollywood Reporter* said that Paramount was considering Marlo Thomas for the lead role in the film. A July 1968 *Daily Variety* article stated that producer Howard W. Koch planned to begin production on the film in October 1968, with exteriors to be shot in San Francisco, the locale of the play. Arnold Schulman was announced in that article as the screenwriter. Barry Shear was then named as the film's director in a December 1968 *Daily Variety* article. The October 1970 *Hollywood Reporter* stated that Joey Heatherton had been "virtually signed" to star in the film.

RELEASE: December 22, 1971, with the taglines "She's Red, White and Blue ... and Funny All Over!" "I may be provincial and old-fashioned. I may believe in a lot of dead things like patriotism and the Constitution, and I like apple pie, because that's the dumb way I was brought up, and that's the dumb way I feel!" and "The story of Amy who loves Andy whose best friend is Norman who chases Amy."

REVIEWS: Praised by Roger Ebert in the *Chicago Sun-Times.* Lambasted by Pauline Kael in *5001 Nights at the Movies,* though Kael says, "Sandy Duncan's comic talent shines through." A mixed reaction from A.H. Weiler in the *New York Times.* He wrote that the direction was lackluster and the film was "like the joke about a chop suey dinner, something that's only momentarily satisfying."

DVD: Released by Paramount on November 25, 2003.

Last of the Red Hot Lovers (1972)

Paramount Pictures/Howard W. Koch Production.

CREW: Gene Saks (Director), Howard W. Koch (Producer), Neil Simon (Screenplay), Victor J. Kemper (Photography), Maury Winetrobe (Editor), Neal Hefti (Music), Ben Edwards (Art Direction), Jack Stevens (Set Decoration), Albert Wolsky (Costumes), David Bennett Ltd. of New York (Miss Kellerman's fur), John Inzerella (Makeup), Vivienne Walker (Hair), Wayne Fitzgerald (Titles). Color, 97 minutes. Filmed in Paramount Studios and on location in Philadelphia, Pennsylvania.

CAST: Alan Arkin (Barney Cashman), Sally Kellerman (Elaine Navazio), Paula Prentiss (Bobbi Michele), Renee Taylor (Jeanette Fisher), Sandy Balson (Charlotte), Bella Brucke (Harriet the Cashier), Frank Loverde (Mel Fisher), Burt Conroy (Bert), Charles Woolf (Jesse), Ben Freedman (Mickey), Buddy Lewis (Waiter #1), Mousey Garner (Waiter #2), Bernie Styles (Man with Boxes), John Batiste (Truckman's Helper), Lois Aurino (Girl in Car), Sully Boyar (Man #1 in Coffee Shop), J.J. Barry (Man #2 in Coffee Shop), Paul Larson (Man #3 in Coffee Shop), Ruth Jaroslow (Lady in Coffee Shop),

Oliver Steindecker (Cabbie), Leonard Parker (Parking Lot Attendant), Liesha Gullisson (Girl on Corner). Uncredited: Gina Smika Hunter (Elevator Girl).

SONGS: "Alfie" (music by Burt Bacharach with lyrics by Hal David), Paula Prentiss; "What the World Needs Now" (music by Burt Bacharach with lyrics by Hal David), Paula Prentiss and Alan Arkin, and instrumental.

SYNOPSIS: Forty-five-year-old, married Queen of the Sea restaurant owner Barney Cashman invites three women to the Manhattan apartment of his seventy-three-year-old mother to have affairs. They are married Elaine Navazio, professional singer Bobbi Michele, and married Jeanette Fisher. However, Barney fails to bed any of the three. He then invites his wife Thelma to join him at the apartment.

NOTES: Simon's adaptation of his play provides new scenes and characters. The treatment features the subject of marriage as family and fidelity, and the theme of radical and conventional behavior. The protagonist is presented as a conventional man of moral ambiguity whose mid-life crisis has him attempting radical behavior. The three women whom he chooses recall the three in *Plaza Suite* as showcases for different actresses, though here they are seen in different stories with the same man. The women are presented as radical in their willingness to have an affair, with Bobbi in particular as radical because she is a professional singer who smokes marijuana. Interestingly Simon drops the word "lesbian" from the play along with Bobbi's comments that the idea of it is "revolting" and "makes her skin crawl."

Simon "opens up" the play with the locations of Barney's suburban home, the expressway, a carpark, on the street in the city, the Queen of the Sea restaurant, a taxi, a park, the Fisher house, a diner, and a telephone booth. We also see the elevator and hallway of the apartment building and the balcony of the apartment. Some new scenes have a narrative payoff. Barney's first drive to the city has him noticing a girl in the next car in traffic and speaking to another girl on the street. Both of these incidents demonstrate his desire to be with a woman other than his wife. The scene where Barney speaks to the girl on the street is interesting in that the girl smiles back at him. She is not repulsed by him, though she is probably aware that Barney is not asking her what he really wants to know. The girl's lack of repulsion is also because Barney's approach reveals that he is not a practiced womanizer and also because of the reality that he is still an attractive man. This scene is echoed in the second story when another girl in a car waves to him and speaks to Barney to tell him that he has a flat tire.

The use of monologues to open each story is a theatrical device, as is the use of characters speaking to themselves, and characters returning after having stated their intention of leaving. Jeanette's repeated returns to the apartment in the third story come from Barney bringing her back, which is different than the theatrical returns of Elaine and Bobbi, which are their ideas, in the first and second stories. Running gags are also used; these are Barney praying to God, talking to Harriet on the telephone, his attempted seduction of women in his mother's apartment, and his promise to never do it again. In the second story there are the running gags of Bobbi asking for a drink, and that the time is twenty to four. Elaine's comment about asking Barney if he wants a copy of her speech is a self-conscious touch, as is her intellectual analysis of his speech, which she describes as "extremely entertaining."

The screenplay adds new funny lines. Elaine asks Barney, at the door to the

Alan Arkin, Sally Kellerman, Renee Taylor, and Paula Prentiss in a lobby card for *Last of the Red Hot Lovers* (1972).

apartment when she arrives, "Any chance of coming in?" When she notices he is wearing a hat she asks if he is staying and then asks, "Are you cold or is that a religious thing?" Barney asks Elaine if her parents were born in this country, and she tells him, "I forget. Would you like me to give them a call and find out?" When Barney repeats that Elaine is an attractive woman, she comments, "We did that line." After Barney tells her that he finds she has a detached attitude towards people, Simon adds to Elaine's response of "You'll get over it" with "and if you don't there are those little pills you can take." After his failure with Elaine, Barney says, "In the next three days, I took twelve baths, nine showers, and I didn't touch anybody in my family for two months." Barney asks if Bobbi's doctor prescribing marijuana is illegal and she tells him, "That's all right. He's not allowed to practice anyway." Jeanette tells Barney in the apartment hallway that she doesn't know what she is supposed to do in an affair and he replies, "You're supposed to go inside. As inexperienced as I am, I know that nothing is going to happen out here." After Jeanette describes melancholia as a quiet, empty, bottomless, relentless, infinite, eternal gloom, Barney comments, "We're in for some terrific afternoon."

Funny lines retained from the play include the exchange after Elaine coughs. She asks Barney for a cigarette and, when he asks her whether she'd rather have water, she replies, "I can't smoke water." After Elaine has another coughing fit, Barney asks her if she has tried sleeping with a vaporizer, and she tells him, "No, but don't worry. I'll get around to everyone." Elaine tells Barney that she doesn't find talking soft sexy but hard to hear. He comments that he is not as staid as she thinks he is and she tells him, "Yes you are. Staid is a very staid word." Elaine asks for a new drink, saying, "I didn't finish it, it evaporated." In line with Barney's paranoia over being found out, Elaine tells Barney that he had better burn the handkerchief he gives her for her bloody lip after their kiss. When Jeanette asks Barney if he is appalled by the times they live in, she comments that promiscuity is everywhere and he replies, "I don't find it anywhere."

In the play Barney's real name is Czernivekovski. The major change in the first story is that Elaine leaves for a second time before reappearing after Barney has called her way of going through life "frightening, sad and pitiful." In the second story, Simon adds the joke that Barney gives Bobbi thirty dollars because, he says, "You'll need cab fare," after he lends her the money for her audition. He has Barney scatter seven packs of cigarettes around the apartment as a lesson learned after Elaine had wanted to smoke when she was in the apartment, although Bobbi will not smoke any of the cigarettes as she prefers her own marijuana. The name of the rock band Bobbi had been asked to sing with is changed from Babylon Revisited to Battle Fatigue, and a joke is added about Barney asking if that is what Bobbi suffered from.

Simon adds a piece of schtick after Bobbi asks Barney the time. As he looks at his watch he also unknowingly pours the contents of one glass into the other, and then sees that one glass is empty and doesn't know where the scotch has gone. Simon's change of having Bobby on the balcony includes Barney's being unable to open the balcony door and thinking he is locked out. When Bobbi suggests breaking the door's glass, he says, "Break the glass? I'm afraid to sit on the cushions." In the third story, for the three people Barney suggests are decent, loving and gentle, Simon changes John F. Kennedy from the play to Albert Schweitzer, and he cuts the plot point that Jeanette can't taste food because of her depression.

The women in the photographs under the opening credits of the film prefigure Barney's desire in the narrative to find a pretty girl. The one he wants is presumably prettier and younger than his forty-three-year-old wife, Thelma. The women in the photographs are idealized and look like models, and are seen in exotic locations and adventures and also kissing men. Barney's mid-life crisis comes from boredom with the repetition of his life. This extends to his marriage; although he is shown to still be attracted to Thelma, she is not as responsive to his needs as he would like her to be. Thelma is never seen fully, but is heard in the transition from the second to the third story and at the third story's party. Barney's attitude to women is influenced by his having lost his virginity to an older woman, and then only having been with one other, that being his wife. The fact that he has decided to try an affair in his mother's apartment is also Freudian. Barney's vanity over aging makes him pray to God for "something terrific" to happen to him, the implication being that another woman will find him physically attractive. Barney is a morally ambiguous character since he wants to cheat on his wife. However, he is not demonized in his desire for something new in his life, and our empathy for him makes the failure of his attempts to seduce other women easier to take. We would like him to be successful in the seductions, but we are glad that he is not. However, our empathy is tested in moments, as when he attempts to leave the apartment before Elaine arrives.

Barney tells Elaine that his turning forty-two began the urge to have an affair. His age made him think about dying. He decided he wanted more in life than being nice, and that he wanted to see if another woman could find him desirable. Barney's middle-age crisis then created self-doubts and gave him a wish to take risks with radical behavior. While having an affair is not that radical in terms of the realm of behavior, it is for a man who has never had one, because he has otherwise led a conventional life. Barney says that in his life he has existed but not lived. Barney's insulting Elaine for her greater willingness to have an affair shows his hypocrisy. He claims to respect women and wants an affair that is memorable, not cheap or sordid. However, what he is looking for can't be found in an affair.

Barney's interactions with Elaine and Bobbi shows him to be reactive to them, presumably because of his inexperience in seducing other women. This passivity makes the failure of his intention inevitable. In the case of Bobbi there are other influencing factors. Bobbi describes herself as a "goofball" to explain her irrational behavior. A modern reading may consider that she is actually mentally ill, evident from her manic talking, stream-of-consciousness thoughts, contradictions, and restless action. Her affect may be explained by her marijuana smoking, since she is also paranoid about men following her. However, her tale of the cab driver who wanted to make it with her under the Manhattan Bridge on his lunch hour is a warning that Bobbi knows how to avoid unwanted advances. Barney fails to even kiss Bobbi because he allows her to take the lead in the relationship. Or perhaps she is so manic that he spends all his effort reacting to her. Bobbi appears not even to be aware of Barney's intention, and her refusal to leave the apartment unless he smokes some of her marijuana shows her domination of the situation. When Barney is stoned he reveals his longings, in that there are many things he wanted to do, and also that he feels he is trapped.

Barney's coupling with Jeanette reveals her ambiguity about having an affair, and as with Bobbi, he initially lets her take the lead. However, what is disturbing in this story is Barney's mounting aggression and the suggestion of the possibility of rape. There is a moment when it appears that Jeanette will agree to the seduction, but after she changes her mind, Barney's frustration is demonstrated by his throwing himself on top of her, locking her into the apartment, chasing her around the living room and into the bathroom and holding her captive. These acts of aggression are only partly relieved by his getting her to admit that she only wants her husband, Mel. Although Jeanette asks Barney at her party if he finds her attractive, she later tells him that she does not find *him* attractive. Added to Jeanette's admission are her further confessions that she doesn't particularly enjoy sex and that is it not important to her any more. Barney's acceptance of this is surprising and a relief. Simon's seemingly happy ending for Barney of inviting Thelma to the apartment is an attempt at mutual radical behavior, and it is revealing that Thelma's presumed response to it is resistance.

Director Gene Saks does not use any of the Broadway cast for the film. Barney is revealed when he looks at himself in the bathroom mirror, and his image is frozen under the opening credits. There is unusual editing in a cut from the sound of Mickey's laughing at Barney in the unpopulated restaurant to Mickey being seen when the restaurant is busy, and a later cut from Thelma, reminding Barney of their dinner with Jeanette and Mel, to a shot of Jeanette answering the door to them. Barney's big speech is the longest monologue to date from one of Simon's plays, and it works as cinema because of Saks' coverage and Arkin's performance. Saks gives Arkin a pause when Barney takes in what Bobbi tells him about her roommate, and uses an out-of-focus transition from the stoned Barney and Bobbi to Barney in bed at home. In the third act, the score employs bullfighter-type music for Barney's entrance to the apartment. Saks has the other people in the diner go quiet in reaction to Jeanette's screaming at Barney the second time they are there, and uses a dissolve to Jeanette sitting in a chair, now holding her pocketbook, when Barney goes to the bathroom, to show that she has retrieved it from the top of the cabinet.

Reportedly, Walter Matthau and Jack Lemmon were wanted but unavailable for the role of Barney. For the part, Alan Arkin grew a black moustache and shaved the mid-section of the top of his head. This look is too calculated to show Arkin as a man older than his years to be believable. However, the actor is funny when Barney is maniacal. He is also funny with his repeated moaning about the taste of the scotch he drinks, which is topped when he does it during Barney's big speech to Elaine. Arkin scores a laugh from the way his eyes move when he hears that Bobbi is prepared to meet him wherever he lives, since we catch what Barney is thinking. He is also funny in his reaction to Bobbi's first outburst of singing, when he puts his hands on his face when he says, "My God, the things that have happened to you," in his fake laugh to Bobbi at the idea of being shot by a "jealous nut," and in the way he shields his face from seeing the scars on Bobbi's wrists. Arkin is hilarious when Barney is stoned from the marijuana, gulping from swallowing the smoke and laughing. The third act has Arkin funny in his embarrassed reaction to Jeanette's screaming at him on the street and in the diner, when Barney grapples for words when reassuring Jeanette, and in his anger when he grabs her pocketbook. However, Arkin is less funny when seen in a towel and shoes and socks, then without the towel in boxer underwear, and later in his mother's bathrobe.

As Elaine, Sally Kellerman's dark sunglasses and fur coat recalls the hooker Barbra Streisand played in *The Owl and the Pussycat* (1970). Kellerman makes Elaine's extended cough funny, and the anger of her frustration is pleasing. However, the nipples seen through her braless dress are distracting. As Bobbi, Paula Prentiss in the park is dressed in short cut-off jeans that recall Sandy Duncan in *Star Spangled Girl* and allow us to see her long legs. Bobbi's faint accent also recalls that of Duncan, although she is said to come from California. Perhaps the accent is explained by Prentiss originating from Texas. Prentiss reveals a surprisingly good singing voice, but the actress doesn't make the impact of Kellerman. Bobbi's goofball charm seems overplayed, and she is more irritating than likeable. This is perhaps due to the changed dynamic, in which our empathy is more with Arkin's Barney and his frustration over her. Renee Taylor makes Jeanette's crying and hysteria funny. Perhaps the least attractive of the three women Barney attempts to seduce, Jeanette, also seems the most Jewish, and Taylor manages to make this woman's grotesque social behavior still sympathetic. She moves back in reaction to Barney's gesture about them plunging right in to the affair, and her screams when being chased by him are both comic and real.

Although the film, as is its source play, is set in New York City, because of a union strike in Manhattan, the majority of the location filming and exteriors had to be shot elsewhere, and Philadelphia, Pennsylvania, was chosen for this.

RELEASE: August 17, 1972, with the tagline "Barney wanted women in the worst way. And that's the way he got them."

REVIEWS: Lauded by *Variety*. Lambasted by Roger Greenspun in the *New York Times* and John Douglas Eames in *The Paramount Story*, with a mixed reaction from Robert K. Johnson.

DVD: Released by Paramount on November 25, 2003.

The Heartbreak Kid (1972) (aka *The Heartless Kid*)
Palomar Pictures International/20th Century–Fox.

CREW: Elaine May (Director), Edgar J. Scherick (Producer), Michael Hausman and Erik Lee Preminger (Associate Producers), Neil Simon (Screenplay, based on the story "A Change of Plan" by Bruce Jay Friedman), Owen Roizman (Photography), John Carter (Editor), Garry Sherman (Music), Richard Sylbert (Art Director), William G. O'Connell (Set Decorator), Anthea Sylbert (Costumes), Irving Buckman (Makeup), Robert Grimaldi (Hair). Color, 118 minutes. Filmed on location at Miami Beach in Florida, Minneapolis, and the University of Minnesota.

CAST: Charles Grodin (Leonard "Lenny" Alan Cantrow), Cybill Shepherd (Kelly Corcoran), Jeannie Berlin (Lila Ina Kolodny), Audra Lindley (Mrs. Corcoran), Eddie Albert (Mr. Dwayne Corcoran), Mitchell Jason (Cousin Ralph), William Prince (Colorado Man), Augusta Dabney (Colorado Woman), Doris Roberts (Mrs. Cantrow), Marilyn Putnam (Mrs. Kolodny), Jack Hausman (Mr. Kolodny), Erik Lee Preminger (Pecan Pie Waiter), Art Metrano (Entertainer), Tim Browner (Kelly's Boyfriend), Jean Scoppa (Flower Girl), Greg Scherick (Young Boy). Uncredited: Neil Simon (Wedding Guest), Joel Thingvall, Jim Westcott (College Students).

SONGS: "Theme from the Heartbreak Kid" (music by Cy Coleman and lyrics by Sheldon Harnick), Bill Dean; "Close to You" (music by Burt Bacharach and lyrics by Hal David), piano at wedding, Charles Grodin and Jeannie Berlin, and heard with an orchestra and chorus; "I'd Like to Teach the World to Sing (in Perfect Harmony)" (The New Seekers), Charles Grodin and Jeannie Berlin.

SYNOPSIS: New York sporting goods salesman Lenny Cantrow marries twenty-one-year-old Lila Kolodny but on their honeymoon soon discovers that he is irritated by her. At a Miami Beach hotel he meets college student Kelly Corcoran from Minnesota and falls in love with her. Lenny lies to Lila so he can be with Kelly and then tells Lila that he wants to end their marriage. He signs an annulment and moves to Minnesota to pursue Kelly. Despite the objection of Kelly's father, Dwayne, Lenny marries her.

NOTES: This adaptation is different from Simon's previous adaptations of his own plays, since here he adapts someone else's material. The narrative is interesting in that it lacks the running witticisms that feature in Simon's play adaptations, which makes it refreshing as new material. The screenplay explores Simon's themes of convention and radical behavior, and presents the subjects of marriage, couple compatibility and falling in love. The narrative juxtaposes the Jewish Lila with the Gentile Kelly, although Simon would say that this was not in his screenplay and is a change that director Elaine May made.

The screenplay's funny lines include Lenny telling Lila, "It's difficult to give out bulletins in the heat of passion," after she tells him that she needs to be reassured in their lovemaking. Another is when Lenny tells Kelly about his wanting to leave Lila: "I had my doubts in Virginia. I was pretty sure in Georgia but you have really settled things for me in Florida." There is a laugh when Kelly tells Lenny that Florida was a long time ago and he reminding her that is has only been two weeks, and when Dwayne tells Lenny, "You could wear two wool sweaters and a raccoon coat, I'd still see through you."

Simon alters some of Bruce Jay Friedman's story. In the story Lenny is only known as Cantrow, the Kelly character is named Sue Ellen Parker, the Lila character is unnamed, and the small Episcopal teacher's college is changed to Minnesota University. Sue Ellen is said to be only eighteen and is physically heavier than Lila, which is seemingly reversed in the film. Cantrow meets her at a pool and not on the beach, and he immediately tells the girl that he is married. Cantrow meets Sue Ellen the day after he has married, as opposed to the film, where it has been five days. Simon adds the idea that Lenny tells Lila that he wants out of the marriage in the public restaurant, whereas in the story Cantrow does so in private. Simon loses the idea of Cantrow's spending a week with his mother before going to find Sue Ellen, and that Lenny's rival for Sue Ellen is "of strange shifting sexuality" and is scared off by Lenny's threats of physical strength.

The screenplay varies Dwayne's response to Lenny's request for approval from the story's more extreme one. In the story the father says, "Not if they stripped me naked and dragged me four times around the world. Over the desert, through the jungle, under the seven seas." In the film Dwayne says, "Not if they tied me to a horse and pulled me forty miles by my tongue" and "Not if they hung me from a tree and put a lit bomb in my mouth." The Dwayne character ultimately gives his blessing to the couple in the story, which is something we don't see in the film, and it is only in the film that Lenny and Kelly marry. In the story it is suggested that Cantrow has changed his mind when he asks to speak to Sue Ellen's mother before the service. This provides a payoff that the film does not.

In the screenplay the character of Lila is alternately attractive and grotesque. She is a conventional girl in refusing Lenny sex before they are married, and clingy in the way she sits under Lenny's arm when he is driving. Lila also talks and asks questions during sex and is a sloppy eater. Lila is juxtaposed with Kelly in the fact that Lila prefers to sit by the hotel pool, while Kelly swims in the ocean. Lila tells Lenny that she can't swim, while Kelly can. Lila refuses sunblock and gets sunburned and Kelly does not appear to. Lila's sunburn results in her appearing smothered in skin cream, which she gets in her hair as well as on her face. Lenny tells Dwayne that Lila is not his type and that he only married her because it was "the decent thing to do." This attitude is usually associated with the girl being pregnant, although that is not the case here. Lenny will also say, "I have learned that decency doesn't always pay off." Ultimately Kelly will come to admit that Lenny is a decent man, which leads her to want to sleep with and then marry him. Because of the way Lila is, we empathize more with Lenny until he starts lying to her about Kelly.

Lenny is unsympathetic over Lila's sunburn, claiming that her being bed-bound will limit his activities, and he goes out to the bar rather than staying with her. Lila repeatedly calls Lenny a "grouch" for his disapproval of her, which prefigures his jilting her. Lenny's duplicity is prefigured by his anger at Lila, which reads as an overreaction although we have to admire his quick thinking in his lies. His convincing Lila that she

Lila Ina Kolodny (Jeannie Berlin) and Leonard Alan Cantrow (Charles Grodin) get married in a still for *The Heartbreak Kid* **(1972).**

must stay in their room all day while he meets Kelly at the beach shows both Lenny's influence on Lila and her gullible belief in him. Lenny plans to see both women at night, but ultimately decides to disappoint Lila when making a choice. What balances the situation is Dwayne's dislike of Lenny, even before he knows that Lenny is married. Kelly calls Lenny a "teddy bear," and his fake laughter at what she says presents him as a pathetic suitor. He is particularly creepy in his aggressive touching of her when they play in the surf together. Lenny's comment to her on the boat, that they will be together for forty years, recalls the same ambition voiced by Lila to Lenny. Kelly continues to toy with Lenny after he tells her that he is married, so we don't know how genuine she is. However, when she tells him that she would dump him if her father told her to, it suggests that Kelly is not as serious about Lenny as he is about her. This is apparent when Lenny tells Kelly that he plans to leave Lila for her. She does not tell Lenny that she is in love with him, as he tells her that he has been waiting for a girl like her all his life. She also does not ask him to leave Lila for him, but Kelly does ask Lenny to go fishing with her group as a sign of interest. Kelly's telling Lenny that she will only be in Florida for a few days presses him to rush his disentanglement from Lila, although he delays doing so by leading Lila on. This can be interpreted to mean that Lenny is being a coward for not immediately telling Lila his feelings, and trying to both appease her and pursue Kelly. We are not surprised when Lila gets sunburned after she refuses the sunblock suggested by Lenny, nor when he does not turn up for the second late dinner date with her. But we are surprised when he meets Lila for dinner in order to tell her that he wants to end their marriage. The scene in which Lenny tells Dwayne that he is married but plans to end it to pursue Kelly is interesting; Kelly is more amused by Dwayne's anger than interested in supporting Lenny.

The dinner scene with Lenny and Lila runs for twelve minutes, so it reads like a theatre scene. Simon gives Lenny misplaced anger towards the waiter about the shortage of pecan pie, presumably because Lenny wants Lila to have a good dinner before he tells her what he wants. Simon also has Lila misinterpret Lenny in thinking that they are over because he is dying. The idea that Lenny refuses to help Lila to the restaurant bathroom, since she claims she is going to be sick, seems cruel, although she does not get sick after all. However, the fact that Lenny has told Lila this in a public place deprives us of any empathy for him when Lila cries. There is some empathy for Lenny over the annulment, since he is willing to pay six thousand dollars in a settlement. After Lenny moves to Minnesota, this empathy increases due to the idea that Kelly is conflicted over him. The narrative also juxtaposes the heat of Florida with the snow of Minnesota, geographically and emotionally. Lenny's stalking of Kelly is also ambiguous since it presents him as desperate and vulnerable. Kelly's kissing him suggests that perhaps she does care for him, as does her invitation for them to go to the family's mountain cabin.

The scene at the cabin shows Kelly's continued ambivalence towards Lenny. She refuses to sleep with him but stills teases him by suggesting they get naked but not touch each other. But they don't have sex or even kiss, although Kelly does keep her word about sleeping with Lenny the next day. The fact that Dwayne does not speak at the dinner when Lenny speaks to Mrs. Corcoran gets paid off when Dwayne later tells Lenny that he was quiet because he was listening. We are surprised when Dwayne comments that he was impressed, but not surprised with his disapproving addition, "I have never heard such a crock of horseshit in my life." Dwayne uses an interesting choice of words when he describes Lenny's behavior as that of a "wise guy," and Simon has Dwayne offer Lenny the same amount of money—five thousand dollars—that Lenny has lost to Lila for him to leave Kelly alone. The increased offer makes us assume that Lenny's resolve is weakened, but when we next see his marriage to Kelly, with Dwayne's new support, it is narratively inexplicable. The Anglican wedding is juxtaposed with Lenny's earlier Jewish wedding to Lila, and the narrative ends with Lenny alone and humming "Close to You." What we are to make of this ending is unclear. Perhaps the song reminds Lenny of when he and Lila sang it, to suggest that he misses her. Dwayne's repeated looking at Lenny after the wedding also suggests that perhaps Dwayne fears that Lenny will run.

Elaine May has Kelly first be seen by Lenny as a vision partly obscured by the glare of the sun, and Dwayne uncomfortably positioned in between Mrs. Corcoran and Lenny when they talk to each over him at the hotel show. May stages the long scene when Lenny breaks up with Lila to show Lila's vulnerability and her excruciating pain. It helps that the narrative not showing Lila in a while makes her appear here to be sweet and likable, which only adds to her humiliation. May cuts to other people in the restaurant hearing Lenny repeat "I want out the marriage" to add to both Lenny and Lila's embarrassment. The scene also appears to have a goof when one of Lila's earrings drop off.

The film features a scene with Nicholas Clay and Susan Macready from the British biographical film *The Darwin Adventure* (1972) on television, a film made by the same Palomar Productions company. May protects the nudity of Cybill Shepherd and Charles Grodin in the mountain cabin scene, where nudity is suggested but not shown. We see the couple advance towards each other from either side of the frame, as they are lit by a fireplace. One source reports that the scene was cut for television and that originally Shepherd was seen nude. Additionally, Kelly is supposed to have had the line, "You're touching me." In the dinner scene where Dwayne eats silently, May has Mrs. Corcoran, Kelly and Lenny jump in shocked reaction when Dwayne clears his throat.

As Lenny, Grodin is funny in his attempt to show off to Kelly when he packs up his towel on the beach to meet Lila, but his anger is not as amusing as Alan Arkin's in *The Last of the Red Hot Lovers*. He also presents Lenny's sincerity as bland. Despite the way May initially presents Jeannie Berlin as Lila as grotesque, we miss her after Lenny leaves her, and the film's energy drops without her. As Dwayne, Eddie Albert is funny displaying his dislike of Lenny, and uses a slow burn reaction to Lenny's pronouncement of wanting Kelly at the dinner.

In the interview with Simon in *American Film*, he says that he tried to buy the rights to the Friedman story to do as a film but found out that Palomar Productions had it in the works. Producer Ed Scherick planned to make a three-part film of various love stories, and the Friedman story was going to be one of them. He asked Simon to write it, but the writer told Scherick that he preferred to write a feature length screenplay and the producer made the deal. Simon says that he tried to write it as Friedman would, with his "very oblique and unique sense of humor," rather than like his own.

In his *Playboy* interview Simon says that he wanted Diane Keaton for the part of Lila. He had a reading with Keaton and she was sensational in the part, and this was before she had made her breakthrough as a leading film actress. Since Elaine May was directing she insisted on casting Jeannie Berlin, her daughter. Simon's choice then became to either have Keaton and lose May or keep Berlin and May. He didn't have a problem with Berlin's acting ability, but he thought she wasn't as attractive as Cybill Shepherd's Kelly. He thought that the screenplay wasn't about a man who leaves an unattractive girl for a beautiful one, because that was too easy. It was about a man who does so because he finds flaws in whatever woman he is married to, no matter how good-looking she is. Simon discussed the issue with May, who planned to go ahead with the idea of Lila as an unattractive girl. When asked why he didn't replace May if he felt so strongly about the problem, Simon said that he thought that May brought things to the film that no one else could. She turned the story into a Jewish versus WASP story, whereas he had written the wedding as more neutral rather than as being Jewish.

In the *American Film* interview Simon says that May got around the clause in Simon's contract that said that no words could be changed by doing a variation on the egg salad scene. He had written that after she took a bite of the sandwich Lila had a small piece of egg salad on her face. May had Lila's face with egg salad all over it. Simon commented that he thought the change was a "little heavy." He also commented that May's directing style gave the impression that the actors were improvising, which they were not.

The *Turner Classic Movies* Web site reports that the film originally concluded with Kelly and Lenny sailing for Europe on their honeymoon. During the cruise, Lenny discovers that he finds Kelly as objectionable as Lila. This sequence was cut before the print was released. According to an August 1971 *Hollywood Reporter* news item, Jerry Orbach had been the "top candidate" for the title role.

The film was parodied by *Mad Magazine* in the October 1973 issue as "The Heartburn Kid." The egg salad scene is commented on when Lenny asks Lila who in the audience is going to believe that such a clean-cut guy married a slob like her. She replies, "The same people who'll believe that we went together for three years, and you never saw me eat!" As expected, the parody uses the fact that Jeannie Berlin is Elaine May's daughter, but this version has a different ending. Rather than having Lenny marry Kelly, he marries into the Corleone family from *The Godfather*, so that his plan to quickly divorce his wife for a financial settlement is predicted to have dire consequences for him.

RELEASE: December 17, 1972, with the tagline "Elaine May directed it. Neil Simon wrote it. Bruce Jay Friedman conceived it."

REVIEWS: Lauded by *Variety*, Vincent Canby in the *New York Times*, Roger Ebert in the *Chicago Sun-Times*, Pauline Kael in *Reeling*, Tony Thomas and Aubrey Solomon in *The Films of 20th Century–Fox: A Pictoral History*, and Robert K. Johnson.

AWARDS: Academy Award nominations for Jeannie Berlin as Best Supporting Actress and Eddie Albert as Best Supporting Actor.

DVD: Released by Starz/Anchor Bay on February 5, 2002.

REMAKE: Remade in 2007. The screenplay was by Bobby and Peter Farrelly, Scot Armstrong, Leslie Dixon, and Kevin Barnett, and was based on Simon's screenplay and the story by Friedman. The film was directed by Bobby and Peter Farrelly and starred Ben Stiller, Malin Akerman, and Michelle Monaghan.

The Prisoner of Second Avenue (1975)

Melvin Frank Production/Warner Bros. Pictures.

CREW: Melvin Frank (Producer/Director), Neil Simon (Screenplay, based on his play), Philip Lathrop (Photography), Bob Wyman (Editor), Marvin Hamlisch (Music), Preston Ames (Art Director), Marvin March (Set Decorator), Joel Schumacher (Costumes), Fred Williams and Harry Ray (Makeup), Sherry Wilson (Hair). Color, 100 minutes. Exteriors filmed on location in New York and interiors at the Warner Bros. Burbank Studios in California. Filmed August to October 1974.

CAST: Jack Lemmon (Mel Edison), Anne Bancroft (Edna Edison, formerly Edna Reale), Gene Saks (Harry Edison), Elizabeth Wilson (Pauline), Florence Stanley (Pearl), Maxine Stuart (Belle), Ed Peck (Man Upstairs, aka Jacoby), Ivor Francis (Psychiatrist, aka Dr. Frankel), Gene Blakely (Charlie), Stack Pierce (Detective), Patricia Marshall (Woman Upstairs), Dee Carroll (Helen), Ketty Lester (Unemployment Clerk), M. Emmet Walsh (Doorman), F. Murray Abraham (Taxi Driver), James McCallion (Mr. Cooperman), Fat Thomas (Bus Driver), Arlen Stuart (Woman in Elevator), Sylvester Stallone (Youth in Park), Alan DeWitt (Wayne Morgan), Harry Ray (Man with Dog). Uncredited: Lonnie Burr (Man on Street), Ben Lautman (NYU Student), Dave Michaels, Gary Owens (Voices of Radio Newscasters), Joe Turkel (Voice of the Man Upstairs).

SONGS: "Night and Day" (Cole Porter), orchestral version heard; "For He's a Jolly Good Fellow," orchestral tune of musical whisky pourer.

SYNOPSIS: Forty-eight-year-old Mel Edison lives in a 14th floor apartment in New York with his wife Edna. In the summer he loses his Madison Avenue advertising executive job, and the apartment is robbed. Edna gets a job as a television studio production assistant while Mel remains unemployed. Mel's brother Harry and his sisters Pauline and Pearl agree to loan him money, but Edna and Mel decline it. Mel goes into therapy with a psychiatrist who prescribes sedatives. Snow falls in the city. Mel plans to use the snow shovel he has bought as revenge upon the couple upstairs who threw buckets of water on him. Mel and Edna pose in a variation of the Grant Wood painting "American Gothic."

NOTES: Simon's adaption includes new lines and characters, cut lines, and rearranged lines from the play. The screenplay continues the subjects of marriage as family and a husband's mid-life crisis. That the husband is unemployed and the wife works as the breadwinner allows for an exploration of a man feeling emasculated by female liberation. The husband's mid-life crisis, which turns into a nervous breakdown and mental illness, is an extension of Simon's characters' usual sense of irritation and conflict in life. The screenplay echoes the impersonal and hostile world of New York that was presented in *The Out of Towners*, and the tone of schaudenfraude echoes that of the same film. The term fag is retained from the play, and there is also a homophobic double entendre used in one of the radio news reports.

The screenplay "opens up" the play by featuring new locations of the street, buses, a taxi, a car, the country house of Harry, a coffee shop, a bottle shop, a television studio, the State Division of Employment, a phone booth, Central Park, the apartment of Pauline and Pearl, a hardware store, and the consulting room of Dr. Frankel. We also see the foyer, the hallway, and terraces of the apartment building. Theatrical devices are used, such as characters returning after their intention to leave is stated, and repeated radio reports. Another theatrical moment occurs in the scene in Harry's living room when Edna appears to hear Harry tell Mel that his being fired is something that Mel has to tell his wife.

The narrative has surprises. Unlike Mel, Edna does not have water thrown on her on the terrace, despite her angry words said to the man upstairs. This surprise gets a later payoff when Edna goes to the terrace to exchange words with the woman upstairs. Despite the water being turned off in the building and the woman's threat to Edna, it is Mel, when moving Edna away from the terrace, who is hit with the second bucket of water. Mel brandishes a knife at Edna, and while she is afraid he will stab her, he only uses it as emphasis for what he is saying and to illustrate the use of the snow shovel. This idea is repeated when Edna brandishes the scrubbing brush at Mel. Another surprise is the youth in the park bumping into Mel in the street, presumably to steal Mel's wallet. It is revealed that the wallet that Mel takes from the youth belongs to the youth and not Mel, which makes us re-evaluate why the youth ran from Mel.

Simon provides some new funny lines. There is a new radio report about the member of the Albanian Diplomatic Corps who was mugged in Central Park despite the fact that twelve mounted policemen were only one hundred yards away. He claimed to have screamed loudly for two minutes but didn't know the English word for help. Harry's

Edna Edison (Anne Bancroft) faces off with Mel Edison (Jack Lemmon), in a still for *The Prisoner of Second Avenue* (1975).

wife's line to Edna that she should paint "up and down, never sideways" is paid off after Edna spills paint on her dress. When the wife tries to clean it off, Edna repeats the line. Mel tells Harry that he has been fired from his job before he tells Edna. Harry initially tells Mel that he thinks that Edna is strong, but after Mel gives Harry the information that he has been fired, Harry says, "Oh my God, I wonder how she's gonna take it?" A new radio report tells that a person mowed obscene words into the grass in Central Park, and another new one provides a gay double entrendre. It is reported that the Harlem Globetrotters are to play a charity baseball game at Nassau Coliseum with members of the gay liberation movement. It is said that the gay team does not expect to win because they are "young and have only been playing with each other since December."

Retained funny lines from the play include Edna's response to Mel's saying is it a wonder he can't sleep at night. She replies, "Don't sleep with your head next to the wall. Sleep in the bedroom." This pays off the fact that Edna can only hear the music and laughter of the neighbors when she puts her head to the wall in the living room. Mel complains, "I haven't had a real piece of bread in thirty years. If I had known that was going to happen I'd have saved some rolls when I was a kid." Mel tells Harry that in order to save money for the company, the vice president of his department used the same paper clip for six months. Mel asks Edna if she told the police that they were robbed when she telephoned them, and she responds, "Why else would I call them? I'm not friendly with the police." Mel tells Edna, "You'll take down the living room drapes, make me a suit, and I'll look for another job."

Changes from the play include the introduction of Harry's wife in the screenplay, and the song that Mel hears his neighbor playing, from "Raindrops Keep Falling on My Head" to "Night and Day." The suggestion that Mel's brother and sisters loan him money is made by Harry, but in the play it is comes from Pauline. The screenplay shows Harry giving Mel the check for twenty-five thousand dollars and Mel tearing it up. The play only has Harry speaking of the check and not giving it to Mel, since he won't accept it. The film has Mel tell Edna that he wants to stay in the city when she tells him that she wants to leave. The play has him agree with her.

Lost in the adaptation is Mel's telling Edna of his concern that he will lose his job, Edna's extended telephone conversation with the police when she reports the apartment being robbed, the mention of the contents of the medicine chest being stolen, Mel's telling Edna what he did during the four days after he was fired and before he had told her, and Mel's painting on a canvas and easel, which is presumably for therapy and also a hobby.

The character of Mel recalls the character of George Kellerman in *The Out of Towners.* This is because Mel has a run of bad luck and also because he complains about things. Mel tells Edna that he fears that he is losing his mind. His unhappiness can be attributed to insomnia and irritation from the heat wave as much as to having a mid-life crisis. Mel's unemployment has led Edna to get a job out of necessity, although we are told that she used to have a career, presumably given up for marriage. This shift in the marriage dynamic is not handled maturely by Mel since he does not perform the home duties that Edna had done when he was working. This leads Edna, who has previously been shown to be sympathetic to Mel, to become less patient and understanding than before and angry at him. Although Mel claims that he has looked for work, his affect of being unkempt suggests depression. Also, it is telling that he cannot occupy himself with other interests such as hobbies, which suggests that his time mainly revolved around his work. Mel's growing madness comes from his being partly "miserable and tormented" and is an extension of his boredom and unhappiness. It is considered mental illness since Harry advises his sisters that Mel has had a nervous breakdown, and also since Mel sees a doctor who is presumably a psychiatrist. Edna's response to Mel's condition is initially disbelief, then concern, so that she arranges for the doctor's appointment. While the psychiatrist is shown to be generally unhelpful in talking to Mel, his prescription of sedatives does make his patient calmer. The fact that the calmer Mel makes cookies that Edna offers to Harry and the sisters suggests that Mel may even perform the home duties he was previously reluctant to do. When Harry and Mel's sisters are visiting, Mel's slow reaction to seeing them is indicative of his drug sedation. While Mel acknowledges Harry's presence, Harry has to point out the additional presence of the sisters.

The second session that we see Mel have with the psychiatrist presents Mel as less calm and more hostile. Despite the doctor's apparent disinterest, Mel has an insight into what he thinks is the root of his hostility. He feels that Harry acted as a father figure to him when they were boys and was always critical of him. Mel did not "fight back" against this treatment but rather repressed his anger towards his brother and everyone else in the world he saw as mistreating him. Mel's breakdown therefore has come from the eventual release of this repressed anger. The sedatives Mel takes again repress these feelings but also allow him to recognize the anger that Edna later expresses after she loses her job. Harry will also later admit to being envious of Mel since he perceived his younger brother as the "favorite," which caused Harry's own anger and resentment.

Mel's position as the mad one of the couple is reversed when Edna loses *her* job and her anger makes her unreasonable. This is shown by her obsession with having a bath, which is heightened by the fact that the water in the building has been turned off. Ironically, her opportunity to have a kind of bath is lost when Mel moves her away from the terrace and she avoids getting hit with the bucket of water by the woman upstairs. Edna's comment to Mel, "Are you out of your mind?" is said from her anger at his unwillingness to bang the pipes after she had banged the wall earlier for him. Her immediate apology for saying it continues the idea that his madness is greater than hers. However, Mel has become lucid and reasonable enough now to comfort Edna in her anger. He expresses this by telling her that he will take care of them, which is underlined by his choice to stay in the city rather than leave, like she wants to. Simon adds to the play's end by having Mel and Edna laughing at each other as they sit on the couch and he holds the snow shovel. This is presumably a realization of the madness of the plan to use the shovel to get revenge upon the man and woman upstairs who threw the buckets of water at them. This laughter may also come from the radio report that advises that citizens are using snow shovels to show how New Yorkers can live and work together in a common cause, although there is no direct indication given that the Edisons have heard the report.

Director Mel Frank uses a montage of high-rise buildings at night, and an echo of the voices of Mel and Harry when they speak in the stairwell. He maintains a tone of sadness for the film despite the screenplay's witticisms, and shows the passage of time only via the dialogue. There is a laugh retained from the play in which Pauline demonstrates that Mel's head is big for his body, and also from her repeating the "nine" for the "nine years" as the last time the sisters were invited to the Edisons.' Frank adds a new moment of humor that pays off the moment when Edna touches Harry's hand when he visits. Harry suddenly is conscious of the touching, and she withdraws it. The director gives Jack Lemmon a long take for the scene in which Mel comes home to find that the apartment has been robbed. This is so that we can observe his initially being unaware of it as he sits on a chair before looking around to see the mess. Frank also holds on Bancroft's Edna when Mel goes to change his clothes and we wait for him to return; we know that the robbers have taken his clothes. Another reveal comes after Mel hears a banging and it is shown that Edna is banging on the bathroom pipes. Lemmon's reaction to Mel's having the bucket of ice cold water thrown on him when he is on his terrace is interesting. As in the play, the reaction is not anger but rather quiet from humiliation. This perhaps makes sense, since the water is thrown at him because he is already yelling in anger so this anger, can only be topped by quiet.

The score of Marvin Hamlisch repeatedly uses military sounding music to suggest a character's anger. This is heard twice: when Mel sees the stewardesses with men in the hallway, and when Edna and Mel climb the stairwell. This style of music is also slowed down to suggest that Edna and Mel are tired from climbing the stairs.

The only cast member from the stage production kept for the film is Florence

Stanley as Pearl. Lemmon and Anne Bancroft show their acting range in presenting the alternate anger and calm of Mel and Edna. Bancroft in particular is touching in Edna's understated compassion for Mel. Her anger at Harry and Mel's sisters is funny, especially with Edna's pride in Mel's homemade cookies. Bancroft is also funny in the way she shakes her body when asking where the upstairs woman is going to get the water that she threatens to throw onto Edna on the terrace. However, the performance of Gene Saks as Harry is problematic since he generally yells and gesticulates in a theatrical fashion.

In his *Playboy* interview, Simon said that he questioned the casting of Lemmon and thought a more ethnic and urban actor was needed for the part, since he finds Lemmon not easily believable as a typical New Yorker. Simon had wanted Peter Falk, but the studio balked because they considered Lemmon to be a bigger box office name. However, Simon observed that since the film was not a financial success, it might have done better with Falk in the lead role. Simon also said that he considered the couple to be Paul and Corie Bratter from *Barefoot in the Park* twenty years later but changed. In the face of the city, which seemed to have become more impersonal and dangerous, people were now more alienated and fearful.

According to Don Widener's book on Lemmon, Bancroft was accidently hit in the shin by the snow shovel in one scene that was shot on a Friday. Franks stopped shooting when he saw that the actress had tears in her eyes. The injury gave Bancroft a big bump on her leg, which was fixed by the following Monday. When the same scene was re-shot, Lemmon did not hit Bancroft. To avoid doing so he had cut himself with a wound worse than he had inflicted on his co-star. It required bandaging but the scene was completed.

RELEASE: March 14, 1975, with the tagline "...and you think you've got problems."

REVIEWS: Lauded by Clive Hirschhorn in *The Warner Bros. Story,* Jerry Roberts in "The Great American Playwrights on the Screen," and Judith McNally in *Filmmakers Newsletter*. A mixed reaction from A.H. Weiler in the *New York Times* and Robert K. Johnson in his book *Neil Simon.* Lambasted by Les Keyser in *Hollywood in the Seventies* and Pauline Kael in *Reeling.*

REMAKE: An East German made-for-TV movie was broadcast on September 7, 1975.

DVD: Released by Warner Home Video on March 30, 2004.

The Sunshine Boys (1975)

MGM/A Ray Stark Production (Rastar).

CREW: Herbert Ross (Director), Ray Stark (Producer), Roger M. Rothstein (Associate Producer), Neil Simon (Screenplay), David M. Walsh (Photography), John F. Burnett (Editor), Albert Brenner (Production Design), Marvin March (Set Decorator), Pat Norris (Costumes), Dick Smith (Makeup), Wayne Fitzgerald (Titles). Color, 110 minutes. Shot on location in New York and New Jersey and on the soundstages of MGM. Filmed starting January 1975.

CAST: Walter Matthau (Willy Clark), George Burns (Al Lewis), Richard Benjamin (Ben Clark), Lee Meredith (Nurse in Sketch), Carol Arthur (Mrs. Doris Green), Rosetta

Le Noire (Odessa, the Nurse), F. Murray Abraham (Mechanic), Howard Hesseman (Mr. Walsk, Commercial Director), Jim Cranna (Mr. Schaefer, TV Director), Ron Rifkin (Eddie, TV Floor Manager), Jennifer Lee (Helen Clark), Jack Bernardi and Fritz Feld (Commercial Auditioning Actors), Garn Stephens (Stage Manager), Santos Morales (Desk Clerk), Archie Hahn (Assistant at Audition), Sid Gould (Patient), Tom Spratley (Card Player), Rashel Novikoff (Woman in Hotel), Sammy Smith (Man on Street), Dan Resin (Mr. Ferranti), Milt Kogan (Doctor), Bob Goldstein (Sam the Waiter), Walter Stocker (TV Executive), Duchess Dale (Ben's Secretary), Bill Reddick (Announcer), Eddie Villery (Delivery Boy), Gary K. Steven (Boy). Uncredited: Steve Allen (Narrator on TV Special), Phyllis Diller (Performer on TV Special), Lois Hamilton, Lauren Simon (Woman in Lobby).

SONGS: "Make 'Em Laugh" (music by Nacio Herb Brown, words by Arthur Freed), heard under the opening credits and at the TV special rehearsal and over the end credits; Lipton Tea jingle, heard on television and sung by Walter Matthau.

SYNOPSIS: Two former vaudeville partners of forty-three years, seventy-three-year-old Willy Clark and Al Lewis, receive an offer to appear in a variety special for ABC about the history of comedy. Willy does not want to do it because he dislikes Al as a person. Willy's agent and nephew, thirty-three-year-old Ben, arranges for the two men to meet and rehearse their old act. The men argue at the rehearsal, but Ben brings them to the TV show dress rehearsal. The rehearsal is cut short when the partners get into another argument and Al walks out. Willy has a heart attack and is told he can't work any longer. Ben arranges to have him live in the New Jersey Actors Fund Home. Al visits and tells Willy that he is also moving into the home.

NOTES: Simon's adaption of his play cuts some lines and adds new scenes and characters. The piece continues the subject of family. Although Willy and Al are not related as family, their long-term partnership makes it seem as though they are. The closeness of the family unit is also presented by Willy's nephew being his agent, and Al's living with his daughter. The screenplay features the themes of aging and the generation gap, with nostalgia as the reason for the vaudevillians getting one last shot at fame.

Left, Walter Matthau, and right, George Burns, in still for *The Sunshine Boys* (1975).

The screenplay "opens up" the play with locations in the street, at a garage, at the office of the commercial audition and ABC television, a restaurant, Al's house in New Jersey, the Friar's Club, Doris' car, a taxi, a television studio and dressing room and backstage stairwell, a hospital, and the Actors Fund Home. We also see the hotel foyer, hallway, and a balcony of the hotel where Willy lives. Some scenes have notable new actions. Simon adds the idea of Al's discomfort at being in Willy's room for the rehearsal since Al refuses to take off his coat when Ben asks, due to Willy's messiness. Al eventually takes it off, and his hat, when the partners set up the furniture for the sketch rehearsal. When Willy and Al have to share a television studio and dressing room, Willy moves Al's makeup over on the table to give him room for his own makeup, which he deposits from a bag. As Al applies his own makeup, Willy squeezes a bottle and white lotion accidently flies onto Al's face and clothes. In response, Al writes "Putz" on the mirror. In his room, Willy's nurse sleeps with a box of chocolates, and he throws cotton balls and a newspaper at her to wake her up.

Simon's new lines include Mr. Gilbert's telling the director that he can't eat the Frumpies potato chips for the ad because, he says, "I got gallstones." The Spanish hotel desk clerk asks Willy, "Don't you understand English?" when Willy repeats his question of whether he has mail. Willy replies, "When you speak it, I'll understand it." In regards to his broken television, Willy says, "Lousy Japs. They lost the war, they send us their junk." There is a new moment when Ben returns to Willy's hotel room door and is about to knock on it when we hear Willy say, "It's still no!" This moment suggests that Willy has some psychic ability to know of Ben's intention. Ben asks Al if he is excited to be doing the old act again with Willy, and Al replies the following: "I did it over eleven thousand times. Eleven thousand and one doesn't get me excited." For the end of the telephone booth scene at the Friar's Club, Ben says, "My God, they're both the same," in reference to Al's seeming as forgetful as Willy. In the sketch rehearsal scene, Willy says that they will stop for the "stupid things." Willy comments that not going out the door for Al's entrance was a stupid thing. Al responds, "Coming in in the first place was the stupid thing." Willy claims that he is still "hot" because he still works, and Al tells him, "If this room were on fire, you still wouldn't be hot." Doris tells Ben when he visits the New Jersey house, "Vaudeville is dead. Thank god my father isn't." Willy tells the nurse, "You owe me fifty dollars. That's what you get for watching me sleep. Why shouldn't I get the same money?"

Witty lines retained from the play include Willy's comment about Al, "As an actor no one could touch him. As a human being, no one wanted to touch him." Ben tells Willy that Al has arthritis, which leads Willy to continue his criticism of Al poking him in the chest: "Instead of a finger, he'll poke me with a cane." Willy's nurse tells him that her husband passed away four years ago and he asks, "You were the nurse?" The use of Sal Burton and Sol Bernstein and Sid Weinstein, and the Belasco and the Morosco, is Simon's word play. This is more word play at the end with the use of Bernie Eisenstein and Sam Hesseltine and Jackie Aaronson.

Changes from the play include some name changes: Ben's name of Silverman is now Clark, Al's character in the doctor sketch is Sylvia and his wife is named Herman, and Willy's Nurse Miss O'Neill in the play is now called Odessa. Notable cuts are the other TV commercials Ben had put Willy up for, the specifics of the night of the Ed

Sullivan show when Al walked out from the partnership, Willy's driving the brandished kitchen knife into a table, and the play's presentation of how the beginning of the sketch is salvaged to be used in the TV special. Simon changes the payoff of the moment when Al is locked out of Willy's apartment during the rehearsal. In the film Willy opens the door, but in the play Al does. Simon also adds an anecdote from Big Bill McCafferey that Al tells Willy for the film's end. The story is about Rosita from Dunlap, who wore a little black velvet ribbon on her neck. She tied it too tight and it affected her breathing so that she couldn't hear the music for her act.

Willy is presented as an old man through his getting the directions wrong for the location of the audition, not listening to people speaking to him, and being forgetful. Willy argues that he says the name of Frumpies wrong for the commercial deliberately because he thinks it's not funny; however, later he admits that can't remember it because it's not funny. Willy's apartment being messy is more an expression of his personality than his age. However, Willy's complaints about Al are balanced by an acknowledgment that Al was the best in the business.

Ben is considered by Willy to be a bad agent, although this is shown not to be true. He gets Willy a second chance for the commercial audition, and also gets Willy the deal for the TV special. Ben quits as Willy's agent but then later continues to convince him to do the TV show. He is also shown to be a good agent when on the telephone he tells ABC's Lester Burns that he had watched the rehearsal, which is a lie, and also when Ben goes to the special's rehearsal. Al is presented to as being as forgetful and unlistening as Willy, although Al's being deaf gives him a better excuse. His general calm and logic in the face of Willy's hysteria and unreasonableness is perhaps more admirable, though we do see Al get agitated and raise his voice. However it is Al's walking out on Willy in the sketch that costs the partners the opportunity on the TV special. Willy finally behaves in a realistic and calm manner at the film's end when tells Al how he is moving to the Actors Fund Home, and thankfully only pauses briefly when he learns that Al will also be there.

Some behavior is predicted and some is a surprise. Willy complains about Al's annoying habits of poking him with a finger and spitting when saying words that begin with the letter "T," so we wait for these to happen when the men reunite. Al's having a walking stick when he arrives at Willy's hotel adds to the predicted threat, although Al will only poke Willy with his finger. At the TV dress rehearsal of the sketch Willy uses "Enter" instead of "Come in" for Al's entrance. Al lets this pass but when he spits and pokes Willy the predicted trouble starts, with Willy stopping the rehearsal twice and Al walking out. The running gag of Willy's room door appearing to be locked but having a sliding latch is used when Ben first visits Willy's apartment. It is not used when Ben answers the door to Al, but it is when Ben tries to leave, which is new for the screenplay. When Willy asks Al to go outside the hotel room door for his entrance in the rehearsal of the sketch, we predict that the door gag will be used again. But it gets a different payoff when Willy opens the door to tell Al to get help in opening the door. The gag is used for the end of the dressing room scene, but not when Ben opens Willy's door twice for Al in the last scene, and not for Ben's exit.

The only member of the Broadway cast that director Herbert Ross uses for the film version is Lee Meredith as the nurse in the sketch. He presents black and white footage of vaudeville performers from early short subjects and the MGM musical *The Hollywood Review of 1929* (1929), seen within a home-movie type smaller screen frame, and *General Hospital* on television, watched by Willy. Ross supplies two interesting shots of Willy. The first shows him as a lonely figure as he looks out his room window onto the street to see Ben arrive in a taxi. The second is a shot of him looking at Al in his living room through the glass kitchen door, where we see only the top of his head and his eyes. For the TV special rehearsal, Ross uses the TV director's point of view on monitors that show two camera angles to the left of the frame and the stage on the right. The dress rehearsal is first shown via a monitor, and later the director and the crew are seen watching nine monitors. Ross also cuts away to Ben's reactions to the sketch. What is interesting is that none of the crew laughs at the sketch, though perhaps this is influenced by the fact of how problematic the partners have been.

Herbert Ross has to work hard to fight against the basic lack of humor in the material. An example is how it is not funny to observe the repetition of statements and questions because of the forgetfulness and not listening of Willy and Al. The unfunny idea of the men in this condition extends to the silent scene of Willy and Al setting up furniture for the sketch, where each one moves the same piece to a different spot. This action is repeated and still fails to be funny. Equally unfunny is the use of slapstick when Ben's hand is caught under Al's room window and Al is squirted with Willy's makeup. When the doctor sketch is finally seen it is equally unfunny, although this is less of a surprise given its dated vaudeville origin. The scene at the Friar's Club telephone booth, in which Willy yells at Ben as he tries to speak to Al, has Simon upstaging his own dialogue, and not even Richard Benjamin's funny, understated anger of Ben at Willy can save it. Benjamin's mime for Al to open his room window is funnier, as is his snarling Al's name at Willy, who pretends not to know it.

To play his role of Willy, Walter Matthau shaved off almost all of his head of hair. However, the obvious effort to make the actor look older than his real age is too apparent, which undercuts the character's believability. Matthau also has a problem when he yells, since it reads as overdone. However, he is funny when Willy dances, as he states that he is "where it's at," and with the noise he makes when Ben kisses him goodbye. Matthau shows vulnerability when Willy lies on the ground with a heart attack, and uses his New York intonation of words like "Jersey" and "first" and "person," and imitates the black nurse's accent. George Burns makes Al more likeable than Willy, though his calm demeanor is naturally upstaged by Willy's attention-getting hysteria.

In his 1991 interview with Alan King for the television series *Inside the Comedy Mind*, George Burns spoke about working with Walter Matthau. Burns said that if he delivered a line in a way that Matthau did not like, Matthau would slap him. Burns said Matthau kept slapping him for twelve weeks. Then after Burns won the Academy Award, he slapped Matthau. Woody Allen had been asked to direct the film, but he declined. He said he would like to have taken the part of Al, a part he would play in the film's made-for-television remake.

Simon is said to have used the Catskill Mountains comedian and former vaudevillian Willie Howard as a model for the characters of Willy and Al. The Simon brothers met Howard when, early in their writing career, they were invited to meet him in his suite at the Astor Hotel on Broadway. They thought that he wanted them to write him new material, but Howard told them that he did not. Rather, he preferred to have them help punch up the old routines he had been doing since his heyday in the twenties. Since it also seemed apparent that he would not be able to pay much for the privilege, the brothers decided that they could not help.

RELEASE: November 6, 1975, with the tagline "For the price of a movie, you'll feel like a million!"

REVIEWS: Praised by Vincent Canby in the *New York Times* and Robert K. Johnson in his book *Neil Simon*. A mixed reaction in *When the Lights Go Down* from Pauline Kael, who lambasted Ross but praised the performance of George Burns.

AWARDS: George Burns won the Best Supporting Actor Academy Award. The film also received Academy Award nominations for Matthau for Best Actor, Simon for Best Adapted Screenplay, and Albert Brenner and Marvin March for Best Art Direction and Set Decoration. Simon won the Writer's Guild of America award for Best Comedy adapted from another medium.

DVD: Released by Warner Home Video on March 30, 2004.

REMAKES: A made-for-television movie broadcast in 1977 starred Red Buttons as Willy and Lionel Stander as Al and was directed by Robert Moore. This version, adapted by Simon, reduced the play to sixty minutes and was reportedly a pilot for a thirty-minute sitcom envisioned to be like the TV series of *The Odd Couple*. However, this pilot did not sell. German made-for-television versions were also broadcast in 1982, 1995, 1999, and 2001. The made-for-television remake that Woody Allen starred in was broadcast in 1996. It co-starred Peter Falk and Sarah Jessica Parker and was directed by John Erman.

California Suite (1978)

Columbia Pictures/Rastar Films.

CREW: Herbert Ross (Director), Ray Stark (Producer), Ronald L. Schwary (Associate Producer), Neil Simon (Screenplay, based on his play), David M. Walsh (Photography), Michael A. Stevenson (Editor), Claude Bolling (Music), Albert Brenner (Production Design), Patricia Norris (Costumes), Ann Roth (Alan Alda and Jane Fonda's Costumes), Marvin March (Set Decorator), Charles Schram (Makeup), Barnandine M. Anderson (Miss Fonda's Makeup), Ruby Ford and Evelyn Preece (Hair), Kaye Pownall (Miss Fonda's Hair), Robert Dawson and Augie Lohman (Special Effects), Wayne Fitzgerald (Titles), David Hockney (Main Titles Paintings). Color, 98 minutes. Filmed on location at the Beverly Hills Hotel, California; the Dorothy Chandler Pavilion of the Los Angeles Music Center; Rodeo Drive; Malibu; and Warner Bros. Studios in Burbank, California. Filmed in April 1978.

CAST in alphabetical order: Alan Alda (Bill "Billy" Warren); Michael Caine (Sidney Cochran); Bill Cosby (Dr. Chauncey Gump); Jane Fonda (Hannah Warren); Walter Matthau (Marvin Michaels); Elaine May (Millie Michaels); Richard Pryor (Dr. Willis Panama); Maggie Smith (Wendy/Diana Barrie); Herbert Edelman (Harry Michaels); Sheila Frazier (Bettina Panama); Gloria Gifford (Lola Gump); Denis Galik (Bunny); David Sheehan (Himself); Michael Boyle (Desk Clerk); Len Lawson (Frank); Gino Ardito (Plumber); Jerry Ziman (Man on Phone); Clint Young (Doorman); David Matthau

(Bellboy); James Espinoza (Busboy); Buddy Douglas (Page); Armand Cerami (Charley); Joseph Morena (Herb); Brian Cummings, William Kux and Zora Margolis (Autograph Seekers); Rita Gomez, Tina Mernard and Lupe Ontiveros (Maids); Bert May and Eddie Villery (Waiters); Army Archerd (Himself); Paolo Frediani (Handsome Actor, aka Adam); Judith Hannah Brown (Oscar Winner); Gary Hendrix (Oscar Winner's Date); Christopher Pennock (Policeman); Jack Scanlan and Bill Steinmetz (PR Men); Dano Plato (Jenny); Nora Boland (Passenger); David Rini (Airline Representative); John Hawker (Sky Cap); Frank Conn (Bobby); Colleen Drape, Linda Ewen, Kelly Harmon, Tawney Moyer, Leslie Pagett, Vicki Stephens and Nan Wylder (Stewardesses). Uncredited: James Coburn (Harold).

SONGS: "Autumn Leaves" (music by Joseph Kosma), orchestral version at the Academy Awards.

SYNOPSIS: Four sets of guests visit the Beverly Hills Hotel in Los Angeles. British actress Diana Barrie is with her husband of twelve years, Sidney, and has come because she is nominated for the Best Actress Academy Award for the film *No Left Turns*. Chicago doctors Chauncey Gump and Willis Panama are there with their wives Lola and Bettina at the end of their vacation. New Yorker Hannah Warren comes to discuss her seventeen-year-old daughter, Jenny, with her ex-husband Bill. Marvin Michaels comes from New York for his nephew's bar mitzvah and is joined by his wife of fifteen years, Millie.

NOTES: This adaptation's intercutting of the play's four stories is a new cinematic device for Simon. This screenplay features the subjects of marriage and friendship and explores the themes of fidelity, aging, New York versus California lifestyle, and professional jealousy. Simon makes some small cuts in the play's dialogue, moves lines around, and adds some new ones. He also uses the homophobic words "queen" and "faggot," in the context of a heterosexual woman who is married to a bisexual man.

Simon employs the theatrical devices of farce, characters speaking to themselves, and the interrupted exit of someone who has stated their intention to leave. The stories of Chauncey and Willis, and Marvin and Millie, are full of farce. The former climaxes in Willis and Chauncey's physically fighting after multiple accidents befall them, and the latter uses extended suspense with the idea that Millie will find Bunny in Marvin's room. The device of someone's exit being interrupted is used when Hannah stops Bill in the elevator and he has to hold the door open to speak to her.

The screenplay "opens up" the play by adding new scenes with locations that include Los Angeles airport, the Dorothy Chandler Pavilion, the highway, a restaurant, the beach, Bill's house, and Rodeo Drive. The hotel entrance, foyer, hallway, and bar are also shown. Some of the new scenes provide narrative payoffs. That Willis and Lola are put in a small hotel room that is undergoing repairs contributes to Willis' hostility toward Chauncey. Millie's stated intention to spend Marvin's money is paid off when we see her return to their hotel room with a trolley of shopping, and later when she emerges from the hotel hair salon. The Marvin and Millie story has a new button involving the taxi that Marvin has ordered being given to Bunny, who has Marvin and Millie share it. The screenplay also provides new endings for the other stories. Hannah is met at the airport by Jenny, and the couples from Chicago all arrive bandaged, with Bettina in a wheelchair. Sidney and Diana leave on the plane that is just about to depart when the hostess announces that *No Left Turns* is the inflight movie; Diana asks to be let off.

Simon supplies some funny new lines. In *No Left Turns*, Diana's character Wendy tells Harold, "Don't shout at me. I'm a first class passenger," and he replies, "You're a first class lunatic." Hannah tells Bob, her Washington lover, on the telephone, "I can't wait to get out of here. It's like paradise with a lobotomy." Bill tells Hannah that she used to be the healthiest girl he knew and she replies, "With Nixon in the White House good health seemed to be in bad taste." The beach scene has Hannah asking Bill, "Can we go? I feel like we're playing 'From Here to Eternity.'" Hannah tells Bill, "I'm out of cigarettes. I can't be expected to give up my daughter and cigarettes on the same day." Willis gets a funny line when he tells the police officer at the scene of the car accident that he is paralyzed: "It's not from the car. It's from sitting in a Japanese restaurant."

Funny lines retained from the play include Hannah's comment about San Francisco—"I was always afraid I'd fall out of bed and roll down one of those hills." After Bill arrives wearing casual clothes she tells him, "When you walked in like that, I thought we were going to play tennis." Bill tells Hannah that he will agree to whatever Hannah decides about their daughter. She replies, "No wonder there's so many used car salesmen out here." Diana has a risqué line when she comments to Sidney about his flirting with Adam, "Discreet?! You did everything but lick his artichoke." Marvin tells Millie that sex with Bunny was meaningless to him and Millie replies, "It's a shame. I always get upset when you don't have a good time."

Simon's other changes from the play include character names. Sidney and Diana Nichols are now Sidney Cochran and Diana Barrie. Sidney's change of name may even be a play on words, since his character is bisexual. He also changes Diana's line about Michael Caine's accepting the award on her behalf to David Niven, obviously in response to Caine's casting as Sidney. Simon changes the visitors being from Philadelphia to being from New York, like Hannah. He makes greater changes to the visitors from Chicago, as Mort and Beth Hollender and Stu and Gert Franklyn, the characters in the play, are all of them white in the film, and none of them a doctor. This story is the one that has the most revisions in the dialogue, with the play version barely recognizable in the adaptation. The other stories have minor changes, the most notable being in the Marvin/Millie story, where Bunny is now unconscious in the hotel room, and the loss of the play's ending of Millie's telephone call from her children.

The screenplay offers two strong female roles in Diana and Hannah. Sidney is equally witty as Diana, while Hannah is wittier than Bill, which unbalances their battle in her favor. Bill's position isn't helped by the fact that he rarely challenges Hannah, and repeatedly compliments her, but Hannah's wit saves her from reading as arrogant and unlikeable. Her fear that California will have a bad influence on her daughter is confirmed when Jenny gives her a map of movie stars' homes as a goodbye present, apparently without irony. This pays off Hannah's earlier line about the map being the state's greatest literary achievement. Regrettably, Diana appears pathetic when she humiliates herself by begging Sidney to make love to her and not to close his eyes when he does so. The Marvin and Millie story has a sour undertaste in light of his sleeping with Bunny. This makes Marvin an ambiguous character, despite our potential empathy when he attempts to make Bunny leave and hides her from Millie.

Michael Caine and Maggie Smith in a still for *California Suite* (1978).

Herbert Ross retains none of the Broadway cast for the film. His treatment sometimes favors score over dialogue. Perhaps this is done to lessens the theatricality of the exchange, but it also overwhelms it. The only interesting visual touch is showing Millie in close-up as she puts her coat in a closet as Marvin is seen behind her, carrying Bunny. Regrettably, Ross fails to make Marvin's whole handling of the unconscious Bunny funny. *Gilda* (1946) is shown on television in the rooms of both Diana and Sidney and Chauncey and Bettina. That film's narrative of a woman mistreated by the man she loves mirrors the limited relationship between Diana and Sidney.

Jane Fonda's Hannah is tense and funny. Though she is burdened with an unflattering hairstyle, her tears at the prospect of giving up her daughter show her vulnerability. Hannah is given an unusual entrance for a star's character; we first see her with the back of her head to the camera. Ross also uses an odd staging effect in which Hannah lies on her bed with her arms up next to her as she speaks. Richard Pryor's Willis is funny in his anger and the weakness of his physical threat against Bill Cosby's Chauncey. Maggie Smith makes Diana funny, especially in her anxiety at appearing at the Academy Awards, in the way she pronounces "bizarre," the way she says, "What's wrong with my hair?" and when she asks Sidney, "What's that green slime you're eating?" She uses physical comedy when Diana is drunk. Michael Caine uses his hooded eyes and effeminate physicality to make Sidney convincingly bisexual and duplicitous. Walter Matthau uses broad comedy for Marvin's reaction to finding Bunny unconscious and in his attempt to give her water and dress her. The noises Marvin makes when Millie inadvertently uncovers Bunny on the bed are also funny. Elaine May pleasingly underplays Millie, and it's a shame that this character has so little to do and say.

In his memoir *The Play Goes On*, Simon states that the character of Diana was "in some sense" based on Glenda Jackson, who won the Best Actress Academy Award for the American comedy *A Touch of Class* (1973). The arrival of Diana and Sidney at the Academy Awards was shot at the actual 1977 Academy Awards ceremony when in real life Michael Caine and Maggie Smith were the presenters of the Best Supporting Actor Award. In her 2013 interview for the television show *60 Minutes*, Smith states that she found Herbert Ross "a bit tricky, a bit spiky.... He was jagged. He was very difficult but when I got upset someone said try not to be because it happens to a lot of people. Walter Matthau left the set the other day in tears." It is said that Catherine Wilkinson was originally cast in the part of Jenny.

In her review of the film, Pauline Kael made the accusation that the treatment of the black couples in the film is racist. In *Jet* magazine, dated March 1, 1979, it was reported that Cosby was incensed by this claim and wrote a letter to producer Ray Stark. Stark then ran the letter in an ad in *Variety*. Cosby's letter speaks of the "projected racism" of white people and claims that he never felt that the film was racist. The article in *Jet* said that the black actors were doing physical comedy, "a legitimate form of the art," and that "black actors must have the same creative freedom as white actors."

RELEASE: December 15, 1978, with the tagline "The best two-hour vacation in town!"

REVIEWS: Praised by Vincent Canby in the *New York Times*, and Clive Hirschhorn in *The Columbia Story*. A mixed reaction from *Variety*, Les Keyser in *Hollywood in the Seventies* and Robert K. Johnson in *Neil Simon*. Lambasted by Pauline Kael in *When the Lights Go Down*.

AWARDS: Maggie Smith won the Best Supporting Actress Academy Award. Simon was nominated for the Best Screenplay Adaptation Award, and Albert Brenner and Marvin March were nominated for the Best Art Direction and Set Decoration Academy Award.

DVD: Released by Sony Pictures Home Entertainment on January 2, 2002.

SEQUEL: The made-for-TV movie *London Suite* (1996) features the characters of Diana and Sidney.

Chapter Two (1979)

Columbia Pictures/Rastar Films.

CREW: Robert Moore (Director), Ray Stark (Producer), Margaret Booth (Associate Producer), Roger M. Rothstein (Executive Producer), Neil Simon (Screenplay, based on his play), David M. Walsh (Photography), Richard Kratina (New York Photography), Marvin Hamlisch (Music), Michael A. Stevenson (Editor), Gene Callahan (Production Design), Pete Smith (Art Direction), Lee Poll (Set Decorator), Oscar De La Renta (Ms. Mason's Clothes), Vicki Sanchez (Costumes), Prasuti (Ms. Harper's Clothes), Tom Case (Makeup), Kathryn Blondell (Hair), Sam Dockrey (Special Effects). Color, 126 minutes. Filmed on location in New York.

CAST: James Caan (George Schneider); Marsha Mason (Jennifer "Jennie" Mac-Laine); Valerie Harper (Faye Medwick); Joe Bologna (Leo Schneider); Alan Fudge (Lee Michaels); Judy Farrell (Gwen Michaels); Debra Mooney (Marilyn); Isabel Cooley (Customs Officer); Imogene Bliss (Elderly Lady in Bookstore); Barry Michlin (Maitre d'); Ray Young (Gary); Greg Zadikov, Dr. Paul Singh and Sumant (Waiters); Cheryl Bianchi (Electric Girl, aka Bambi); George Rondo (Martin, aka Marty, Joe Papp's Stage Manager); Elizabeth Farley (Actress); Sunday Brennab (Tina); Cari Jones (Girl at Dinner Dance); Danny Gellis (Bucky); Henry Sutton (Judge); E.D. Miller (Umpire); Howard Jeffrey (Director); Marie Reynolds (Barbara).

SONGS: "The Man I Love" (music by George Gershwin with words by Ira Gershwin), Joe Bologna; "Isn't It Romantic" (music by Richard Rodgers), French restaurant; "Red Sails in the Sunset" (Hugh Williams, aka Wilhelm Grosz), West Indies hotel restaurant; "I'm on Your Side" (music by Marvin Hamlisch with words by Carole Bayer Sager), Marilyn McCoo under end credits.

SYNOPSIS: A forty-two-year-old widowed New Yorker, novelist George Schneider, is introduced to thirty-four-year-old actress Jennifer MacLaine by his press agent brother Leo. George has recently lost his wife of twelve years, Barbara, and Jennie has recently divorced her ex-baseball player husband, Gus Hendricks. Jennie's married friend Faye Medwick asks to borrow her apartment to have an affair with Leo, who is separating from his wife, Marilyn. George marries Jennie but he gets depressed on the honeymoon in the West Indies and cuts it short. Back in New York the couple fight. George leaves to go to Los Angeles on business but returns to work on the marriage with Jennie.

NOTES: This screenplay is about marriage and how a widower's new wife can be challenged by the memory of her predecessor. The autobiographical aspect of the material is well known; Simon married Marsha Mason too soon after he lost his first wife. The adaptation creates new scenes and lines, and moves some of the play's lines.

The screenplay "opens up" the play with scenes at the airport, a park, a French and Indian restaurant, Joseph Papp's The Other Stage, the Public Library, a flea market, a bookshop, Carnegie Hall, a deli, a ladies gym, Leo's house where his backyard and horse stable are shown, the judge's chamber and courthouse where George and Jennie are married, and the West Indies for their honeymoon. Some of the new scenes have narrative payoffs and differences from the source play. In the Indian restaurant scene George has a bad reaction to the spicy food, whereas in the play he got fish food poisoning. In the café where they don't speak, Jennie comments, "Maybe we should always keep quiet like this." After they walk out of the Carnegie Hall piano concert, George remarks, "Infatuation makes you stupid." The scene gets a later repeat when Jennie and Faye walk out of a concert by the Polish chamber orchestra. The West Indian hotel restaurant where the couple meet Lee and Gwen Michaels gets a payoff because it helps to remind George of Barbara, since the Michaelses were at the same hotel during George's first honeymoon.

The narrative uses the device of George and Jennie's being at the same place at the same time before they meet. The locations of the airport and the French restaurant show their social alignment, since both return to New York after trips and both have bad dates at the restaurant. The sense of timing also prefigures their telephone conver-

Jennifer MacLaine (Marsha Mason) and George Schneider (James Caan), in a still for *Chapter Two* (1979).

sations, in which their witty banter indicates that they are intellectually compatible. Bad timing comes into play when George sees a photograph of Barbara while he is in bed with Jennie, and when Jennie catches Faye and Leo in her apartment.

The idea that George mistakenly telephones Jennie when he means to contact a research librarian is a romantic comedy contrivance. However, his continuing to call Jennie demonstrates his interest in her. That the characters sometimes speak to themselves is a theatrical device. George is humanized by the shaving cuts he sustains on his wedding day, which show his nerves. After Jennie's big speech, the film's climax, we assume that George will apologize and go to her but he does not, and it is only after his trip to Los Angeles that he comes back to her physically and emotionally.

A funny new line comes when Leo sees George's shaving cuts and asks, "What is that, a suicide attempt?" Jennie asks the name of Leo's horse, and Leo replies, "Who cares? You call him and he doesn't move." After Faye tells Leo that she told her analyst about her intention to have the affair, he asks, "Did you name names?" Funny lines retained from the play include one that concerns Leo's wife Marilyn having a list of reasons why she is leaving him: "Ask her, she'll show it to you." Leo refers to George's trying to open the cellophane wrapper on a carnation as "What is that, a forest fire?" The noise is particularly annoying because George makes it when Leo is on the telephone with their mother. Faye expresses her paranoia about meeting Leo in Jennie's apartment, saying, "I changed taxis three times and walked with a limp into the building, and you gave out this number." He tells her, "You're so much more interesting-looking than you were eight years ago. You have so much character in your face," to which Faye replies, "Why does that not overjoy me?" Jennie tells Leo that Faye told him about their meeting in her apartment. She says, "[Faye] was completely honest and straightforward. She told me she was drugged." This line is a variation on one of Faye's lines in the play.

The play's character of Jennie Malone is renamed Jennie MacLaine. One of George's spy novels read by Jennie on the honeymoon in the film is *Queen of Zanzibar*. George also mentions two other titles that appear in the play—*The Duchess of Limehouse* and *Falling into Place*. The rain retained from the play when the couple return to New York from their honeymoon is a narrative harbinger of the trouble to come. Jennie's line in the play about how she can still smell her ex-husband's cigar gets a payoff in the screenplay when Faye finds the cigar that is causing the smell. Jennie asks, "When does that go away?" and Faye answers, "When you throw it out." Jennie says that it is there because he must have come by to pick up the rest of his things, and we see the new action of Faye throwing the cigar away. In another change from the play Simon has Jennie call George back after he telephones her when she is in bed. Before she does, she takes aspirins for a headache. Her spraying herself with perfume before George arrives for the five-minute meeting gets a new payoff when he admires it and Jennie replies, "I may have overdone it. I didn't know how much to put on for five minutes." There is a new exchange between Jennie and Marilyn. Jennie says that she intends to keep her career as an actress when she marries, whereas Marilyn had abandoned her college thesis on political history to marry Leo.

Simon gives a line to Jennie that is spoken by Faye in the play. It is concerning Faye's marriage; she says that you can tell it is bad when things at home are worse than on the soap. Simon's moving the scene where Jennie and George exchange presents to the public library gets a line payoff. In reaction to a woman who is exasperated by the sound of the presents being unwrapped, George says, "They don't make quiet paper." Simon also makes additions to the end of the play for the film. George tells Jennie after her big speech that he would like to go and get a chili burger. George telephones the restaurant when Jennie and Leo are and asks for Bambi. He suggests that Jennie come back to the house so that they can try another of those five-minute dates that worked last time. At home George tells Jennie, "You not the only one that's wonderful. I'm wonderful too."

Cut from the play are the scenes in which Faye tells Jennie that she wanted to have an affair with Gus, and in which Jennie returns to live in her apartment when George goes to Los Angeles. Simon also loses the second kiss between Faye and Leo, and Leo's long speech where he tells Jennie about Barbara's death and George's reaction to it.

The narrative centers on the issue of George's grief at his previous wife's death being an obstacle to his new marriage to Jennie. Although Jennie is also suffering the loss of a partner, through divorce, George's grief is given far more weight, creating an uncomfortable imbalance in the relationship. That George wallows in his grief can read as self-indulgent, and he admits it to be self pity. It also requires a level of patience from Jennie that he is doesn't offer to her, since he never considers her own grief. Neither George nor Jennie listens to the warnings from George's brother Leo and Jennie's best friend Faye that the marriage is premature. George's choice to not change Barbara's decoration of the house and to book the same hotel in the West Indies for his second honeymoon as for his first appears inconsiderate and self-indulgent. He stops speaking to Jennie on their honeymoon, both blaming and punishing her by not expressing his feelings to her. He also judges her when he accuses her of over-drinking on the trip back from their honeymoon, which he has selfishly cut short. Jenny leaves her *Cherry Orchard* audition, showing her willingness to sacrifice her career for her marriage. George's sacrifice for the marriage is not as big since the meeting he forsakes at Paramount in Los Angeles can presumably be rescheduled, while Jennie apparently has only one shot at the audition. George resents Jennie for being so understanding and for not behaving like Barbara, who he implies was more violent in her reaction to him. This is paid off in the narrative climax when, in the face of George's leaving for Los Angeles, Jennie hits him. This is her effort to act more like Barbara, and also to express her frustration at how he is behaving. The issue is resolved on George's terms. He finally realizes what Jennie has to offer him, and the narrative concludes with his reading her his new novel, which implies an opening up to her. Images under the end credits of Jennie in period costume also suggest she has been cast in the production of *The Cherry Orchard* after all.

Director Robert Moore keeps the pivotal telephone scenes between George and Jennie from becoming dull talking heads, though the wit in the dialogue also helps. Moore suggests the physical attraction between the couple by showing them touching each other in public, their holding hands, and George with his arm around Jennie. The use of score is too intrusive in Jennie's run through the street back to George, but the dark tones in the music generally help to match George's depression. The stable scene is unbalanced by the lights on Mason seen in the reflection of her sunglasses, and in a scene in George's office the squeaking of George's chair as he rocks back and forward obscures what Jennie is saying to him.

None of the Broadway cast were retained for the film. James Caan and Marsha Mason make George and Jennie equally likeable. The autobiographical aspect of the narrative is added to by Caan's wearing Neil Simon–style spectacles, though his movie star looks makes this George an idealized version of Simon. Caan shown semi-naked also adds beefcake to the image of George. Mason's performance overcomes the awkward autobiographical element of her character, which apparently stopped her from wanting to do the play version. She makes Jennie's long, climactic speech to George moving, even if she is mannered in the use of her hands. Regrettably, Moore violates Jennie's speech with a shot of the back of her head for Caan's face to be seen in close-up for George's reaction.

It has been said that the skinniness of Valerie Harper's Faye makes her look anorexic, though it is believable for her character, who is an actress on a New York television soap opera. Harper's Faye is funny with her pronunciation of "badly" when she says that Leo's taking the telephone call during their tryst is badly timed. Joe Bologna makes Leo likeable in the role of an unfaithful husband who could be otherwise played as a sleazeball.

RELEASE: December 14, 1979, with the tagline "It's not supposed to happen twice in your life, but it can."

REVIEWS: Praised by *Variety*. A mixed reaction from Janet Maslin in the *New York*

Times, Roger Ebert in the *Chicago Sun-Times,* Clive Hirschhorn in *The Columbia Story,* and Robert K. Johnson in *Neil Simon.*

AWARDS: Marsha Mason was nominated for the Best Actress Academy Award.

DVD: Released by SPE on April 3, 2012.

Only When I Laugh (1981) (aka *It Hurts Only When I Laugh*)
Columbia Pictures.

CREW: Glenn Jordan (Director), Roger M. Rothstein (Producer), Neil Simon (Producer/Screenplay, based on his play *The Gingerbread Lady*), David M. Walsh (Photography), Warren Rothenberger (New York Photography), John Wright (Editor), David Shire (Music), Albert Brenner (Production Design), David Haber (Art Director), Marvin March (Set Decorator), Ann Roth (Costumes), Tom Case (Makeup), Kathryn Blondell (Hair). Color, 120 minutes. Filmed on location in New York; on location at a theatre in Wilshire Boulevard, Los Angeles; and at Warner Hollywood Studios, California, in October 1980.

CAST: Marsha Mason (Georgia Hines/Carol), Kristy McNichol (Polly), James Coco (Jimmy Perino), Joan Hackett (Toby Landau), David Dukes (David Lowe), John Bennett Perry (Vincent Heller/Lou in play), Guy Boyd (Man at Bar), Ed Moore (Dr. Bob Komack), Bryan Webster (Tom), Peter Coffield (Mr. Tarloff), Mark Schubb (Adam Kasabian), Ellen La Gamba (Sandy the Receptionist), Venida Evans (Nurse Garcia), John Vargas (Manuel), Nancy Nagler (Heidi Stanton), Dan Monahan (Jason), Michael Ross (Paul), Tom Ormeny (Kyle, bartender at Joe Allen), Ken Weisbrath (Waiter), Henry Olek (George De Vane, the Director), Jane Atkins (Doreen), Kevin Bacon (Don Holcroft), Ron Levine (Gary Chandler), Rebecca Stanley (Denise Summers), Nick La Padula (Bartender), Phillip Lindsay (Charlie the Super), Birdie Hale (Super's Wife), Wayne Framson (Polly's Father).

SONGS: "Theme from New York, New York" (music by John Kander and lyrics by Fred Ebb), James Coco; "Heart" from *Damn Yankees* (Richard Adler and Jerry Ross), Kristy McNichol and Nancy Nagler; "Machine Gun," Storm, heard when Polly makes pancakes; "Take the 'A' Train" (Billy Strayhorn), Joe Allen's; "I Guess I'll Have to Change My Plan" (music by Arthur Schwartz with lyrics by Howard Dietz), Marsha Mason and Kristy McNichol.

SYNOPSIS: Thirty-eight-year-old, divorced, alcoholic actress Georgia Hines comes back to her New York apartment after having spent three months at a Long Island sanitarium. Her estranged seventeen-year-old daughter Polly is in her last year of high school and moves in with her mother. Georgia accepts the lead in an autobiographical play by her ex-boyfriend, David Lowe. Six weeks away from opening night, her friend Toby Landau has a party for her fortieth birthday. Before the party Toby's husband tells her he wants a divorce after twelve years of marriage, and Georgia's other friend Jimmy Perrino gets fired from his acting job in another play. George starts drinking again and gets beaten up by a man in a bar. Polly also drinks martinis so she can know why her mother likes to drink. Georgie asks Polly to move out, but meets her and Polly's father for lunch sporting the bruised eye she got from her night off the wagon.

NOTES: Simon's adaptation features the most changes to one of his source plays

Georgia Hines (Marsha Mason, left) in bed with her daughter, Polly (Kristy McNichol), in a still for *Only When I Laugh* (1981).

to date. He makes large cuts, overhauling most of *The Gingerbread Lady*, moves some lines, and introduces a lot of new material. A pivotal new character is Adam, who helps Polly try drinking so that she knows what about it appeals to Georgia. The screenplay explores the subject of alcoholism and its effect on family and friends, in particular the relationship between an estranged mother and her teenage daughter. It also explores the difference between friends and family as people you can rely upon.

The play is "opened up," with the screenplay providing new locations of the sanitarium, Polly's school, Joe Allen's bar, the theatre where David's play is in rehearsal, restaurants including Tavern on the Green, Toby's apartment, a park, and a bar. While Toby's apartment is like Georgia's in that we can view private protected behavior, the public places allow for other behavior to be observed in the context of society. Examples are how at Joe Allen's, Georgia "makes a scene" with David, how she and Mr. Tarloff are embarrassed when they realize that they have been fixed up at the coffee shop, how Toby swears at the lunch she has with Georgia and Jimmy, how Georgia embarrasses Polly at the lunch when the two college boys try to pick them up, Georgia's abusing the person at the sanitarium on the telephone because she only wants to speak to her doctor, Georgia's being attacked in the street by the man from the bar, Polly's vomiting in the park after drinking, and Georgia's meeting Polly and her father for lunch at Tavern on the Green when Georgia has a black eye. Some interior scenes also provide awkward behavior, as when Georgia meets Denise at the theatre, when David apologizes to Georgia in her dressing room, and when Georgia gets drunk at Toby's party, spills champagne on Toby, and is told off by Polly for being drunk.

Georgia attends Polly's school rehearsal of *Damn Yankees*, which allows us to see that Polly wants to be a performer like her mother. This scene is juxtaposed with the rehearsal for David's play when we see Georgia acting. The Joe Allen scene gets two payoffs in Georgia's deciding to act in the play, and then later finding that her personal problems are an obstacle to doing so. The scene of Polly recommending that Georgia buy a Donegal jacket that Georgia feels is too young for her gets a payoff when the women are followed in the street by the college boys, with the idea that Georgia can pass for Polly's older sister. The lunch scene also prefigures Georgia's hypocrisy in her use of language. She ridicules the college boy Gary for his use of being "into" something and then she uses the same expression when giving David the 1942 Mickey Mouse watch she buys him.

Simon's funny new lines include Jimmy's comment on Georgia's coat, "She looks like she's wearing the drapes from Radio City Music Hall," and his asking Georgia, "Do you know what it feels like to be turned down for a haemorrhoid commercial?" Georgia asks Jimmy about the woman he says he saw David with, and Jimmy says, "What am I, a police reporter? She was a female Caucasian. That is the best I can do." Jimmy comments about the house painting he has done with Georgia, "It took me all night to get the roller out of my hand." Georgia tells Polly, "I know it's only been four minutes, but I think we're getting along beautifully." Toby tells Georgia, "I found a long gray hair on Kevin's jacket last night. If it's another woman's I'll kill him. If it's mine I'll kill myself." Jimmy tells Georgia, "The putz producer just fired the scenery. I swear to God, he pointed to the scenery and said, "You're out!" Jimmy tells Georgia that he forgot to bring his gift to Toby's party: "I was coming up in the elevator with two old ladies and I suddenly yell out 'Oh Shit!'" Jimmy sees that Toby looks "radiant" for the party and tells Georgia, "She dresses up for depression." Toby reminds Georgia of her promise that she would never drink again. Georgia replies, "That was in the car. I am not drinking in a car." When Polly applies some makeup to try to conceal Georgia's bruised eyes, Georgia tells her, "We couldn't get away with this on Halloween." Polly tells Georgia, "I'm going to move back here one day, even if I'm eighty-three years old." Jimmy sees Georgia's bruised eye and asks her if she is "trying to commit suicide one feature at a time."

Funny lines retained from the play include Georgia's telling Polly about not wanting to have lunch with her father because of her hangover shakes: "The minute I start spilling water on the man's lap he's going to notice something." Jimmy tells Georgia that she should see a doctor about her bruised eyes, and Georgia says, "I already had medical attention. A dog licked me when I was on the ground."

Simon makes many changes to the play. His updates include references to Bo Derek and Xerox. The play's singer, Evy Meara, is now actress Georgia Hines. In the play Evy is forty-three, and in the film Georgia is thirty-eight. This matches the respective ages of Maureen Stapleton and Marsha Mason for the play and film versions. The Lou Tanner musician character is now David, a playwright, and Jimmy Perry is now Jimmy Perino. Toby's husband Marty is changed to Kevin, though neither is seen in the play or film. In the play it is Lou who punches Evy in the face, offstage, but in the film it is done by the man in the bar, also offstage. Simon cuts the telephone call Jimmy takes from the telephone company, the return of Manuel to talk to the Evy character, and Evy's singing for herself. We also lose Evy's later listening to one of her albums after Toby's party. Simon cuts the lines that reference the film's title, in which Polly reminds her mother that when she was nine she gave her a gingerbread house with a gingerbread lady inside. Instead, Simon explains the film's title as the name of the play that David writes about Georgia. That title is said to come from an old joke about a man who has a spear sticking through his chest and tells someone else that it hurts only when he laughs. The title gets another airing when Polly says that she is worried only when she laughs about the romantic triangle of herself, Adam, and Heidi. The screenplay shows Georgia drinking, whereas the play initially had Evy tell Polly that she drank offstage before we see her drink at Toby's party. The location of Toby's party is Evy's apartment, whereas it is at Toby's apartment in the film. We lose the plot point of Toby's husband being a television salesman, and although the screenplay doesn't specify his job, we assume that her Park Avenue apartment means that he is financially successful.

The narrative contrasts Georgia's family of Polly with Georgia's friends in Toby and Jimmy. Polly is a teenager mature beyond her years. However, at the climactic party scene, she rejects Georgia and leaves. Polly does forgive her mother and return to her, but her judgment of Georgia is harsher than that of Toby and Jimmy, perhaps because Georgia has cost her more. Georgia's friends don't reject her, but Toby and Jimmy have their own problems. Toby's sense of superior beauty comes with arrogance and insecurity. She comments that her sister-in-law knows about sympathy because of the two huge warts on the side of her nose. Her speech about her past and the men who have desired her is both boastful and pathetic. We see Toby's vanity in trying to hide the fact that she uses glasses to read the menu at the lunch restaurant. Toby also has an interestingly contemptuous reaction to Georgia's bloodied face after she has been attacked, although Toby does treat the wound.

Jimmy describes the three friends as the three comrades: Hedy Lamarr, Margaret Sullavan and Beulah Bondi. But his sense of self-involvement has him soon crying to Toby over the pain of his failed acting career, suggesting it is greater than her pain over her pending divorce. Jimmy as a gay man can only give Georgia limited physical comfort and cannot be a romantic companion. In his chapter on the film in his book on Simon, Robert K. Johnson suggests that the narrative's end has Georgia choosing Polly over Toby and Jimmy. Johnson claims that Jimmy's remark to Georgia that she will always have her friends is what makes her decide to reject them.

The subject of alcoholism is explored with Georgia's addiction. Her low self-esteem is probably the reason for her drinking. Bob at the sanitarium comments that she doesn't take compliments well, and she dismisses David's praise of her acting in the rehearsal of his play. Toby tells Georgia she has noticed she hates to accept applause from an audience after a performance. Georgia rationalizes this by saying that people applaud trained seals and that's how she sees herself as an actress. Georgia also likens herself to Toby and Jimmy in being "weak and helpless." She asks Jimmy why Polly won't give up on her, and he tells her it's because Georgia is special: "Crazy, lunatic, disgusting but special." She summons inner strength to meet Polly and Polly's father at the Tavern on the Green, despite her bruised eye and hangover.

Georgia's willingness to change her behavior is shown by her stint at the sanitarium, her new sobriety, and loss of weight. David's play highlights her former self, and it's probably a mistake for Georgia to accept the part in the production. Her penchant for masochism resurfaces when she makes assumptions about David, knowing that he has a new girlfriend, Denise. Georgia's friends have their own crises, giving her the excuse to drink again. When David tries to apologize to Georgia for bringing Denise to meet her at the theatre, Georgia can conveniently deny her feelings since she also has Toby's situation to feel bad about. Her weakened state of resolve is demonstrated when, walking to Toby's apartment, she is tempted by the bars she passes along the way. She also fails to reach her sanitarium doctor since he is unavailable when she calls for counseling. At Toby's party Georgia pours Toby a glass of champagne and encourages her to drink it, apparently so that Georgia can see it gone and also enjoy it by proxy. Georgia then succumbs to drinking, alone in the kitchen. Back at the party, she then drinks openly in front of the others.

Since the narrative establishes that Georgia is a struggling alcoholic, we predict that she will fall off the wagon. She does, and the narrative gives a new dimension to the character. In the film's opening scene Georgia tells the sanitarium counselor that she is funny when she drinks, and this is proven to be true at Toby's party. Georgia is elsewhere shown to have a good sense of humor but, at the party, her humor comes at the expense of others. She uses sarcasm to attack Toby and Jimmy, when she jokes about their not knowing what it is like to have a daughter. She tells Toby to let Jimmy help her get the cake rather than Polly, "since he is not working anyway," and she offers to buy Toby's ruined dress, observing, "It's not worth much. It's got a big goddamn wine stain on it."

Georgia's drinking also provides narrative consequences. Polly points out that her mother's drinking only makes her think of herself, and that her mother knows that her friends will be there to look after her. Georgia is seemingly not too drunk to hear Polly and feel ashamed, telling Jimmy "I think I fucked up." The fact that Jimmy is in the taxi, taking her home, shows that Polly is right about Georgia's having people to look after her. Polly has Adam buy her a bottle of Martini's so that she can feel what Georgia feels when she drinks. Polly later tells Georgia that she learned what she predicted: that when drunk all she cared about was herself, feeling nothing for anybody else. Georgia goes out at night to buy cigarettes—her second form of addiction—at a bar where she drinks and flirts with a man. When she later rejects him, he pushes her into a car park and we assume she is raped, although she is only beaten up. The bloodied eye she receives is used as a plot point, allowing Polly to see the extent to which Georgia has slipped. The attack on Georgia also has two interesting effects. She doesn't want to report it the police since the publicity might be bad for the show she is to be in, and she tries to use it as an excuse not to have the scheduled lunch with Polly's father.

None of the Broadway cast was used for the film version. Considering that almost ten years had passed since the production, this is not a surprise. Director Glenn Jordan opens with the sound of a cigarette lighter and the screen black as the back of a chair that Georgia sits in as she speaks to a doctor at the sanitarium. He lights David half in shadow when David calls Georgia from a bar, which suggests that the ex-boyfriend has a dark agenda. This will turn out to be true, since David has written a play about her.

In the montage of Georgia and Polly shopping the score is overdone, but it *is* effective in its use of an unresolved musical cord to show Georgia's state of mind when she is tempted to drink. *Gilda* (1946) is seen on television in Georgia's apartment, another story of a masochistic woman. Jordan illustrates the scene of the man following Georgia from the bar like a thriller; the man is shown compartmentalized as a pair of legs, and the sound of his footsteps is heard by Georgia. Her increased steps are matched by his increased steps until he calls out to her. The man's pushing Georgia into a fenced car park suggests that he will rape her. Jordan cuts away to Toby talking to Jimmy on the telephone, and the doorbell ringing at Toby's apartment reveals it to be the battered Georgia.

Wearing her hair longer than it was in *The Goodbye Girl* and *Chapter Two*, Marsha Mason makes Georgia very likeable and sympathetic. The character is funny when presenting herself to Jimmy with, "Ok, say it. I'm goddamn gorgeous." Some of Mason's overplaying can be understood, given the context of Georgia as an actress. Mason holds a smile when David brings Denise to meet Georgia, but we know that she is faking it since her façade drops when she watches David walk Denise away. Mason supplies a mix of anger and anxiety when Georgia telephones the sanitarium and her doctor is not available. She shows how Georgia "acts" calm for Polly on the telephone, with her tears and the anxiety she shows Toby after the call revealing what she has covered up for her daughter. The smeared mascara and bruised face of the attacked Georgia have an ironic effect since they seem to make Mason's clown face even more apparent. Jordan gives Mason a long close-up of reaction when Jimmy tells Georgia that the three friends have each other to lean on. He then dissolves to the last scene at the Tavern on the Green, where Georgia makes a star entrance wearing dark glasses.

James Coco makes Jimmy funny in his speech about wanting to be a star and with his cynical reaction to seeing Georgia's bruised eye, although his tears of self-pity lack empathy. Joan Hackett shows the insecurity underneath Toby's lacquered surface, although her performance of Toby's anger at Georgia is disappointing. Conversely, Kristy McNichol brings conviction to Polly's anger at Georgia, which is a relief after Polly's previous supreme understanding for her mother. McNichol also supplies tears when Polly confronts Georgia about what she experienced while drinking.

In his *American Film* interview, Simon said that at the time of the play's production he received an offer for it to be filmed by Hallmark Hall of Fame as a two-hour special. However, he was told that he would have to eliminate certain things, so he refused. He held out hope for a film version in which he could do it the way it was meant to be done, without the restrictions that television imposed. In his 1976 *Playgirl* interview, Simon said that he could then not interest Hollywood studios in a film of the play because the central character was a forty-two-year-old actress. He said he could have sold it if he had been willing to forgo a salary in lieu of box office profits, and if he could have found an actress who would accept the same arrangement. The studios were also not interested because they saw the story as "a downer" and specifically a female downer. Additional box office insurance was required by casting a bankable female star, such as Streisand or Liza Minnelli, although both were then too young for the part. More age-appropriate was Maureen Stapleton, who had done the play on Broadway, and Anne Bancroft, although neither was then seen by the studios as bankable.

In the article on the film by Frank Miller on the *Turner Classic Movies* Web site, he quotes Simon on why he decided to produce the film: "to avoid any of the confrontations I've had with producers in the past over casting. I didn't want anyone telling me we had to have superstar names." The fact that Simon had Mason cast, his wife at the time, is hardly a surprise. Simon changed the character from a singer to an actress, presumably because Mason is not a singer. Miller claims that the play's protagonist was based on Judy Garland. Miller also says that David Shire wrote a title song with words by Richard Maltby, Jr. for the film that was not used. It would be recorded by Brenda Lee, promoted as "From the Columbia Motion Picture," and nominated for a Razzie Award for the Worst Original Song from a movie.

In Marsha Mason's memoir *Journey* she comments that Simon did not think at first that she was right for the part and felt she would have to work hard to act it. Mason knew better, because her parents were "glow drinkers," people who behaved in a socially acceptable manner in front of others but changed when they were in their own home. The actress wanted to put this "turn-on-a-dime" quality on the screen, rather than play the character as a generic drunk. Mason writes that the telephone scene between Georgia and the sanitarium, presumably the one when her doctor is not available, is one of her favorite scenes.

RELEASE: The film premiered at the Toronto Film Festival on September 13, 1981, and was released in the United States on September 23. The taglines were "It'll make you laugh ... till you cry" and "Kristy McNichol's a daughter who never had a childhood.... Marsha Mason is a mother who never grew up. For 16 years, they've been practically strangers.... And when they get together, they're the most mismatched roommates since *The Goodbye Girl*."

REVIEWS: Praised by Vincent Canby in the *New York Times*, though he had misgivings about Kristy McNichol. Canby also reported that the screenplay only retained fifteen lines from the source play. Lambasted by Roger Ebert in the *Chicago Sun-Times*, though he praised the performance of McNichol. A mixed reaction from Clive Hirschhorn in *The Columbia Story* and Robert K. Johnson in *Neil Simon*.

AWARDS: Academy Award nominations for Marsha Mason for Best Actress, James Coco for Best Supporting Actor and Joan Hackett for Best Supporting Actress. Coco also received a Razzie Award nomination for Worst Supporting Actor.

DVD: Only available on video; released by Sony Pictures on June 24, 1994.

I Ought to Be in Pictures (1982)

20th Century–Fox.

CREW: Herbert Ross (Director/Producer), Rick McCallum and Charles Matthau (Associate Producers), Roger M. Rothstein (Executive Producer), Neil Simon (Producer and Screenplay based on his play), Sidney Levin (Editor), Marvin Hamlisch (Music), Albert Brenner (Production Design), Garrett Lewis (Set Decorator), Ruth Morley (Costumes), Frank Griffin and Ron Snyder (Makeup), Allen Payne and Carol Meikle (Hair), Al Lorimer (Special Effects). Color, 107 minutes. Filmed on location in Brooklyn, New York and Los Angeles.

CAST: Walter Matthau (Herbert "Herb" Tucker); Ann-Margret (Steffy Blondell);

Dinah Manoff (Libby Gladyce Tucker); Lance Guest (Gordon Zaharias); Lewis Smith (Soldier, aka Jeffrey McKecknie); Martin Ferrero (Monte Del Rey); Eugene Butler (Marty); Samantha Harper (Larane); Michael Dudikoff (Boy on the Bus); Gillian Farrell (Waitress); Santos Morales (Mexican Truck Driver); David Faustino (Martin); Shelby Balik (Shelley); Bill Cross (Truck Driver); Virginia Wing (Auto Cashier); Larry Barton (Harry the Waiter); Jose Rabelo and Norberto Kerner (Groundskeepers); Calvin Ander (Rabbi); Muni Zano (Motel Cashier); Allan Graf, Art La Fleur, Nomi Mitty, Charles Parks, Wayne Woodson and Tom Wright (Baseball Fans).

SONGS: "One Hello" (music by Marvin Hamlisch with words by Carole Bayer Sager), Randy Crawford, heard under end credits.

SYNOPSIS: Nineteen-year-old Libby Tucker travels from Brooklyn to Hollywood to visit her screenwriter father, Herb, who has abandoned his family. She has not seen him for sixteen years and hopes that he will help her with her acting career. Libby moves into Herb's house and starts taking acting classes. Herb has a casual girlfriend, studio hairdresser Steffy Blondell, who is sixteen years his junior. Libby realizes that she doesn't want to be an actress after all and decides to go back to Brooklyn. Steffy tells Herb that she has the chance to go away for three weeks with another man, and Herb tells her not to go.

NOTES: Simon's screenplay includes new scenes and lines, and moves some lines from where they appeared in the play. The treatment explores the subject of family, in particular estranged family. The estranged father and daughter recalls the estranged mother and daughter of *Only When I Laugh.* The screenplay also comments on the differences between New York and California. The radical behavior of those in Hollywood is demonstrated via the bare-breasted appearance of Larane, with this kind of screen nudity being something new for Simon. Radical behavior is also demonstrated in the form of artistic expression, in that Libby desires to be an actress and Herb has chosen to be a writer over a conventional domestic life. The screenplay includes poetry and letters of Emily Dickinson, credited as being from *Letters to Dr. and Mrs. Josiah Gilbert Holland.* The dialogue credits the William Luce play *The Belle of Amherst,* with Dickinson's writing on her father related to the theme of the lost father.

The play is "opened up" with new locations at a cemetery, on a bus, a motel, a café, in Herb's car, an auto shop, Hollywood Park Racetrack, Steffy's studio trailer, a restaurant, Dodger Stadium, the Actors Center of Hollywood, a supermarket, parking lots, and a bus terminal. Of the new scenes, some have character observations and narrative payoffs. Libby is first seen talking to a soldier on a Greyhound bus, and the film ends with her talking to a boy on another bus. These express her self-confidence, as does the way she has decided to cross the country to see her father. At the racetrack Steffy tells Libby that she is a failed film actress because she "didn't have the gift." Steffy's paying off Herb's debt to the man who comes to the house to collect gets two narrative payoffs. At the racetrack when the man tells Herb what Steffy has done, Herb tells the man to tear up the check. We then see Herb paying Steffy back the money and telling her not to do that again. The second time Herb waters the trees gets a payoff in the dialogue, since he does it after the rain storm. Libby comments, "I thought it just rained," and Herb tells her, "It might not rain again for a year." The idea of Libby's speaking to her dead grandmother operates as the theatrical device of her talking to herself, which

Ann-Margret, Walter Matthau and Dinah Manoff in a still for *I Ought to Be in Pictures* (1982).

is also used as Libby's voice-over in one scene. Another theatrical device is Libby's stated intention of leaving Herb's house and then returning to continue the conversation.

Some of the new lines include Herb's response to Libby's comment that Robby and Grandma think she has talent: "Unless they own a studio out here I wouldn't rush into anything." Herb tells Libby she has a chip on her shoulder, and she replies, "You're the one who dumped it there." Herb asks Libby, "Why do you talk like Humphrey Bogart?" when she objects to his taking her from the motel by yelling, "I'm not going widcha!"

Funny lines retained from the play include Libby's line about the juicy orange she is given by Herb, "You need a bathing suit to eat it." Lost in the adaptation is the play's plot point that Libby is fat, and Herb's long speech about why he left Libby's mother and his marriages to Patty and Veronica. The screenplay makes Steffy ten years younger than she is in the play, perhaps because Ann-Margret is seven years younger than Joyce Van Patten, who originated the part on stage. Simon changes the telephone conversation Herb has with Blanche and Robby. In the play Libby leaves Herb to make the call alone, but in the film he has her stay with him. She feeds him lines to say to Blanche but then tells her, "Would you keep your voice down. She's gonna hear you." Libby tells Herb to ask Blanche if he can speak to Robby, and then Herb tells Libby to leave him alone when he talks to his son. Simon does a variation on the play's moment of Libby taking a photograph of Herb. In the screenplay Libby also takes one of Herb with Steffy.

The storm in the narrative, when Herb says how rare rain is in California, could be considered a portent for the trouble in his relationships with Steffy and Libby. Steffy decides that she wants more of a commitment from him, and she also criticizes him for not writing. This leads to Steffy's leaving. She returns under the pretext of saying goodbye to Libby, and then wants Herb to tell her not to go away with another man to prove his attachment to her. Since Herb does tell her not to go, she stays with him. Libby's return from being out late also incurs Herb's anger, but it is underplayed so that the anticipated argument doesn't happen. She will only leave when she decides she has gotten what she came for, but she does not leave with rancor.

Libby is demonstrated to have mixed agendas in regards to Herb. She wants a relationship with him and his help in getting into pictures, though she denies both. The narrative ends with Libby having secured a relationship with Herb, strong enough that she doesn't need to live with him. She also realizes that she doesn't really want to be in pictures or be an actress. Libby being a virgin at nineteen adds to her vulnerability as a sexual child, although it is given no narrative payoff. We don't see Libby's opportunity to lose her virginity in her follow-up date with Gordon. The emotional demands Libby makes on Herb suggest what his former wife may have also demanded. However, Libby's desire to be an actress also suggests that she has inherited the need for creative expression that Herb has pursued.

Herb is a morally weak figure since he has abandoned his family in favor of an individual life, and also because he now seems no longer able to be creative. His being estranged from his family is evident from his first kiss to Libby, and his not knowing that his wife has renamed his son Carl as Robby. He is also shown to be careless in thinking that Steffy's son Martin is named Warren. Herb is also presented as a failed writer who would rather gamble than pitch ideas, although Simon adds contempt for the modern Hollywood executives that Herb has to deal with. Herb's rundown car is a symbol of his low status, and Libby's renovation of it and of the house shows her effect on his life. This effect also extends to the second kiss that Herb gives Libby, when he also hugs her.

Director Herbert Ross only retains Dinah Manoff from the Los Angeles and Broadway productions. Manoff had won the Tony Award for her performance. The casting of Ann-Margret over Joyce Van Patten, who appeared in both stage productions as Steffy, is a problem. Steffy as a failed film actress would seem to fit better with Van Patten. Ross first shows Libby at the café at a table talking to the waitress in the reflection of Monte's sunglasses, which prefigures his approach to Libby. He lets us hear some dialogue between Libby and Herb as Steffy returns to the house, and the point is paid off when Steffy tells them that their yelling can be heard outside. Ross also uses a black screen for the start of the scene in which Libby comes home late at night and Herb speaks with her.

The director's greatest achievement with the film is providing a showcase for Walter Matthau's range. Matthau appears wearing a beard and dyed black hair as Herb, although his beard has some gray in it. He provides emotion when he first meets Libby and when he leaves her the first night she stays in his house, but he also shows emotional distance in the detached first kiss he gives her. Matthau is funny when Herb is sarcastic about Libby's leaving her name on the back of cards on parked cars, and tender in his expression of love for his daughter. He is touching in the disappointment over Libby's deciding to leave and when Herb speaks to Robby on the telephone.

Ann-Margret's flat line readings may be accepted as an expression of Steffy's depression over unhappiness with Herb. Dinah Manoff sometimes resembles Kristy McNichol from *Only When I Laugh*. Her accent recalls her mother, Lee Grant, and Manoff is most like her mother when she cries. She is pleasing in Libby's amusement at Herb's sarcasm and never makes Libby's Brooklyn accent or her hostility towards Herb strident.

RELEASE: March 26, 1982, with the tagline "Libby Ticker hitchhiked from Brooklyn to take Hollywood by storm. And her father by surprise."

REVIEWS: Lambasted by Vincent Canby in the *New York Times*, who wrote, "*I Ought to Be in Pictures* ought not to be."

DVD: Only available in PAL DVD format, released by Koch Media. Released on American video by Fox Home Entertainment on December 1, 1982.

Brighton Beach Memoirs (1986)

Universal/Rastar.

CREW: Gene Saks (Director); Ray Stark (Producer); Joseph M. Caracciolo (Associate Producer); David Chasman (Executive Producer); Neil Simon (Screenplay based on his play); John Bailey (Photography); Carol Littleton (Editor); Michael Small (Music); Stuart Wurtzel (Production Design); Paul Eads (Art Director); George DeTitta Jr. and Gary Jones (Set Decorators); Joseph G. Aulisi (Costumes); Joseph Coscia, Lyndell Quiyou and Bill Farley (Hair); Allen Weisinger and Mickey Scott (Makeup). Color, 105 minutes. Filmed on location at Brighton Beach, Brooklyn; Ridgewood, Queens; and Kaufman Astoria Studios, New York.

CAST: Blythe Danner (Kate Jerome), Bob Dishy (Jack Jerome), Brian Drillinger (Stanley Jerome), Stacey Glick (Laurie Morton), Judith Ivey (Blanche Morton), Lisa Waltz (Nora Morton), Jonathan Silverman (Eugene Morris Jerome), Richard Bright (Recruiting Sergeant), James Handy (Frank Murphy), Bette Henritze (Mrs. Matthew Murphy), Steven Hill (Mr. Stroheim), David Margulies (Mr. Farber), Fyvush Finkel (Mr. Greenblatt), Kathleen Doyle (Mrs. Laski), Alan Weeks (Andrew), Marilyn Cooper (Woman in Street), Jason Alexander (Pool Player #1), Christian Baskous (Pool Player #2, aka Gootch), Brian Evers (Policeman #1), Ed Deacy (Policeman #2), Wanda Bimson (Dance Teacher).

SONGS: "Good Morning Glory" (Mack Gordon and Harry Revel), George Hall; "You and the Night and the Music" (music by Arthur Schwartz and lyrics by Howard Dietz), radio in Jerome house; "A Doinele A Volechl Gelt" (Ray Musiker), Neshoma Orchestra and the New York Klezmer Ensemble; "Infatuation" (Walter G. Samuels and Leonard Whitcup), George Hall and his orchestra, radio; "Home" (Geoffrey Clarkson and Harry F. Clarkson), Mildred Bailey; "Jungle Drums (Canto Karabalij)" (Ernesto Lecuomo, Carmen Lombardo and Charles O'Flynn), Guy Lombardo and his Royal Canadians.

SYNOPSIS: In 1937 fourteen-year-old Eugene Morris Jerome lives with his Jewish family in Brighton Beach, Brooklyn, New York. They are his mother, Kate; his father,

Jack; his eighteen-year-old brother, Stanley; Kate's widowed sister, Blanche; and her daughters, thirteen-year-old Laurie and sixteen-year-old Nora. Nora wants to go to Philadelphia to be in a show. Stanley is threatened with being fired by his employer, Mr. Stroheim, unless he writes a letter of apology for being rude. Jack has a heart attack and is no longer able to work. Mr. Murphy stands up Blanche on a date after he is caught driving drunk. Stanley leaves home to join the army after losing his salary playing pool, but decides to come home. Blanche has a fight with Kate and wants to move out, but stays.

NOTES: Simon features the subject of family again, and the coming-of-age of a teenage boy. The boy's interest in baseball recalls the same interest of the teenage Michael McPhee in *Max Dugan Returns*, and the baseball player Daryl Palmer in *The Slugger's Wife*. The protagonist's coming-of-age allows Simon to include risqué topics such as masturbation and incest, and Simon uses the "F" bomb to express a character's anger rather than to define the person's class. The screenplay also features Jewish racism in Kate's fear of the neighborhood Irish and in her disapproval of Mr. Murphy's dating Blanche. The autobiographical elements of the story include Eugene's character as a writer with an older brother, and a father, Jack, who has a weak heart. In his adaptation for the screen, Simon has cut lines from the play, moved some, and added new ones.

The narrative demonstrates Eugene's adolescent sexuality through his interest in breasts. He draws them, looks at pictures of bare-breasted tribeswomen in *National Geographic*, and uses a telescope to spy on Mrs. Laski, his neighbor, undressing. His voyeurism gets a payoff when he sees Mrs. Laski's son spy on Eugene's cousin, Nora. Eugene also has a sexual curiosity about Nora, and he looks up her dress under the dinner table. That Stanley has fixed the bathroom door lock so he can walk in on Nora in the shower to see her naked gets an ironic twist when Nora walks in on Jerome on the toilet. The narrative climaxes with Stanley's giving Eugene a French postcard with a picture of a naked woman, and ends with Eugene announcing that puberty is over for him now that he has seen "the golden palace of the Himalayas." The character of Jack is different than Simon's earlier fathers. For example, compared to the controlling Harry Baker in *Come Blow Your Horn*, Jack is more reasonable, and he gives advice as opposed to orders to his children.

Simon uses the theatrical devices of narration, direct address, and soliloquy. Eugene has a "memoir" book, where he sometimes writes down lines he has heard spoken by his family. He comments in a funny line from the play: "I'm putting this all down in my memoirs so if I grow up twisted and warped the world will know why." Simon changes the play to dramatize moments that are otherwise only spoken of. These include Stanley's confrontation with Mr. Stroheim, the family visit to the cemetery, Stanley playing pool, Blanche putting on makeup under her glasses for her date, and Stanley at the army recruiting office. The most effective of the new scenes have Kate knowing about the second cookie that Eugene takes, and Eugene's comment in monologue after Jack's heart attack. Eugene says he is glad that he doesn't have to put a stone on the grave of his father as we see the family do for Uncle David.

New funny lines include a payoff to the plot point that Laurie has a heart condition. Eugene says, "She better have a bad heart or I'm going to kill her one day." Laurie asks Eugene why Mrs. Murphy wants to see her and he replies, "She wants you to taste her

From left: Stacey Glick, Brian Drillinger, Blythe Danner, Bob Dishy, Judith Ivey, Lisa Waltz and Jonathan Silverman in a still for *Brighton Beach Memoirs* (1986).

spider soup." Funny lines retained from the play include the exchange between Eugene and Kate when she asks him to get a second quarter pound of butter from Greenblatts. He asks her why she doesn't buy a half pound at a time. Kate replies, "And suppose the house burned down this afternoon. Why do I need an extra quarter pound of butter?" Stanley comments on the fact that Eugene doesn't know what puberty is and asks him if he ever reads books. Eugene replies with a variation from the play, "The Count of Monte Cristo. It never mentioned puberty." Stanley asks Kate if he can talk to her and she replies, "Where am I going? To a nightclub?" The screenplay also retains the play's only bad line: Blanche's "I already buried someone I love. Now it's time to bury someone I hate."

In the interview with Jackson R. Bryer in Gary Konas' book, *Neil Simon: A Casebook*, Simon claims that Gene Saks cut three major scenes from the play for the film adaptation. This is an exaggeration. While there are cuts made from the play, they are not major scenes; rather, small parts of scenes with inconsequential dialogue. The most notable losses are Stanley's description for Eugene of the naked Nora, and the issue of Stanley's smoking. Other plot points are transformed. The letter about Frank that Blanche receives from Mrs. Murphy is replaced by Blanche's visit to her. While Stanley tells Eugene that he is leaving in the play, in the film he writes Eugene a letter. Eugene's gambling losses comes from his playing poker in the play but from pool in the film.

None of the Broadway cast was used in the film. Director Gene Saks makes the treatment not stagebound, although he overuses score, which drowns out dialogue.

Jonathan Silverman is funny showing Eugene's angry denial to Stanley of "diddling with himself," and his Brooklyn accent is effective. Blythe Danner is not an obvious casting choice for Kate, but she delivers on the character's annoyance of Eugene and tenderness towards Jack and Blanche. However, it's hard to believe that Danner's Kate would be considered the lesser beauty to sister Blanche, as played by Judith Ivey. Ivey is funny showing Blanche's nervousness over her date with Frank, but she falters in Blanche's climactic scene with Nora. Steven Hill as Mr. Stroheim gives funny and delicate line deliveries to his stylized performance of a German hat salesman.

RELEASE: December 25, 1986, with the taglines "Meet Eugene Jerome and his family, fighting the hard times and sometimes each other," "It's about laughter, tears and love," and "The heart-winning story based on his award-winning play."

REVIEWS: Praised by Janet Maslin in the *New York Times.* Lambasted by Roger Ebert in the *Chicago Sun-Times*—"Everything is by the numbers"—and Rita Kempley in the *Washington Post* as "an amorphous hybrid that's stagey and forced."

DVD: Released by Universal Studios on July 1, 2003.

Biloxi Blues (1988)

Universal/Rastar.

CREW: Mike Nichols (Director); Ray Stark (Producer); Joseph M. Caracciolo and Marykay Powell (Executive Producers); Neil Simon (Screenplay based on his play); Bill Butler (Photography); Sam O'Steen (Editor); George Delerue (Music); Paul Sylbert (Production Design); John Alan Hicks (Set Decorator); Ann Roth (Costumes); Frank Bianco (Hair); Jay Cannistraci (Makeup); Daniel Ottesen, Kevin Brink and John Ottesen (Special Effects). Color, 102 minutes. Filmed on location in Fort Smith and Van Buren, Arkansas, from April 18 to June 24, 1987.

CAST: Matthew Broderick (Eugene Morris Jerome), Christopher Walken (Sgt. Merwin J. Toomey), Michael Dolan (James J. Hennesey), Markus Flanagan (Roy W. Selridge), Penelope Ann Miller (Daisy Hannigan), Matt Mulhern (Joseph T. Wykowski), Park Overall (Rowena), Corey Parker (Arnold B. Epstein), Casey Siemaszko (Donald J. Carney), Alan Pottinger (David P. Peck), Mark Evan Jacobs (Pinelli), Dave Kienzie (Corporal), Matthew Kimbrough (Spitting Cook), Kirby Mitchell (Digger #1), Allen Turner (Digger #2), Tom Kagy (Digger #3), Jeff Bailey (Mess Hall Corporal), Bill Russell (Rifle Instructor), Natalie Canerday (Girl at Dance), A. Collin Roddey (Private Roddey), Christopher Ginnaven (Corporal Ginnaven), Morris Mead (Corporal Mead), David Whitman (Tower Officer), Norman Rose (Newsreel Announcer), Michael Haley (Corporal Haley), Ben Hynum (Private Lindstrom), Andy Wigington (Corporal Wigington), Christopher Phelps (Private Phelps), Scott Sudbury (Private Sudbury). Uncredited: There is a rumor that David Schwimmer plays a soldier on the train, but the actor denies it is him.

SONGS: "How High the Moon" (Nancy Hamilton and William Lewis), Pat Suzuki, opening credits and at USO dance; "Bourbon Street Parade" (Paul Barbarin); "Fellow on a Furlough" (Bobby Worth), Mark Warnow and His Orchestra; "Blue Moon" (Richard Rodgers and Lorenz Hart), Jo Stafford and Her V-Disc Playboys, radio in brothel; "Marie" (Irving Berlin), Tommy Dorsey and His Orchestra; "Solitude" (Duke Ellington,

Irving Mills and Eddie DeLange), the Dorsey Brothers Orchestra; "Brass Boogie" (Phil Moore), Bob Crosby and His Orchestra; "Goodbye Dear, I'll Be Back in a Year" (Mack Kay), Dick Robertson and His Orchestra, closing credits; "Chattanooga Choo Choo" (music by Harry Warren and lyrics by Mack Gordon), Casey Siemaszko; "Don't Sit Under the Apple Tree" (music by Sam H. Stept and lyrics by Charles Tobias and Lew Brown), Casey Siemaszko.

SYNOPSIS: In 1945 recruits from the Fort Dix, New Jersey, army platoon are sent to Biloxi, Mississippi, for ten weeks of basic training under Sgt. Merwin J. Toomey. On a two-day pass, Eugene visits a brothel and loses his virginity to Rowena. At a USO dance he meets a convent girl, Daisy, whom he dates on the weekends. When Toomey learns that he is to be retired from his position, he threatens to shoot Eugene. Fellow recruit Arnold Epstein gets help, and Eugene is rescued. The end of the war is declared before Eugene sees active duty overseas.

NOTES: The screenplay features the subjects of relationships between army recruits as substitute family members and friends, conventional versus radical behavior, and adolescent desire. As a sequel to *Brighton Beach Memoirs*, the film also presents the continuation of Eugene Morris Jerome's coming of age, in which he loses his virginity, falls in love for the first time, and learns to participate in life rather than just witness it. In this adaptation, Simon cuts lines and moments from the play, moves scenes and lines, and adds new elements. Homophobic terms are used in the context of the exploration of homosexuality in the military. Simon employs self-reference at the conclusion when the Eugene comments that he became a playwright and wrote a play called *Biloxi Blues*, and also mentions how he could adapt it to make a movie.

Simon continues the device of narration and Eugene's use of a memoir book from *Brighton Beach Memoirs*. The book is utilized in the narrative as a weapon against Eugene when fellow recruit Wykowski steals it and reads from it to the others. Because he writes, Eugene is criticized by Epstein for being a "witness" to events, rather than a participant. This distancing tactic of Eugene's also makes him less of a target than Epstein, whose principles get him into trouble. The climax shows Eugene taking the opportunity to defend Epstein against Toomey, sacrificing himself, thereby giving him the participatory experience that Epstein has told him he needs in order to grow as a writer.

Of the new scenes, the play's march through the swamp is dramatized in the screenplay. This gives Toomey another opportunity to harass Eugene, pretending that Eugene has volunteered Wykowski to walk into the swamp to see how deep the water is. The scene where Lindstrom and Hennessey are discovered in the latrine together is another scene dramatized for the film that was only spoken about in the play. The firing range scene gets a payoff after Eugene's gun breaks, when Toomey throws it at Epstein with orders to reassemble it, and a shot fires off, blowing one of the tires on Toomey's jeep. In the USO dance scene Daisy tells Eugene that he has a "birthday look" on his face, as if something special has happened to him. This pays off his coming to the dance from Rowena's room. Rain is added to the scene where Toomey threatens Eugene. This is paid off when Toomey speaks to the platoon outside, wearing nothing to protect himself from getting wet, and when he does push-ups in the mud.

Some of the recruits demonstrate adolescent male behavior including spitting,

1988

U.S.A.

COMÉDIE

BILOXI BLUES
BILOXI BLUES

RÉALISATEUR
Mike Nichols

French movie card for *Biloxi Blues* (1988).

hitting, and swearing. This sets them up to be made into adults through the army's training, which Toomey tells Epstein is designed to make them obedient, disciplined fighting soldiers. Wykowski is presented as the strongest and most feared recruit of the platoon, and his behavior includes racism towards Hennesey, who admits to having a "colored" mother. The idea that Rowena is a much older woman than the recruits who frequent her is paid off when she tells Eugene, "Come to Momma," and he comments, "Would it be okay if we did not use the word momma. Makes me think of my mother and that sort of kills it."

The character of Sgt. Toomey is interesting since he appears affable but uses mind games to torture the recruits. The supposed plate in his head may suggest that he is mentally unbalanced. This is paid off when at the climax he is to be forcibly retired and sent to a veterans' hospital. But even when drunk, Toomey is not the violent threat that is expected, since he allows Eugene to take his gun away from him and agrees to Epstein's idea that he should do push-ups in front of the platoon.

The screenplay presents Epstein as an effeminate man with a "nervous stomach." This stereotypical presentation of homosexuality gets a twist in the idea that Epstein is also the smartest man in the platoon, and initially the only one who has the courage to stand up to Toomey. Epstein also shows concern for Eugene when he goes to tell the other recruits that Eugene is being threatened by Toomey, and brings them back to help. The recruits use homophobic terms such as "homo" and "fruit" and "fairy" to show their negative opinion of homosexuality. This opinion is shared by the U.S. Army, which does not accept open homosexuals and punishes homosexual behavior with imprisonment. Although Eugene thinks that Epstein is homosexual, Epstein does not confirm this. Later Epstein asks Eugene why he thinks he is gay, and Eugene replies because Epstein never talks about girls. The plot point of Epstein's possibly being gay is paid off with the two men being caught together having sex. Private Lindstrom is identified, but the second man runs away with his identity unknown. Since Epstein has been outed by Eugene, the recruits expect him to have been the second man, although we know he is not. Hennesey is later taken away by MPs, presumably identified as the second man by Lindstrom. Hennesey had not been known to be gay by the other recruits. Wykowski had commented that he thought there was something different about him, though what Hennesey admits to is having a black mother. It is also noteworthy that Hennesey is the one person who objects to Wykowski's reading from Eugene's memoirs.

A funny line retained from the play is Eugene's comment about army food: "I saw this stuff in the Bronx zoo once. Gorillas were throwing it at each other." The character of Toomey is changed from the play, where he was more the stereotypical hard-ass. In the screenplay he is less devious, and Eugene will ultimately describe him as "eccentric." Simon also concentrates the sergeant's focus of harassment on Eugene rather than sharing it more equally among the recruits, so that Toomey can disassociate Eugene from the others. This focus is highlighted in the climax, which features Eugene and Toomey, unlike in the play where it occurs between Toomey and Epstein. However, Simon returns the focus to Epstein for the end of the scene, when it is he who suggests that Toomey be punished only by doing push-ups.

The play's midnight march in the swamp is changed to an early morning one, and

Simon cuts the play's plot points of Epstein's refusing to eat his meal and of Eugene's telling us of Epstein's being put on KP duties and being harassed by three men when he cleans the latrines. Simon also cuts the last line of the play's scene between Rowena and Eugene. When she asks if there is anything else he wants after his orgasm, he replies, "I'd like two bottles of perfume and a pair of black panties." Other cuts include Eugene's telling us that he visited Rowena a second time, his explaining to Carney why he wrote what he did about him, the goodbye scene between Daisy and Eugene, the dialogue scene between the recruits on the train, and the play's ending, when Carney sings "Tangerine." Simon interrupts the play's scene of the recruits' fantasy game with Toomey walking past them to his room, the retreat bugle being heard, and Toomey's turning off the lights in the quarters before he returns to confront the men over Wykowski's racist tirade to Epstein. Eugene's last monologue in the screenplay also reports different fates for Selridge, Wykowski, Carney, and Epstein than those in the play. The most notable is for Epstein. In the play we are told he is missing in action, but in the film he has returned and become a lawyer.

Only Matthew Broderick, Matt Mulhern and Penelope Ann Miller were retained from the Broadway cast. This is the only film version of a Simon play that Mike Nichols has directed, although he has directed the plays *Barefoot in the Park, The Odd Couple, Plaza Suite, The Prisoner of Second Avenue,* and *Fools.* Nichols' use of the beautiful song "How High the Moon" under the opening credits creates a mood of period and nostalgic romance that is also appropriate for the song's reprisal at the USO dance, when Eugene and Daisy dance together. In the scene in the mess hall where the corporal and Toomey inspect the recruits' plates for uneaten food, Nichols has steam from the kitchen in the foreground partially covering our view of the action. Nichols makes Eugene's sex scene with Rowena subtly funny in its awkwardness, and he uses the same delicacy in the private moment of Eugene and Daisy dancing together. Nichols introduces Daisy as a reflection in a window at the USO dance when she asks Eugene to dance. *Buck Privates* (1941) is watched by the recruits, as well as *Movietone News* with the headline "Allies hurl back Nazis in Italy." There is also footage of soldiers' coffins and burial grounds, which changes the response of the watching recruits from laughing and cheering to silence.

Matthew Broderick's Eugene is less the wise-guy that Jonathan Silverman's Eugene in *Brighton Beach Memoirs.* Broderick expresses the pain in Eugene's exposure when his memoir book is read by Wykowski to the other recruits. However, his Eugene doesn't show real fear in the climax when he is threatened by Toomey. Christopher Walken underplays Toomey, making him a more frightening figure than if his hostility were played on the surface. In the climax, Walken also doesn't play drunk in an obvious fashion, and Toomey's good humor is mixed with the pain of the character's fate. Marcus Flanagan's yelling at Selridge during the scene when the recruits tell their fantasies of the last day of their life reads as too theatrical.

In his memoir *The Play Goes On,* Simon writes that, in 1945, he was in an army boot camp in Biloxi. The only experience he describes that is similar to something in the film is the heat of Biloxi. However, in Jerry Roberts' *The Great American Playwrights on the Screen*, he claims that Simon in camp did experience tyrannical sergeants, prejudices, fights, lousy food, and seeing a pal dishonorably discharged. Elsewhere Simon reports that Christopher Walken first rehearsed Toomey's introductory speech to the recruits by improvising, not saying a word that was written. The writer thought what the actor said was brilliant and infinitely better that what was in the script and urged him to use it. However, Walken insisted that this was only his acting process and that he would perform Simon's words for the film.

RELEASE: March 25, 1988, with the tagline "The Army made Eugene a man. But Daisy gave him basic training!"

REVIEWS: Praised by Vincent Canby in the *New York Times*, Michael Wilmington in the *Los Angeles Times* and Rita Kempley in the *Washington Post*. A mixed reaction from *Variety*. Lambasted by Roger Ebert in the *Chicago Sun-Times* as "pale, shallow, unconvincing and predictable."

DVD: Released by Universal Studios on January 27, 2004.

Lost in Yonkers *(1993)*

Columbia Pictures/Rastar.

CREW: Martha Coolidge (Director), Ray Stark (Producer), Emanueal Azenberg (Co-Producer), Joseph M. Caracciolo (Executive Producer), Neil Simon (Screenplay based on his play), Johnny E. Jensen (Photography), Steven Cohen (Editor), Elmer Bernstein (Music), David Chapman (Production Design), Mark Haack (Art Director), Marvin March (Set Decorator), Shelley Komarov (Costumes), Don Striepeke (Makeup), Carol Schwartz (Ms. Ruehl's Makeup), Susan Germaine (Hair), Susan Kalinowski (Mr. Dreyfuss' Hair), Daniel Ottesen and Bill Myatt (Special Effects). Color, 114 minutes. Filmed on location in Augusta, Boone County; Ludlow, Kentucky; Cincinnati; and Wilmington, Ohio; and at Sony Pictures Studios, Culver City, California.

CAST: Richard Dreyfuss (Louie), Mercedes Ruehl (Bella Kurnitz), Irene Worth (Grandma Kurnitz), Brad Stoll (Yakob "Jay" Kurnitz), Mike Damus (Arthur "Arty" Kurnitz), David Strathairn (Johnny), Robert Guy Miranda (Hollywood Harry), Jack Laufer (Eddie), Susan Merson (Gertrude "Gert" Kurnitz), Illya Hasse (Harry's Crony), Calvin Stillwell (Gas Station Attendant), Dick Hagerman (Truck Driver), Jesse Vincent (Danny Petrillo), Howard Newstate (Kid in Store), Peter Gannon (Cop), Lori Schubeler (Teresa), Jean Zarzour (Flo), Mary Scott Gudaitis (Celeste).

SYNOPSIS: In 1942 recently widowed Eddie Kurnitz leaves his sons, fifteen-year-old Jay and thirteen-year-old Arty, at their Grandma's house in Yonkers while he goes off to earn money. The boys live in the house and work in Grandma's Kornitz Kandy Store with Eddie's thirty-six-year-old mentally challenged sister, Bella. Bella dates forty-year-old movie usher Johnny. The boys learn from Bella that Grandma has money hidden in the house, but they cannot find it. Eddie's brother Louie arrives to stay at the house also, and he is monitored by Hollywood Harry and his crony. Jay acts as a decoy so Louie can get away. Bella disappears after the family disapproves of her wanting to marry Johnny but comes home again when Johnny decides he cannot marry her. Eddie returns and takes the boys with him. Bella leaves Grandma and moves to Florida.

NOTES: This screenplay features the subjects of family, including estranged children, and mental illness. The use of children as protagonists recalls the scenarios in *Only When I Laugh, I Ought to Be in Pictures,* and *Brighton Beach Memoirs,* and the character of Arty can be interpreted as another self-portrait by Simon, since he has an older brother. In the adaptation, Simon incorporates new scenes and new dialogue; includes characters such as Johnny and Hollywood Harry, who are only spoken of in the play; moves lines and makes line cuts.

Simon again uses narration as a device; letters written by Jay, Eddie and Bella are used as voice-overs. The theatrical device of a character stating their intention to leave and then returning is used three times: twice when Louie wants to leave when Bella tells the family about Johnny, and when Bella threatens to leave the house after she confronts Grandma. Simon also delays paying off the vocal condition of Gert until late into the narrative, when its repetition becomes a running gag.

The play is "opened up" with the use of locations in the street

From left: **Richard Dreyfuss, Mike Damus, Mercedes Ruehl (seated), Brad Stoll and Irene Worth** in a still for *Lost in Yonkers* (1993).

around the store; Eddie on a train, a bus and a ferry; Bella at the cinema; Bella and the boys at a cemetery; Bella and Johnny walking in the park; and Louie, Jay and Arty at a swimming hole and campfire. The rooftop of the store is also used, as is an underground tunnel that travels from a wall into the store's basement to the side of the house.

Some of the new scenes provide narrative payoffs. Arty is shown to steal candy from a jar in the store. When he again steals a candy bar from the storeroom basement, he breaks a tooth from eating it and is taken to the dentist by Grandma. Louie subsequently tells Arty that when he was kid they couldn't afford a dentist and that Grandma removed his molars with an open Coke bottle. The store-watching by Hollywood Harry and his crony has some payoffs. Harry offers Jay a one-dollar note to tell him when he sees Louie, but Harry crumples up the note and throws it onto the ground rather than actually hand it to the boy. The scene also gets a follow-up when Jay tells Arty about Harry, and Grandma admonishes the boys for talking as they work in the store. This leads Arty to say to Jay, "I wonder what those guys would give us for Grandma?" When Harry returns and puts a five-dollar note in Jay's pocket, Jay throws it back at him. This is perhaps because Harry slaps Jay in the face after he gives him the money. Jay tells Harry that he doesn't want his money, and Harry says that Jay can pass on the message for free. There are more scenes showing Harry and his crony watching the house, and a new one where we see Jay as a decoy when Louie steals the men's car to get away.

The scene in which Bella and Johnny walk in the park features a funny line when, after she has had to convince him to kiss her, Johnny repeatedly does so so passionately that she has to fight him off to make him stop. Bella then comments, "I don't know why they wouldn't take you in the army." There is a new scene where Bella hangs up washing with Jay and Arty. It gets a payoff when rain forces them to take the clothes down. Grandma sees the clouds in the sky and after watching the clothes being removed, she calls Bella "Stupid Dummkopf." Bella also has a new line regarding the rain falling on the washing: "This always happens to me."

The montage of Jay's searching rooms in the house for Grandma's money has a surprise. A shadow appearing in a doorway with a cane is expected to be Grandma catching Jay but is revealed to be Arty playing a trick. Arty gets the attention of Jay, who has his back to the door, by banging the cane on the floor. Later when the boys see how Grandma hits the boy who steals a comic from her, Arty tells Jay, "I don't think we should look for her money anymore." Another surprise is that Louie sleeps in the same bed as the boys and takes Arty's pillow for himself. There is a laugh after Bella asks Arty to mind the store and he tells her he can't make sundaes; he can only pour a glass of water. When a policeman in the store asks how he is, Arty asks him if he would like a glass of water. That Bella meets her friend Teresa and her baby at a clothes store is paid off in the climactic scene when Bella tells the family about Johnny because she wants to get married to have babies.

A funny line is retained from the play after Bella tells the boys that she doesn't think Grandma will give her the money she wants to open a restaurant with the movie usher Johnny. Arty comments, "I don't think she's going to let you go to the movies much anymore." Simon's cuts from the play include Arty's collar getting torn in a fight with Jay, some of Eddie's voiced-over letters to his sons, Grandma's finding money in her pocket that Louie has slipped to her and her rejecting it, and Eddie's thank-you to Grandma for keeping his boys. Arty's fever is changed to a toothache after eating stolen candy and results in his being taken to the dentist by Grandma. Grandma's hiding place for the money is changed from behind the malt machine in the store to the boy's mattress. Simon also loses a funny exchange in which Jay tells Arty that Grandma is in a rotten mood today and Arty replies, "You mean all those other days she was in a *good* mood?" Simon also changes the ending, adding new scenes in which Grandma looks at the thank-you card the boys leave for her, Bella asks if she can play music at dinner, and Bella leaves home for good.

Bella's mental illness is shown by her seemingly smiling at nothing in the street, and by her absentmindedness, which makes her walk past the Kandy Store. However, despite her condition, she is seen to be attractive to men. This point is explored when Bella says that she allowed men to make love to her because she wanted to be touched. Her condition is later defined by Grandma not as being crazy or stupid but being a child. This is also evident from the way Bella dresses, since her choices appear too young for a woman of her age. Bella's condition apparently comes from her being born with scarlet fever. Bella's confiding in Jay and Arty also suggests her childlike nature, since she appears to consider them her peers. Johnny is shown to be a match for Bella in that the army won't take him and he has trouble learning things such as reading. He also has spent time in the same "home" as Bella, presumably a home for mentally challenged people.

Bella is also shown to be brave. She tells Grandma that she has to let the boys stay or she will leave, helps Jay by giving him back his dinner after Grandma tells her to take it away, leaves the house for four days after Grandma disapproves of her desire to have babies, and eventually leaves Grandma's house for good. Johnny proves not to be as brave as Bella, since ultimately he chooses to remain working as an usher and living with his parents rather than attempting a new life with her.

Grandma's disdain for crying exemplifies her German, autocratic manner. She also disapproves of Bella's buying movie magazines and is shown to be aware in knowing when a boy steals a comic from her store, a crime she punishes by hitting him on the head with the comic she retrieves. However, Grandma's tart manner can be funny. An example is when she asks Louie how long he is staying; when he replies, "A couple of days. Maybe a week," she says, "A couple of days is better." Another example is when Jay thanks her for letting the boys stay with her, saying, "I know it wasn't easy for you," and she replies "That's right. It wasn't." The darker side of her manner is revealed when Louie tells the boys that she used to lock him in a closet for hours as a punishment when he was a child. That Grandma throws tea in Bella's face after she assumes that Bella has stolen money from her provides a dramatic demonstration of her violent nature. She is also said by Bella to be vulnerable in being afraid of being left alone, although this is not demonstrated in the narrative.

Louie is shown to be a manipulator by breaking into the store, helping himself to a sundae, and slipping money into the pockets of Jay and Arty without them realizing. He doesn't ask Grandma if he can stay at the house; he just assumes that he can. She is awakened by his voice when he arrives at the house, but although she recognizes it, she doesn't get out of bed to see him. He tells Bella that he is home, but he does not go into his mother's room to tell *her*. Louie demands that the boys hug him, and he carries a gun for protection as a mob "bagman" and bodyguard for a henchman. He is unselfconscious about undressing in front of the boys, and sleeps in the same bed as them. He shows the boys the tunnel he and Bella dug from a wall of the storeroom up to the side of the house, and uses Jay as a decoy to help him get away from Hollywood Harry. Simon doesn't show Louie discussing this plan with Jay in advance, but Louie must be aware that Jay's cooperation puts him in danger. This will be shown to be the case when we see Harry slap Jay when he sees that he is not Louie.

Director Martha Coolidge succeeds in making the material more realistic than theatrical, until the climactic scene. The narrative becomes less interesting once Louie appears since he is a less compelling character than Grandma, even though in the climax it is he and not Grandma who is more vocal against Bella's desire to marry Johnny. The problem may be due to fact that Richard Dreyfuss is miscast as Louie. Coolidge introduces Grandma as if she is a horror movie antagonist. We see a door knob turn, a door open, and Grandma's cane and feet as she enters the room before we see her in full form as she limps down the hallway. Coolidge uses the whistle of a train over Grandma's open-mouthed reaction to Bella's threat of leaving. She also first presents Louie in shadow in the Kandy store when he speaks to Jay and Arty, and presents only the back of Gert's head. The film *Now, Voyager* (1941) is shown at the cinema. That tale of an unattractive woman dependent upon her mother who changes into a beautiful, independent person presumably strikes a chord with Bella. The score by Elmer Bernstein is often too theatrical for the material. It overwhelms the dialogue in the last scene between Bella and Johnny, and when in the scene Bella tells Grandma that Johnny doesn't want to marry her.

Only Mercedes Ruehl and Irene Worth are retained from the Broadway cast. Richard Dreyfuss as Louie is not believable, despite his use of accent and tough-guy physicality. Ruehl as Bella uses odd mannerisms to show the character's mental condition. She cries in the climactic family scene and when she confronts Grandma alone, but Ruehl fails to deliver empathy. However, Irene Worth's Grandma arouses our empathy when she cries after Bella confronts her. Mike Damus as Arty inexplicably talks like Humphrey Bogart, but he is funny when he imitates Louie's impression of "moxie."

RELEASE: May 14, 1993, with the tagline "This summer there's no better place to find yourself."

REVIEWS: Praised by Janet Maslin in the *New York Times* and Roger Ebert in the *Chicago Sun-Times.* A mixed reaction from Rita Kempley in the *Washington Post.* Lambasted by Peter Travers in *Rolling Stone* as "sitcom phoniness."

DVD: Released by Sony Pictures Home Entertainment on January 1, 2002.

PART TWO

Original Screenplays

After the Fox (1966) (aka *Caccia alla volpe*)

Cinecitta Italiana Stabilimenti Cinematografici/ Compagnia Cinematografica Montoro (CCM) Productions/Nancy Enterprises/United Artists. Uncredited: Brookfield Films.

CREW: Vittorio De Sica (Director), John Bryan (Producer), Maurizio Lodi-Fe (Associate Producer), Neil Simon (Uncredited Co-Producer/Screenplay), Leonida Barboni (Photography), Russell Lloyd (Editor), Burt Bacharach (Music), Mario Garbuglia (Production Design), Piero Tosi (Costumes), Maurice Binder (Main Titles), Dick Horn (Main Title Animation), Stuart Freeborn and Amato Garbini (Makeup). Color, 99 minutes. Filmed at the studios of Cinecittia in Rome and on location in Naples and Umbria, Italy, from June to July 1966.

CAST: Peter Sellers (Aldo Vanucci, aka The Fox/Federico Fabrizi), Victor Mature (Tony Powell), Britt Ekland (Gina Vanucci/Gina Romantica), Martin Balsam (Harry Granoff), Akim Tamiroff (Fred Okra), Paolo Stoppa (Polto), Lydia Brazzi (Mamma Vanucci, aka Teresa), Tino Buazzelli (Siepi), Mac Ronay (Carlo), Maria Grazia Buccella (Bikini Girl), Lando Buzzanca (Police Chief Rizzuto), Maurice Denham (Chief of Interpol), Tiberio Murgia (1st Detective), Francesco De Leone (2nd Detective), Nino Musco (Mayor Giuseppe Molini), Carlo Croccolo (Café Owner), Pier Luigi Pizzi (Doctor), Lino Mattera (Singer), Piero Gerlini (First Jailer), Daniele Vargas (Prosecuting Counsel), Franco Sportelli (Judge), Guistino Durano (Mario Stravol, Film Critic), Mimmo Poli (Fat Actor), Enzo Fiermonte (Raymond), Roberto De Simoni (Marcel Vignon), Angelo Spaggiari (Felix Kessler), Mario Del Vago (Manuel Ortega). Uncredited: Timothy Bateson (Michael O'Reilly), Vittoria De Sica (Himself as Director of *Flight from Egypt*), Carlo Delle Piane, Daniela Igliozzi, David Lodge (Police Officer), Enrico Luzi (Movie Director on Via Veneto), Carlo Pisacane (2nd Judge), Marcella Rovena (Salvatore's Wife), Nino Vingelli (3rd Judge).

SONGS: "After the Fox" (music by Burt Bacharach and lyrics by Hal David), The Hollies and Peter Sellers; "You Make Me Feel So Young" (music by Josef Myrow and lyrics by Mack Gordon), Victor Mature.

SYNOPSIS: Three hundred gold bullions have been stolen from Cairo by Okra and his gang. Umbrian criminal Aldo Vanucci escapes from prison and is offered the job of importing and delivering the gold to Rome. He accepts the offer and plans to move the gold in daylight under police protection while pretending to be the movie director making *The Gold of Cairo* in the town of Sevalio. When the ship arrives with the gold it is loaded into a truck, but the truck is stolen by Okra. After a car chase Aldo is arrested with the townspeople of Sevalio. The film is screened as evidence of the gold robbery, but the footage does not show the gold. Aldo admits to the theft and is imprisoned again. He is sentenced to five years but vows to escape again.

NOTES: Simon's first original screenplay continues the subject of the importance of family, which he had previously covered in his plays *Come Blow Your Horn* and (to a lesser extent) *Barefoot in the Park.* Aldo takes the job of smuggling gold to assure the financial security of his widowed mother and his sister Gina. The screenplay also makes a distinction between radical and conventional lifestyle choices. Aldo's life as a criminal is seen to be more radical than that of his conventional mother, while Gina's desire to be an actress can also be read as being radical and unconventional. However, Aldo's objection to Gina's playing a prostitute in a film shows his conventional side in regards to his sister. His desire towards the woman contact also changes to fatherly outrage when he learns that she is the sister of Okra. Aldo expresses his concern for family when he admits to stealing the gold and asks that Gina write to him every day and that the other gang members take care of Mamma.

Director Vittorio De Sica insisted that Simon collaborate on the screenplay with De Sica's usual writer, Cesare Zavvattini. Simon was apparently concerned that Zavvattini's political and social consciousness would require him to alter the narrative. However, this concern must have been unfounded, given the way the people of Sevalio and Umbria are depicted. For example, that the Sevalio townspeople all want to be in the movie being made there portrays them as equally shallow as the people in Umbria who crowd around Tony when he arrives. What's worse is that we see the Sevalions abandoning their homes and their jobs to go to Aldo as Federico Fabrizi. The people scramble to get the sandwich that one of the gang throws away, and when they are asked to walk slowly across a square as extras, they run and swamp the lead actors. They also allow Aldo to use them to help him transport the gold. That they sing a work song as they load the truck adds to the naivety of their response to this manipulation. Thankfully, the narrative redeems the people when Aldo accepts lone responsibility for the theft of the gold.

The screenplay has two devices that are each used only once: it opens with a narration and ends with a to-camera line. Simon employs a lot of slapstick moments, the funniest of which is the reaction of the speaker at Interpol to the unexpectedly heavy weight of a gold bar. Simon pays off Tony tripping over a footstool when he has him comment, "I was only trying to prove to you how agile I am." The most extreme slapstick is when Tony backs away from Gina and falls out of his hotel room window. Since none of the slapstick results in real injury, it is acceptable to laugh at it.

There is also a set piece and a running gag. Aldo's escape from prison is a set piece that gets a repeated payoff at the end of the narrative. Aldo reads the book *Stanislavsky on the Art of the Stage* before his escape. He puts on a fake beard and spectacles to impersonate the doctor who has just visited him. The guards then chase the real doctor, thinking he is Aldo. The scenario gets a funny payoff when the guards with the doctor and the guards with the disguised Aldo meet, revealing Aldo's ruse. This ruse gets

Federico Fabrizi (Peter Sellers, left) offers actor Tony Powell (Victor Mature) a new movie role, while Tony's agent, Harry Granoff (Martin Balsam) observes, in a still for *After the Fox* (1966).

repeated for the film's end, although Simon gives it a twist and then a resolution that cannot be explained. After Aldo has vowed that he will escape again and we see the doctor in the prison we wait for ruse to be repeated, with Aldo once again reading Stanislavsky. The Doctor is tied up in Aldo's cell but when he calls for help, the guards think he is Aldo and say they will not fall for the same trick again. We then see the disguised Aldo successfully leaving the prison, but when he tries to remove the fake beard it won't come off. Then he looks into the camera and says, "My God. The wrong man escaped," supposedly believing that he is the real doctor.

The smuggling contact is a buxom woman who speaks in a man's voice, a running gag that raises the portrayal above the cliché of a female spy's being buxom. The initial assumption that she is a man in spectacular drag is not met when we see that she mimes for Okra, who sits back-to-back behind her. Simon pays off Aldo's kissing the woman after Okra offers Aldo fifty percent of the profits when Okra asks, "What more do you want?" and Aldo replies, "More meetings." Aldo also gets a funny last line to the woman when he tells her, "It has been a great pleasure doing business with a man as beautiful as you." The miming device is repeated when we see two horses drinking from a water fountain and hear the voices of Okra and Aldo, with a cut to the two men showing that they are in the carriages that the horses are tied to. We assume the device is repeated when Federico is called to the telephone and we hear the voice of Okra. Federico stands in front of a curtain so we imagine Okra will be behind it. But when the curtain is pulled back, we see Okra and the contact woman. This time the woman does not mime for Okra; she says nothing. The device gets a funny payoff when the woman contact comes to see Aldo. She says, "I must talk to you," and he replies, "Who's talking, you or him?"—the "him" referring to the unseen Okra.

There is other comedy in the screenplay. The passenger in the car that carries the gold reads a *Playboy* magazine, which prefigures the woman in head-to-toe black clothes that appears on the road. Her undressing to her underwear creates the shocked reaction that results in the car being driven off a ramp into the waiting truck. Three of the four men that Interpol consider to be possible gold smugglers are comic figures. Marcel Vignon, described as being "now perhaps a little past his prime," steals a woman's purse and tries to get away unsuccessfully in a slow-moving wheelchair. Michael O'Reilly's failing eyesight has him trying to hold up a police station, and Felix Kessler proves too fat to escape through the door of a bank he has just robbed. Aldo announces his name outside Mamma's window, just as the detectives arrive at the house looking for him. There is an aural gag in the sound of a snarling dog heard when a detective looks for Aldo behind a clothes closet, and another gag with a surprise. Aldo on the telephone accepts the smuggling job, and it is revealed that he has spoken to a child and asks that the message be passed on.

Tony is presented as an aging, vain actor, and there is a funny exchange on this between him and Harry. Tony asks, "How many people in the world over forty can still say they have their own teeth?" Harry replies, "How many people over fifty can still say they are only forty?" At first, Tony laughs when Harry accepts his invitation, and punches him in the stomach to show how fit he is, but when Tony is alone we see that the punch has really hurt him. Tony also colors his hair and eyebrows, which gets a payoff when Gina comes to seduce him. When she kisses his ears some of the newly applied dye from his sideburns gets on her hands, and she inadvertently runs it down her face. The scene has Tony admitting to being fifty-seven before catching himself to tell Gina that he is thirty-seven. His reluctance to accept Gina's advance is a refreshing narrative touch, partly explained by the fact that she has gotten him out of bed and he is tired.

A further amusing exchange is when Harry asks about Tony's contract for the film with Fabrizi. The director kisses Tony on the cheek and says, "There is my contract." Harry asks, "Do I get a copy for my lawyer?" and Fabrizi throws him a dispirited kiss. There is another funny exchange when Harry tells Tony that the film Fabrizi is making uses "neorealism." When Tony asks what that is, Harry replies, "No money." The concept of neorealism gets a further payoff when *The Gold of Cairo* is screened at the court hearing. Badly photographed in black and white, the clip is a series of jump cuts, camera jerks and out-of-focus close-ups that make those filmed appear to be comic grotesques in an unintelligible home movie. The film is praised by the film critic, who calls it a classic and hails Federico as a "primitive genius." At the arrival of Tony, the mayor of Sevalio tells Federico, "This is a golden day." Federico as Aldo responds, "Yes. Golden," and rubs his hands together, referencing the gold he is expecting. Aldo tells the woman contact that Okra is a swine, and De Sica cuts to Tony snorting in bed. The car chase in smoke results in a gag. One police car asks, "Car 17. Where are you?" The detectives in Car 17 reply with "This is Car 17. We are right behind you." We see a crash and the police car rear-ends the detective's car. The detective then re-advises, "No. We are in front of you."

Simon uses wordplay and misdirection in the dialogue. Aldo accuses one of his three gang members of lying about Gina when they visit him in prison. Also chokes the man, telling him, "You're lying. Say you're lying." The man answers, "All right, I'm lying." Aldo then responds with, "Liar, you're not lying." Mamma tells Aldo that Gina is "on the streets." He comments, "You mean my sister is a..." and a woman playing bingo then announces, "Bingo!" Simon pays off this joke further when Aldo finds Gina behaving like a hooker, although it is only for a film she is making. A misdirection comes in an exchange between Aldo and Rizzuto about Rizzuto giving Aldo the application form for a permit. Aldo tells him, "In films you either have a face or you don't got a face. Can I have it please? The application form."

There is also some mild humor and some that does not work. Aldo sinks into a bubble bath when he is told that the detectives have come to the house where he is staying. This gets a payoff when a detective says to the other gang members, "I'm going to get him because one of these days he's going to expose himself." We then see Aldo naked and covered in suds hiding on the roof. When Tony Powell drives into Umbria, his identity is not immediately apparent since the view of him is obscured by an accompanying crowd. Someone says that the man's nose looks like Marlon Brando, and when someone else asks who is in the car, Aldo remarks, "Marlon Brando's nose." Aldo helps Tony flee from the policemen by throwing Tony's torn collar at them. This is a clever move, since the crowd runs after the collar and blocks the policemen. Another gag that is only mildly amusing is how Federico holds an ice cream, instead of his viewing lens, to his eye when he gets distracted. The humor that does not work includes the business of Aldo and the gang stealing the camera, the lamps, the unit truck, the assistant director's clothes, a crane with platform and a directing chair during the sandstorm. This is a joke that doesn't pay off because of its lack of logic. Also unsuccessful is the repeated gag of Federico's pretending to receive a telephone call from a Sophia, presumably Sophia Loren.

The direction is uneven. Pacing becomes a problem once the locale changes from Umbria to Sevalio, and the narrative's initial promise is only paid off in mild effects. The score helps a little to add to the farcical tone, especially during the climactic car chase. However, the film is ultimately not as funny as we would like it to be. There is obvious rear projection for the gang's getaway from the prison and through the streets of Umbria, a device that is not apparent in the climactic car chase.

De Sica provides a visual gag when Aldo comes to Tony's hotel room. Aldo calls out, "Where's Tony?" and Tony is seen to peek behind a vase of flowers to look at Aldo. De Sica intercuts between Gina in Tony's room and the woman contact in Federico's room, with both Vanuccis playing the sexual aggressors. Gina tells Tony that she wants him to teach her how to kiss like an actress, which somewhat diminishes her advance, but perhaps this is wise considering that she is only sixteen. The editing improves a joke about the ugliness of the wife of the Sevalio restaurateur. When she is introduced to Federico, he looks at her and comments, "Very pretty." We are then shown her laughing at his compliment and we see that she is mature-aged and gap-toothed.

De Sica casts himself as the director of the film *Flight from Egypt*, which sabotaged by the gang. This self-reference gets no payoff apart from making him look ridiculous after the theft of his chair during the sandstorm; he goes from being on a chair in a raised platform to sitting on the ground. Peter Seller's performance as Federico Fabrizi may be a parody of De Sica, though if so, this is perhaps too much of a production in-joke.

The film includes a scene from *Easy Living* (1949), featuring Victor Mature and Lizabeth Scott. The scene features a perverse moment when Mature kisses Scott after slapping her, and her fighting him off in self-defense before succumbing to the kiss. This action presumably demonstrates Mature's character's ultra-masculine appeal, though a modern reading makes it seems more like assault.

The screenplay presumably attracted Sellers because it allows him to present multiple national identities, accents, and disguises. His Aldo poses as a priest, a Carabinieri officer, an actor playing a slave in the Biblical epic *Flight from Egypt*, and the director Federico Fabrizi. Seller's Aldo is appropriately passionate and impulsive for an Italian, and he uses garbled speech in his portrayal of an American tourist in the scene at the Red Grotto restaurant. Sellers' Adlo is funny when he shakes as he holds the viewfinder lens when he sees Rizzuto, and in the way he says, "He's rotten. Rotten," in desire to the woman contact. Sellers' characterization is also good in the climactic courtroom scene in showing the sincerity of Aldo's confession. However, he overacts Aldo's anger in reaction to Rizzuto's line reading.

Martin Balsam's performance as Harry seems too broad, despite his yelling "required by the screenplay" when Aldo asks why he does so. De Sica directs other performances to be excessive, with Daniele Vargas as the prosecuting counsel also yelling, and Britt Eckland's Gina crying petulantly, though perhaps the latter has the context of her age. Victor Mature makes Tony likeable, using a smile to demonstrate his vanity and good humor. Mature is said to have come out of retirement to appear in the film.

The production was plagued by problems. Simon was moved from the first hotel room he stayed at in Ischia when strange sounds were heard on the rooftop at two in the morning. After a Fiat arrived for him, Mature demanded that he be transported in a limousine, despite the fact that it wouldn't fit down the narrow roadways to the beach location. When a white limousine was provided, it took four times as long as the fiat would have done to complete the journey. Sellers, too, demanded a white limousine, but since the island did not have two, he was given a black one. To balance out the delays caused by using the limos, the actors' calls were made earlier. Mature was picked up at five a.m., which made him irritable. One day he got angry at having to do a take five times as he stood in water up to his knees. No scene of Mature in water appears in the film. Mature walked off the set after throwing his script into the sea. The crew were furious at this, for they saw it as a huge sign of disrespect and they all wanted to quit. Thankfully, they changed their minds after De Sica had a local priest bless the sun-dried script. United Artists then paid for the road to be widened for the limousines. The crew also walked off the set when the wife of a visiting government official arrived wearing purple, a cardinal sin in Italian filmmaking. They returned when it was promised there would be no more visitors, although an exception was made for Princess Margaret.

Accidents were also a problem. A camera was knocked over by a large wave, and the expensive lens was ruined. The crew suffered cuts, broken bones, concussions, and a collision in which a truck hit a car that then went through a store window. Doctors were sent daily to the set.

Simon reports that Peter Sellers had demanded that his wife Britt Ekland be cast in the part of Gina. Her lack of acting experience did not worry De Sica, who had directed people who had never acted before in *Bicycle Thieves* (1948). Eckland wore a brown wig over her blonde Scandinavian hair in an attempt to make look more Italian, although nothing was done about her blue eyes. Lydia Brazzi, actor Rossano Brazzi's wife, was also not a professional actress. De Sica spotted her in a restaurant and thought she looked perfect for the part of Mamma Vanucci.

In his memoir, *Rewrites*, Simon writes that he believed that because De Sica's English was not good enough for him to appreciate certain nuances of the language, he missed some of the intended humor in the screenplay. He also claims De Sica's editors, not being able to speak English well, cut some of the dialogue scenes and that these could not be recovered by Russell Lloyd when he reassembled footage in London.

In his biography of Peter Sellers, *Mr. Strangelove*, Ed Sikov writes that the actor was an uncredited executive producer on the film. He also claims that Sellers wanted De Sica replaced by Joseph McGrath but that McGrath refused the assignment.

RELEASE: December 15, 1966, with the taglines "Watch your girl, guard your gold, hold your jewels ... the fox is loose!" and "You caught the 'Pussycat' ... now chase the Fox!"

REVIEWS: Critically acclaimed by *Variety* but lambasted by Bosley Crowther in the *New York Times* and Ronald Bergan in *The United Artists Story.* Crowther called it "amateurish" and "unfunny." In *5001 Night at the Movies* Pauline Kael wrote that the film had a surprisingly number of funny moments, and that Mature earned the biggest laughs. Simon said that the critics thought the film to be "the work of a Chinese cook making an Italian dinner for a Jewish family" and that more people would come to see it if it had been described as such in the ads.

DVD: Released by MGM (video and DVD) on February 5, 2002.

The Out of Towners (1970)

Paramount Pictures/Jalem Productions.

CREW: Arthur Hiller (Director), Paul Nathan (Producer), Neil Simon (Screenplay), Quincy Jones (Music), Andrew Laszlo (Photography), Fred Chulack (Editor), Charles Bailey (Art Director), William Farley (Hair), Clay Lambert (Makeup), Don Record (Titles). Uncredited: Arthur Jeph Parker (Set Decorator), Forrest T. Butler and Grace Harris (Wardrobe). Color, 93 minutes. Filmed in Massachusetts and New York from April to August 1969.

CAST: Jack Lemmon (George Kellerman), Sandy Dennis (Gwen Kellerman), Sandy Baron (Lenny Moyers, TV Man), Anne Meara (Purse Snatching Victim in Police Station), Robert Nichols (Mr. Cooper, Boston Airplane Passenger), Ann Prentiss (1st Stewardess), Graham Jarvis (Murray the Mugger), Ron Carey (Barney Polacek, Cab Driver in Boston), Phil Bruns (Police Officer Meyers), Carlos Montalban (Manuel Vargas, United Nations Cuban Delegate), Robert King (Agent in Boston), Johnny Brown (Waiter—Train),

Dolph Sweet (Police Sergeant Kovalevski), Jack Crowder (Police Officer), Jon Korkes, Robert Walden (Looters), Richard Libertini (Baggage Man—Boston), Paul Dooley (Hotel Clerk—Day), Anthony Holland (Winkler, Waldorf Astoria Night Desk Clerk), Billy Dee Williams (Clifford Robinson, Lost and Found—Boston), Bob Bennett (Man in Phone Booth—Boston). Uncredited: Ray Ballard (Attendant), J. French (Cleaning Woman), Maxwell Glanville (Redcap), Hash Howard (2nd Hippie), Paul Jabara (1st Hippie), Milt Kamen (Counterman), Norma Jean Kron (Flight Attendant #1), Alfred Mazza (Bellhop), Mary Norman (Flight Attendant #2), B. Paipert (Sweeper), Ronald Porter (Man in Airport), Philip Suriano (Liquor Store Looter), Arthur Tovey (Man in Diner Car), Meredith Vincent (Washroom Lady), A.P. Westcott (Porter).

SYNOPSIS: Gwen and George Kellerman leave their home town of Twin Oaks, Ohio, to travel to New York City. George has a job interview as the new vice president in charge of sales for his company, Drexel. The trip is a disaster. The couple are rerouted to Boston because of fog, their baggage is lost, New York has a transit strike, and their hotel room is given away. They get mugged, kidnapped, and robbed as they sleep in Central Park; they fight with a dog and are chased by a horse; Gwen loses her wedding ring; and George breaks a tooth and loses his hearing. They are rescued from a demonstration and George goes to his interview. He gets the job but Gwen asks that he does not take it. On the way home, their plane is highjacked.

NOTES: Simon's next original screenplay continues his exploration of the subject of family with the married Kellerman couple, who unite together against fate, which wreaks havoc on them in their trip to New York. The Kellermans are also offered as conventional people, with Jack Lemmon and Sandy Dennis playing an idealized, middle-aged married couple the way that Robert Redford and Jane Fonda play an idealized younger couple in *Barefoot in the Park*. Simon's twist on the Midwestern, seemingly mild personas of Lemmon and Dennis is in how quickly Lemmon's George turns hostile. The narrative also reads as a hate letter to New York and a warning to out-of-towners, within the context of a comedy.

Apart from the Kellerman's general bad luck there are running gags. They repeatedly catch the same taxi of Barney Polacek in Boston, and this carries over the gag about George not having change to pay for it. Another repeated gag is George telling someone, "My wife will verify that," and Gwen responding, "I can verify that." There are shifts of point of view, plot payoffs, and ambiguity, but also narrative surprises. George and Gwen get on the train at Boston only to be told that they are on the wrong train. There is a funny payoff when George asks the cleaning woman to retrieve Gwen from the ladies' room, and Gwen appears outside and tells George that she could not find it. A second payoff comes when the cleaning woman then produces a woman from the ladies' room that is not Gwen, though this is less of a surprise. When George awakens without Gwen in the park, after the appearance of the man in the black cape at night, we assume the man has taken her, which proves not to be true. Gwen having the box of Cracker Jack upon her return makes us assume that she will be able to feed George, but the appearance of Corky, the dog who takes the box, stops the couple from having all that was in the box.

Although the narrative has the unpleasant flavor of schadenfreude, there is still plenty of humor. George asks Gwen to feel his chest. When she asks whether he is having

George Kellerman (Jack Lemmon) eats stale Cracker Jack in Central Park with his wife, Gwen (Sandy Dennis), in a lobby card for *The Out of Towners* (1970).

a heart attack, he tells her, "I just want to make sure we got the tickets," since they are in his coat pocket. When the stewardess on the plane tells George, "I imagine we're run into some bad weather," he replies, "You don't have to imagine. Just look out the window." Gwen tells George that the airline can't find their bags, to which he replies, "What do you mean they can't find our bags?" Gwen then comments, "I can't say it simpler, George. They can't find the bags." In the dining car on the train to New York from Boston, George tells Gwen, "I was going to take you to one of the best restaurants in the world. Here you are eating peanut butter on white bread with nothing to drink. If you ever get your mouth open again, I wouldn't blame you if you never talked to me." Gwen claims that Murray was six feet tall, but George says she is wrong and tells her, "You got a broken heel. Everybody looks bigger to you." George tells Gwen, "You can't walk with a bleeding foot," and she replies, "Well I would fly, but New York is fogged in." When Gwen hears the lost Spanish boy crying, George comments, "Maybe it's the man with the black cape and he doesn't like my watch." When George asks Gwen how her wedding ring could have slipped off, she replies, "I haven't had any food. My fingers are thinner." Gwen also gets a laugh from the way she covers her left eye when she and George attend the front desk of the Waldorf Astoria. This pays off her earlier observation in the train window reflection that she had lost her left false eyelash.

George is an intelligent man who is a control freak, and he recalls Lemmon's Felix Ungar from *The Odd Couple.* His anger is counterproductive to solving the problems he is faced with, and it often presents as sarcasm. He pointlessly argues logic with people who are less smart than he, and this makes him appear to be arrogant and unlikable. His anger is justified given the context of what occurs to him, but it is exaggerated to the point of unreasonableness. George's paranoid overreactions are aimed at people who are trying to help him, although there are exceptions such as Murray the mugger and the man in the black cape in Central Park who gets George's watch.

Gwen describes George as being "sourcastic [*sic*], whining, irritable, insensitive, and intolerant." She believes she does not behave in any of these ways, although she admits to being sarcastic. Gwen is presented at first as George's placator and more optimistic and accepting of situations than he. Her stance as an observer is demonstrated by her repeated utterance of "Oh my Gawd," which becomes a narrative running gag. Gwen's stopping to appreciate the pile of garbage in the street as it rains presents her as having a childlike innocence. George's stomach ulcer, which his anger aggravates, doesn't result in the assumed empathy that he would otherwise be entitled to. Perhaps it is easier to empathize with Gwen because she has not behaved as unreasonably as George has. It is when Gwen becomes more assertive that the narrative adds dimension to the main characters, since this creates conflict between them rather than having bad luck inflicted upon them. The turning point for Gwen is when she loses a shoe getting out of the police car that the looters have stolen. She refuses to get involved with George's paranoid rants, and perhaps for the first time he asks her advice. Gwen's giving the man in the black cape George's watch, without asking George's permission, is another step. We assume that she knows that George would have refused to hand over the watch willingly and that her doing so may have spared George the consequence of his pig-headedness. Gwen is assertive in showing her compassion for the lost Spanish boy in the park, in telling George that she plans to stay with the boy, and freeing George to go to his interview. She condemns George's behavior in not wanting to help the boy as being the same as everyone else in New York, where people only care about themselves. Additionally, the climactic scene in which Gwen tells George that she hopes he will not accept the job he has been offered shows her in her final narrative act of assertiveness.

Some of the bad choices of George and Gwen would seem to make them complicit in their own undoing. Rain begins as George and Gwen decide to walk to the Waldorf Astoria from the train terminal, but it is George who leads them in the wrong direction. Murray produces a gun and attempts to mug them but is only successful after Gwen reveals that the wallet George has denied having is in fact in his pocket. She rationalizes this action by saying that this saved their lives and stopped them from being shot, an idea continued by Gwen's giving the man in the black cape George's watch. She steps on a broken bottle and breaks the heel of one of her shoes because she isn't looking where she is going. George refuses to get out of the police car, allowing him and Gwen to be kidnapped by the liquor store robbers. Gwen takes off the remaining shoe after one has been run over by a car and cuts her foot as a consequence of walking barefoot on the road. Because George and Gwen are in Central Park at night, they become the victim of theft by the man in the cape. George takes the lost Spanish boy into the bushes, which sets him up to be accused of being a pervert by an unseen woman and leads George and Gwen to be chased by a policeman on horseback. He refuses to take his hands off Gwen after she asks him to; this leads the two Clansy Bar joggers to punch him. His idea to get on a bus without the money to pay for tickets is met with the couple being thrown off. George stands on top of a manhole that explodes and temporarily deafens him. He stops the car of Manuel Vargas in the street to get help, only to have it attacked by demonstrators because Vargas is the United Nations delegate for Cuba. The final payoff for the bad luck is Drexell's comment to George that he had not expected George to be on time given that there were problems on the transit system. The narrative ends with a further example of George's culpability and bad choices when he declines the dinner on their flight back to Boston: if he hadn't gone to get Gwen coffee on board, he wouldn't have faced the hijackers.

Director Arthur Hiller's presentation of the two leads is unconventional, since he begins with them in an extended, extreme long shot when they leave their house. This shot is perhaps to signify how small they will become in the face of the giant monster, New York. An alternative reading is that this view of them is that of God, detached and amused by what he is about to put them through. Hiller then has the camera behind them in the back seat of the car during the drive to the airport for a medium two-shot, though Gwen can be seen in profile. He uses a close-up on Gwen when George is in the bushes with the lost Spanish boy, searching his pockets and caught by the off-screen woman. For Gwen's climactic speech about why she hopes George won't take the New York job, Hiller favors Lemmon in close-up. This is presumably a sign of Lemmon's perceived greater box office appeal. Hiller also ends the film strangely, providing a close-up of Gwen after George meets the hijackers, then using her aural "Oh my gawd" over a shot of the plane.

Hiller uses reduced images under the film's opening credits, and employs an aural point of view for the sound of the ringing in George's ears after he is temporarily deafened by the exploding manhole cover. When we hear George being told of the transit strikes by a Grand Central Station Redcap in the background, there is a simultaneous foreground-reveal shot of a man reading the *Daily News* with the headline "Transit Strike Hits!" Hiller shows Murray in the foreground of the foyer watching George and Gwen before he speaks to them. For the scene with the man in the black cape in Central Park, Hiller shows the man's feet first walking, then appearing next to the sleeping George and Gwen. The camera pans up the man's back, and we see that he also wears a hat. He leans down toward the couple before his black cape covers the screen, and we hear Gwen's "Oh my Gawd" spoken. Hiller has an image, obviously manipulated in editing, of Corky's head moving back and forward to make his growling at Gwen more aggressive. He uses depth of field for Gwen standing in long shot at the right of the frame behind George in close-up at the left of the frame, for George eating and the slow realization that he has swallowed the Cracker Jack box toy and has broken a tooth. The score is also notable with a military drumbeat when George goes to his job interview.

Jack Lemmon makes George funny in the look he gives and his saying, "I don't want to hear this," to the announcement of the plane captain that all the New York airports are closed and that the plan is to proceed to Boston. He makes George's display of stomach pain, as with the moment where he breaks a tooth from eating the toy in the Cracker Jack box, more comic than real. In contrast, Dennis makes Gwen's pain at cutting her foot more real than comic. Lemmon is equally funny in the way George laughs at Gwen's suggestion to sleep under the tree in Central Park at night, and his running about when he is looking for her the next morning. He is also funny in the sideways glance at the little Spanish boy George gives to suggest his idea of searching the boy's pockets, when George kneels to pray in the church in defiance of the order to leave, and when he crosses himself in front of Lenny Moyers as the couple leave the church.

Playing second fiddle to Lemmon, Dennis has an inconsistent New York accent, and her character doesn't make comic impact until the second half of the narrative. The white color scheme of her wardrobe helps to present Gwen as the more innocent and reasonable of the couple. Dennis is funny when Gwen covers her left eye because she has lost her false eyelash when she and George attend the front desk of the Waldorf Astoria and in Gwen's smug smile when George thinks that he has called the bluff of the night desk clerk, Winkler. She is also funny in her second reading of the line about the man in the black cape, "I told you it all happened so quickly." Dennis gets another laugh from her delivery of Gwen's line, "A man does not stand over you at four o-clock in the morning if he doesn't have a knife, does he?" and from her head-nodding and smiling when she tells George that she doesn't hear his whistling through his broken tooth. Dennis' best scenes are when Gwen has lost her wedding ring and is angry at how indifferent George is to it, and in the limousine and in the street afterwards in reaction to the demonstrators.

In his memoir *Rewrites*, Simon says that the inspiration for the story came from an incident circa 1967 when he flew to Boston to work on David Merrick's musical *How Now Dow Jones*: "Flying up there, I was caught in a major snowstorm, lost my luggage, spent three hours getting to the hotel on icy streets, a trip which normally was a ten-minute ride." Simon also reports that Lemmon committed to the film at a lunch they had together in the Polo Lounge of the Beverly Hills Hotel after only hearing the story and not having read a script. The writer had completed a first draft but didn't want to show the actor unpolished work. When Simon asked Lemmon if he wanted to read a second draft before committing, Lemmon told him he didn't need to. He already liked the sound of the first draft and believed that the second would only be better. The actor told Simon, "Tell me when you want to start and I'll bring my face and my makeup."

In an article on the Turner Classic Movies Web site, Bret Wood reported that Lemmon was unsatisfied with the film. He said he loved Neil Simon, Dennis was quite good in it, and Hiller was "a ball to work for.... Unfortunately, he's no flaming genius as a filmmaker." Lemmon described a five-minute sequence that was cut, a scene he considered important for character motivation, as being better than anything left in. No further clues are offered as to the content of the missing footage.

Many of the incidents depicted in the film referenced real-life events going on in New York. There was a transit strike in 1966 and a sanitation strike in 1968. The dilapidated condition and overcrowding of the train the Kellermans take from Boston to New York mirrored the decline in passenger rail service throughout the entire country in the late 1960s. The muggings and robberies experienced by the Kellermans mirrored the rising crime rate, and the portrayal of Central Park as a haven for crime reflected its reputation at the time.

The screenplay originated as a monologue that was one act of Simon's four-act play *Plaza Suite*, which was cut in rehearsals so that the play would only have three acts. In their book *Video Versions: Film Adaptations of Plays on Video*, Erskine and Welsh claim that the play that was adapted for British television in the late 1960s and starred Ed Begley and Margaret Johnston, though this cannot be verified.

RELEASE: May 28, 1970, with the tagline "When they take you for an out-of-towner, they really take you."

REVIEWS: Lauded by *Variety* but lambasted by Roger Greenspun in the *New York Times*, John Douglas Eames and Robert Abele in *The Paramount Story*, and Robert K. Johnson in *Neil Simon*.

DVD: Released by Paramount on November 25, 2003.

REMAKE: Remade as *The Out-Of-Towners* by director Sam Weisman in 1999 with a screenplay by Marc Lawrence, based on Neil Simon's screenplay.

Murder by Death (1976)

Columbia Pictures/Rastar Pictures.

CREW: Robert Moore (Director), Ray Stark (Producer), Roger M. Rothstein (Associate Producer), Neil Simon (Screenplay), David M. Walsh (Photography), John F. Burnett (Editor), Dave Grusin (Music), Stephen Grimes (Production Design), Harry Kemm (Art Director), Marvin March (Set Decorator), Ann Roth (Costumes), Joseph Di Bella (Makeup), Vivienne Walker (Hair), Augie Lohman (Special Effects), Wayne Fitzgerald (Titles), Charles Adams (Title Drawings). Color, 91 minutes. Filmed on location in Berkshire, England, and at Warner Bros. Studios in Burbank, California, from fall to December 1975.

CAST in alphabetical order: Eileen Brennan (Tess Skeffington/Vilma Norman), Truman Capote (Lionel Twain), James Coco (Milo Perrier), Peter Falk (Sam Diamond/J.J. Loomis), Alec Guinness (Jamesir Bensonmum/Irving Goldman/Marvin Metzner/Irene Twain/Rita/Sam Diamond), Elsa Lanchester (Jessica Marbles), David Niven (Dick Charleston), Peter Sellers (Sidney Wang), Maggie Smith (Dora Charleston), Nancy Walker (Yetta the Maid/Rita), Estelle Winwood (Miss Withers, the Nurse), James Cromwell (Marcel Cassette), Richard Narita (Willie Wang).

SYNOPSIS: Seventy-six-year-old Lionel Twain invites the world's five greatest detectives to his country castle for dinner. He hopes to ruin their reputations of never having failed to solve a crime by staging a murder that they cannot solve. However, he also offers one million dollars to the person who can solve the crime. Bensonmum is found dead and Lionel also appears dead. The detectives are all revealed to have personal motive for killing Lionel. They retire to their rooms and they are all subjected to murder attempts. Bensonmum appears to be behind the plan, until he is unmasked as Lionel. The guests leave the house thinking that there has been no murder, and Lionel is unmasked to be Yetta.

NOTES: Simon's screenplay parodies the literary and film detectives and private investigators Nick and Nora Charles, Charlie Chan, Hercule Poirot, Sam Spade and Miss

Marple. He presents a murder mystery complete with characters with multiple identities, multiple victims, attempted murders, and a convoluted resolution. The screenplay is made of bad jokes with some funny lines mixed in. Simon also employs the homophobic terms "pansy" and "queeries."

The narrative provides the atmospheric conventions of the mystery genre, including a lightning storm, fog, and a doorbell that sounds like a screaming woman. The score adds to this effect. Though hardly subtle, we don't expect it to be. The use of an unknown gloved person seen performing tasks such as cutting the telephone wire, loosening a door hinge, and pushing gargoyles from the roof introduces an anonymous antagonist. Of these tasks, only the loosened door hinge fails to get a narrative payoff. Simon expresses his dislike of the conventions of mystery literature through Lionel, who admonishes the detectives for the surprises in their stories and the illogical endings, characters that are introduced only in the last pages, and clues and information that are withheld to make it impossible to guess who the murderer is. This prefigures Simon's own convoluted and ambiguous narrative conclusion.

That the character of Bensonmum is blind allows for the expected jokes, although the first one undermines the narrative. He is seen to apply licked stamps to a table and not to the invitations, so that we question whether they have actually been delivered. However, his condition gets a funny reference. Dick asks him if the house has other servants and Bensonmum replies, "I'm not sure. I've never seen anyone." Lionel tells Sidney that his use of language drives him crazy and Sam comments, "Sounds like a short ride to me." After Lionel's chair speeds out of the dining room backwards, Dora comments, "I hope he knows how to stop that thing."

The parodies of the detectives have some inconsistencies. Nick and Nora Charles are American and their dog is named Asta, whereas Dick and Dora Charleston are British and their dog is Myron. The characters Sam Diamond and Tess parody Sam Spade and Effie Perine from *The Maltese Falcon* (1941), and Sam references the film when he tells Tess to fill a gas can. He says, "I want you to know that I'm going to be waiting for you," which is what Sam Spade says to Brigid O'Shaughnessy after he gives her up to the police in that film. Sam also references Humphrey Bogart's Rick from *Casablanca* (1942) when he tells Tess about a woman who left him in Paris when war was declared, and Lauren Bacall's "Slim" in *To Have and Have Not* (1944) when he tells Tess that all she has to do is whistle to get him to come to her and then asks her if she knows how to whistle.

The Sidney Wang character speaks in Charlie Chan aphorisms that are generally amusing. Examples are "Conversation is like television set on a honeymoon. Unnecessary," "Questions like athlete's foot. After a while very irritating," "Man who argue with cow on wall is like train without wheels. Very soon get nowhere," and "Bickering detectives like making lamb stew. Everything go to pot." Simon also points up Wang's use of aphorisms by having Willie drive away as Sidney starts to say to Dick, "Treacherous road is like mushrooms ..." He also has Lionel Twain criticize Sidney's speech for lacking prepositions, articles and pronouns.

The doorbell's sound of a screaming woman becomes a running gag. This gets a payoff when Dora screams at a mouse in her room, and Bensonmum thinks it's the doorbell. There is also a matching joke of a man's moan being the sound of the dinner

Clockwise from left: Willie Wang (Richard Narita), Sidney Wang (Peter Sellers), Tess Skeffington (Eileen Brennan), Marcel Cassette (James Cromwell), Milo Perrier (James Coco), Jessica Marbles (Elsa Lanchester), Miss Withers (Estelle Winwood), Sam Diamond (Peter Falk), Dick Charleston (David Niven), Dora Charleston (Maggie Smith), with Lionel Twain (Truman Capote) inset, in a still for *Murder by Death* (1976).

gong. Another running gag is that a gargoyle is pushed off the roof each time one of the guests comes to the front door. This gag gets a twist when Sam is hit instead of Tess. A third running gag is real eyes seen behind the eyes of a painting. This gets a payoff when we also see a tongue through the painting's mouth. A fourth gag is that the guests remaining in the dining room are not seen by those who leave and then return to the room. This also operates as a narrative mystery that gets an explanation that is not confirmed.

The fire on Sidney's bed, which Bensonmum has accidently lit, sparks a funny line when Sidney says, "At least the bed will be warm." Yetta's notes that say she cannot speak, or hear, or read English get payoffs, particularly as she has to work with the blind Bensonmum, who shows her the menu without knowing that she cannot read it. He also tells her that when he needs her he will ring bells in the kitchen. When he does so, Yetta can neither hear nor even see the bells, as she is sitting with her back to them. Yetta scores a laugh when she screams silently, and there is only the audience to witness her cackle at the film's end.

The title drawings by Charles Adams are amusing caricatures of the main actors.

Director Robert Moore makes an unusual choice of blocking when Sam stands with his back close to the camera as he speaks to Bensonmum. There is a pan over the listening characters as Dick makes a toast at dinner followed by a matching pan over animal heads mounted on the wall. Moore uses quick cuts for the appearance of Lionel and the guests' reaction to him, and an aerial view of the guests all holding hands at the dinner table. The director can't do much with the screenplay, which is essentially an over-extended skit with juvenile antics. However, he does manage to bring some energy into the climactic revelations.

Most of the actors have little opportunity to rise above the material, but there are two exceptions. As Milo, James Coco gets a laugh from the moan he makes to indicate that the wine he drinks is a bad vintage. As Sam, Peter Falk is funny with his off-screen crying, and is better as the earnest actor J.J. Loomis than in his parody of Bogart.

In the DVD featurette, "A Conversation with Neil Simon," Simon notes that the film is staged almost like a play. Simon's screenplay was written as if he were fifteen or sixteen years old, as a take-off of the films he had seen at that age. Opinions differ on the controversial casting of Truman Capote as Lionel. Some sources say that Simon wrote the part for Capote, but in his memoir *The Play Goes On* Simon calls the casting a mistake, and says that it came from producer Ray Stark, who saw the publicity value that Capote attracted. Simon is quoted in George Plimpton's book on Capote as saying that Capote was a great raconteur but "he got stuck when he had lines to say." The interview on the DVD featurette has Simon saying that he was unhappy with Capote's performance, as was director Robert Moore. Moore is quoted in the Turner Classic Movies article by Deborah Looney on the film as saying, "To put Capote at a table with international stars was too much of a test for any literary figure to withstand." Simon diplomatically said that ultimately Capote's performance was passable because "it represented a very unique, idiosyncratic character."

It is said that Orson Welles was wanted for the part of Sidney but was unavailable. Myrna Loy was offered the part of Dora but turned it down. Katharine Hepburn was to play a character named Dame Abigail Christian, which was to be a parody of Agatha Christie. When Hepburn withdrew, the character was changed to Abigail Christmas and Estelle Winwood was to play her. However, after a rewrite Simon dropped the character altogether and Winwood was cast as Miss Withers instead. Peter Sellers also played Jessica Marbles' taxi driver, but the scene was deleted. Additionally, Phil Silvers was filmed in a role that was deleted.

Peter Sellers originally had a percentage share in the film, but later, thinking it didn't work, he sold back his investment. When the film became a hit he regretted his decision. The screaming woman sound of the doorbell is said to be Fay Wray from *King Kong* (1933). In the television version of the film there are two characters who appear at the end, arriving by car at the house. They are Sherlock Holmes, played by Keith McConnell, and Doctor Watson, played by Richard Peel.

Three other scenes ended up on the cutting-room floor. In the first, the Charlestons narrowly avoid hitting Tess when she is walking back to Sam's car with the can of gasoline. Dick makes sure that she is not hurt but does not offer her a lift. The second scene shows Willie finding a note Lionel has in his hand when he is covering up the body. Willie tells Sidney that he is a better detective than his father. Sam takes the note from

Willie and finds that it says, "Please call dairy and stop deliveries of milk. Lionel Twain deceased." The third scene has the Wangs passing the car of Holmes and Watson *en route* to the house. Sidney gives them the directions they ask for. Willie asks Sidney why he didn't tell them the truth about the house, and Sidney replies. Sources differ as to what Sidney says. The possibilities include "Let idiots find out for themselves," "Let fools find out for selves. Drive, please," and "If he world's greatest detective, let him figure it out."

RELEASE: June 23, 1976, with the taglines "By the time the world's greatest detectives figure out whodunnit ... you could die laughing!" and "You are cordially invited to dinner ... and a murder!"

REVIEWS: Praised by *Variety*, with a mixed reaction from Vincent Canby in the *New York Times* and Robert K. Johnson in *Neil Simon*.

DVD: Released by Sony Pictures Home Entertainment on December 18, 2001.

Bogart Slept Here (*not released*)

Warner Bros/Rastar.

CREW: Mike Nichols (Director), Ray Stark (Producer), Robert Schultz (Associate Producer), Howard W. Koch (Executive Producer), Neil Simon (Screenplay), Robert Surtees (Photography), Dede Allen (Editor), Anthea Sylbert (Costumes).

CAST (character names unknown): Robert DeNiro, Marsha Mason, Elaine Stritch, Richard Romanus, Linda Lavin, Tony Lo Bianco.

SYNOPSIS: A struggling off–Broadway actor is cast in a Hollywood film and becomes an international star. He moves to California with his ex-dancer wife and two children but has trouble coping with his new-found success. The title of the film refers to a room in the Chateau Marmont Hotel in Hollywood in which Bogart and the protagonist both stayed.

NOTES: The screenplay for this film is not available, so information about its content and the behind-the-scenes events that caused the film to be abandoned has been compiled from other sources. These include Simon's memoir *Rewrites* and Marsha Mason's memoir *Journey*.

Simon revealed in an interview in *Filmmakers Newsletter* that the screenplay was originally entitled *Clark Gable Slept Here*. He changed the hook from Gable to Bogart after the film *Gable and Lombard* came out in 1976. The story is said to have been partly based on that of Dustin Hoffman, who lived across the street from Simon, with his wife and two children. Hoffman was a talented but struggling Off Broadway actor that no one in Hollywood had heard of when Mike Nichols tested him to star in *The Graduate*. At the time it was thought that Hoffman didn't have much chance of getting the part since the studio was more interested in more established actors such as Robert Redford and Warren Beatty. When Hoffman got the telephone call telling him that he had got the part, he was at home with his dancer wife, Anne Byrne. When he told her the news he could tell from the look on her face that their lives had changed forever.

In his *Playgirl* interview Simon says that he wrote the role of the actor's wife for Marsha Mason and that the story was as much about her as it was about him. In the story the character of the wife copes better with the actor's success than he does, and

NOW SHOOTING

A
MIKE NICHOLS
FILM

Bogart Slept Here

BY
NEIL SIMON

STARRING

ROBERT DE NIRO
MARSHA MASON

ELAINE STRITCH · RICHARD ROMANUS
LINDA LAVIN
and TONY LO BIANCO

Film Editor DEDE ALLEN · Director of Photography ROBERT SURTEES · Associate Producer ROBERT SCHULTZ · Executive Producer HOWARD W. KOCH, JR. · Written by NEIL SIMON · Produced and Directed by MIKE NICHOLS · RASTAR · From Warner Bros. W A Warner Communications Company.

it is his problems that lead to the breakdown of their marriage. Simon says that the wife was intellectually brighter than the actor, and that she kept the house and the family together while working as a reader for a book publisher and writing a novel.

Hoffman was the first actor offered the lead role in the proposed film, but Mason says that he took too long getting back to Simon and Ray Stark, the producer. This led them to go to Robert De Niro, who was considered very hot at the time just after coming off *Mean Streets* (1973). He would subsequently become even hotter after winning the Academy Award for Best Supporting Actor for *The Godfather: Part II* (1974) in April 1975. De Niro wanted to shoot *Taxi Driver* before starting *Bogart Slept Here*. Since it was considered a coup to get De Niro, the rehearsals were postponed for a few days to accommodate him. He would finish *Taxi Driver* on a Friday in New York and be in Los Angeles for rehearsals for *Bogart Slept Here* on the following Monday. *Taxi Driver* was filmed from June to September 1975 in New York and released the following February.

In her memoir, Mason reports that Simon once got angry in a pre-production meeting with director Mike Nichols and clenched a soda can so tightly that he cut his thumb. Mason also claims that several days before the film was to begin shooting, Nichols' previous title, *The Fortune*, premiered in Los Angeles. It starred Jack Nicholson, Warren Beatty, and Stockard Channing. Nichols, Mason and Simon attended the premiere, and from the audience reaction it was clear to Mason that the film was a failure. Nichols was devastated, and perhaps this caused him to lose confidence as a filmmaker, which would spill over into *Bogart Slept Here*.

Since De Niro finished *Taxi Driver* in September 1975 and went straight into this film, late September/early October is the presumed start of production. This is despite Mason's claim that it was around May 1975. Mason says there were two weeks of rehearsals scheduled. Simon writes that there was very little rehearsal because Nichols believed that De Niro would be better without it. However, neither Simon nor Mason comments specifically on De Niro's behavior in the rehearsal period. Mason does report that by this time, Simon and Nichols were barely speaking.

Once shooting began, Simon writes that De Niro spent an entire day searching for the right earring for his character, which seemed to try Nichols' patience. He also says that De Niro sometimes strayed from his lines because he felt his paraphrased versions sounded just as good. Mason went along with this improvisational acting. However, it became clear to Simon in the dailies that the humor that the writer was going for was being lost. He felt that De Niro could be funny but that the humor came from particular nuances that were different from those in the script. For example, in the first scene shot, De Niro's character told Mason's that he had received the film offer. The actor delivered the news without the script's required happiness, which then affected Mason's response. Simon told Nichols that maybe the interpretation was valid, but Nichols disagreed and claimed that happiness was essential for the narrative's setup. Shooting continued for five more days, and Simon says that Mason felt lost because the film seemed to be going in different directions.

Mason believed that De Niro hadn't had enough time in between films to help him create this new role, which she described as "funny, sunny, upbeat and ebullient." Perhaps

Opposite: Variety ad for Bogart Slept Here.

because he had just come off *Taxi Driver*, his approach to the new character was too grim and humorless. De Niro told her he needed time to "live" the character and asked Mason to move in with him. She declined, knowing that Simon, her husband, would hate her leaving him at night. Mason said she could feel the tension between Nichols, Simon and De Niro, and things were not helped when Nichols insisted on calling her "Mason" as a nickname. She hated it and eventually asked him not to, which seemed to affect their working relationship.

They shot a breakfast scene in which the wife (Mason) was cooking bacon and eggs while her two children were at the table eating cereal. When the actor (De Niro) entered, the wife was required to answer a question from him while doing the cooking, as well as speaking to their children and her mother on the telephone. Mason also had to cope with complicated use of props and movement around the room. De Niro only had to speak one line, but he had trouble with the timing. After a few attempts Mason lost her patience and left the set to go to her trailer. Nichols came to her and told her that she had to apologize to De Niro. Mason felt abandoned by Simon because she says he had refused to come to the set. He had written her a letter, concerned that their marriage would not last because *he* felt abandoned, and he also did not understand the friendship she had maintained with her ex-husband. Mason knew that she couldn't confide in Nichols about her problem with Simon because they had their own conflicts. She was conscious of Nichols' anxiety over his perceived previous failure, and DeNiro's anxiety about the character he was trying to create. Despite everyone having told Mason that this film role was a great opportunity, she felt miserable and was intimidated by all the male energy surrounding her. She used meditation and the teachings of Baba Muktananda to help her get through it and eventually did apologize to De Niro.

The film was shot on location in a house in the Hollywood Hills. In the script, the house that the studio had provided for the actor and his family was all yellow, and one scene required the family to react to the color. Mason does not report that there was any problem with the scene, but she says that the day after it was shot, the decision was made to fire De Niro.

Simon writes that after seven days of shooting, Nichols invited two Warner Bros. executives, John Calley and Frank Wells, to view the footage. They recognized that there was a problem. Nichols suggested stopping the film since he had decided De Niro was miscast. Simon writes that his opinion was not asked and even if it had been, he wouldn't have known what it was. The next day, the film was shut down and De Niro was told he was to be replaced. The shot footage was relegated to a shelf in the Warner Bros. archives, and it has not been seen since.

Mason says De Niro had asked for her help, wanting her to rehearse more with him. He told her that he knew he could play the part but that he needed more time. Mason had seen the dailies and knew that they were not good. However, she felt she could not fight for him given that she was married to Simon. If the project had been a play, there might have been time to work on it. However, as a film that was costing thirty thousand to forty thousand dollars a day, there was not. Mason reports that two weeks of filming had taken place and the film had already cost around two million dollars. Simon writes that upon hearing he was to be let go, De Niro was livid. The screenwriter felt lucky that he was not in the room when the actor was told the news. The story of De Niro's firing made headlines in *Variety.*

Nichols tried to carry on with the film. He considered casting Raul Julia and other actors but then withdrew. Simon thought Nichols' withdrawal was a smart but brave act. This was because the director was sure to get bad press about dropping the film straight after the failure of *The Fortune.* Warner Bros. wanted to continue with the film and approached other directors, but after a month no one had committed. Mason says Stark and Simon hired Howard Zieff, and he stayed on the film for two weeks. Some of the actors considered as potential replacements for De Niro were Jack Nicholson, James Caan, and Tony Lo Bianco. Simon thought of Richard Dreyfuss, but he had been told that the actor wasn't interested or available, which turned out not to be true on either count. With Zieff as director Simon had a reading with Dreyfuss and Mason at Stark's office. The writer had become fearful that if the script didn't work with De Niro, whom he thought to be a brilliant actor, then maybe something was wrong with it.

The reading showed that Dreyfuss and Mason had great chemistry together. Dreyfuss later commented in his Mark Twain Award speech for Simon that the writer had said that the script didn't work but *they* did. Simon decided to write a new script for them, keeping the idea of the struggling young actor, so *Bogart Slept Here* became *The Goodbye Girl.* The scene in *The Goodbye Girl* in which the Hollywood film director comes backstage into the actor's dressing room to offer him a film part was how *Bogart Slept Here* had begun. To write the new story, Simon worked backwards from that moment to create a romance showing how the two people met. It took him six weeks.

In his *American Film* interview, Simon says that the first reading of the new script with Mason and Dreyfuss revealed that about fifty percent of it worked. After a rewrite three months later there was another reading, and Simon felt seventy-five percent of it worked. At a final reading on the first day of production of *The Goodbye Girl,* another three months later, Simon felt that the script was structurally right and just needed some minor work to be done.

In later years both Simon and Mason attempted to resolve their differences with DeNiro. When the writer saw him again he found it hard to look him in the eye, but he did buy two paintings by De Niro's father for his home. Years later, Mason was interviewed by Danny DeVito for the film *The War of the Roses.* He asked her if she knew whether the character of Tony DeForrest in *The Goodbye Girl* was based on De Niro. She told him that she did not know and that she had never before made the association. Mason obtained an address for De Niro and wrote him a letter, apologizing for what had happened to him on *Bogart Slept Here.* He telephoned and thanked her, saying he understood the situation she had been in and did not blame her.

In his 1989 *Playboy* interview with Lawrence Grobel, DeNiro spoke about the experience. He said, "It didn't work, just didn't work out." He said that the producers tried not to pay him, but they were unsuccessful. Grobel tells the actor of an eyewitness story of De Niro, Mason and Nichols in the studio commissary having lunch. Supposedly Mason accused De Niro of not showing enough respect to Nichols as the director attempted to tell him what comedy was. De Niro then reportedly left the table, walked out the door, went to the airport and flew to New York. The actor does not confirm or deny the story. He asks Grobel who the eyewitness was—a question presumably not answered by Grobel—and comments, "People think what they want, so what the hell's the difference? Those who know don't say; those who say don't know. "

RELEASE: Film abandoned during production.

The Goodbye Girl (1977)

MGM/Warner Bros. Picture/Rastar.

CREW: Herbert Ross (Director), Ray Stark (Producer), Roger M. Rothstein (Associate Producer), Neil Simon (Screenplay), David M. Walsh (Photography), John F. Burnett (Editor), Dave Grusin (Music), Albert Brenner (Production Design), Jerry Wunderlich (Set Decorator), Ann Roth (Costumes), Allan Whitey Snyder (Makeup), Kaye Pownall (Hair), Carrie White (Miss Mason's Hair), Albert Griswold (Special Effects), Wayne Fitzgerald (Titles). Color, 110 minutes. Filmed at MGM Studios in Culver City, California, and on location in New York.

CAST: Richard Dreyfuss (Elliot Garfield); Marsha Mason (Paula McFadden); Quinn Cummings (Lucy McFadden); Paul Benedict (Mark Bodine); Barbara Rhoades (Donna Douglas); Theresa Merritt (Mrs. Crosby); Marilyn Sokol (Linda); Michael Shawn (Ronnie Burns); Patricia Pearcy (Rhonda Fontana); Gene Castle (Eddie, Assistant Choreographer); Daniel Levans (Dance Instructor); Anita Dangler (Mrs. Morganweiss); Victoria Boothby (Mrs. Bodine); Robert Costanzo (Liquor Store Salesman); Pancho Gonzalez, Jose Machado and Hubert Kelly (Muggers); Dana Lurita (Cynthia Fein); Dave Cass (Earl the Drunk at Strip Club); Loyita Chapel and Caprice Clark (Strip Club Dancers); Esther Sutherland (Strip Club Manager); Clarence Felder (Critic); Kensuke Haga and Ryohei Kanokogi (Japanese Salesmen); Ruby Holbrook (Woman in Audience); Kristina Hurrell (Gretchen); David Matthau and Milt Oberman (Furniture Movers); Eddie Villery (Painter); Joseph Carberry and Eric Uhler (Strip Club Customers); Ray Barry, Powers Boothe, Tom Everett, Janice Fuller, Munson Hicks, Robert Kerman, Jeanne Lange, Robert Lesser, Fred McCarren, Nicholas Mele, Maureen Moore, Joseph Regalbuto, and Peter Vogt (*Richard III* Cast); Wendy Cutler, Susan Elliot, Andy Goldberg, and Paul Willson (The Inventory Improvisation Group). Uncredited: Charles Silvern, Nicole Williamson (Oliver Fry).

SONGS: "Goodbye Girl" (David Gates), guitar by Richard Dreyfuss, and David Gates over end credits; "How About You" (music by Burton Lane with lyrics by Ralph Freed), record, and Richard Dreyfuss.

SYNOPSIS: Thirty-three-year-old ex-dancer Paula McFadden lives with her ten-year-old daughter Lucy and actor Tony De Forrest in an apartment in New York. They plan to move to Hollywood where Tony has a job, but he goes alone to Italy instead for a better one. He sublets the apartment to Chicago actor Elliot Garfield. Refusing to leave, Paula agrees to share the apartment with Elliot. He is cast in an off–Broadway production of *Richard III*, but the play closes after opening night. Elliot seduces Paula and they begin a romance. He gets an acting job in a film in Seattle and leaves his guitar behind to prove to Paula that he will return.

NOTES: Simon's original screenplay offers the subject of family, with an unmarried mother who finds romance with a new man in whom she sees a potential new husband and father. The idea of conventional and radical behavior is explored through the differences between the two main characters. Simon attaches a lot of curse words to the child Lucy to present her as precocious, but instead it just makes her appear to be brattish. Other unfortunate choices are using the word "gimp" to describe Richard III, and the idea of playing the character as gay, which allows for an inherent level of homophobia in the discussion.

Since the film is a romantic comedy, Simon has some funny lines. They include Paula's telling Lucy to shut up after she has told her daughter that possession is nine-tenths of the law, and Lucy asks what the other tenth is. Elliot asks Mark how far off the diving board he wants him to jump in playing Richard III as gay. Mark replies, "Don't give me Bette Midler, but let's not be afraid to be bold." Lucy gets a stomachache from eating ice cream and says to Elliot, "Did you see *The Exorcist*?

Paula McFadden (Marsha Mason) is hugged by Elliot Garfield (Richard Dreyfuss) in a still for *The Goodbye Girl* (1977).

Then you better get out of the room." Elliot asks her if his playing the guitar soothes her better than medicine, and Lucy replies, "And it tastes better too." Elliot asks Paula why he lets her daughter read pornography, referring to a bad newspaper review she reads aloud. He comments, "I'm beginning to think my Richard wasn't that bad," after seeing Paula trying to cover forgetting her lines at the auto show. Paula accuses Lucy of pushing her to Elliot and says, "Your fingerprints are all over my back." Paula tells Elliot that she is glad to be over the period where she likes macho men and he responds, "I think I'll let that remark pass."

Simon creates the necessary obstacles of the genre for the two main characters to get together. However, while Paula is presented as the protagonist, she is strangely unlikable and our preference goes instead to the antagonist, Elliot. Paula's reaction to being abandoned by her boyfriend Tony presents her as weepy, self-deprecating and self-pitying. Additionally, her behavior in not letting Elliot into the apartment that he has leased makes her unreasonable. Our sympathy, then, is more with him. This empathy for Elliot persists despite his annoying habit of playing his guitar at night, and chanting and using incense in the morning. The attraction between Paula and Elliot is obvious from the beginning, when he comments on her attractiveness and she is shown to be amused by him. This attraction prefigures the romance between them, the obstacles being their objections to each other's behavior when they are forced to live together.

Elliot is presented as a more radical character than Paula, and she calls him "weird." However, his mild form of radicalism says more about Paula's judgment than it does about him. Paula disapproves of Elliot's taking Rhonda to his room in the apartment, despite the fact that he is paying the rent. Elliot points out her hypocrisy in having lived with Tony, a married man. When Paula is mugged she behaves unreasonably to Elliot. When he reluctantly chases the speeding car in which the muggers have fled and attempts to rescue her stolen purse, she is not grateful, because he fails. Although he gave up only when the muggers brandished a knife, Paula refuses even to let him walk home with her. Her behavior to Elliot changes after she gets a job at the auto show, possibly because of her need for him to look after Lucy when she is working. However, the continuation of the obstacle to the couple getting together is that Elliot does not hear her apologize to him for her hostile behavior, as he falls asleep while she is speaking. When Paula and Lucy go to see Elliot play Richard III, we question whether Paula's praise is genuine, since she is shown to cover her face at his performance. However, she does stay with Elliot when he is drunk and humiliated after the show. She blames him for making her forget her lines at her auto show job when he appears to watch her, but then she is appreciative after he tells her Japanese bosses that they should keep her.

Paula is shown to be more likeable in her interaction with Lucy, and she is finally likable with Elliot when he seduces her. However, her neurotic rejection of him the next morning reverses this impression, and she presents herself as a martyr when she tells him that she is willing to let him go to Seattle and leave her. The narrative concludes with Paula's being happy about Elliot going once he asks her to come with him, an idea she rejects because it is enough for her that he asked. His leaving the guitar behind is supposedly confirmation that he will return for her.

The plot point that Elliot's director, Mark, wants him to play Richard III as gay is another demonstration of the difference between conventional and radical behavior. Even for an Off Broadway play, the interpretation is deemed to be radical. Elliot objects to it because he prefers the hump and club foot of the conventional Richard III interpretation. A clue that Mark is misguided is that he initially sits with his back to the actors during a rehearsal. Elliot's walking out on the rehearsal because of his disagreement over characterization seems petulant and a risky move for an actor who can be replaced. Luckily for Elliot, Mark goes after him and does not fire him. Elliot asks that Mark not let him look foolish, and Mark compromises by allowing Elliot to incorporate the hump and club foot into the gay interpretation.

The homophobia is not in the idea of playing Richard as gay as much as in the homophobic comments it provides an excuse for. Lucy responds when she hears Elliot, "Sounds like that guy in the beauty parlor." This is a weak joke on the stereotypical "gay voice," even if it is meant to come from the honesty of a child. There are equally homophobic comments made by critics about Elliot's Richard, such as "Britain's first badly dressed interior decorator" and "The Wicked Witch of the North." Simon also demonstrates a low opinion of people who frequent strip clubs by showing their offensive behavior to Elliot. They applaud when he is punched by the drunken customer Earl, tell Earl that they want him to hit Elliot again when asked, and applaud again when he does. Simon tries to make the situation funny but fails with Elliot's pathetic button line, "My first standing ovation."

Director Herbert Ross opens the film with an unusual medium shot of the front of a bus in whose windscreen the city is seen reflected. He gives Marsha Mason, as Paula, a long reaction shot after Elliot has told her that the only thing likeable about her is Lucy, and a similar long shot when Paula apologizes to Elliot. Ross provides an extreme long shot of Elliot and Paula on the rooftop for their dinner scene, and a montage for Paula's redecorating the apartment.

Richard Dreyfuss makes Elliot likable and more reasonable than Paula, and overcomes the pretentiousness of Elliot as an actor. Dreyfuss is funny when he realizes how terrible his performance is as the gay Richard III, when he pretends to attempt to strangle himself with his own scarf, and when he leaps up on the bedroom door frame like a monkey. He also looks convincingly miserable after the play's performance, and his calm in the face of Paula's rejection of him the morning after their lovemaking again shows him to be the more reasonable of the couple.

Mason's Paula may be considered too old to succeed in her audition for a Broadway musical. However, one's eye goes to her among the group of dancers in her audition group when they perform the required routine. Mason scores a laugh from the nod of her head in reaction to the instructor in her dance class. She is funny when Paula asks Elliot, "Is that the last chorus?" of his chanting, the way she repeats "rising young actress," and the way she says, "No, I see you took everything," regarding Elliot's having packed to leave. The bathroom seduction and rooftop dinner scenes work because of Mason's reactions; her mild anger is funny in the former and her tears effective in the latter.

Quinn Cummings overcomes some of the bad idea of Lucy as a precocious wise-guy with charm, and is funny when Lucy imitates Paula's fake voice when she asks why her mother wants her to wait downstairs for her. She also supplies tears for Lucy's hansom cab scene with Elliot.

The character of Paula's ex-boyfriend, Tony DeForrest, may have been inspired by Robert De Niro. De Niro was cast and fired from *Bogart Slept Here*, Simon's screenplay that filming had been abandoned on. De Niro's similarity to Tony includes having a "De" name and also because Tony, like De Niro, had gone to Italy to make the film *1900* (1976) with director Bernardo Bertolucci. In his headshots in the apartment Tony also resembles De Niro. Lucy will say that Tony was sexy but not classy, presumably alluding to an Italian working-class sensibility. De Niro has displayed a range of performance that includes his playing Italian and working class characters. The *Bogart Slept Here* connection is also evident from Elliot doing a Bogart impression for the dinner with Paula.

The film was co-produced by Warner Bros and MGM. This is because the rights to the original screenplay for *Bogart Slept Here* was held by Warners. Since they had little faith in the script for *The Goodbye Girl*, they wanted to sell the rights to MGM. MGM would only agree to split the costs and the anticipated profits. When the film became a box office hit, both studios profited.

In his memoir *The Play Goes On*, Simon advises that Mason was deglamorized for her character. She was dressed as if her clothes had been purchased in thrift shops and her hair was cut short to make it appear cheaper to manage. In his interview for *American Film* magazine, Simon says that he started writing the screenplay about California but that he changed it because he thought that there was something more interesting in the conflicts inherent in living in New York.

In the *Intimate Portrait* documentary on Mason, she says that making the film was a "perfect experience." because it was a good film and hugely successful. In the same episode Herbert Ross says that Mason and Dreyfuss were doing good work, "were in a special light," and were endlessly inventive. However, Mason also tells the story of how she and Dreyfuss rehearsed their first scene together, adding improvisations and making it heavily dramatic. They were both shattered with Simon's response when, after viewing what the actors had come up with, he said, "Well, it's terrible." In her memoir *Journey*, Mason writes that Dreyfuss had gone on a fish diet because he felt that he needed to lose weight for the role. He ate only sushi. He reeked of it, but he didn't lose any weight, so he stopped the diet.

RELEASE: November 30, 1977, with the taglines "He's moving in ... she's not moving out ... it's love at first fight!" and "Thank you Neil Simon for making us laugh at falling in love ... again."

REVIEWS: Praised by Clive Hirschhorn in *The Warner Bros. Story*. A mixed reaction from Vincent Canby in the *New York Times*, Roger Ebert in the *Chicago Sun-Times* and Robert K. Johnson in *Neil Simon*. Lambasted by Pauline Kael in *When the Lights Go Down*.

AWARDS: Richard Dreyfuss won the Best Actor Academy Award. Also nominated were Marsha Mason for Best Actress, Quinn Cummings for Best Supporting Actress, Ray Stark for Best Picture, and Simon for Best Original Screenplay.

DVD: Released by Warner Home Video on November 9, 2010.

REMAKES: Three television pilots were made by NBC, but only one was screened. Karen Valentine starred in two of them and Jobeth Williams in the third. The screened pilot was entitled *Goodbye Doesn't Mean Forever* and was written by Allan Katz. It starred Valentine and Michael Lembeck and was directed by James Burrows. It was broadcast as a made-for-television movie on May 28, 1982. A musical version of the film adapted by Simon was produced on Broadway in 1993 and starred Martin Short and Bernadette Peters. It was remade as another made-for-television movie in 2004 with Jeff Daniels and Patricia Heaton. The teleplay was written by Simon and the movie was directed by Richard Benjamin.

SEQUEL: A proposed sequel for the film was written by Simon but never made. In his book *The 50 Greatest Movies Never Made*, Chris Gore says that the sequel was a reworking of *Bogart Slept Here*. It was to be called *Mr. Famous*. It was centered on Elliot becoming a success and not being able to cope with it, a scenario that Richard Dreyfuss experienced in real life. The project was cancelled because it was thought that people would not care about a movie star who had everything but was still miserable.

The Cheap Detective (1978)

Columbia Pictures/EMI/Rastar Films.

CREW: Robert Moore (Director), Ray Stark (Producer), Margaret Booth (Associate Producer), Neil Simon (Screenplay), John A. Alonzo (Photography), Sidney Levin and Michael A. Stevenson (Editors), Patrick Williams (Music), Robert Luthardt (Production

Design), Phillip Bennett (Art Director), Charles Pierce (Set Decorator), Theoni V. Aldredge (Costumes), Joe Di Bella (Makeup), Kathryn L. Blondell (Hair), Augie Lohman (Special Effects), Wayne Fitzgerald (Titles). Color, 92 minutes. Filmed at Warner Bros. Studios in Burbank, California.

CAST: Peter Falk (Lou Peckinpaugh); Ann-Margret (Jezebel Dezire, aka Nadia Gladdia Poppenescu); Eileen Brennan (Betty DeBoop); Sid Caesar (Ezra Dezire); Stockard Channing (Bess Duffy); James Coco (Marcel); Dom DeLuise (Pepe Damascus); Louise Fletcher (Marlene DuChard); John Houseman (Jasper Blubber); Madeline Kahn (Mrs. Carmen Montenegro, aka Denise Manderely/Wanda Coleman/Gilda Dabney/ Chloe LaMarr/Alma Chalmers/Alma Palmers/Vivien Purcell/Diane Glucksman/Mrs. Danvers/Natasha Ublenskaya/Sophie DeVega/Mary Jones/Lady Edwina Morgan St. Paul/Norma Shearer/Barbara Stanwyck); Fernando Lamas (Paul DuChard); Marsha Mason (Georgia Merkle); Phil Silvers (Hoppy); Abe Vigoda (Sgt. Rizzuto); Paul Williams (Boy); Nicol Williamson (Colonel Schlissel, aka Colonel Prince Count Baron von Schlisseldorf); Emory Bass (Butler); Carmine Caridi (Sgt. Crosetti); James Cromwell (Schnell); Scatman Crothers (Tinker); David Ogden Stiers (Captain); Vic Tayback (Lt. DiMaggio); Carole Wells (Hat Check Girl); John Calvin (Qvicker); Barry Michlin (Bandleader); Jonathan Banks (Cabbie); Lew Gallo (Cop); Lee McLaughlin (Fat Man); Zale Kessler and Jerry Ziman (Couriers); Wally Berns (Floyd Merkle); Bella Bruck (Scrub Woman); Henry Sutton (Desk Clerk); Maurice Marks (Doorman); Joe Ross (Michel); Dean Perry, George Rondo and Ronald L. Schwary (Cab Drivers); Louis H. Kelly and Charles A. Bastin (Croupiers); Armando Gonzalez (Bartender); Gary L. Dyer and Steven Fisher (Men in Crusades Bar); Laurie Hagan and Nancy Warren (Elegant Ladies); Nancy Marlowe Coyne and Lynn Griffis (Ladies of the Night); Paula Friel, Sheila Sisco and Lauren Simon (Military Wives); Cindy Lang (Navy Wife); Tina Ritt (Army Wife); David Matthau (Military Man); Garyl Alexander and Michele Bernath (Dancers); George F. Simmons (Reporter); Joree Sirianni (Cigarette Girl); Cornell Chulay (German Singer).

SONGS: "Taking a Chance on Love" (music by Vernon Duke with lyrics by John La Touche and Ted Fetter), Nix; "La Vie en Rose" (music by Marguerite Monnot and Louis Guglielmi with lyrics by Edith Piaf), Eileen Brennan; "Bye Bye Blackbird" (Ray Henderson), Rix; "Ain't She Sweet" (music by Milton Ager and lyrics by Jack Yellen), Nix; "Deutschlandlied" (music by Joseph Haydn and lyrics by August Heinrich Hoffmann von Fallersleben), Nicol Williamson, James Cromwell and John Calvin; "Les Marseillaise" (Claude Joseph Rouget de Lisle), Fernando Lamas, James Coco, David Ogden Stiers and Louise Fletcher; "Deep Purple" (music by Peter DeRose with lyrics by Mitchell Parish), Peter Falk and Eileen Brennan; "Jeepers Creepers" (music by Harry Warren and lyrics by Johnny Mercer), piano and Scatman Crothers and orchestra under end credits; "I'm Getting Sentimental over You" (music by George Bassman and lyrics by Ned Washington), Rix; "Ain't Misbehavin'" (Fats Waller and Harry Brooks), Crusades bar; "Mimi" (music by Richard Rodgers with lyrics by Lorenz Hart), Maurice Chevalier as tune on Paul's golden watch; "Heigh-Ho" (music by Frank Churchill and lyrics by Larry Morey), Peter Falk; "Georgia on My Mind" (music by Hoagy Carmichael and lyrics by Stuart Gorrell), Oakland Ferry Station.

SYNOPSIS: In 1939, Floyd Merkle, the partner of San Francisco private investigator Lou Peckinpaugh, is found murdered. At Nix Place Lou reunites with his former lover,

Marlene DuChard, who is now married to Paul. News comes that Paris has fallen to the Germans. Lou is contacted by Jasper Blubber, who tells him of a missing Albanian diamond necklace that he wants, which has been stolen by the Romanian Vladimir Tserijemiwtz. The name is unscrambled to be Ezra C.V. Mildew Dezire, Jr. Lou visits Dezire, who is shot before he can shoot Lou. Marcel appears at Lou's office with a wrapped parcel that is thought to be the diamonds. Lou gives the parcel to Jasper in exchange for the papers, but inside are only eggs with baby chicks. At Oakland Ferry Station, Colonel Schlisser is shot by Georgia, and Paul catches a ferry, leaving Marlene with Lou.

NOTES: In another spoof like *Murder by Death,* Simon mixes the plot and characters from *The Maltese Falcon* (1941) and *Casablanca* (1942) together with characters and lines from *The Big Sleep* (1946), *To Have and Have Not* (1944), *A Streetcar Named Desire,* and *Chinatown* (1974) for comic effect. The narrative leaves a lot of unresolved plot points and the end is particularly inexplicable; however, such slight material is easily forgiven because of its comic genre.

The main characters recall those in the films being parodied. Lou is a mixture of Sam Spade from *The Maltese Falcon* and Rick Blaine from *Casablanca.* Other character matches from *The Maltese Falcon* are Mrs. Montenegro as Brigid O'Shaughnessy, Georgia Merkle as Iva Archer, Pepe Damascus as Joel Cairo, Jasper Blubber as Kasper Gutman, Bess as Effie Perine, Boy as Wilmer Cook, Lt. DiMaggio as Tom Polhaus, Sgt. Rizzuto as Dundy, and Floyd Merkle as Miles Archer. Nix Place recalls Rick's Café Americain from *Casablanca,* and other *Casablanca* character substitutions are Tinker as Sam, Colonel Schlissel as Major Heinrich Strasser, Marlene DuChard as Ilsa Lund, Paul DuChard as Victor Lazlo, and Marcel as Carl. Betty DeBoop replaces Marie "Slim" Browning from *To Have and Have Not.* Jezebel and Ezra Dezire channel Carmen Sternwood and General Sternwood from *The Big Sleep,* and their butler is modelled on Norris the butler. Jezebel and Ezra have also been likened to the characters Velma Valento/ Helen Grayle and Lewin Lockridge Grayle from *Murder, My Sweet* (1945).

Simon also references a number of other features from the earlier films. For example, Lou reminds the pianist Sam that he is never to play "Jeepers Creepers." Sam's saying that Marlene told him to is a parody of the use of "As Time Goes By" in *Casablanca.* She later says to Lou, "Of all the cheap gin joints in the world I picked this one," which is a variation on Sam's line in *Casablanca*: "Of all the gin joints, in all the towns, in all the world, she walks into mine."

The wrapped parcel recalls the bird statuette from *The Maltese Falcon,* though here the contents are baby chicks inside a dozen eggs. The self-slapping that Lou makes the boy do recalls the slap Sam Spade gives Joel Cairo in the same film. The competitive singing at Nix parodies the singing of "Deutschlandlied" and "Les Marseillaise" in *Casablanca.* The plane that Ilsa and Victor catch at the end of *Casablanca* is replaced by a ferry, and here only Paul catches it. Also the climax has Paul more concerned about getting the papers than Marlene. The papers in *Casablanca* are letters of transit, but here they are a liquor license for Paul's Oakland French restaurant. Mrs. Montenegro's claim that Tserijemiwtz is her husband and father recalls Evelyn Mulwray, whose sister is also her daughter in *Chinatown.*

Simon mixes bad lines with mainly mildly funny ones, although there are some

Clockwise from middle left: Marsha Mason, Madeline Kahn, Louise Fletcher, Stockard Channing, Eileen Brennan, Ann-Margret, and Peter Falk at center, in a still for *The Cheap Detective* (1978).

occasional good ones. Marcel tells Colonel Schlissel that Betty has returned from the islands. The colonel asks her, "Caribbean or Virgin," and she replies, "Well, let's just say I came back a Caribbean." Marlene delivers metaphorical platitudes and the colonel comments, "There goes a brave, beautiful and extremely boring woman."

The farcical nature of the material is evident from the nonsensical opening scrawl, which references both the opening scrawl of *The Maltese Falcon* and the opening narration of *Casablanca*. The opening scene is also farcical since the shooting victims are all shown to be frozen in positions that they would not be able to maintain after actually being shot in the head. This becomes a running gag, since Marcel and Colonel Schlissel each remain standing after being shot later. There are several other running gags: Lou always refuses to leave tips for cabbies and he produces a ready-made drink from his top drawer; women tell Lou of their sexual encounters, which he does not want to hear; and Mrs. Montenegro uses a false name fifteen times, exaggerating Brigid's behavior in *The Maltese Falcon*, in which she did it twice. Mrs. Montenegro's changes of identity often come with a change of hair color, which gets a payoff in the parcel-opening scene, when her hair is shown to be multi-colored and she says that she plans to use her share of the money to get her hair done.

More farcical touches are Mrs. Montenegro, first seen in Lou's office lying back in a chair and thought to be dead but later revealed to only be asleep. Simon prefigures Lou telling Lt. DiMaggio to tell Sgt. Rizzuto to get off his back after the sergeant literally leans on Lou's back. Jasper Blubber asks Lou to meet him at the Crusades bar, and when he enters asking for "Blubber," many fat men turn around to him. Lou gets punched by one of them who considers the term blubber to be an insult. Lou is told that someone has broken into his apartment, and inside separately are Marlene, Betty and Georgia. The gag is that Bess arrives at the door just as Marlene asks if there have been any other women in his life, and Bess is still there when Georgia leaves. Another gag demonstrates the duplicity of Ezra and Jezebel when Ezra slips Lou a note that reads, "Don't trust her," and Jezebel slips Lou a note that reads, "Don't trust him either."

Director Robert Moore plays with the visual conventions of the genres, with much use of Venetian blinds, film noir lighting and fog in the street. He first presents Mrs. Montenegro in an extreme close-up of her mouth when she talks on the telephone, and Jasper is seen only as an arm when he is on the telephone with Lou. However, Moore cannot enliven the film's third act, which is a letdown. Some of the actors make more of an impression than others. Louise Fletcher does a spot-on imitation of Ingrid Bergman's earnestness, and Ann-Margret's brief use of Jezebel's Romanian accent is pleasing. Dom DeLuise has a good moment when Pepe winces at the boy slapping himself and yells, "He's had enough!" Madeline Kahn supplies an amusing scream of excitement from Mrs. Montenegro when the parcel is being opened, Marsha Mason over-emotes appropriately as Georgia, and Eileen Brennan is funny as the masochistic Betty.

In the DVD featurette "A Conversation with Neil Simon," the writer says that *The Maltese Falcon* is his favorite film. He advises that the scene at Nix was filmed at Warner Bros., using some of the light fixtures and props from *Casablanca* and also some of the same actors as waiters. The final scene was shot on the same soundstage as the final scene in *Casablanca*. Simon says the studio was reluctant to approve the film, believing spoofs never really worked, since they rely on the audience knowing the original to appreciate the references. However, he felt that this film was an exception as the humor worked independently of the original sources.

RELEASE: June 9, 1978, with the taglines "Who dunnit? This time it's Neil Simon who's really dunnit" and "He knows every cheap trick, cheap joke, cheap shot and cheap dame in the book."

REVIEWS: A mixed reaction from Vincent Canby in the *New York Times*, Clive Hirschhorn in *The Columbia Story*, Les Keyser in *Hollywood in the Seventies* and Robert K. Johnson in *Neil Simon*.

DVD: Released by Sony Pictures Home Entertainment on November 13, 2001.

REMAKES: A television pilot was broadcast by NBC on June 3, 1980, loosely based on the film. Flip Wilson starred as Eddie Krowler (sometimes sourced as Eddie Krowder), a Los Angeles private detective. It was written by Richard Powell and directed by Edward H. Feldman.

Seems Like Old Times (1980)

Columbia Pictures/Rastar Films.

CREW: Jay Sandrich (Director), Ray Stark (Producer), Margaret Booth (Associate Producer), Roger M. Rothstein (Executive Producer), Neil Simon (Screenplay), David M. Walsh (Photography), Michael A. Stevenson (Editor), Marvin Hamlisch (Music), Gene Callahan (Production Design), Pete Smith (Art Director), Lee Poll (Set Decorator), Betsy Cox (Costumes), Tom Case (Makeup), Kathryn Blondell (Hair), Bob Nolan (Special Effects). Color, 102 minutes. Filmed in April 1980 on location at Carmel, California, and at the Warner Bros. Studios in Burbank.

CAST: Goldie Hawn (Glenda "Glen" Parks), Chevy Chase (Nicholas "Nick" Gardenia/Harris J. Friedlander), Charles Grodin (Ira J. Parks), Harold Gould (Judge John Channing), George Grizzard (Governor, aka Stanley), Yvonne Wilder (Aurora), T.K. Carter (Chester), Robert Guillaume (Fred), Marc Alaimo (Bee Gee Ramone), Judd Omen (Warren "Dex" Dexter), Joseph Running Fox (Thomas Jefferson Wolf Call), Ray Tracey (Robert Broken Feather), Bill Zuckert and Jerry Houser (Gas Station Attendants), David Haskell and Ed Griffith (Policemen), Chris Lemmon (Charlie, Policeman), Fay Hauser (Anne), Carolyn Fromson (Ellen, Bank Teller), Sandy Lipton (Jean), Herb Armstrong (Jack), Natividad Rios Kearsley (Rosita), Dolores Aguirre (Conchita), Rosanna Huffman (Court Clerk), Edmund Stoiber (Ezra), Alice Sachs (Mrs. Ezra), Ann Cooper (Jackie, Ira's Secretary), Shirley Anthony (Bank Customer), Denise Franc (Stenographer), Roberta Storm (Party Guest).

SONGS: "I'm on Your Side" (Marvin Hamlisch), party; "Theme from *The High and the Mighty*" (Dimitri Tiomkin), whistled by Chevy Chase.

SYNOPSIS: Writer Nick Gardenia is kidnapped from his Big Sur cabin by Bee Gee and Dex and forced to rob the Carmel bank. After being released by the bandits, Nick seeks shelter at the Brentwood house of his ex-wife lawyer Glenda, who is married to Ira Parks, the Los Angeles district attorney. The governor comes to dinner and Nick is apprehended. Bee Gee and Dex attempt to rob another bank with the Parks' cook, Aurora, as their victim. The men are caught and they make a bargain plea in exchange for their admission that Nick is innocent. Nick leaves the Parks at the courthouse. When the couple go on a vacation and have a road accident, Glenda finds Nick in the nearby Big Sur cabin.

NOTES: Simon's screenplay presents the subjects of marriage and ex-boyfriends, and explores the themes of jealousy, fidelity, and the difference between conservative and radical behavior. Simon features a combination of wit and bad jokes.

Bad timing and farce are used as narrative devices. The best example of bad timing is when Nick hides in the back of Glenda's car and it is stopped by police, who then attempt to escort it to the hospital after Nick lies that he is sick. A funny example is when the governor's chauffeur throws coffee out of his car window as Nick crawls past. The best example of the use of farce is the dinner scene, in which Nick fights offstage with Ira, and after Glenda rings the serving bell, Nick is pushed into the dining room where the governor is. The courtroom climax tries for farce, with a topper where Glenda's dogs appear in court, but fails. The scene recalls the climax of the comedy *What's Up, Doc?* (1972), since again all the previous narrative is explained for a judge.

From left: Chevy Chase, Charles Grodin, and Goldie Hawn with their dog co-stars in a still for *Seems Like Old Times* (1980).

However, the dogs' appearances don't have the comic payoff that the earlier film has when the judge's desk collapses. Here the judge gets a mild laughline, "Something fascinating has just come up, which in this case is redundant."

Simon uses running gags, which include Nick's repeatedly telling Glenda what to say, the same judge turning up for different trials, and the dogs—used generally as a disturbing force—always barking at Ira. Simon supplies expected narrative points such as Nick's appearance at the house when the governor comes for dinner, and Glenda's temptation to be with Nick again, but also a comic payoff when we see Nick under Glenda's bed. Ira repeatedly re-enters the room to be with Glenda, who knows that Nick is there, and she refuses to have sex with him because of it.

Glenda is the object of desire of two men, and is shown to be eccentric in her ownership of six dogs and several rabbits, by her growing corn in her rose garden, and by hiring probationary defendants as employees. This behavior suggests she is better matched with the innocent fugitive Nick than with the more conversative Ira. Conversely, her role as the pampered wife of the district attorney suggests a closer alignment with Ira. The idea that Nick is more radical than Ira is offered in the narrative by the way he hides in Glenda's house and attempts to romance her and steal her away from her husband. The narrative setup, though, has Nick as the victim of circumstances rather than the instigator of the crime that he is being pursued for. After the climax Glenda tells Nick that she chooses Ira over him. However, the ending is more ambiguous: Glenda smiles when she sees Nick in the cabin, which suggests that she might have a future with him after all.

Despite the romantic-comedy contrivance of Nick's going to Glenda for help, presumably because he still has feelings for her, we do wonder why he doesn't just go home to his own house. This is established as being on loan to Nick from a friend, so it is doubtful that the police would know to look for him there. The best narrative idea is the delayed reveal of the black eye that Ira gets from the fight with Nick. We don't see it in the bedroom scene after the dinner scene, and it is only shown when Ira gets a close-up in court.

Despite Simon's use of comic devices, director Jay Sandrich fails to make the film funny. However, he does features some clever cuts. He transitions from a photograph of Glenda in Ira's office to a close-up of the real Glenda, and from Glenda looking at a photograph of Nick in her garden to her looking at it in her bedroom. There is another clever transition from Nick eating stale candy from a vending machine to Chester eating hors d'oeuvres at the Parks' party.

There is something lacking in the performances of all three lead actors that contributes to the failure of the comedy. As Nick, Chevy Chase does demonstrate a talent for physical comedy with pratfalls, but while Nick's sensual nature is revealed when he kisses Glenda, the character lacks charm. Goldie Hawn's Glenda is funny when she coughs to cover up the sound of Nick's handling a paper bag in the car, and she looks great in a black nightgown, yet she only gets to laugh once in the entire film. Charles Grodin underplays Ira's anger, but perhaps the character dynamic would have worked better if he had not. The best performance is that of Yvonne Wilder, who brings a more accomplished farcical style to her portrayal of Aurora.

In his book on Simon, Robert K. Johnson claims that the screenplay was inspired by the comedy *The Talk of the Town* (1942), directed by George Stevens. In that film Cary Grant plays a man falsely accused of crimes, hidden in the home of a vacationing judge (Ronald Colman) by the judge's landlady (Jean Arthur).

Marsha Mason and Burt Reynolds were originally announced to play the leads in the 1980 film. Paul McCartney recorded a title song that was not used. In his book *Being Hal Ashby: The Life of a Hollywood Rebel*, Nick Dawson claims that the narrative was based on Simon's marriage with Marsha Mason and, perhaps specifically, the retained friendship with her first husband.

RELEASE: December 19, 1980, with the tagline "alone—at last...."

REVIEWS: Praised by Janet Maslin in the *New York Times* and Clive Hirschhorn in *The Columbia Story*. A mixed reaction from Roger Ebert in the *Chicago Sun-Times* and Robert K. Johnson in *Neil Simon*.

AWARDS: Charles Grodin received a Razzie Award nomination for Worst Supporting Actor.

DVD: Released by Sony Pictures Home Entertainment on January 1, 2002.

Max Dugan Returns (1983)

20th Century–Fox.

CREW: Herbert Ross (Director/Producer), Neil Simon (Producer/Screenplay), Richard Marks (Editor), David Shire (Music), Albert Brenner (Production Design), Garret Lewis (Set Decorator), David Haber (Art Director), Bob Mackie (Costumes), Giorgio Armani (Mr. Sutherland's Clothes), Dan Striepeke (Makeup), Barbara Lampson (Hair), Alan Lorimer (Special Effects), Kurtz and Friends (Title Animation). Color, 98 minutes. Filmed on location at Alexander Hamilton High School and in California in April 1982.

CAST: Marsha Mason (Nora McPhee, née Dugan); Jason Robards (Max Dugan/Mr. Parker/Gus Wittgenstein); Donald Sutherland (Lieutenant Brian Costello); Matthew Broderick (Michael "Mike" McPhee); Dody Goodman (Mrs. Litke); Sal Viscuso (Coach Roy); Panchito Gomez (Luis); Charley Lau (Himself); Mari Gorman (Pat); Brian Part (Kevin Costello); Billie Bird (Older Woman); Tessa Richarde (Blonde at Shoe Store); James Staahl (Man at Shoe Store); Duke Stroud and Sondra Blake (Teachers); David Morse and Howard Himelstein (Shoe Store Cops); Santos Morales (Grocer); Irene Olga Lopez (Grocer's Wife); Tom Rosales, Jr. (Robber); Tommy Fridley (Steve); Kiefer Sutherland (Bill); Bill Aylesworth (Chris); Lydia Nicole (Celia); Elisa Dolenko (Maria); Marc Jefferson (Wendall); Tom Spratley (Truck Washer); Ray Girardin (Umpire); Joey Coleman (3rd Baseman); Bradley Lieberman and Devoreaux White (Boys); Pop Attmore (Baseball Player); Grace Woodard (Maitre d'café); Ken Neumeyer (Waiter); Frank D'Annibale (Bears Coach); John Corvello (Basketball Coach), Carmen Silveroli, Sr. (Shoe Store Manager); George Wilbur (Cop in Car); Robert D'Arcy (Cabbie); Shelley Morrison (Mother); John Moio and Gary Coombs (Policemen); Benjie Bancroft (Policeman at Station); Della Thompson, Ty Fredericks, Kent Freutziger, Patrick Rodriguez and Dorian Turner (Students).

SYNOPSIS: Widowed English literature teacher Nora McPhee lives in Venice, California, with her fifteen-year-old son, Michael. Her sixty-three-year-old ex-con father, estranged for twenty-eight years, appears and asks to spend his last six months with the family. Max brings a suitcase with stolen money totaling $687,000, buys extravagant presents and redecorates the house. Nora agrees to let him stay if he tells Mike the truth about himself. Nora's new boyfriend, police lieutenant Brian Costello, meets Max and discovers he is a fugitive. Max leaves for Brazil, but not before watching Mike play a baseball game.

NOTES: Simon's screenplay recalls his prior film *I Ought to Be in Pictures* with its subject of a family's estranged father. Here the difference is that the father returns to the family rather than the family to him. The fact that Max is dying adds an urgency to his agenda that the scenario in the previous film lacks; however, the material presented remains slight. In his memoir *The Play Goes On*, Simon draws parallels between the narrative and his own life; he had a father with a weak heart who abandoned his family.

Although Simon apparently intended the film to be a comedy, he only supplied one funny line. Nora asks Max how she knows he has six months to live, and he replies, "We could sit here and wait." There is one visual gag. Max is shown seemingly playing the violin until he turns off music, revealing that the sound has not been coming from him. Simon attempts a running gag of Nora having vehicles stolen from her. However, the Mercedes apparently being stolen at the climax is a surprise when we see that Max has taken the car so he can drive to Brazil.

The theatrical device of a false exit is used twice. Nora stops Max after he has left her house, since she decides that he can stay after all, and later Max states his intention

Left: Marsha Mason and Jason Robards, and right, Donald Sutherland in a composite still for *Max Dugan Returns* (1983).

of leaving the family but reappears to see Mike's baseball game. The narrative includes instances of fate and portent. Fate provides Nora with the windfall of Max's money, although the fact of the money's being stolen means that it comes with consequences. Fate also allows Brian to catch a store robber when he is out teaching Nora how to ride the motorbike he has lent her. The rain that prefigures Max's appearance is a dramatic portent of both good and bad fortune for Nora. Another portentous touch is the man seen watching Mike's second baseball game. At first we think that someone is chasing Max, but the man is Charley Lau, the Chicago White Sox coach. We assume that Mike's game will improve with Charley's coaching, and it does since in the third baseball game he hits a home run. The fact that Nora, Brian, Charley and Max are watching, and that Brian's son Kevin is the pitcher, adds to the payoff.

The screenplay's main characters are of varied morality. Nora is a middle class schoolteacher living in conditions that mark her as a person ready for financial improvement. However, she demonstrates poor judgment and carelessness with valuable possessions. She leaves her keys in the car's ignition, which allows it to be stolen outside Carmen's Shoe Repairs; leaves the motorbike unchained so that it too is stolen, from the Sharpe Field parking lot; and leaves her home door unlocked, allowing Brian to enter and find Max. Nora is also careless in getting a speeding ticket on the motorbike. Despite these setbacks Nora refuses to accept Max's money and the gifts he buys her with it. When she lies to Brian about Max it reads more as her protecting her father than wanting to deceive her boyfriend, and her willingness to sacrifice a potential romantic partner also adds to the sense of her moral strength.

Mike's initially bad performance at baseball suggests that he has inherited Nora's carelessness. As a child we don't expect he will also refuse Max's gifts. But the fact he chooses to keep Plato the dog in preference to all the gadgets Max has given him is somewhat redeeming of the boy.

Max is presented as equal in moral ambiguity to Herb Tucker in *I Ought to Be in Pictures.* Max has both abandoned the family and stolen money, and he continues to lie to Nora. He promises not to buy more gifts but he doesn't keep his promise. He also promises that he will tell Mike the truth about himself and the stolen money, but he initially does not. Max's duplicity continues when he leaves alone after Nora has suggested that the family all leave the country together. His purchase of the video equipment and big-screen television gets narrative payoff when Max records a goodbye video, since it appears that he cannot say goodbye to Nora and Mike face-to-face.

Brian is also a character with mixed morality. His romantic interest in Nora is expressed by his generosity in loaning her his motorbike. Being a policeman he is a narrative threat to Max, which is apparent when Brian meets him at the house and later follows him. Brian investigates Max's identity, but he chooses not to pursue him in the end, instead choosing his romance with Nora over his duty as a police officer.

Director Herbert Ross shows the theft of Nora's car in the window reflection of Carmen's Shoe Repair. He uses a split screen effect for a scene of two simultaneous dialogues between Max and Mike in the kitchen and between Nora and Brian on the telephone. Regrettably, this effect undermines both dialogues so that we can't understand either. Ross also has music overwhelming dialogue sometimes, and it swamps the montage of Charley coaching Mike. He uses slow motion for the climactic baseball game where we see the reaction to Mike hitting the ball on his third attempt.

Marsha Mason, as Nora, appears as an ash blonde in an unflattering hairstyle that is presumably designed to present her character as an ordinary woman. She is funny in her angry frustration over Max and in the suspicious looks she gives him, and pleasingly calm when rejecting Brian. Jason Robards makes Max likeable, and Donald Sutherland's Brian is funny in his reaction to Nora's rejection of him on their date. Sutherland nearly makes the lieutenant unlikeably aggressive when pursuing his police agenda, but Simon, in having Brian choose Nora over the hunt for Max, returns the character to a conventional romantic-comedy sweetheart.

RELEASE: March 25, 1983, with the taglines "Prices are double. Your love life's in trouble. The car won't start. Your boss has no heart. The door squeaks. The roof leaks. Your stereo just went mono. All you need is a little Max Dugan" and "It's time to feel good again."

REVIEWS: Praised by Janet Maslin in the *New York Times.* A mixed reaction from Roger Ebert in the *Chicago Sun-Times.* Ebert writes that the film is "watchable and sort of sweet" and thinks that Robards gives a poignant performance. But he also writes, "There's hardly a moment in the whole movie that would be confused with daily life as it is really lived."

DVD: Released by Starz/Anchor Bay on July 12, 2005.

The Slugger's Wife (1985)

Columbia Pictures/Delphi Productions II/Rastar.

CREW: Hal Ashby (Director), Ray Stark (Producer), Margaret Booth (Executive Producer), Neil Simon (Screenplay), Caleb Deschanel (Photography), George C. Villasenor and Don Brochu (Editors), Patrick Williams (Music), Michael Riva (Production Design), Bruce Weintraub (Set Decorator), Rick Carter (Art Director), Ann Roth (Costumes), Kaye Pownall (Hair), Lee C. Harman and Barbara Maggi (Makeup). Color, 104 minutes. Filmed on location in Atlanta, Georgia, including the Atlanta-Fulton County Stadium, from March 14, 1984.

CAST: Michael O'Keefe (Daryl "Slugger" Palmer); Rebecca De Mornay (Debbie Palmer, née Huston); Martin Ritt (Burley De Vito); Randy Quaid (Moose Granger); Cleavant Derricks (Manny Alvarado); Lisa Langlois (Aline Cooper); Loudon Wainwright III (Gary); Georgann Johnson (Marie De Vito); Danny Tucker (Coach O'Brien); Lynn Whitfield (Tina Alvarado); Al Garrison (Guard); Nicandra Hood (Nurse); Ginger Taylor (Sherry); Kay McClelland (Peggy); Julie Kemp (Paloma); Tina Kincaid, Martha Harrison and Becky Pate (Baseball Wives); Dennis Burkley (Chuck); Alisha Das (Lola); Dan Biggers (Preacher); Justine Thielemann (Iris Granger); Marc Clement (Mr. Davis); Richard Alan Reiner (Patron at Zelda's); Valerie Mitchell (Waitress at Limelight); Edwin H. Cipot (Cuneo); Stephen H. Stier (Varsity Patron); David R. Yood (Cop in Varsity); Wallace G. Merck (Fan in Limelight); Johnny B. Watson Jr. (Gateman); Alex Hawkins ("Hawkins"); Mort Schwartz (Man); John B. Sterling (Himself); George Stokes (Stage Manager); Harmon L. Wages (Interviewer); John W. Bradley (Himself); Jerome Olds (Musician); Starshower (Band); Erby Walker and Phillipe Fontanelli (Waiters); Steve Daniels, Jr., Henry J. Rountree, George Jack Klarman, Collin Fagan and David M. Pallone (Umpires); Kevin James Barnes (Public Address); John Lawhorn (Coach Reckon); Douglas Garland Nave and Bill G. Fite (Catchers); Al Hrobosky and Mark Fidrych (Baseball Players); Pete Van Weiren and Ernie Johnson (Baseball Narrators); Skip Caray and Nick Charles (Sportscasters); Chico Renfroe, Anthony Peck, Corey B. McPherrin, Paul S. Ryden, Charles Darden, John Buren Solberg and Brad Nessler (Reporters); Helen Dell (Stadium Organist).

SONGS: "Love (It's Just the Way It Goes)" (music by Quincy Jones, Glen Ballard and Clif Magness, and lyrics by Carole Bager Sayer), John Farnham and Sarah M. Taylor, heard under end credits; "Oh Jimmy" (Sarah M. Taylor), Rebecca De Mornay; "Hungry Heart" (Bruce Springsteen), Lisa Langlois; "Little Red Corvette" (Prince), Rebecca De Mornay; "All American Boy" (Van Stephenson and Dave Robbins), Van Stephenson in Varsity restaurant; "Ragtop Day" (Jimmy Buffet, Michael Utley and Will Jennings), Jimmy Buffet; "Singin' in the Rain" (Arthur Freed and Nacio Herb Brown), Michael O'Keefe; "Hey Hey My My" (Neil Young), Loudon Wainwright III and Rebecca De Mornay; "Love the One You're With" (Stephen Stills), Lowden Wainwright III and Rebecca De Mornay; "Party Animal" (James Ingram, Mark Vieha and Richard Page), James Ingram; "Human Racing" (Nik Kershaw), Nik Kershaw; "When I Need You" (Carol Bayer Sager and Albert Hammond), Rebecca De Mornay; "Stray Cat Strut" (Brian Setzer), Lisa Langlois; "The Men All Pause" (Bernadette Cooper and Joyce "Fenderella" Irby), Klymaxx at Daryl's party; "El Rancho Grande," aka "I Love My Rancho Grande" (music by Silvano Ramos with Spanish lyrics by J.D. Del Moral), Freddy Fender at Daryl's party; "Summer in the City" (John Sebastian), Lisa Langlois; "Love Potion Number Nine" (Jerry Leiber and Mike Stoller), Lisa Langlois; "Wild Life" (Don Felder and Mark Jordan), Don Felder.

SYNOPSIS: Atlanta Braves baseball player Daryl Palmer sees Debbie Huston singing at the Limelight club and is infatuated with her. He scores two home runs and wins a dinner with her, and after dating, the couple get married. Daryl asks Debbie to stop working so she can be with him as his team travels in the season. She gets an opportunity to make an album, but needs to go on the road to write new songs. Debbie leaves Daryl but returns for the last game of the pennant, in which he scores a record-breaking home run. She then leaves again to make her album.

NOTES: This screenplay explores the subject of marriage and the question of whether a woman who gets married should be willing to sacrifice her career in order to devote herself to her husband. The scenario echoes the reported relationship between Simon and Marsha Mason, who at first agreed to stop working when they married, but later refused to do so. Other sources suggest that the story was inspired by the relationship of Go-Go singer Belinda Carlisle and Los Angeles Dodgers player Mike Marshall. Baseball is strongly present in the narrative, coming after its use as a smaller plot point in *Max Dugan Returns*. The screenplay's interest in baseball, however, is just about the only thing that makes it recognizable as a Neil Simon project, since it is otherwise a negligible piece of work.

There is little genuine wit, although there are a few amusing touches. A screen at the baseball game where Daryl hits two home runs has "Palmer Power" shown with an open hand, and the final game has another screen image of an anguished-looking ball when Daryl again hits a home run. There are clever allusions to oral sex in Daryl's explanation of baseball to Debbie in bed, but the closest Simon comes to a funny line is an exchange between Daryl and his teammate Manny. Daryl says that his heart isn't in getting laid by a groupie, Peggy, and Manny replies, "Your heart ain't gonna get anywhere near it."

The narrative has several surprises. The Braves do not win the climactic pennant game, despite Daryl's achieving his goal of breaking the home run record. Debbie does not return to Daryl permanently, though we are led to believe that she will eventually do so. Another surprise is that Daryl does not want to have sex with another woman when he gets the opportunity, because he is still married. Interestingly, Debbie is not offered the same test, despite Gary's romantic attraction to her. Additionally, Daryl's punching Gary when he is provoked and breaking the windows of the Kansas City restaurant is violent behavior that is not continued.

The main character of Daryl is presented as loutish, chauvinistic, and not too bright. This seems to make Debbie his perfect match, since she presents as equally dim. Daryl's interest in her at first reads as obsessive, since his pursuit of her causes Debbie to crash her car. We assume that he does not do so deliberately to compromise her ability to travel for work; that's just a bonus. Daryl is shown to be a good baseball player who is able to hit two home runs out of the park to get a date with Debbie. She, on the other hand, is presented as a moderately successful club singer, with a mediocre voice, in a band that performs mostly cover songs.

After the couple are married Debbie agrees to put her career on hold so that she can go on tour with the team and watch Daryl play baseball. Interestingly, Debbie never thinks to ask him if he would be willing to stop playing to tour with her band. The implication is that Daryl's career is the more important. Since Daryl plays during the day and Debbie performs at night, we do wonder why both jobs can't be accommodated, although travel is clearly an issue. The conflict arises when Debbie gets an opportunity to make an album, providing that she has new material to record. She feels that the only way to accomplish this is to go on the road herself and polish new material on tour, instead of following Daryl to his ball games. Debbie is unsure what to do, although she tells her friend Tina that she

Daryl "Slugger" Palmer (Michael O'Keefe) flirts with Debbie Huston (Rebecca De Mornay) in a still for *The Slugger's Wife* (1985).

feels her husband has her on a "leash" and she is losing her identity. Finally she decides to go ahead with the tour, but rather than tell Daryl to his face, she leaves him a cowardly letter.

Simon may seem to empathize with both individuals, but Debbie's leaving is shown to have the expected detrimental effect more on Daryl's performance than hers. Unlike her husband, Debbie does not need to have her partner watching her perform to give her confidence. This idea of Daryl being the weaker player is important since he states an ambition to break the existing Hall of Fame record for home runs in a season, something that his broken confidence calls into question. His confidence is restored thanks to a ruse arranged by coach Burley, who passes off another singer, Aline, as Debbie to visit Daryl in the hospital after he has been hit by a ball during game practice. As we note Aline's physical resemblance to Debbie before the ruse, this plot point is not a surprise. Daryl's injury makes the charade more probable, assisted by Aline's being kept in shadow. It is a surprise that Debbie is not angry when Aline tells her of the ruse, which has seemed to help Daryl score a home run in the next game. Simon provides a twist on the ruse when Daryl realizes that Aline is not Debbie from her cold hands, and this is paid off later when he confronts Aline at the Limelight nightclub.

It is said that the film was taken away from director Hal Ashby in postproduction, which may explain how ordinary it mostly is. Nonetheless, there are some noteworthy elements. Intercuts are used between Debbie singing in clubs and Daryl playing baseball to show the characters' respective work. The music often upstages dialogue and the full playing of songs that Debbie's band performs reads as filler. However, two songs are used to make an impact. "When I Need You" is the best presented, since we see Daryl's reaction to Debbie having left him intercut as she sings it. Also the song has some emotion to it, unlike the others that Debbie performs. "Hey Hey My My" adds to the scene where Aline tells Debbie by telephone that she had impersonated her, and the camera is on Daryl playing ball when Aline breaks the news. Ashby gives himself a cameo in the Kansas City restaurant scene, sitting at the same table as Daryl but saying nothing.

Michael O'Keefe expresses pain and vulnerability when Daryl goes to see Debbie in Kansas City, before the moment is undermined by the character's violence. Rebecca De Mornay as Debbie uses a slow, soft speech pattern that suggests that her character is not too bright, although she has the street smarts to deal with unwanted admirers at her gigs.

It was rumored that producer Ray Stark had interested Warren Beatty in playing Daryl but that Beatty had subsequently turned down the part because he wanted more creative input and disagreed that Simon should have complete control. Daryl Hannah initially accepted the role of Debbie, then changed her mind, whereupon Stark is said to have sent her a bouquet of dead flowers. Stark originally hired Martin Ritt to direct, but ill health forced Ritt to withdraw, although he still agreed to take an acting part. Ritt is quoted as saying that he was relieved not to be the director, since he found that Stark "had no taste." In his book *Picking Up the Tab: The Life and Movies of Martin Ritt*, Carlton Jackson says that Simon also wanted Ritt for the film, because the two frequently participated in Hyde Park Sunday morning baseball games together.

In November 1983 Ashby was announced as director. In his book *Being Hal Ashby: Life of a Hollywood Rebel*, Nick Dawson devotes a chapter to the film. He claims that Stark had admired Ashby's work on *The Last Detail* (1973) and *Being There* (1979). He also quotes director of photography Caleb Deschanel, who claims that Ashby was hired by Stark because the director was "down and out" and Stark thought he could "push him around." Stark insisted that Ashby include product placement for certain companies and baseball teams. The setting for the film was changed from Houston to Atlanta because the Huston Astros' ground was not a hitter's park. Dawson thinks that the fact that Atlanta was the home of Coca-Cola, which owned Columbia Pictures, may also have been a factor. Debbie was also changed from being a country-and-Western singer to a pop singer.

Ashby is said to have been displeased with De Mornay's Southern accent and reshot work with her speaking without one. Dawson quotes Michael O'Keefe, who said that the actress was in over her head with the singing and acting aspects of the role. Tornadoes hit the set on three different occasions, and De Mornay was trapped in her trailer once when the wind picked it up and landed it with the door facing upward. De Mornay says it was Ashby who fought through the rain to pull her out to safety. She escaped with only a bruised eye, though her drama coach, who was also in the trailer, had torn arm ligaments.

The director was removed from the film by the producers because he had cut much of Simon's dialogue, preferring his actors to improvise their lines. This action by Ashby was a violation of his contract, which prohibited him from changing the script. Dawson claims that Ashby voluntarily withdrew from the film twice during the editing process. He asked that his name be removed from the film, and after going to the Director's Guild of America was awarded $2,500 in minimal damages since it was agreed that his directorial rights had been infringed upon. However, the viewed DVD shows that Ashby's name remains on the film, which is credited as "A Hal Ashby Film." Additionally, Dawson claims that producer Ray Stark punished Ashby by having his directing credit in the film moved from the opening to the closing credits. However, the viewed DVD has Ashby's name in the opening credits.

Dawson says that Simon was depressed after having divorced Marsha Mason, which resulted in the downbeat and humorless script, and his on-set rewriting changed the story from a romantic comedy to a bittersweet romance. Another problem was that Ashby was apparently indulging in drinking and cocaine use after hours, and he was found more than once by the film's security guards in an intoxicated state.

The legal agreement between Ashby and Stark had a disparagement clause that prohibited Ashby from bad-mouthing the film. However, this did not apply to Simon, who commented two weeks after it opened that the film is not what he wrote. He claimed that fifty pages of his script were cut, and that he had envisaged there would be very little music in the film. Simon felt that a perceived need to appeal to the MTV generation had led to the inclusion of all the songs. Dawson thinks that Simon's distaste for the film is why it is not mentioned in either of his memoirs. Stark would later comment publicly that he thought the film was terrible, that he regretted his participation in it, and that he blamed himself for hiring Ashby.

Dawson also writes about a cut scene, and about the original script's flashback structure, which Ashby insisted should be changed. The cut scene is said to have featured Atlanta Braves owner Ted Turner giving a pep talk to the team in the locker room.

RELEASE: March 29, 1985, with the taglines "How can a woman walk out on a love like this? Just Watch!" and "A love story about two of America's greatest pastimes."

REVIEWS: Lambasted by Janet Maslin in the *New York Times,* Clive Hirshhorn in *The Columbia Story,* and Nick Dawson in *Being Hal Ashby: Life of a Hollywood Rebel.* Maslin described the film as "resoundingly unfunny." A mixed reaction from Roger Ebert in the *Chicago Sun-Times.*

DVD: Released by Sony Pictures Home Entertainment on March 9, 2004.

The Marrying Man (1991)

Hollywood Pictures/Silver Screen Partners IV/Odyssey Entertainment.

CREW: Jerry Rees (Director); David Permut (Producer); David Streit (Co-Producer); Donald Kreiss (Associate Producer); Neil Simon (Screenplay); Donald E. Thorin (Photography); Michael Jablow (Editor); David Newman (Music); Stan Getz (Tenor Saxophone Solos); William F. Matthews (Production Design); Mark Mansbridge (Art Director); Jim Duffy (Set Decorator); Ruth Myers (Costumes); Jim Kail, Lisa Pharren and Monty Westmore (Makeup); Stephen A. Abrums (Ms. Basinger's Makeup); Jan Alexander,

Richard Sabre and Robert L. Stevenson (Hair); Judy Alexander Cory (Ms. Basinger's Hair); Jeffrey Hornaday (Choreography); Seth Riggs (Ms. Basinger's Vocal Consultant). Color, 118 minutes. Filmed on location at Greystone Park and Mansion, aka the Doheny Mansion, Beverly Hills; the Wilshire Ebell Theatre; the "Valentino Gate" at Paramount Studios; Castillo del Lago; Lancaster and Los Angeles, California. Interiors shot at the Ambassador Hotel in Los Angeles. Filming took place from May 19 to September 2, 1990, and in January 1991.

CAST: Kim Basinger (Victoria "Vicki" Rosemary Anderson), Alec Baldwin (Charles "Charley" Raymond Pearl), Robert Loggia (Lew Horner), Elisabeth Shue (Adele Horner), Paul Reiser (Phil Golden), Fisher Stevens (Sammy Fine), Peter Dobson (Tony Madden), Steve Hytner (George), Armand Assante (Benny "Bugsy" Siegel), Big John Studd (Dante), Jeremy Roberts (Gus Dinato), Tony Longo (Sam), Tom Milanovich (Andy), Tim Hauser (Woody), Carey Eidel (Cab Driver), Marla Heasley (Sheila), Karen Medak (Sherry), Rebecca Staab (Arlene), Melissa Behr (Dee), Paul Collins (Butler), Dave Florek (Gas Attendant), Geof Prysirr (Charlie the Bartender), Teresa Gilmore-Capps (Bugsy's Blonde), Alan Mandell (Justice #1), Elly Enriquez (Woo Ling), Joe Guzaldo (Announcer/Manager), Shanti Kahn (Nurse), Clarke Gordon (Charley's Father), Gretchen Wyler (Gwen), Susan Kellermann (Bobbie), Kathryn Layng (Emma), Janni Brenn (Liz), Joe Bellan (Waiter), Don Keefer (Justice #3), Jules I. Epstein (Maitre'd), Robin Frates (Grace), Kristen Cloke (Louise).

SONGS: "Let's Do It" (Cole Porter), Kim Basinger; "Murder, He Says" (Frank Loesser and Jimmy McHugh), Kim Basinger; "Why Can't You Behave?" (Cole Porter), Kim Basinger; "Honeysuckle Rose" (Andy Razaf and Thomas Waller), Kim Basinger; "Satisfy My Soul" (Buddy Johnson), Kim Basinger; "Love Is the Thing" (Ned Washington and Victor Popular Young), Kim Basinger; "Stompin' at the Savoy" (Benny Goodman, Edgar Sampson and Chick Webb); "L.D.'s Bounce" (Tim Hauser); "You're Driving Me Crazy (What Did I Do?!)" (Walter Donaldson) Alan Paul; "Mama Look a Boo Boo" (Lord Melody) (Fitzroy Alexander), Tim Hauser; "You Can't Be Mine (And Someone Else's Too)" (J.C. Johnson and Chick Webb), Billie Holiday in Vicki's bungalow; "Yardbird Suite" (Charlie Parker), Charlier Parker. Uncredited: "The Bridal Chorus" ("Treulich geführt"), aka "Here Comes the Bride" (Richard Wagner), wedding chapel; "Wedding March" (Felix Mendelssohn), wedding chapel.

SYNOPSIS: In San Francisco in 1956 Phil Golden sees band singer Vicki Anderson perform at Dexter's nightclub and tells his friends the story of her and "Toothpaste King" Charley Pearl. In 1948 Charley is in Hollywood and engaged to Adele Horner. His male friends take him to Las Vegas for a bachelor party. At the El Ranch Vegas club he meets Vicki, who he learns is the girlfriend of "Bugsy" Siegel. They get caught having sex by Bugsy, who forces them to get married. After three months the marriage is annulled and Adele again agrees to marry Charley. But instead he remarries Vicki after finding her at the St. Tropez nightclub. The couple move to Boston after Charley's father dies. After two years Vicki leaves him. Charley again finds her in Las Vegas and they remarry again. After she bears him four children, Charley goes bankrupt when his venture into Pearl Pictures fails. Once again, Vicki leaves Charley and he asks her to marry him for the fourth time in 1956 in San Francisco.

NOTES: This screenplay presents the subjects of marriage and physical attraction, and explores the theme of conventional versus radical behavior. Simon features the "F" bomb to demonstrate the lowbrow expression of certain characters. The plot point of a woman sacrificing her career to be a housewife evokes that in *The Slugger's Wife*, which recalled what Marsha Mason did for Simon, and the idea of a man remarrying the same woman reflects Simon's own two marriages to Diane Lander in 1987 and 1990.

Simon uses the device of narration by Phil and a narrative of flashback. That the barman that Vicki speaks to is named Charlie allows for a romantic comedy introduction to Charley, who is also there. The screenplay includes Charley's gnomic line, "Every woman I've ever been with has made her living from disappointments." The narrative includes historical inaccuracies in regards to the film career of Rita Hayworth, including the fiction of her making a film entitled *That Girl from Chile* in 1954 with Charley's friends, Tony and Phil. There is also an odd moment when Charley laughs because he is scared of what Bugsy will do to him. Narrative surprises include Bugsy's punishment of forcing Charley and Vicki to marry, Vicki's temporary disappearance from the narrative although we assume that she will return, and Vicki's pause during the third marriage ceremony to Charley before she agrees to remarry. Simon also uses a comic cliché regarding Charley's father wanting to meet Vicki before he dies, since she leaves his bedside after he comes out of his coma and she returns after he dies.

The screenplay has some wit. When Sammy tells his friends that Esther Williams likes one of his songs and MGM wants her to sing it in her next picture, George responds, "Where? Underwater?" On learning that Charley is in the toothpaste business, Vicki comments, "No wonder you smile so much." Lew comments to Adele about Charley remarrying Vicki, "Last time he tells us he got married at gunpoint. What did they have this time? A cannon up his ass?" Adele hopes that Charley will change his mind again and her father, Lew replies, "What the hell did he see in you in the first place?" Sammy can't believe that he is to marry his girlfriend, Sherry, and comments to his friends, "I think she had a hypnotist come over while I was sleeping." Charley criticizes Gus' suit by saying that it "looks like the lining of a better suit." There is a funny payoff to Charley being in the toothpaste business when we see him brush his teeth to give feedback to his associates on a proposed flavor, and Tony's toupee is said to be made from his own hair.

The narrative distinguishes between women who are "hot" and those who are not. A "hot" woman in the film is physically attractive but "trouble." Vicki is assumed to be hot and therefore trouble. The trouble in the three marriages that Vicki and Charley enter into is caused by her only the first time, since it is a marriage the couple are forced into by Vicki's ex-boyfriend, Bugsy. Although Vicki leaves Charley in the second and third marriages, she does so as a justifiable reaction to his behavior. In the second marriage he makes her give up her singing career and then neglects her at home, and in the third, he attempts to promote her career by building the Hollywood studio but blames her for his bankruptcy when it fails. Ultimately the pair is shown to be willing to marry for a fourth time because they have both overwhelming physical attraction and love for each other.

In his first engagement to Adele, Charley chooses to marry her because she is "dependable" rather than hot. He wants to put his days as a playboy behind him and become conventional, though when Charley and Adele are kissing he asks her to bite his mouth, which suggests that he wishes to retain some radical behavior. The fact that Charley's mother abandoned the family when he was young may explain his lack of faith of women and this need for dependability. Charley's behavior changes from relative conventionality to radical recklessness when he decides to reject Adele for the second time and remarry Vicki. However, he returns to convention when he assumes leadership of his father's business in Boston, has Vicki sacrifice her career for him, and prefers to work in bed rather than have sex with her. Charley makes a radical move in building the Hollywood studio for Vicki, and the decision to have four children in lieu of a Hollywood career is the epitome of a conventional lifestyle. The narrative's conclusion implies that Charley will regain his conventional business success after he marries Vicki for a fourth time.

Vicki's beauty puts her in the category of a "hot" woman, but the idea that she is "trouble" is shown to be misleading. Her initial hard-boiled attitude and rude rejection of Charley is presumably because she thinks that he is coming on to her, though the fact that Vicki already has a boyfriend may be another factor. It seems that it is only when Vicki learns Charley has money and can help her career that she is more civil to him. We assume she only agrees to meet him later because she thinks she can use him. Despite Charley's good looks, Vicki does not express a physical attraction to him, which makes us question her sexual assertiveness towards him in her bungalow. Another possible reason that Vicki has sex with Charley is because she thinks Bugsy has a new woman and she feels rejected and jealous. Vicki's attraction to Charley appears to change because they have sex, when she calls him an "animal." After their first marriage is annulled, they both retain a mutual physical attraction. However, Vicki's manipulation of Charley changes after they are married and she walks away from him without seeking a settlement. She also sacrifices the screen test for a Monogram movie musical when she goes with Charley to Boston to see his ailing father. Additionally, Vicki gives up her potential Hollywood career when she stays in Boston for two years. Since Vicki is said to wait for Charley to come home at night, the assumption is that she cannot be a nightclub singer there either. She walks away from the second marriage, again with no apparent financial settlement, and in the third, she couldn't get one even if she wanted to, given Charley's bankruptcy. The screenplay does not explain the custody arrangements for the couple's children, but it is implied that leaving the third marriage means Vicki sacrifices her children to Charley. This is despite the fact the Charley would not seem to be able to support them financially. The narrative also implies that Vicki does not take up with another romantic partner, despite her divorces from Charley, which attests to her continuing love for him.

Director Jerry Rees employs black and white stock for the home movies shot by Phil, which allows Charley to look into the camera. This footage is intercut with newsreel footage for a montage of Charley's sporting accidents. Rees' use of score is obtrusive, and his attempt to use it to make scenes of violence funny fails. This is evident in the scenes in which Charley is being beaten up, Charley and Vicki physically fight, and the climactic car chase occurs. However, Rees does provide some clever editing. A shot of Charley's car moving is followed by one of Charley walking in the same direction; a shot of Charley in his hospital sickbed is replaced with one of him lying on an inflatable bed in his pool; and Rees intercuts between Tommy singing "You're Driving Me Crazy"

Top: Vicki Anderson (Kim Basinger) sings; and at bottom, from left, she is watched by Phil Golden (Paul Reiser), Charles Raymond Pearl (Alec Baldwin), and Sammy Fine (Fisher Stevens) in a still for *The Marrying Man* (1991).

and Charley and Vicki making love. Vicki's performance style appears to be more contemporary than period in the undulating way she moves when she sings, and Rees creates the same impression when Tony performs "You're Driving Me Crazy," since he moves like Elvis Presley.

As Charley, Alec Baldwin is funny in his first reaction to seeing Vicki, asking, "Who is that?" and looks convincingly infatuated with her. He supplies tears in the climactic car park scene, though his use of his hands when angry can be mannered. Kim Basinger as Vicki reveals a serviceable singing voice, and she provides some pleasingly understated anger and surprise reactions in the car park argument scene. Rees features a lot of shots of Basinger's (clothed) posterior, as if he thinks that it is her greatest asset, though he allows her repeated hysterical screaming to become tiresome.

In the film's pressbook Simon is quoted as saying that his inspiration for the story came from overhearing a conversation between friends in which it was mentioned that someone had married the same woman four times. He later discovered the relationship between shoe store tycoon Harry Karl and the 1950s singer/actress Marie McDonald, who was nicknamed "The Body Beautiful" and "The Body." The couple were married twice, and she also was reportedly one of the mistresses of Bugsy Siegel. Simon says that the story of Karl and McDonald was not the story he wanted to tell but was rather just the starting point for him. Another fact that hit close to home also piqued his interest in the new story—that he recently remarried his own ex-wife, Diane, because, he said, "We didn't get it right the first time. But we aren't headed for four marriages!" McDonald released an album of standard ballads in 1957 entitled *The Body Sings*, which can be seen to be imitated by Vicki's album, *Vicki Anderson Sings*. It's a pity that the screenplay doesn't use a remark allegedly made by McDonald about the idea of a reconciliation with Karl: "You can't heat up yesterday's mashed potatoes." Charley's four friends are believed to be loosely based on comedian Phil Silvers, songwriter Sammy Cahn, singer Tony Martin and baseball manager Leo Durocher.

In the pressbook Simon speaks about the casting of the leads: "Alec has a lot of the character's qualities. He's also adept at both comedy and drama, something many of today's stars can't claim." Of Basinger Simon says, "I thought Kim was perfect. She is beautiful, but she doesn't play on her sex appeal. It's just there." Later Simon is quoted as saying about the film, "With a play, I have only two people to please—myself and the director. With this movie, it was nineteen executives, a director who'd never done anything but animation before, and two stars who would tell you what lines they'd say and what lines they wouldn't say."

An on-location article in *Premiere* magazine reported that Basinger and Baldwin were "demanding and unreasonable" and made life miserable for the crew during shooting. In an interview with Alex Witchel in the *New York Times* on May 20, 1992, Baldwin insisted that they only wanted to make the best movie possible. Basinger is said to have told Simon, "This isn't funny. Whoever wrote this doesn't understand comedy." Simon is reported to have left the set in response. Simon denies that this incident took place, but apparently he only returned to the set once during the remainder of the shoot. Baldwin said that when the article came out, "I looked at it and said, 'It's nothing,' and then the media picks it up like it was a trial transcript." One finer point made in that transcript was that Basinger had the habit of washing her hair in Evian water. Not true,

Baldwin said, claiming that Basinger made this demand as a joke after she was criticized for spending too long on her hair.

An article in *People* magazine by Elizabeth Sporkin on April 22, 1991, describes the alleged on-set offensive behavior. One senior member of the production crew is quoted as saying, "Honest to God, if I were destitute and living on the street with no food and somebody offered me a million dollars to work with Alec and Kim, I'd pass.... Their actions were vile, deplorable, despicable." Sporkin says that Basinger demanded that Ian Baker be replaced as the film's director of photography as she didn't like the way she looked in test shots. She also claims that the actress refused to wear underwear under her costumes, which had her assistant scampering for towels to throw over her legs. For her part, Basinger told *USA Today* that making the movie was "the worst situation anyone could imagine—ever. I thought hell was below us, but it fell right on my head."

Michael Gross wrote an article on Baldwin in *New York Magazine* on November 24, 1997, and said that love led the actor into career hell. Baldwin and Basinger were accused of "going on a rampage" on the set of the film. Gross says that articles in *Premiere* and *People* magazines claim that Basinger was accused of habitual lateness, flashing the crew (presumably because of her lack of underwear), using filthy language on open walkie-talkies, refusing to shoot in sunlight, and demanding that no one look at her. Baldwin supposedly smashed the cell phones of Disney executives because he did not have one, punched dents in walls, kicked over a case of lenses, and threw his director's chair. Baldwin denies many of the charges and claims that promises that were made to the couple were not kept. He railed against the studio for cost-cutting, calling its executive Jeffrey Katzenberg "the eighth dwarf, Greedy," and fired his publicist for counseling him not to respond to the bad press.

RELEASE: April 5, 1991, with the taglines "Every man has a weakness. For millionaire Charley Pearl she's blonde, beautiful, and loves to say 'I DO' (there was also a variation on this line with the end being "YES") and "About to marry the perfect girl, he suddenly meets the girl of his dreams."

REVIEWS: Lambasted in *Variety* as a "stillborn romantic comedy of staggering ineptitude." A mixed reaction from Roger Ebert in the *Chicago Sun-Times* and Vincent Canby in the *New York Times*, who comments that the film "keeps shooting itself in the foot, and elsewhere, until all life has gone."

AWARD: Kim Basinger nominated for Razzie Award for Worst Actress.

DVD: Released by Walt Disney Video on April 8, 2003.

The Odd Couple II (1998)

Paramount Pictures and Cort/Madden Productions.

CREW: Howard Deutch (Director), Robert W. Cort and David Madden (Producers), Elena Spiotta (Associate Producer), Neil Simon (Producer and Screenplay), Jamie Anderson (Photography), Seth Flaum (Editor), Alan Silvestri (Music), Dan Bishop (Production Design), Jeff Knipp (Art Director), Kristen Toscano Messina (Set Decorator), Lisa Jensen (Costumes), Michelle Johnston (Choreography), Steve Artmont (Makeup), Steve LaPorte (Makeup for Mr. Lemmon), Linda Melazzo (Makeup for Mr. Matthau),

Janis Clark (Hair), Linda Rizzuto (Hair for Mr. Matthau), Gloria Ponce (Hair for Ms. Baranski), Robert L. Knott (Special Effects). Color, 92 minutes. Filmed on location at Crazy Otto's Diner, Lancaster, and Los Angeles International Airport; and in Bakersfield, Los Osos, Santa Maria, San Luis Obispo, Palmdale, Shafter, Arcadia, Pomona, Hidden Valley, Santa Menendez, and Guadalupe, California, from June 9 to September 19, 1997.

CAST: Jack Lemmon (Felix Unger), Walter Matthau (Oscar Madison), Christine Baranski (Thelma), Barnard Hughes (Beaumont), Jay O. Sanders (Leroy), Jonathan Silverman (Bruce Madison), Jean Smart (Holly), Ellen Geer (Frances Unger Melnick), Estelle Harris (Peaches, aka Flirting Woman), Mary Beth Peil (Felice Adams), Florence Stanley (Hattie), Alice Ghostley (Esther), Lou Cutell (Abe), Doris Belack (Blanche Madison Povich), Rex Linn (JayJay), Richard Riehle (San Menendez Sheriff), Lisa Waltz (Hannah Unger), Rebecca Schull (Wanda), Mary Fogarty (Flossie), Peggy Miley (Millie), Joaquin Martinez (Ricko the Truck Driver), Amy Yasbeck (Stewardess), Francesca P. Roberts (Woman Passenger), Amy Parrish (Computer Girl), Liz Torres (Maria), Myles Jeffrey (Little Boy), Carmen Mormino and Chuck Montgomery (California Troopers), Earl Boen (Fred), Ron Harper (Jack), Edmund Shaff (Ralph), Daisy Velez (Conchita), Beecey Carlson (Waitress), Terry L. Rose (Bartender), Alfred Dennis (Morton), Armando Ortega (Detective #2), Peter Renaday (Justice of the Peace), David Jean-Thomas (Bus Driver), Daniel Zacapa (Lead Cop), Cliff Bemis (Dance Partner), Frank Roman (Bellman), Lonnie McCullough (Roadblock Officer), Matt McKenzie (Pilot), Heath Hyche (Policeman), Irene Olga Lopez (Café Waitress), Jerry Rector (Detective), Martin Grey (Immigration Officer), Michelle Johnston (Bridesmaid), Michelle Matthow (Wedding Guest), Mark McGee (Wedding Bartender), Barry Thompson (Male Passenger), Joanne Sanchez and Catherine Paolone (Passengers), Michelle Johnston (Airline Employee), Laura Russo (Stewardess #2).

MUSIC/SONGS: "The Odd Couple" (Neal Hefti); "The Village Inn" (Henry Mancini), Henry Mancini and His Orchestra; "The Good, the Bad and the Ugly" (Ennio Morricone), Ennio Morricone; "Old Time Rock and Roll" (George Jackson and Tom Joneds III), Bob Seger and the Silver Bullet Band in bar; "It's Too Late" (Crit Harmon, Barbara L. Jordan and William Peterkin), Crit Harmon; "Play Fair" (Crit Harmon and Barbara L. Jordan), Crit Harmon; "I Like It I Love It" (Steve Dukes, Jeb Stuart Anderson and Markus Anthony Hall), Tim McGraw in bar; "In the Mood" (Joseph Garland), Glenn Miller; "Little Sister" (Doc Pomus and Mort Shuman), Elvis Presley; "Don't Get Around Much Anymore" (Duke Ellington and Bob Russell).

SYNOPSIS: Oscar Madison, now living in Sarasota, Florida, hears from his son, Bruce, that he is to marry Hannah in Los Angeles. She is the daughter of Felix Unger, who still lives in New York. The old friends have not seen each other in seventeen years. Oscar meets Felix at Los Angeles airport and they attempt to drive to San Malina, but they come across all manner of obstacles in San Menendez. They meet Felice Adams, the widowed sister of Oscar's ex-wife Blanche, on a flight, and Felix is smitten. All three attend the wedding, and Felix and Felice go to San Francisco. Felix then appears at Oscar's house, having rejected Felice, and asks to stay with him while he settles in Florida.

NOTES: Simon's screenplay for this sequel retains some of the plot points of the original film. The treatment presents a road trip with the pair the victims of misfortune.

The subjects featured are friendship, family, and marriage. Simon uses the "F" bomb twice for Felix's expression of anger, which can be considered an updated reference, and there is also the potential for a variation on one of the stories from *Plaza Suite* that is not exploited.

The screenplay opens and closes with poker games that recall the original film, with the concepts of Oscar serving food carelessly and then Felix cleaning up and offering to serve better food being repeated. The difference in the setup here is that the two men do not live together, although their traveling together has the same effect. As in the original film, the narrative ends with Oscar agreeing to let Felix move in with him, although Felix's doing so after moving from New York to Florida seems a contrivance. The misfortunes that befall Oscar and Felix recall the predicament of the couple in *The Out of Towners* more than those in the original *Odd Couple* film, though unlike *The Out of Towners*, the misfortunes here cease after the climax. These misfortunes include the leaving of Felix's suitcase at the Budget rental office, Felix having a sprained ankle, their rental car falling over a cliff and exploding, the pair being lost in the desert, their riding in the car of a dead man, and their being kidnapped by the husbands of Thelma and Holly. Regrettably, a lot of these incidents come with little logic and provide no narrative payoff.

Simon uses running gags. The main one is the appearance of Oscar and Felix in front of the San Menendez sheriff after being arrested on three separate occasions. Felix's making moose noises to relieve his sinus problem is repeated four times, once in a restaurant with Oscar to recall the same scenario in the first film. Other gags include their being unable to remember the name of San Malina as the wedding location, how a closed window is thought to be open where something is thrown at it and bounces back, and a car driving rapidly past the pair as they look out for a car in the desert. This gag has a variation in the crowd of cars, cyclists, joggers and walkers that passes Beaumont's slowly driving car in which Oscar and Felix are passengers.

The screenplay is grimly unfunny, and the closest it gets to a laugh line is when in response

From left: Jack Lemmon, Neil Simon and Walter Matthau in a portrait for *The Odd Couple II* (1998).

to Abe's comment about the crowd in the opening baseball game, Oscar replies, "What crowd? We could all go home in one car." The plot point of Bruce's hiding on the roof of his house because he is afraid of getting married has the potential to be a variation on the story of Mimsey Hubley in *Plaza Suite*, but Simon ends the dilemma quickly by having Oscar talk Bruce down and help him change his mind. The crop-duster that drops white powder on the men makes no sense, since it does not fly over any crops, though the pancaked effect on Oscar and Felix gives them an amusing vaudevillian appearance. The men being given a lift by Ricko, who then lets them take the truck alone, gets an odd payoff when they are arrested for supposedly transporting illegal aliens, although we don't see evidence of it. The inclusion of the female bikers Thelma and Holly gets a payoff after their boyfriends kidnap Felix and Oscar, but the kidnapping is brief and the women's roles are basically forgettable. There is an ambiguity to the women's attraction to Felix and Oscar anyway, because their apparent age difference means we can't tell whether they find the men genuinely attractive or if they are just manipulating them. The appearance of Felice as a romantic interest for Felix would seem to confirm that he still has an attraction for women, and it is a narrative surprise that he and Oscar don't compete for her.

As old men Oscar and Felix are shown to be still active and contributing to society. Oscar appears to be still working as a sports writer, and Felix volunteers part time at a hospital. Felix is shown to now take medication. This may seem to be appropriate for an aged man, although we don't see Oscar do the same. However Felix's hypochondria in the earlier film positions this medication as an extension of his younger self's neurosis. Felix also appears to be calmer than in the original film, perhaps due to the mellowing effect of age, but he stills gets annoyed by Oscar and even swears at him. Equally, Oscar is shown to be more tolerant than in the first film, when he threw Felix out of his apartment because he could not live with him.

None of the supporting cast from the first film return for the sequel. Director Howard Deutch overuses an awful score, with the theme from the original film employed *ad nauseam*. Since the first film was released thirty years ago, it is interesting to see how the two leads have changed in looks. Both actors remain pleasant company even if they have little to do that is extraordinary. Of note is that as Oscar, Matthau twice uses a funny stylized anger, and as Felix, Lemmon gets a laugh from his obsequious smile at Thelma's and Holly's husbands, who appear on the bus brandishing guns.

In the book *Matthau: A Life*, Edelman and Kupferberg say that Simon began writing a film sequel to *The Odd Couple* in 1988. However, after completing thirty-eight pages to see if the premise would work, he put it away and moved on to other things. Another obstacle was that Simon and Paramount Pictures could not reach a deal for the film. However, the box office success of the film *Grumpy Old Men* (1993) and its sequel *Grumpier Old Men* (1995) revived Lemmon and Matthau's box office appeal, leading to a renewed interest in the sequel. Matthau had proposed a new plot in which Oscar dies at the beginning of the film and returns as a ghost to torment Felix. However, Simon did not use it.

Prior to the film's release Lemmon was quoted as saying that the new screenplay was "funnier and more touching than the first, and how often can you say that about a sequel?" He said it was the second best comic script he had ever read, after *Some Like*

It Hot. Matthau also said that the writing was much funnier than the original. This reaction of the actors is dumbfounding. While publicizing the film, Lemmon suggested that a second sequel might be in the works, something Matthau said was as true as the idea that he had had an affair with Marilyn Monroe. The box office failure of the film killed any notion of a further sequel.

RELEASE: April 10, 1998, with the tagline "Some arguments stand the test of time."

REVIEWS: Lambasted by Stephen Holden in the *New York Times* as a "dispiriting, flavorless travesty" and by Roger Ebert in the *Chicago Sun-Times.* A mixed reaction from Ruthe Stein in the *San Francisco Chronicle*, who wrote that Matthau and Lemmon have "terrific chemistry."

DVD: Released by Paramount on October 21, 1998.

PART THREE

Television Specials
and Adaptations

The Trouble with People (1972)

CREW: Danny Simon (Director/Producer), Neil Simon (Teleplay). 60 minutes.

CAST in order of appearance: James Coco, Dena Dietrich, Joseph Campanella, George C. Scott, Elaine Shore, Renee Taylor, Gene Wilder (Ernie), Jack Weston (Ben), Valerie Harper (Rita Mindlin), Alan Arkin (Dave).

SYNOPSIS: Five short sketches with the theme of urban nightmares. They are "The Greasy Diner," "The Man Who Got a Ticket," "The Night Visitor," "The Officer Sharers," and "Double Trouble."

NOTES: This special, which is made up of a series of revue-style sketches, was not available to view, so comments on its content are limited to information mentioned by John O'Connor in his review in the *New York Times.* The sketches seem to explore the themes of urban isolation, fear and paranoia. In an interview with Al Morgan for *TV Guide* Simon says that he wrote them to illustrate the frustrations of everyday life.

O'Connor describes the sketches as follows. In "The Greasy Diner" a man and his wife go to a seedy restaurant and are threatened by three leather-clad toughs, two of whom are named Diablo and Slicer. The couple pay the waitress $100 to let them stay there for the night, while the wife complains that "nothing is safe anymore." Notable funny lines from the sketch include, "You could get hepatitis just from the napkins," and "As soon as the food comes, we'll eat, get sick, and go." In "The Man Who Got a Ticket," a timid, law-abiding man is harassed by a female police clerk who claims that he has broken the law. In "The Night Visitor" an unmarried woman in Queens agrees to help a police detective capture a sexual molester. In "The Office Sharers" Ernie has been annoyed for eight years by the habits of his co-worker Ben. Ernie believes that Ben has a deliberate plan to secure Ernie's desk, which is two feet closer to the window. Ben's alleged tactics include not saying "good morning" first, chewing on pencils, picking his ear, and ordering a prune danish every day. In "Double Trouble" Dave goes to shut his apartment window in the middle of the night because his wife is cold and wrenches his bad back. The couple attempt to get a doctor to do a home visit, but fail to do so. A funny line from this sketch is, "The flu is good compared to this."

Top: left, Elaine Shore and George C. Scott; right, Alan Arkin and Valerie Harper; bottom: James Coco and Dena Dietrich; Joseph Campanella and Neil Simon in a composite still for *The Trouble with People* (1972).

In his *TV Guide* interview Simon advises that the special came from a conversation he had with his brother Danny about writing some new sketches. Danny felt that the theatre revue form was dead and suggested television as the ideal medium. Morgan asked the writer why, if he thought the sketches were first rate, he didn't want to put them on stage. Simon declared the question condescending and patronizing towards television and said he could not have got such a good cast for the stage, as television reached a bigger audience than plays or film. However, Simon comments on the problems that had driven him out of the medium earlier: the need to cut the sketches down to fit them into the allotted airtime and the threat of censorship by the sponsors and network, which meant he had to take the word "pervert" out of the show.

RELEASE: Broadcast by NBC on November 13, 1972.

REVIEWS: A mixed reaction from John J. O'Connor in the *New York Times.* O'Connor asked if Simon would be at his most effective in the medium that nurtured his gift for comedy. The answer from these sketches is "sometimes yes, sometimes no." O'Connor wrote that while the first three sketches had funny bits and pieces, the best were the last two. He concluded, "Simon and television can be rewardingly compatible."

DVD: Not available.

The Good Doctor (1978)

Broadway Theatre Archive.

CREW: Jack O'Brien (Director), Lindsay Law (Producer), Phylis Geller (Associate Producer), Jac Venza (Executive Producer), Neil Simon (Teleplay, adapted from and suggested by stories by Anton Chekhov), Danny Franks (Photography), Conrad Susa (Music), David Jenkins (Art Director), Bob Checchi (Set Decorator), Noel Taylor (Costumes), Michael Westmore (Makeup), Renata (Hair), Audrey Levy (Lee Grant's Hair). Color, 88 minutes.

CAST: Richard Chamberlain (The Writer/Peter Semyonych/Kistunov/The Writer's Father), Marsha Mason (Madame Sonya Cherdyakov/Actress/Julia/Irena/Nina Mikhailovna Zarechnaya/Girl), Bob Dishy (Ivan Ilyitch Cherdyakov/Nikolaich/Tramp), Lee Grant (Madame Brassilhov/Actress/Mistress/Woman, aka Mrs. Schukin), Edward Asner (General Mikhail Brassilhov/Policeman), Gary Dontzig (Assistant, aka Pochatkin/Antosha, aka Anton, aka The Writer).

SYNOPSIS: A theatre in Russia, 1898. A theatre writer narrates and presents a collection of short stories. They are entitled "The Sneeze," "The Governess," "The Seduction," "The Drowned Man," "The Audition," "The Defenseless Creature," and "The Arrangement."

NOTES: The source play had a reasonably successful run on Broadway of six months, but the fact that the adaptation was made for television rather than film comes with the assumption that the film would not have been a box office hit. Perhaps this material was considered too specialized, which may also why the made-for-TV version was produced so long after the theatrical run of the play. Simon adapts his own play, which was itself an adaptation of some of Chekhov's short stories.

"The Sneeze" is an adaptation of Chekhov's 1883 short story "The Death of a

Government Clerk," also known as "The Death of a Civil Servant." "The Governess" is an adaptation of the short story "The Ninny," also known as "The Nincompoop," the publication date of which is unknown. "The Seduction" appears to be an adaptation of an 1887 story entitled "The Boa Constrictor and the Rabbit." "The Drowned Man" appears to be an adaptation of the 1885 story "Drowning." "The Audition" is not an adaptation of any particular Chekhov story, as Simon notes in his memoir *The Play Goes On*. Rather it takes the last scene from Chekhov's play *The Three Sisters* and presents it as a showcase for an actress. "The Sneeze" is referenced in "The Audition" when Nina tells the writer that she likes the story. "The Defenseless Creature" is an adaptation of the 1887 short story of the same name, but "The Arrangment" does not appear to be an adaptation of any particular Chekhov story.

Two of the play's stories, "Surgery" and "Too Late for Happiness," are cut from the teleplay. Because of cutting "Surgery" the title *The Good Doctor* is meaningless, since no doctor appears in any of the remaining stories. The themes of class struggle, obsession and mental imbalance, ageism and gender manipulation, sexual coming-of-age and theatrical ambition are presented.

As the narrator of the teleplay, the writer writes for the theatre, so it is easy to see him as an extension of Neil Simon the playwright. The writer says that his work has

been described as "charming and clever but nothing more," which also reflects the perception of Simon as a writer being better suited to comedy than dramatic material. In "The Sneeze" and "The Governess" there is a running gag. The writer offers alternative endings in which Ivan and the governess inherit five million rubles. This gag is not used in the other stories, and is cut from the end of the play's story "The Arrangement." Another gag is used for the ending of "The Drowned Man," which reads as the most curious story, in which the writer apparently forgets the name of the man who is supposed to save the tramp from drowning at the waterfront dock. It is not clear why the writer should have such bad listening skills, nor why he should be so callous as to make no attempt to save the tramp. In "The Arrangement" Simon uses the theatrical device of having a character state an intention and

The writer (Richard Chamberlain) in a still for *The Good Doctor* (1978).

then change their mind. This is first employed by Antosha, who is afraid to meet with the prostitute, then by the father, who stops Antosha from going to the prostitute's room after having sent him there. The second use provides for an unexpected resolution to the episode in which the boy agrees to delay losing his virginity.

Some funny lines are retained from the play. "The Audition" retains the last funny line of the story, which pays off Nina's saying that she walked all the way from Odessa for the audition. The writer, desperate to cast her, tells his assistants, "Will someone go get her before she walks all the way back to Odessa?" "The Defenseless Creature" retains two funny lines. The manager refers to the woman as a "balding lunatic," which pays off her showing him that her hair is falling out. He also comments, "It's women like you who drive men like me to the condition of husbands like yours."

Changes from the original play include Simon's losing the opening lines about the writing being in his study, and replacing them with new lines about the theatre. The short story that "The Sneeze" is based on does not feature the second sneeze that Simon has, and this plot point redeems the otherwise humorless story. Other new elements include Ivan throwing items from the general's desk and the general pinching Ivan's ear. The story also has a new exchange in the theatre when Madame Brassilhov asks the general who Ivan is and the general replies that he does not know. In "The Governess" there are new actions, the most significant being how the governess pretends to give back the ten rubles when the mistress calls her back, but then pockets them as well as taking the eighty rubles in the envelope. The writer introduces this story as one about a woman trapped, but the ambiguous resolution brings this premise into question. In "The Drowned Man" Simon provides a new line in regards to the tramp's notion that his drowning act spares him the thing that every other working man faces—that he eventually touches something filthy. The tramp asks the writer his profession, and notes that ink is the filthy thing that he touches. Simon's adaptation differs from the short story, since Chekhov has the hustler surviving his drowning demonstration to get out of the water and be paid by the observer. "The Defenseless Creature" also includes new actions, the most significant being the manager pouring himself a glass of water, which the woman drinks. The end of the story is retained from the play, though this action is not in the Chekhov story. This is where the manager farcically hits his own foot over the idea that the woman will return to bother him again. In "The Arrangement" the prostitute does not smoke, and she has a new line. After the father cries at the prospect of Antosha going to her, she tells him, "I never had anybody cry over me before."

The issue of class difference is presented in "The Sneeze," "The Governess," "The Defenseless Creature" and "The Arrangement." It is most noteworthy in three of the stories. In "The Sneeze" Ivan blames his sitting in the front stalls of the theatre where the wealthy are, rather than in the balcony seats with the common people, for his being behind the general, whom he sneezes on. In "The Governess" the mistress repeatedly tells the governess to keep her head up and make eye contact. There is some humor in the mistress' explanation of how she is reducing the governess' pay for two months' work, from eighty to ten rubles. The mistress eventually reveals that she does this only to teach her governess to be assertive, before paying her both the expected ten rubels and the original eighty. However, the governess still judges her employee by telling her that it is possible for her to be a "simpleton." Unlike the other stories, in which the upper class character takes advantage of a lower class one, "The Defenseless Creature" features the reverse situation. The peasant woman gets the better of the bank manager because he is overwhelmed by her persistence in achieving her goal of remuneration for her husband's lost wages, even though the loss is not the responsibility of the banker. This victory is perhaps made because the manager's vulnerability to the woman is shown to be greater than presumably normal because he suffers from gout and an injured foot.

The only actor retained from the Broadway production is Marsha Mason. Director Jack O'Brien uses self-conscious touches of music and staging. In "The Sneeze" he replays the play's action of the first sneeze seen in slow motion. In "The Seduction" the writer also plays Peter Semyonych and has asides to the camera. A mirror is used by O'Brien in this episode both to show Peter talking to himself and us, and to show Irena and Nikolai having a conversation with each other as she looks into it. In "The Drowned Man" we see the theatre mechanics of creating fog. The writer's face is obscured by smog when he speaks to the camera, and fog is also seen on the ground in "The Arrangement."

Marsha Mason supplies tears in "The Governess" and "The Audition," and funny duplicitous playing in "The Seduction." She also cleverly differentiates the three sisters' speeches in "The Audition." However, her performance in "The Arrangement" is odd since she presents with a strange affect as the prostitute. Bob Dishy makes "The Drowned Man" very likeable, which adds to the poignancy of his character's fate. Lee Grant and Richard Chamberlain overplay the overbearing woman and bank manager from "The Defenseless Creature," which regrettably makes this story the least enjoyable.

RELEASE: Broadcast by Public Broadcasting Service (PBS) on November 8, 1978, as part of the *Great Performances* television series.

REVIEWS: Lambasted by John J. O'Connor in the *New York Times* and Jerry Roberts in *Encyclopedia of Television Film Directors*. O'Connor wrote that neither Chekhov nor Simon is served to advantage, and "the misbegotten venture is best forgotten."

REMAKE: The play was remade for Spanish television and broadcast on October 12, 1987.

DVD: Released by Kultur Video on June 11, 2002.

Broadway Bound (1992)

ABC Productions

CREW: Paul Bogart (Director), Terry Nelson (Producer), Michael Brandman and Emanuel Azenberg (Executive Producers), Neil Simon (Screenplay based on his play), Isidore Mankofsky (Photography), Andy Zall (Editor), David Shire (Music), Ben Edwards (Production Design), Richard Johnson (Art Director), Sharon Bonney (Set Decorator), Rita Riggs (Costumes), Deborah Larsen (Makeup), Claudia Diaz (Hair), John K. Stirber (Special Effects). Color, 90 minutes.

CAST: Anne Bancroft (Kate Jerome), Hume Cronyn (Poppa, aka Ben), Corey Parker (Eugene Morris Jerome), Jonathan Silverman (Stanley "Stan" Jerome), Jerry Orbach (Jack Jerome), Michele Lee (Blanche), Marilyn Cooper (Voice of Mrs. Morris Pitkin), Pat McCormick (Voice of Announcer), Jack Carter (Voice of Charles "Chubby" Waters).

SONGS: "It Had to Be You" (music by Isham Jones and lyrics by Gus Kahn), Benny Goodman on radio.

SYNOPSIS: In Brighton Beach, New York, 1948, twenty-two-year-old stockroom worker Eugene Morris Jerome lives at home with his older brother, twenty-eight-year-old Stan, who works selling boys' clothes at Gimbels. The brothers write a comedy sketch for television that is eventually broadcast on the radio. Eugene's mother, Kate, tells him about the night she danced with George Raft when she was a girl. Eugene's father, Jack, walks out on the family to be with his mistress. Stan and Eugene get jobs as writers on Phil Silver's television show and move to Manhattan.

NOTES: Coming after a string of film versions of his plays, this made-for-TV movie adaptation is a step down in status for Simon, despite the play's having had a run of nearly two years on Broadway. The demotion would also seem to indicate a decline in interest from Hollywood and the general public in Simon as a screenwriter. As the third part of Simon's trilogy about Eugene Morris Jerome, this film about the Jerome family resembles *Brighton Beach Memoirs* more than *Biloxi Blues*. The adaptation includes line cuts, line relocations, and new lines. The treatment explores the themes of aging, a husband abandoning his family, and the career ambition of children.

Narration is again used by Simon as a device, and he adds to and cuts that in the play. Autobiographical elements are again present in the play. Eugene and Stan are clearly based on Neil and Danny Simon. There are obvious parallels in their careers as comedy writers, the fact that their father abandoned his family, and the fact that Eugene, like Neil, gets married and has two daughters. Simon also has some points of self-reference. The television comedy sketch re-uses the story "Double Trouble" from Simon's TV special *The Trouble with People*. A further example of Simon's self-reference is Jack's line to Kate about the woman he had an affair with: "Don't make me say nice things about her," which recalls a line spoken in *Plaza Suite*. Eugene's response to Kate's story about her dancing with George Raft, "This is a movie and one day I'm going to write it," is another line of self-reference, given that the play was made into a TV movie.

Simon opens up the play by providing additional locations around the exterior of the Jerome house, which is shown when Ben leaves to go to the Chinese laundry, Ben and Stanley come home, Blanche's Cadillac arrives, Kate smokes on the back porch, and the taxi takes the boys away, and in the final shot of the house on the street. We also see a photograph of Kate as a girl that Ben shows to Eugene. Simon's main cuts from the play are the telephone call Stan receives from Joe Pinotti and the one Kate has from her mother. Simon adds the new action of Kate's leaving the house after the radio broadcast and returning after Jack's argument with the boys. The teleplay also changes the plot point of Jack's leaving. In the play Ben tells Kate about it, but in the teleplay she knows because she sees him leave.

The sketch that Stan and Eugene write is unfunny, but because it is listened to by the family allows for the plot point of Jack's recognizing how he and Kate and Ben are parodied in it. Kate, however, is unaware of this, despite her comment that the voice of Mrs. Pitkin reminds her of someone but she doesn't know who. Simon seems to comment on people's ambivalence about comedy through Ben after the radio sketch is heard. Ben makes the highbrow comment that he thinks comedy should do more than just make people laugh; it should make a point and educate. However, he is still amused

Clockwise from left: Michele Lee, Hume Cronyn, Jerry Orbach, Anne Bancroft, Jonathan Silverman, and Corey Parker in a still for *Broadway Bound* (1992).

by the lowbrow humor of a dog that barks in Spanish, which follows Stan referring to the lowbrow comedy of the Three Stooges as "for morons." This point gets a new payoff when Eugene tells Ben that the brothers are going to write a sketch for him with a dog that barks in Russian.

 New lines include Ben's comment after he takes some medicine Kate gives him: "Your mother used to cook like that." A funny line retained from the play is Kate's remark to Jack, "I say what I'm thinking, you're liable to tell me what I don't want to hear." Another is Kate's line about how the women in her family cried when they got to American and saw the Statue of Liberty, thinking, "That's not a Jewish woman. We're going to have problems again." Kate also delivers a howler to Jack, retained from the play: "You break what was good between us and you leave me to pick up the pieces."

The only actor retained from the Broadway version is Jonathan Silverman, though in the play he was Eugene. Director Paul Bogart makes the treatment more realistic than theatrical, except for the moments of confrontation. These include Blanche's speech to Ben about how he doesn't give her affection, Jack telling Kate about his affair (though here Bogart uses cutaways to the others in the house listening), and Stan's speech to Jack about his disappointment in him. Bogart provides a two-minute pan from the exterior of the house that follows Kate through windows as she moves from room to room. However, Bogart's coverage of Kate and Eugene dancing, which is the climax of the play, is photographed badly and disappointingly edited. Bogart shoots Jack in shadow when he cries so that we cannot see whether there are tears. The score by David Shire is mostly understated except for the scene where Eugene packs to leave, when it overwhelms both narration and dialogue.

After his playing Eugene in *Brighton Beach Memoirs*, it's interesting to see Silverman play Stan as a grown man here. As Eugene, Corey Parker isn't as memorable as Silverman was in *Brighton Beach Memoirs* or Matthew Broderick was in *Biloxi Blues*, but he demonstrates the character's wit and tenderness towards his mother. As Kate, Anne Bancroft's casting after Blythe Danner played the role in the film of *Brighton Beach Memoirs* replaces one good actor with another. That Kate is dealing with two adult sons now, rather than the two adolescents in *Brighton Beach Memoirs*, allows her to express more affection for them, giving the actress more scope to show emotional range. Bancroft supplies some shocking moments of anger, and a convincing physicality of defeat for a woman who learns that her husband has lied and cheated on her. The casting of Michele Lee as Blanche, however, jars with the memory of Judith Ivey from *Brighton Beach Memoirs*, despite Lee's giving a better performance than Ivey did. As Jack, Jerry Orbach provides a darker character than Bob Dishy did in *Brighton Beach Memoirs*, and Orbach's Jack is frightening in his rage at Stan.

On the 2006 Mark Twain Award show, Jonathan Silverman claimed that Jason Alexander, who had played Stan on Broadway, was unable to do the film version of the play because of his commitment to the television series *Seinfeld*. Alexander corrected him by saying that he was in fact available but had turned down the part.

Paul Bogart is interviewed by Peter Bogart on the Director's Guild of America Web site. One part of the interview covers Simon's reaction to the made-for-TV movie. The director says that Simon couldn't get the funding to make a feature of the play and had to accept a low-budget "art house" television movie. Bogart filmed the play as is, but found that it was twenty minutes too long. He provided Simon with a script of all the cuts he made. Bogart said that Simon was deeply moved by the film and accepted all the cuts.

RELEASE: March 23, 1992, with the tagline "From the creator of *The Odd Couple* and *Barefoot in the Park* and *The Goodbye Girl*."

REVIEWS: Praised by John J. O'Connor in the *New York Times*: "Cast to near perfection, it's a show very much worth catching" and "Bogart has directed the production with his customary skill and sensitivity." Lambasted by Ken Tucker in *Entertainment*

Weekly as "flat, artificial, and, well, stagy." Tucker writes, "Watching it on TV, where the camera's close-ups insist on intimacy and naturalism, you think, 'Sorry, people just don't talk like that.'"

DVD: Not available on DVD. VHS released by Buena Vista Home Entertainment on August 11, 1993.

AWARDS: Emmy Award to Hume Cronyn for Outstanding Supporting Actor in a Miniseries or Special. Emmy Award nominations for Paul Bogart for Directing, Neil Simon for Writing, Jerry Orbach for Supporting Actor and Anne Bancroft for Supporting Actress.

Jake's Women (1996)

RHI Entertainment/Hallmark Entertainment.

CREW: Glenn Jordan (Director and Producer), Robert Bennett Steinhauer (Co-Producer), David Simmons (Associate Producer and Editor), Robert Halmi, Sr. (Executive Producer), Neil Simon (Teleplay based on his play), James Glennon (Photography), David Shire (Music), Fred Harpman (Production Design), Linda Donahue (Costumes), Pat Gerhardt (Makeup), Nina Paskowitz (Hair). Color, 89 minutes.

CAST: Alan Alda (Jake), Anne Archer (Maggie), Lolita Davidovich (Sheila), Julie Kavner (Karen), Mira Sorvino (Julie), Joyce Van Patten (Edith), Kimberly Williams (Molly), Ashley Peldon (Young Molly), Perry Anzilotti (Waiter), Aasif Mandvi (Driver), Steven M. Porter (Hal), Yul Vazquez (Luigi), Hynden Walch (Server).

SONGS: "Oh, Lady Be Good" (Ira and George Gershwin), opening credits.

SYNOPSIS: Jake is a successful, fifty-six-year-old New York novelist and a teacher of writing, who has been married to Maggie for eight years. Maggie is unhappy and wants a separation. They have both had affairs, and Jake is still grieving his deceased first wife of ten years, Julie. After six months, Jake has writer's block and is dating the decorator, Sheila. Jake creates fantasy conversations with women from his life, to experience an intimacy that he feels he does not have in his real life. This culminates in the fantasy of his twenty-one-year-old daughter Molly re-uniting with Julie. Jake finds he can no longer create the fantasies, and Maggie returns to try to make their marriage work.

NOTES: This television adaptation of one of Simon's plays is a further sign of his inability to secure funding for a feature adaptation. This comes after the source play had enjoyed a seven-month run on Broadway; a reasonable season for any playwright but disappointing given Simon's pedigree. The adaptation has line cuts, lines moved, new lines, new action, and a new ending. The piece presents the subject of marriage and the mental state of a misunderstood writer who is accused of critical observation and a lack of intimacy. The autobiographical elements of the narrative are that the protagonist is a writer, has remarried after being widowed, still harbors feelings for his dead wife, and is resentful of his wife's career because it keeps her away from him. The last point echoes Simon's supposed complaint about his marriage to Marsha Mason.

Simon has Jake talk directly to the camera, and this is as much as a theatrical contrivance as characters appearing out of Jake's imagination. The device is parodied when Karen says, "Look, I'm walking through walls," and "I wish you would stop flying me in

Clockwise from bottom left: Kimberly Williams, Lolita Davidovitch, Anne Archer, Julie Kavner, Mira Sorvino, Joyce Van Patten and Ashley Peldon, and at center, Alan Alda, in a still for *Jake's Women* (1996).

and out of your mind. I'm getting airsick." Edith compliments Jake and then undercuts it: "They're your words, I'm just moving my lips," and she says, "I love how my voice trails off" when she leaves Jake. Another example is that Edith and Karen have to stop talking about Jake while he cleans his teeth in the bathroom.

Jake and Maggie meet in a cute way when she spills a drink on him after he bumps into her at a party, and there is a running gag of Jake's having women dressed in clothes they resent. The highlight of this gag is when Edith and Karen both appear wearing the Laura Ashley dress and white hat Maggie had worn when Jake first met her. Another repeated gag is the action of having an imagined person appearing ahead of Jake in multiple rooms in his apartment. Jake also has to protect the real person from the imagined, when he stops Sheila from sitting on top of the imagined Maggie. He also speaks back to the imagined Maggie, and Sheila naturally assumes he is talking to her, while Maggie imitates Sheila's gestures and mimes her words. (This gag is flawed because Maggie is able to do the gestures and mime the words in unison with Sheila, although Maggie cannot see what Sheila is doing as she stands in front of her.)

The play is "opened up" by the screenplay, which includes scenes in the street and in Jake's car, as well as at a luncheonette, an East Hamptons party, Jake's writing class, a Vermont cabin by the lake, Molly's campus at Brown, Sung Foo's restaurant, and Geppeto's restaurant. The Hamptons party scene features a new gag in which Maggie thinks that the waitress who offers her sushi is named Suzie. The waitress is used to offer Jake sushi to distract him so that he bumps into Maggie. The rain and lightning in the second campus scene with Jake and Molly pays off the imagined Maggie's comment that he needs a "catharsis, a bolt of lightning, a miracle" to change his life. This miracle is that he seemingly loses the ability to create the imaginary meetings after the one between Molly and Julie, although Jake will later call the fact that he catches Maggie at Geppeto's alone another miracle.

New funny lines include Karen's referring to the black dress with white spots Jake has her wearing as a trick-or-treat costume. Funny lines retained from the play include Karen's objection to the dress Jake has her in ("Bette Midler does a concert in a dress like this") and Jake's comment, "Analysts don't work nights. That's when they have their own breakdowns." Another is Edith's observation of Jake and Julie talking: "This is interesting. This is fascinating. I can't follow it but it's riveting." Simon also retains the play's howler in Jake's question to Maggie, "Do I sense something important is about to get said?" Simon scores another laugh at the climax when he calls out for help from all his women, but when he thinks of Sheila, says, "No, not Sheila." This references the earlier scene in which he had broken off their relationship.

Simon's cuts from the play include the telephone call Jake gets from Karen, and Molly's call to Jake when he is with Julie. Also gone is Jake's showing Julie photographs of Molly, the appearance of both Mollies together to Jake, which is the end of the play's first act, and Jake's imagined Maggie returning to him in the play's opening of the second act. The gift Maggie gives Molly is changed from an atlas to a book on baseball, and Simon changes Jake's taking sleeping pills to get rid of Edith and Karen in the play to having Molly appear to scare them away. Sheila's first appearance is also changed. In the play she is buzzed into Jake's apartment; now she is already in the apartment when Jake comes home so that he can initially think she is another imagined person. Simon also cuts a funny line when Molly and Julie leave; he says in the play, "I feel like Ethel Merman's going to come out and sing "Everything's Coming Up Roses." He also changes the play's ending, cutting Jake's speech about seeing his father with another woman when he was a boy and Jake's hearing the voice of his mother. We also lose the return of the imagined Edith, Karen, young and old Molly, Julie, and Sheila, and then their disappearance, and the return of the Maggie to Jake's apartment. The screenplay ends with Maggie and Jake at Geppeto's where she agrees to come back to their marriage. Simon also has the film end of a note of ambiguity when Jake looks back in the street when he is with Maggie. We don't see anybody that might be from his imagination, but his second look back as he kisses Maggie suggests otherwise.

The dramatic conceit of the material is that Jake as a writer is able to imagine conversations with people from his past and others who are not physically with him at the time. The idea is that he invents what the other people say, but he can be surprised by what he invents. This device exists as memory and also as new conversations. The deceased Julie is imagined by Jake as when he first knew her when she was twenty-one, but she sees him as he is now, and the device is extended to allow Julie to speak to Molly, her daughter. Simon also has the device turn against Jake in the way people start to appear when he has not summoned them and also to speak for themselves. An example of this is when Karen and Edith appear and refuse to leave until Jake summons Molly as a child to scare them away. Simon also parodies the device when Jake telephones the real Edith at her work while her imagined incarnation sits in front of him. Jake speaks to both Ediths at once; however, Simon wiggles out of realizing the scenario's full potential since Jake later admits that he didn't actually ring Edith but only pretended to. A payoff to an imagined character saying their own words happens when the imagined Maggie makes suggestions to Jake that he repeats to Sheila. This scene begins with the assumption that Maggie is undercutting Jake's relationship with Sheila, but ends with Maggie's assertion that she was acting as Jake's proxy, to help him break it off with Sheila, which is what he wanted to do. The climax of the appearance of the imaginary characters is the reunion between Molly and Julie. Molly is upset that she has such little time with her mother and demands that Jake stop imagining the encounters. After Jake fails to win back Maggie because she still objects to the observing writer side of him, he finds he can no longer create the imaginary people. The imagined women reappear to wave goodbye to Jake as he leaves the restaurant with Maggie at the narrative conclusion, though with Jake's last look the suggestion is created that his visions are not over.

Maggie's role as a career woman produces some interesting plot points. She likes working because she finds her relationship with Jake "claustrophobic, airless and suffocating" and working allows her to spend months away. She has an affair with a coworker, and has her assistant buy Molly a birthday present rather than buy it herself.

The only actors retained from the Broadway show are Alan Alda and Joyce Van Patten. Director Glenn Jordan uses Alda's voice and a younger body double to show Jake as a younger man in flashback. Jordan uses simple special effects for the appearance and disappearance of the imaginary characters, though the imagined Molly is given a realistic exit via a door that she opens and walks through. However, he errs with Julie's exit by having her exit the frame and then be seen walking through the door that Jake opens to let Maggie in.

The casting is interesting. While Alan Alda played Jake in the Broadway show, as an actor he is primarily known for television work. The other actors are better known as film performers, except for Julie Kavner, who has a television association from her work on *The Simpsons*. This demonstrates that despite Simon's diminishing status as a screenwriter, he was at this time still able to attract movie stars to his material. As Jake, Alda gives a magnificent performance. He is affable and also expresses pain at the idea of Maggie's wanting to separate from him, and at the loss of Julie. He produces tears when telling Julie about Molly, and has teary eyes watching the reunion of Molly and Julie, and when Maggie returns. Alda's Jake is funny in his anger at Edith and in his farcical fear of commitment to Sheila. The actor also demonstrates physical comedy skills in the way Jake jumps on the bed that Karen makes and in how he fights to open a locked door. As Edith, Joyce Van Patten uses a funny smile to convey the character's unctuousness, and Julie Kavner as Karen uses her New York intonation for comic effect. As Julie, Mira Sorvino overuses her hands, but she lowers her voice for Julie to age from twenty-one to thirty-five and supplies tears.

RELEASE: March 3, 1996, on the Columbia Broadcasting System Playhouse '90 (CBS) with the tagline "Jake Loves Women. His Sister, His Daughter, His First Wife and His Second. They all live in his heart. Can he make room for one more?"

REVIEWS: A mixed reaction from Jeremy Gerard in *Variety*, who describes it as "oddly cast and surprisingly claustrophobic" and John J. O'Connor in the *New York Times*, who calls it "leaden."

DVD: Released by Platinum Disc on October 5, 2004.

London Suite (1996)

RHI Entertainment/Hallmark Entertainment.

CREW: Jay Sandrich (Director), Greg Smith (Producer), Robert Halmi, Sr. (Executive Producer), Neil Simon (Teleplay based on his play), Denis Lewiston (Photography), John Michel (Editor), Lee Holdridge (Music), Brian Ackland-Snow (Production Design), Peter James (Set Decorator), "Tiny" Nichols (Costumes), Pat Hay (Makeup), Stephen Rose (Hair). Color, 86 minutes. Filmed on location at Grosvenor House, London Heathrow Airport, Theatre Royal Haymarket, the Tower Bridge restaurant, and Westminster Park, London; and at Shepperton Studios, Surrey, England.

CAST: Kelsey Grammer (Sydney Nichols), Julia Louis-Dreyfus (Debra Dolby), Michael Richards (Mark Ferris), Jane Carr (Mrs. Sitgood), Patricia Clarkson (Diana Nichols), Julie Hagerty (Anne Ferris), Kristen Johnston (Grace Chapman), Madeline Kahn (Sharon Semple), Richard Mulligan (Dennis Cummings), Paxton Whitehead (Dr. McMerlin), William Franklyn (Widley), Deborah Moore (Meg Dolby), Rolf Saxon (Carl Dolby), Margot Steinberg (Lauren Semple), Robert McBain (Hobwick), Janine Duvtiski (Emma—Nanny), Eileen Dunwoodie (Jane—Nanny), Mathew Ashford and Michael Hobbs (Bellboys), Alisa Bosschaert (Hotel Assistant), David Mulligan (Hotel Waiter), Cathy Murphy (Hotel Waitress), John Marquez (Hotel Plumber), Virginia Stride (Beatrice), Jack Mackenzie (Walter), Hilary Crane (Woman in Restaurant), Dorothea Phillips (Woman at Airport), Stewart Harwood (Cab Driver), Jonathan Stratt (Hotel Doorman). Uncredited: Jonathan Silverman (Paul Dolby).

SYNOPSIS: The Grosvenor House hotel in London is visited by four groups of people. Americans Mark and Anne Ferris have come for Wimbledon, but Mark hurts his back and is seen by Dr. McMerlin. American Debra Dolby has come for her honeymoon, but her new husband Paul is missing. Paul appears at the hotel after having been arrested at the airport for smuggling cocaine and then cleared of the charge. British actress Diana Nichols has come to promote her television series and to meet her British ex-husband, Sydney, who is now gay and living in Greece with his lover, Max. Sydney tells Diana that he is dying of cancer and she agrees to take him and Max back to America with her. American tourist Lauren Semple arranges for a date between her widowed American mother Sharon Semple and Scotsman Dennis Cummings.

NOTES: This is another example of Simon's fallen status as a writer whose play adaptations now become television films rather than movies. However, that this material finds its home on television is less of a surprise than for some of his other screenplays. This is because the source play itself ran only Off Broadway, though it had a respectable five-month season. The adaptation employs the same device of divided stories that was used in *California Suite.* Simon cuts one of the four stories of the play, loses two characters, relocates lines, and introduces new scenes and characters. The subjects featured are marriage, sexuality, and romance in later life. Simon also makes some pointed criticisms of television via the character of Sydney, which is ironic given how the material ended up on television.

The play is "opened up" with locations that include the airport, a cab, the street, a shoe store, a restaurant, a park, a church cemetery, a pub, and the Theatre Royal Haymarket. In the airport scene, Mark mistakes someone else's luggage for Anne's, and this prefigures the misfortune of his back accident in the hotel room. The luggage mix-up also prefigures Paul's being caught with cocaine in luggage that he claims is not his. Also at the airport, Mark says that sleeping on the plane has hurt his back, which gets a later payoff when it disables him.

There is a new scene of a fire in Sharon's room that makes her hair smell of smoke. This gets paid off for her date with Dennis when she gets her hair done, tilts her head away from him, and lets the air blow through it as they drive in his car. Another new scene has Debra talk in short sentences to two nannies in the park where she asks herself, "Why are we talking like this? We sound like we're in a musical." In one hotel room scene, Debra's self-declaration of how she yearns and aches for Paul is met with the somewhat contrived surprise appearance of the hotel plumber from her bathroom.

New funny lines include Sydney's telling Diana that the people on Mykanos are not bitchy, but straightforward: "If they don't like you, they stone you to death." In another, Mrs. Sitgood sees Mark lying on the floor and asks, "Your back, is it?" to which he replies, "No, it's my first time here." When Mrs. Sitgood stands on Mark's hand, he cries, "My hand," to which she replies, "My error."

The narrative scores laughs from the impenetrability of some British accents, such as those of Mrs. Sitgood, Dennis and Dr. McMerlin. There is also a laugh from Debra's misinterpreting Meg's London pronunciation of "And I you" as "And are you," and "the firm" as "the farm." There is a running gag in which Mrs. Sitgood walks on Mark's hands as he lies on the floor, and another in which Lauren and then Dennis fail to recognize Sharon with her new hairstyle. This gets a payoff in Sharon's remark to Dennis after

From left: Kelsey Grammer, Kristen Johnston, Julia Louis-Dreyfus, Jonathan Silverman, and Michael Richards in a still for *London Suite* (1996).

her hair is disheveled from the car ride, "I'm just amazed that you recognize me." There are also visual gags, such as Sharon's windblown hair from her drive in Dennis' car. The best one is when, after telling Sharon, "I need ... I've got to have it," Dennis lunges at her and grabs a mask attached to an oxygen tank in his car. Simon also repeats the bathroom slapstick from *California Suite,* when Anne bumps her head on the bathroom medicine cabinet, and uses other slapstick in Dennis' snorting and eye twitching mannerisms.

Funny lines retained from the play include an exchange between Diana and her assistant, Grace. Grace tells her that she is still a beautiful woman and Diana replies, "What a sweet thing to say. All except the 'still are' part." A funny variation on a line from the play is that when Sharon hits her head as she exits Dennis' car. He comments that it must have hurt and she replies, "My hair is so stiff it took most of the blow," referring to her having just been seen to spray it.

Regrettably, Simon also retains a variation on the howler also used in *Jake's Women*, with Diana's "I sense something important coming up." Equally bad is her line to Sydney, "We've been prisoners since the day we met."

Simon changes the names of two characters common to *California Suite* from Diana Barrie and Sidney Cochran to Diana and Sydney Nichols. He also gives the mother character in the play's *London Suite* "Going Home" the name Sharon Semple. Simon's cuts include the play's first story, "Settling Accounts," with the characters Billy Fox and Brian Cronan; this is replaced with the story of Debra Dolby. This provides for three stories with farce, perhaps thought to be needed to buffer the more serious story of Diana and Sydney. In other changes, Simon loses the plot points of Sydney's showing Diana a photograph of his lover, and of Mother telling Lauren that she is seeing a married man. Simon also adds new endings to the stories of "The Man on the Floor," in which Anne joins Mark lying on the floor, and "Diana and Sydney," which has Simon repeat a line about Los Angeles in *California Suite.*

Unlike Simon's prior television production, *Jake's Women*, this movie features a lot of actors known primarily for their work on television. They are Julia Louis-Dreyfus and Michael Richards from *Seinfeld*, Kelsey Grammer from *Frasier*, Jonathan Silverman from *The Single Guy*, and Kristen Johnston from *3rd Rock from the Sun*. This places the production more comfortably in the television realm. The only actor who is retained from the off–Broadway show is Paxton Whitehead, who played three roles on stage but here is reduced to a supporting one. That director Jay Sandrich has the characters laugh at each other's witticisms is a self-conscious touch, though it was done presumably in lieu of an audience laugh track. The score overwhelms the dialogue in the scenes between Diana and Sydney, and is also too loud for the two scenes of Dennis' driving.

The material gives the actors plenty of opportunities to demonstrate their comic talents. Michael Richards as Mark gets to show his gift for physical comedy, and Madeline Kahn makes practically everything Sharon says funny. It's interesting to compare the comedy styles of Kahn, who uses tiny inflections, with Julia Louis-Dreyfus, who favors hysteria with exaggerated gestures. This is not to say that Kahn cannot do broad comedy, as she demonstrates in the way Sharon sprays her hair after it is disheveled from her car ride with Dennis and in her cough in reaction to her hairspraying. Richard Mulligan, as Dennis, gets to play broad comedy with his snorting laugh and eye twitch. As Diana and Sydney, Patricia Clarkson and Kelsey Grammer suffer in comparison to the memory of Maggie Smith's and Michael Caine's portrayal of the same characters in *California Suite*. While both Clarkson and Grammer are proficient, she doesn't have Smith's eccentricity, and he lacks Caine's edge.

RELEASE: Broadcast on September 15, 1996, on National Broadcasting Company (NBC) with the tagline "Do Not Disturb!"

REVIEWS: A mixed reaction from Jeremy Gerard in *Variety*, who praises the performance of Patricia Clarkson but otherwise calls the film "sub-par Simon" and says, "Viewers may experience an unsettling sense of déjà vu hearing a kind of boulevard-comedy writing as faded in the memory as boulevards themselves." Another mixed reaction from Robert Koehler in the *Los Angeles Times*, who praises Kahn as a comic genius who "wills the situation to ironic life," and Louis-Dreyfus for "extending her usual man-trouble dilemmas on 'Seinfeld' into an aria of brilliant timing and borderline insanity."

DVD: Released by Platinum Disc on August 31, 2004.

The Sunshine Boys *(1997)*

RHI Entertainment/Hallmark Entertainment.

CREW: John Erman (Producer and Director), Gerrit Van Der Meer (Co-Producer), Robert Halmi, Sr. (Executive Producer), Neil Simon (Teleplay based on his play), Tony Imi (Photography), John W. Wheeler (Editor), Irwin L. Fisch (Underscore), Ben Edwards (Production Design), Beth Kuhn (Art Director), Susan Kaufman (Set Decorator), Helen Butler (Costumes), Bob Laden (Makeup), Greg Cannon (Peter Falk's Makeup), Colleen Calaghan (Hair). Color, 85 minutes.

CAST: Woody Allen (Al Lewis), Peter Falk (Willie Clark), Michael McKean (Scott Grogan, Director of Camera Test), Liev Schreiber (Ricky Gregg, Commercial Director), Edie Falco (Carol), Sarah Jessica Parker (Nancy Davison), Tyler Noyes (Peter), Olga Merediz (Sue), Andy Taylor (Michael Davison), Jose Soto and Kirk Acevedo (Hispanic Boys), William Hill (Hal Jenks), Herbert Rubens (Murray), Merwin Goldsmith (Harry), David Lipman (Jerry), Ray Anthony Thomas (Limo Driver), Peter Appel (Anton Black), Jennifer Esposito (Jeannie, Stage Manager), Jim Bracchitta (Assistant), Michael Badalucco (Sound Man), Stephen Singer (Paul Zumat, Camera Operator for Camera Test), Carlos Rafart (Desk Clerk). Uncredited: Whoopi Goldberg (Nurse).

SONGS: "Old Friends" (Stephen Sondheim), Liza Minnelli in main titles and orchestra in end titles.

SYNOPSIS: Agent Nancy Davison tries to persuade her uncle, comedian Willie Clark, to reteam with his ex-partner Al Lewis for a film appearance. Al agrees to the deal but is exasperated by Willie's behavior when they try to rehearse their scene in the script. Nancy arranges for the two men to meet for lunch and they agree to continue. However, at the camera test they argue and Al walks out. Willie has a heart attack, and the partners lose the film job. Al visits Willie in his hotel room, where they learn that they are both moving to Los Angeles.

NOTES: Simon adapted his own play for this television remake. He provides some changes to the play and the 1975 screenplay, the most important one being the change of the Ben character into a woman. Simon also provides some new lines that are noticeably funnier than the earlier screenplay, and one new scene.

The main characters of Willie and Al are also presented differently in this version, since neither is as forgetful or such a bad listener as he was in the film. Willie's habit of renaming people may be due to his being forgetful or may be a deliberate attempt at humor, and an extension of his cantankerous nature. The Ben character is changed to Nancy, as Willie's niece, and it is noteworthy that she is amused at Al's but not Willie's jokes. She gets stomach pains from dealing with Willie whereas Ben, in the play and movie, got chest pains. The ex-partners are now comedians from the 1960s who had worked together for twenty-three years before Al quit the act because he could see that comedy styles had changed. The job offer they now receive is to appear in one scene of a Christmas comedy film entitled *Peter Piper*. In it they would play a comedy team performing one of their old routines for a sick boy in hospital. The characters in the film are named Phil and Jack.

There are other plot changes. Willie hides in the bathroom when Al enters his hotel room for the rehearsal, and Willie emerges with his face covered in shaving cream, which he only partially removes. Al shows a note to Willie that he had written to himself that reads, "This will never work. I give it, the most, twelve minutes." This prediction is shown to be correct. Willie begins the reading on the wrong page, does not take any notice of the stage directions, changes lines and characters names, and wants to switch parts. All this occurs before Willie insists on changing "Come in" to "Enter," which is retained from Simon's play. Al stays for a second try; Willie then objects to Al's supposed spitting and finger poking, also retained from the play, and Al gives up and leaves. As in the original material, these provocative actions are also repeated in the screen test, so that again Al walks out and this costs the ex-partners the job. Simon's new scene involves a lunch at the Friars Club that Nancy sets up after the disastrous rehearsal in Willie's hotel room. Willie and Al attend with Nancy and Al's daughter, Doris. Regrettably, the scene comes to an abrupt end once the two men agree to go ahead with the test.

The teleplay's funny new lines include Nancy's asking Al if it was his idea to be the straight man to Willie. Al tells her, "No, he just said the jokes before I could get them out." She tells him that Willie told her that their team had had some occasional differences, and Al tells her, "And every day was an occasion." In reference to Willie's appearing with shaving cream, Al tells him that he takes his tea "without shaving cream." Willie, who is clumsy with a kettle, questions why Al wants so little hot water for his tea, and Al tells him, "It's better than having scalding feet." The tea gag is repeated in Al's line, "I don't feel like sitting here breathing in ten year-old dust with a finger-full of hot water and a used tea bag." Willie also gets a funny line in reference to Al's deceased wife, Dede: "Was Dede her name or her initials?" Al tells him both, since her name was Dede Doris Davis.

The new comedy lines continue when Willie advises Al to tell him when he is ready for the reading, and Al replies, "What do you want me to do? Shoot off a pistol?" Willie's changing his film character name of Jack to Chuck pays off the earlier plot point that words with a "K" sound are funny. Al references this name change with his line "If you make one more change I'm chucking Jack out the window and Phil is going home with Al." Al repeats with disbelief Willie's accusation that he looks for words with a "T" in them so he can spit, and adds, "I can't even get a cup with tea in it." Nancy describes Al's rehearsal with Willie as a difficult day, to which he responds with the following: "The day that I swallowed a Szechuan spare rib at the Chinese restaurant was a difficult day. The day it was twelve degrees and my eyebrows froze to my eyeglasses was a difficult day. Today was more like the Hundred Years' War." Al says, "If Willie had tact he would nail it to my head with a hammer," and Willie asks Nancy what he could possibly do all day in Los Angeles, saying, "There's just so long you can sit and watch mudslides." The character of the nurse uses the modern slang term "dissing," and gets the following new line: "You don't wanna know what I got up under my white uniform cos I don't just treat heart attacks, I give heart attacks."

Shown from left: Al Lewis (Woody Allen), Nancy Davison (Sarah Jessica Parker) and Willie Clark (Peter Falk) in still a for *The Sunshine Boys* (1997).

Modern updates for the teleplay include Al's watching the Home Shopping Network on television, his grandson playing Nintendo with him, and topical references to David Letterman, Robin Williams, Arnold Schwarzenegger, Princess Diana, Steve Martin, John Candy, Jackie Mason, Carol Burnett, Oprah, *The Terminator* and *Seinfeld*. Other changes include that the potato chips in the commercial that Willie auditions for are now called "Chumpies" when they were "Frumpies" in the film. Here we don't see the audition, only Willie suggesting changes to the director, which implies that he did not get the job. At the Friars' Club, Willie's friend Murray tells Willie that he got it. An interesting new moment is when, after Nancy pays for a taxi for Willie and leaves, Willie gets out of the car and gets his money back, having decided to walk instead. The telephone conversation scene between Al and Ben that was so undermined in the film version by Willie's interruptions is better here, as the characters no longer speak simultaneously. Nancy is not speaking with Al on the telephone in the moments that Willie is speaking to her.

The running gag of Willie's door being stuck gets some variations. Willie now has a large collection of keys, which gets a payoff. He cannot open his door with the only key he tries in the lock, but Nancy can. The gag is not repeated for Nancy's exit as in the film; however, it returns for the rehearsal when Al has a hard time getting back into the room after his exit. Simon also has Al go outside the door for a second attempt at the rehearsal entrance, but he does not repeat the gag, nor when Al finally exits the hotel room. The gag *is* repeated for Nancy's final exit from Willie's hotel room, but not for when she opens the door for Al to enter. The stuck makeup-room door gag is retained from the screenplay, but we don't see how the men are freed.

Two plot points from the play and screenplay are lost in this version. They are Al's requirements for the sketch, including the blonde woman, and the partners moving furniture for the rehearsal set. However, Simon provides new dialogue to introduce the doctor sketch, which is never gotten to in the test. The kid in the screen test, Peter, laughs at Willie and Al's scripted lines, which recalls Nancy's laughing at Al. The end of the teleplay is also varied. The offer in the play and the screenplay of Ben having Willie come live with him is changed because Nancy offers to have Willie do so since she is moving to Los Angeles to head her agency's local branch. The plot point of the Actors' Home as an alternative dwelling is lost, and instead she says that he can entertain at the local Friars' Club. Al is also moving to Los Angeles because Carol is moving there as her husband has a new job. Further, Al advises that he has a new agent, whom we assume is Nancy. The closing moments have Al remind Willie how they first met at a benefit show and decided to become working partners, rather than having them reminisce about vaudeville performers. This reflects the updated period of the comedians' heyday.

Director John Erman uses an incongruous fade-out and fade-in for the moment when Willie retrieves his script from the bathroom for the hotel room table rehearsal. He has another fade-out and fade-in for Al coming up from the hotel foyer to Willie's hotel room to visit after Willie's heart attack. These are presumably designed for commercial breaks for television, but they interrupt the flow of the drama.

Peter Falk, as Willie, appears to use a fake nose, perhaps to make his appearance look more stereotypically Jewish. Falk's Willie isn't as overbearing as Walter Matthau's is in the film version, but Woody Allen's performance as Al is more successful than Falk's because he makes Al's exasperation at Willie funny. He also uses a stylized body language, with his right arm held raised, for his performance in the screen test to suggest a comedian of the past.

In his book *The Great American Playwrights on the Screen*, Jerry Roberts writes that the telefilm was made in 1995 but held back for broadcast. This is because the executives who originally green-lighted the production were gone by the time it was completed, and their replacements had only a tepid response to the material.

RELEASE: Broadcast December 28, 1997, on CBS television.

REVIEWS: Lambasted by Jerry Roberts, Matthew Gilbert in the *Boston Globe,* and Steve Linan in the *Los Angeles Times.* Gilbert wrote that the film "is as dreary as a rainy day." Linan describes it as "a thoroughly exasperating film devoid of humor or pathos," and says it is best to avoid these boys, "whose brand of sunshine can only bring you gloom."

DVD: Released by Platinum Disc on August 17, 2004.

Laughter on the 23rd Floor (2001)

Paramount Pictures/Showtime/Neil Simon Production.

CREW: Richard Benjamin (Director), Jeffrey Lampert (Producer), Mike "Spud" Spadone (Associate Producer), Emanuel Azenberg (Executive Producer), Neil Simon

(Executive Producer and Teleplay, based on his play), Danny Nowak (Photography), Jacqueline Cambas (Editor), Joseph Vitarelli (Music), Franco De Cotiis (Production Design), Cheryl Toy (Art Director), Megan Less (Set Decorator), Tamara Winston (Costumes), Ava Stone (Makeup), Katarina Chovanec (Hair), Brauhaus Productions (Special Effects). Color, 102 minutes. Filmed on location at the Tivoli Theatre, Toronto, Canada.

CAST: Nathan Lane (Max Prince), Mark Linn-Baker (Val Skolsky), Victor Garber (Kenny Franks), Saul Rubinek (Ira Stone), Peri Gilpin (Carol Wyman), Dan Castellaneta (Milt Fields), Richard Portnow (Harry Prince), Zach Grenier (Brian Doyle), Mackenzie Astin (Lucas Nader), Sherry Miller (Faye Prince), Colin Fox (Cal Weebs), Ardon Bess (Cecil), Roy Lewis (Alfred), Craig Eldridge (Lawrence the Observer), Karyn Dwyer (Toga Girl), Keith Knight (Brutus), Steven Morel (Reporter/Cassius), Shannon Rowe (Gail), Irene Lopez (Carla), Samantha Espie (Helen McGovern), Robert Bidaman (Brad), Victor A. Young (Harley), Gerry Quigley (Aaron), Frank Proctor (Walter Winchell), Johnny Guardhouse (Dresser), Alex Fallis (Waiter), David Gow (Dave), Neil Foster (Stage Manager), Philip Craig (Dennis), Brian Heighton (Friend of Walter's), Jake Golsbie (Pauly), Heather Paine (Elly), Marcia Bennett (Cal's Secretary), Shaun Smyth (Warren Wyman), Ian D. Clark (Doctor), Kristi Angus (Darleen Drew), Jack Jessop (Cemetery Keeper), Tamara Hickey (Diner Waitress), Roger Dunn (Bartender), Michael Hanrahan (Policeman #1), Jeffrey Lampert (Policeman #2), Kelsey Matheson (Girl in Elevator).

SONGS: "I Remember You" (music by Victor Schertzinger and lyrics by Johnny Mercer), saxophone by Max Prince at party and end credits.

SYNOPSIS: In 1954, in New York, NBC's *The Max Prince Show* is the number one comedy on television. Lucas Nader is the newest writer on the show. Max is told by the network executives that the show is losing ratings, and its running time is reduced from ninety to sixty minutes. The executives also fear that the show is too urbane for middle–Americans, and they send an observer into rehearsals. With ratings falling further, the show is eventually canceled by the network.

NOTES: The television home of the last of Simon's plays to be adapted to date further confirms the playwright's loss of screen status, despite the source play having a nine-month-long season on Broadway. The film's subject is a television comedy show of the 1950s, an obvious reference to Simon's own experience as a writer on *Your Show of Shows*. The main theme is the struggle between art and commerce, represented by the fact that the television show is ultimately considered too highbrow for middlebrow tastes. Another theme is the role of co-workers as friends and family.

The adaptation has sizable cuts to the source play, comparable to the major revision Simon did to develop his play *The Gingerbread Lady* into the film *Only When I Laugh*. There are new scenes and new characters, and lines and scenes relocated. Simon uses the "F" bomb liberally here, presumably getting past the television censor on the grounds that the production was made for cable and not network television. Narration is used as a theatrical device, though to a lesser extent than in the play. The teleplay "opens up" the play by setting scenes in the television studio where we also see the audience, in restaurants, at Max's home and in his car, in a doctor's surgery, on the Staten Island ferry, and in a cemetery. The new scenes show action that is only described in the play, such as Max's meeting with the NBC executives, and the show observer at work. Other new scenes have narrative payoffs. The restaurant scene in which the overmedicated Max falls into his dinner plate shows a consequence of his pill-taking, as does Faye's telling Max that he made love to her when he was apparently asleep from the pills. Another new scene pays off the play's plot point of Milt wearing a white suit in front of Max, when Lucas tells Lawrence at the Christmas party that he should wear a white suit at the next rehearsal he observes, for Max, as thanks for the watch he has been given. Simon also provides new gags, such as how Brian's hacking smoker's cough stops after he takes a drag on a cigarette, and Max squirting water on Milt when he crushes a paper cup.

A new funny line pays off the "funny contest" when Milt threatens to pee in a plant in the office and Carol says, "Put it away. The funny contest is over." Simon's changes the name of the play's Lucas Brickman to Lucas Nader, but he is reduced to being a minor character in the narrative. Other changes include how Ira's heart palpitations are given to Max, and that we don't see the writer's contributions to the show so that the impression is given that all the sketch ideas come from Max. Simon also changes the ending, where Harry tells the writers about himself and Max as brothers, and Max plays the saxophone.

Max is presented as the tortured artist, a genius who is self-destructive from an excess of work, liquor and pill-taking. However, interestingly, one device he does not indulge in is womanizing. He is most comfortable in fantasy on-camera, and has trouble with reality in dealing with the television executives. His marriage and children do not give him the emotional grounding he needs; his brother, Harry, who lives and works with him, is the person closest to him. Max's eccentricity is demonstrated by his wearing only underwear in his office. He is both passive-aggressive in the way he delays going into Cal Weebs' office for a meeting as a revenge for previously being kept waiting by Cal, and violent when he breaks his office chair, punching holes in the walls of the writers' room, and attacks Lawrence. However, Max is also heroic in wanting to do a sketch that attacks Joseph McCarthy, something the writers all consider a bad idea because they are afraid of the consequences, and firing himself when he is told that he must fire one of the writers on the show.

The writers are presented as eccentric artists in their vulgarity and swearing, and in the fanciful way Milt dresses in cape and mink coat, and bright colors. Carol is the only female writer, and she is the pacifier of the group, though she objects to the men's swearing. When Max refuses to fire Carol because she is pregnant, she objects because she wants to be retained because she is a good writer. Lucas is presumably based on Neil Simon, although there is no accompanying character based on his brother, Danny, who worked on the real-life show with him. Lucas is intimidated by the other writers, although he does speak, despite the fact that Simon was reported to have only whispered his suggestions.

The material is biased in favor of the artists compared to the network executives, who get a further strike against them when they get Harry's name wrong. Max holds the executives in contempt despite the fact that the network owns the show and provides him and his writers with work. He never considers that they may be right in thinking that some of the show's sketches are too highbrow for their market. Rather, Max humiliates Lawrence, the observer, which is counterproductive. The executives are proven

Clockwise from left: Saul Rubinek, Dan Castellaneta, Zach Grenier, Richard Portnow (standing), Victor Garber, Mackenzie Astin (standing), Mark Linn-Baker, Peri Gilpin and Nathan Lane in a still for *Laughter on the 23rd Floor* (2001).

to be right when the show loses more ratings after Max does a Julius Caesar parody, which leads to the show being canceled.

The only actors retained from the Broadway show are Mark Linn-Baker and Nathan Lane. Director Richard Benjamin uses period footage of New York, newsreel footage of Senator Joseph McCarthy and the House Un-American Activities Committee hearings, and extracts from *The Lawrence Welk Show* and *Miracle of Morgan's Creek* (1944) on television. Benjamin's direction adds to the humor of the piece after Val tells Max on the telephone that the writers have five or six wonderful ideas, and we cut to the writers all looking at Val to tell us that this is not true. However, he missteps with the use of score, which overwhelms the dialogue in a lot of scenes, and also in having the characters laugh at each other to show us how amusing they are. The nadir of the use of this effect is when the writers laugh at Max's very unfunny remarks at the climax.

As Max, Nathan Lane is funnier than Sid Caesar was in *Your Show of Shows*, though Max fails with his Marlon Brando impersonation. Lane adds gravitas to Max's suffering, underplays his rage at the NBC executives, and scores a good laugh when Max grabs Milt to look at the suit he wears.

The play's main characters are said to be inspired by people Neil Simon knew when he worked on *Your Show of Shows*. Max Prince is based on Sid Caesar, Kenny Franks on Larry Gelbart, Val Slotsky on Mel Tolkin, Brian Doyle on Tony Webster, Milt Fields on Sheldon Keller, Carol Wyman on Lucille Kallen, Ira Stone on Mel Brooks, and Harry Prince on Sid Caesar's brother, Dave Caesar.

Mel Brooks also made a film based on his experience of working on the show, *My Favorite Year* (1982), which was also directed by Richard Benjamin. The character of Stan "King" Kaiser is like Sid Caesar, a short-tempered autocrat but also generous in sending gifts to his staff. At one point King shoots down a monologue that he dislikes with an invisible air rifle, a gesture that Caesar was known to have performed. The narrative has the freshman Benjy Stone, presumably based on Brooks, working on the NBC sketch show *Comedy Cavalcade* in 1954. Benjy is given the job of looking after the show's guest star, Alan Swann, an Errol Flynn–type movie star who is a drunken womanizer. Flynn didn't ever appear on the show in real life, so it is hard to know what guest star the character is based on, if it is meant to be based on a real incident. Selma Diamond, who was another writer for Caesar, plays a supporting role in the film as the wardrobe mistress, Lil; the show's head writer, Sy Benson, appears to be based on Mel Tolkin; and the character of Herb Lee is presumably based on Simon's reputation of being a shy whisperer. The film's climax has Herb speak out loud for the first time, and Benjamin gives a double-take reaction to the others in the television studio control room.

Sid Caesar was interviewed by Susan King for the *Los Angeles Times* on June 6, 2001, about the television production of *Laughter on the 23rd Floor*. He commented that it was more dramatic than the play: "There is a lot of fiction in there, but there is a lot of truth in there. It was more of a piece you could relate to; it wasn't just laughs."

RELEASE: Premiered on January 14, 2001, at the Palm Springs International Festival. Broadcast on May 26, 2001, on Showtime Television with the tagline "TV's top comic has everything. Except his sanity."

REVIEWS: A mixed reaction from Steven Oxman in *Variety*, who says that Benjamin and Simon transform a "pretty plotless piece into a barely coherent one. And yet, Nathan Lane and a superb group of supporting players mine this stuff expertly." Howard Rosenberg wrote in the *Los Angeles Times* that the exaggerated behavior is better suited to stage than the intimate small screen, and as a result, "Max and his bickering gang are much less funny than grating, no recipe for comedy."

AWARD: Nominated for the Outstanding Made for Television Movie Emmy Award.

DVD: Released by Paramount Entertainment, date unknown.

The Goodbye Girl (2004)

TNT/Warner Bros. Television/Ron Ziskin Productions.

CREW: Richard Benjamin (Director and Producer), Timothy Marx (Producer), Simon Abbott (Co-Producer), Ron Ziskin and Dave Collins (Executive Producers), Don Safran (Co-Executive Producer), John Forrest Niss (Associate Producer), Neil Simon (Executive Producer and Teleplay, based on his screenplay), Danny Nowak (Photography), Jacqueline Cambas (Editor), John Frizzell (Music), Franco De Cotiis (Production Design), Susan De Laval (Costumes), Suki Parker (Art Director), Penny Chalmers (Set Decorator), Odessa Munroe (Choreography), Faye Von Schroeder (Vancouver Makeup), Patty Bunch (Ms. Heaton's Makeup), Michael Bigger (New York Makeup), Forest Brooke Sala (Vancouver Hair), Stephan Lempire (New York Hair). Color, 102 minutes. Filmed in Vancouver and New York.

CAST: Patricia Heaton (Paula McFadden), Jeff Daniels (Elliot Garfield); Hallie Kate Eisenberg (Lucy McFadden); Lynda Boyd (Donna Douglas); Alan Cumming (Mark Bodine); Oliver Frey (Richard Benjamin); Sharon Wilkins (Mrs. Crosby); Zak Santiago (Dance Class Instructor); Marco Soriano (Ronnie Burns); Woody Jeffreys (Eddie, Ronnie's Assistant); Panos Grames (Pianist); Jessica Van der Veen (Stage Manager); Emily Holmes (Rhonda Fontana); John Shaw (First Gentleman); Jack O'Connell (Liquor Salesman); Dominic Colon, Wass M. Stevens and Joseph D'Onofrio (Muggers); Ron Halder (Lovell); John B. Lowe (Man in Audience); Katey Wright (Duchess); Ross Benjamin (Catesby); William Samples (Critic in Audience); Kurt Max Runte, Marcus Hondro and Kwesi Ameyaw (*Richard III* Troupe); Marie Stillin (Mark's Mother); Warren Takeuchi and Kevan Ohtsji (Auto Executives); Telly Kousakis and Andrew Francis (Young Men Outside Club); Jenn Griffin (Club Manager); Brian Lydiatt and Jimmy Broydon (Club Waiters); Paige Gray and Tai-Monique Kristjansen (Club Dancers); Alyssa May Gold (Cynthia Fein); Christine Lippa, Patricia Idlette, Zahf Paroo and Chris Gauthier (Improv Troupe); Margaret Zag (Gretchen).

SONGS: "Cheek to Cheek" (Irving Berlin), uncredited singer, Jeff Daniels; "Goodbye Girl" (David Gates), Hootie and the Blowfish end credits. Uncredited: "Laughter in the Sunshine" (Patrick Woodland); "Heaven" (John Frizzell and Dee Carstensen).

SYNOPSIS: Ex-dancer Paula McFadden lives in a Manhattan apartment with her ten-year-old daughter Lucy. Her lover actor Tony DeForrest leaves for a film role in Italy and sublets the apartment to Chicago actor Elliot Garfield. Refusing to move out, Paula makes a deal to share the apartment with Elliot. Elliot is cast in an off–Broadway production of *Richard III*, which is cancelled after opening night. She gets a job at the auto show and he joins an improv group. Elliot romances Paula and they make love. He gets a film job offer in Seattle and promises Paula that he will return, leaving his guitar behind.

NOTES: The last to date of Simon's work to be made into a film, this adaptation of his own 1977 screenplay for a made-for-television remake is perhaps the final confirmation of the playwright's loss of screen status. For the adaptation Simon introduces three new scenes and some new dialogue. As the second new scene and some of the new dialogue appears in the screenplay's novelization, it suggests that they were cut from the original screenplay. However, there are other lines that are completely new.

Some of the changes from the original screenplay include updated references and technology. The Italian director that Tony goes to work with is now Roberto Benigni. Elliot has a cell phone and the apartment key has been FedEx'd from Tony to Elliot. Further, the off–Broadway theatre where Elliot performs is shown to be more professional looking; Elliot references show reviews on television's Discovery Channel, the Chinese channel, the cooking channel and ESPN; and a dancer at the strip club is shown to pole dance. Paula was thirty-three in the original film and here she is thirty-six. Her apartment is shown to be larger than it was in the original film. To do his morning meditative chanting Elliot now wears a camp headdress, which prefigures the feather boa he wears as *Richard III* in rehearsal and in performance. The boa is presumably to reinforce Richard's being gay, as is his lisping. The *Richard III* cast laugh when hearing Mark's idea that Richard was gay, and Mark is shown to be a fool by his dropping a cookie and then loudly eating another during the first rehearsal. A major change for Elliot is that he is shown here as a more pretentious actor, repeating "now," the first word in the play, twenty-five times. Simon now also has the cast of *Richard III* take bows at the end of the disastrous opening night performance.

The bathroom scene that begins the romance between Paula and Elliot is altered. Now Paula kisses Elliot back when he kisses her so that their attraction is shown to be mutual, and she dresses up for the rooftop party, which is something that the original Paula did not do. Elliot sings "Cheek to Cheek" and not "How About You" to Paula on the rooftop. However, the line about James Stewart playing Lindbergh in a film, retained from the screenplay, doesn't work here since the actor died in 1997. Simon loses the plot point of Elliot's being short, presumably made to accommodate Richard Dreyfuss' height at five foot five inches, since Jeff Daniels is six foot three inches. This lost point is apparent when Paula no longer comments that Elliot is too short to play Stanley in *A Streetcar Named Desire,* and when he later describes himself as "thin of stature." A similar lost point is Paula's having a pug nose, presumably written specifically for Marsha Mason. Another lost moment is Paula's telling Elliot backstage after *Richard III* that she thought he was wonderful.

There is a new scene in which Paula checks to see how much money she has left after Tony has gone, and tells Lucy to kick her the next time she sees Paula talking to an actor. The scene also pays off the loan shark line from the letter Tony has written her, with Lucy suggesting they could borrow money from the sharks. The second new scene has Paula shown coming out of Elliot's room after they have presumably made love. She tells Lucy that she spent the night reading the life of Lincoln and Lucy asks her when Lucy has to move back into her old room. The final new scene shows Elliot with the Improv Group and has Elliot jokingly telling the audience not to applaud or else the management will have to pay the actors. The new lines in which Paula comments that Elliot doesn't touch her the morning after their lovemaking provide two payoffs: he tells her that she doesn't like how he touched her at first, and also suggests that they can spend the day touching each other.

Simon's new plot points include Elliot's stating that he has gay friends as part of his objection to playing Richard as gay, and having someone walk over a *Richard III* program on the floor after the show. He also has the revolving car at the auto show that Paula is working at bump into her (and less interestingly, has her trip over her high heels)

Patricia Heaton and Jeff Daniels in a still for *The Goodbye Girl* (2004) (Photofest).

to emphasize her faltering delivery of sales spiel. Another good choice is to have Elliot climb back into the apartment using the fire escape ladder he has used to appear to Paula in the street. This pays off when Paula is shown at his bedroom door as he climbs back through the window. Simon's best new line has Lucy commenting that she thought they didn't do homework in California but just skateboarded all day. Another amusing line comes from a man in the audience at *Richard III*. He references Richard's line about "my kingdom for a horse" when he comments, "That's what I'd give for a taxi."

Director Richard Benjamin uses repeated fast motion with shots of the New York skyline and rolling clouds for the passage of time. At one point the screen is misty from a glass door that is being cleaned before Paula walks through it. In the scene played under the opening credits, the dialogue reads as blather and the music used is distracting. The score's incorporation of guitar is another misguided choice, given that Elliot plays one. This is a problem in two scenes: when a cue is heard after Elliot falls asleep in Lucy's bed, and when Paula and Lucy visit him backstage after *Richard III*. Benjamin also overdoes the lightning in the scene when Elliot arrives so that the tone is more suggestive of a horror movie. He appears to use a dance double for Paula's audition and over-edits the sequence so that we don't get any sense of her as a dancer.

A major difficulty with the adaptation is that Simon does not do what he did for the television remake of *The Sunshine Boys*, in which he made the two main characters different from those in the original film. As a result the two lead actors here have to fight against our memory of Richard Dreyfuss and Marsha Mason. Jeff Daniels suffers the most by comparison, since he lacks Dreyfuss' charm and likeability. A more mannered actor, he also seems a bit old at forty-eight, compared to Dreyfuss' thirty years of age for an up-and-coming actor. Instead, the character now reads more as a mature man who has been an unsuccessful actor for a long time. Daniels also loses the sexual innuendo suggested in Elliot's request for Paula to be nice to him, so that her subsequent anger makes no sense. Daniel's Richard III in performance is worse than Dreyfuss', who made the interpretation work. Perhaps to demonstrate that his Elliot is a bad actor, Daniel's attempt at Richard's limp is awkward, with the result that the gay issue is the lesser problem. The upstaging of the other actors during the applause at the Improv Club may also be a sign of Elliot's lack of professionalism. Daniels' general overuse of gesturing hands may be another sign that Elliot is supposed to be a bad actor, though it reads as more of an indictment of Daniels.

Patricia Heaton was 45 at the time of filming, while Marsha Mason was 33. Heaton's age is more apparent in close-ups, but otherwise she passes for the mother of a ten-year-old. She can be as mannered an actor as Daniels, and her performance is inconsistent. She makes Paula more likeable than Elliot, which reverses the original film's greater likeability of Elliot over Paula. In Paula's reading of Tony's farewell letter, Heaton shows depth of emotion. She is also funny when crying, "Isn't it terrible?" and in her strained smile when saying hello to Elliot's date, Rhonda. Heaton also makes Paula's emotional transitions more believable than Daniels', particularly in her change to being romantically interested in Elliot. As Lucy, Hallie Kate Eisenberg is less of a wise-acre than Quinn Cummings was, and lacks the individual personality of her predecessor. However, she does provide tears in the hansom cab scene. In his small role, Alan Cummings makes Mark funny in an arch way.

RELEASE: Broadcast January 16, 2004, with the tagline "A story about love at first fight."

REVIEWS: Lambasted by Terry Kelleher in *People* as "optional" rather than "must-see," and Robert Bianco in *USA Today*. Bianco writes, "More than just superfluous, [it] is one of those misbegotten remakes that make you rethink the original. This is, in part, because the actors aren't up to the roles, or at least aren't able to make you look past the material."

DVD: Warner Home Video on July 20, 2004.

Appendix: Theatre Credits
(Chronological)

Catch a Star!

CREW: Danny Simon (Director), Sy Kleinman (Producer), Danny Simon and Neil Simon (Writers), Lee Sherman (Dances and Musical Numbers Stager), Sammy Fain and Philip Charig (Music), Paul Francis Webster and Ray Golden (Lyrics), Herb Schutz (Ballet Music), Milton Greene (Musical Director), Ralph Alswang (Scenic Design), Thomas Becher (Costumes).

CAST: Elaine Dunn, Jack Wakefield, Helen Halpin, Marc Breaux, Undine Forrest, Sonny Parks, Wayne Sherwood, Kay Malone, Denny Desmond, Calvin Holt, Lynne Bretonn.

SEASON: Broadway from September 6 to 24, 1955, at the Plymouth Theatre, New York.

NOTE: The sketches were entitled "To Be or Not To Be in Love," "Twist My Arm," "Room for Rent," "Las Vegas," "Arty," "Fly Little Heart," "Gruntled," "Matrimonial Agency," "One Hour Ahead of the Posse," and "Carnival in Court."

New Faces of 1956

CREW: Paul Lynde (Director); Leonard Sillman and John Roberts (Producers); Yvette Schumer (Associate Producer); Paul Lynde, Richard Maury, Louis Botto, Neil Simon, Danny Simon, Terry Ryan, and Barry Blitzer (Writers); David Tihmar (Musical Numbers Director); Peter Larkin (Scenic Design); Thomas Becher (Costumes); Peggy Clark (Lighting).

CAST: Jane Connell (Madame Interpreter).

SEASON: Broadway from June 14, 1956, to December 22, 1956, at the Ethel Barrymore Theatre, New York.

NOTE: The Simons' sketch was entitled "Madame Interpreter."

Come Blow Your Horn

CREW: Stanley Prager (Director), William Hammerstein and Michael Ellis (Producers), Neil Simon (Writer), Ralph Alswang (Scenic Design and Lighting), Stanley Simmons (Costumes).

CAST: Hal March (Alan Baker), Arlene Golonka (Peggy Evans), Warren Berlinger (Buddy Baker), Lou Jacobi (Mr. Baker), Sarah Marshall (Connie Dayton), Pert Kelton (Mrs. Baker), Carolyn Brenner (A Visitor).

SEASON: Broadway from February 22, 1961, to October 6, 1962, at the Brooks Atkinson Theatre, New York.

Little Me

CREW: Cy Feuer and Bob Fosse (Directors), Cy Feuer and Ernest H. Martin (Producers), Neil Simon (Book based on a novel by Patrick Dennis), Cy Coleman (Music), Carolyn Leigh (Lyrics), Ralph Burns (Music Orchestrator), Charles Sanford (Musical Director), Bob Fosse (Choreography), Robert Randolph (Scenic Design and Lighting), Robert Fletcher (Costumes).

CAST: Peter Turgeon (Patrick Dennis), Nancy Andrews (Miss Poitrine, Today), Adnia Rice (Momma), Virginia Martin (Belle), Sid Caesar (Noble Eggleston/Mr. Pinchley/Val du Val/Fred Poitrine/Otto Schnitzler/Prince Cherney/Noble Junior), Nancy Cushman (Mrs. Eggleston), Mickey Deems (Pinchley Junior), Joey Faye (Bernie Buchsbaum), Mort Marshall (Benny Buchsbaum), Swen Swenson (George Musgrove).

SEASON: Broadway from November 17, 1962, to June 29, 1963, at the Lunt-Fontanne Theatre, New York.

AWARDS: Tony Award to Bob Fosse for Best Choreography. Nominations for Best Musical, Cy Feuer and Ernest H. Martin for Best Musical Producer, Simon for Best Musical Author, Cy Coleman and Carolyn Leigh for Best Score, Sid Caesar for Best Actor in a Musical, Swen Swenson for Best Featured Actor in a Musical, Virginia Martin for Best Featured Actress in a Musical, Cy Feuer and Bob Fosse for Best Musical Direction, and Robert Fletcher for Best Costume Design.

Barefoot in the Park

CREW: Mike Nichols (Director), Saint Subber (Producer), Ellen Enterprises (Associate Producer), Neil Simon (Writer), Oliver Smith (Scenic Design), Donald Brooks (Costumes), Jean Rosenthal (Lighting).

CAST: Elizabeth Ashley (Corie Bratter), Herbert Edelman (Telephone Man), Joseph Keating (Delivery Man), Robert Redford (Paul Bratter), Mildred Natwick (Mrs. Banks), Kurt Kasznar (Victor Velasco).

SEASON: Broadway from October 23, 1963, June 25, 1967, at the Biltmore Theatre, New York.

AWARDS: Tony Award for Mike Nichols for Best Direction of a Play. Nominations for Best Play, Saint Subber for Best Dramatic Producer, and Elizabeth Ashley for Best Actress in a Play.

The Odd Couple

CREW: Mike Nichols (Director), Saint Subber (Producer), Neil Simon (Writer), Oliver Smith (Scenic Design), Jean Rosenthal (Lighting), Ann Roth (Costumes).

CAST: Art Carney (Felix Ungar), Walter Matthau (Oscar Madison), Nathaniel Frey (Murray), Paul Dooley (Speed), Carole Shelley (Gwendolyn Pigeon), Monica Evans (Cecily Pigeon), Sidney Armus (Roy), John Fiedler (Vinnie).

SEASON: Broadway from March 10, 1965, to July 30, 1966, at the Plymouth Theatre, and from August 1, 1966, to July 2, 1967, at the Eugene O'Neill Theatre, New York.

AWARDS: Tony Awards for Simon for Best Dramatic Author, Walter Matthau for Best Actor in a Play, Mike Nichols for Best Director of a Play, and Oliver Smith for Best Scenic Design. Nomination for Best Play.

Sweet Charity

CREW: Bob Fosse (Director/Choreography); Robert Fryer, Lawrence Carr and Joseph P. Harris (Producers); John Bowab (Associate Producer); Neil Simon (Book based on the screenplay *Nights of Cabiria* by Federico Fellini); Cy Coleman (Music); Dorothy Fields (Lyrics); Ralph Burns (Music Orchestrator); Robert Randolph (Scenic Design and Lighting); Irene Sharaff (Costumes).

CAST: Gwen Verdon (Charity), Michael Davis (Dark Glasses/Mike), John Stratton (Bystander/Waiter), Bud Vest (Married Man/Manfred), Elaine Cancilla (Married Woman/Old Maid), Ruth Buzzi (Woman with Hat/Receptionist/Good Fairy), John Sharpe (Football Player), Gene Foote (Ice Cream Vendor), Harold Pierson (Ballplayer/Brother Harold/Policeman), Eddie Gasper (Ballplayer/Brother Eddie), Barbara Sharma (Career Girl/Rosie), Lee Roy Reams (Young Spanish Man), John Wheeler (First Policeman/Herman), David Gold (Second Policeman/Barney), Thelma Oliver (Helene), Carmen Morales (Carmen), Helen Gallagher (Nickie), I.W. Klein (Doorman), Sharon Ritchie (Ursula), James Luisi (Vittorio Vidal), John McMartin (Oscar), Arnold Soboloff (Daddy Johann Sebastian Brubeck).

SEASON: Broadway from January 29, 1966, to July 15, 1967, at the Palace Theatre, New York.

AWARDS: Tony Awards for Bob Fosse for Best Choreography. Nominations for Best Musical, Gwen Verdon for Best Actress in a Musical, John McMartin for Best Featured Actor in a Musical, Helen Gallagher for Best Featured Actress in a Musical, Fosse for Best Direction of a Musical, Cy Coleman and Dorothy Fields for Best Score, and Irene Sharaff for Best Costume Design.

The Star-Spangled Girl

CREW: George Axelrod (Director), Saint Subber (Producer), Neil Simon (Writer), Oliver Smith (Set Design), Ann Roth (Costumes), Jean Rosenthal (Lighting).

CAST: Anthony Perkins (Andy Hobart), Richard Benjamin (Norman Cornell), Connie Stevens (Sophie Rauschmeyer).

SEASON: Broadway from December 21, 1966, to August 5, 1967, at the Plymouth Theatre, New York.

Plaza Suite

CREW: Mike Nichols (Director), Saint Subber and Nancy Enterprises (Producers), Neil Simon (Writer), Oliver Smith (Scenic Design), Jean Rosenthal (Lighting), Patricia Zipprodt (Costumes).

CAST: "Visitor from Mamaroneck": Bob Balaban (Bellhop), Maureen Stapleton (Karen Nash), George C. Scott (Sam Nash), Jose Ocasio (Waiter), Claudette Nevins (Jean McCormack). "Visitor from Hollywood": Jose Ocasio (Waiter), George C. Scott (Jessie Kiplinger), Maureen Stapleton (Muriel Tate). "Visitor from Forest Hills": Maureen Stapleton (Norma Hubley), George C. Scott (Roy Hubley), Bob Balaban (Borden Eisler), Claudette Nevins (Mimsey Hubley).

SEASON: Broadway from February 14, 1968, to October 3, 1970, at the Plymouth Theatre, New York.

AWARDS: Tony Award for Mike Nichols for Best Direction of a Play. Nominations for Best Play, and Maureen Stapleton for Best Actress in a Play.

Promises, Promises

CREW: Robert Moore (Director), David Merrick (Producer), Samuel Liff (Associate Producer), Neil Simon (Book based on the film *The Apartment* by Billy Wilder and I.A.L. Diamond), Burt Bacharach (Music), Hal David (Lyrics), Harold Wheeler (Musical Director), Jonathan Tunick (Music Orchestrator), Michael Bennett (Choreography), Robin Wagner (Scenic Design), Donald Brooks (Costumes), Martin Aronstein (Lighting).

CAST: Jerry Orbach (Chuck Baxter), Edward Winter (J.D. Sheldrake), Jill O'Hara (Fran Kubelik), Ken Howard (Bartender Eddie), Paul Reed (Mr. Dobitch), Adrienne Angel (Sylvia Gilhooley), Norman Shelly (Mr. Kirkeby), Vince O'Brien (Mr. Eichelberger), Donna McKechnie (Vivien Della Hoya), A. Larry Haines (Dr. Dreyfuss), Marian Mercer (Marge MacDougall), Dick O'Neill (Jesse Vanderhof), Rita O'Connor (Dentist's Nurse), Gerry O'Hara (Company Doctor), Carole Bishop (Company Nurse), Millie Slavin (Peggy Olson), Baayork Lee (Lum Ding Hostess), Scott Pearson (Waiter), Michael Vita (Madison Square Garden Attendant).

SEASON: Broadway December 1, 1968, to January 1, 1972, at the Shubert Theatre, New York.

AWARDS: Tony Awards to Jerry Orbach for Best Actor in a Musical and Marian Mercer for Best Featured Actress in a Musical. Nominations for Best Musical, Jill O'Hara for Best Actress in a Musical, A. Larry Haines and Edward Winter for Best Featured Actor in a Musical, Robert Moore for Best Direction of a Musical, and Michael Bennett for Best Choreography.

Last of the Red Hot Lovers

CREW: Robert Moore (Director), Saint Subber (Producer), Neil Simon (Writer), Oliver Smith (Scenic Design), Donald Brooks (Costumes), Peggy Clark (Lighting).

CAST: James Coco (Barney Cashman), Linda Lavin (Elaine Navazio), Marcia Rodd (Bobbi Michele), Doris Roberts (Jeanette Fisher).

SEASON: Broadway from December 28, 1969, to September 4, 1971, at the Eugene O'Neill Theatre, New York.

AWARDS: Tony Award nominations for Best Play, James Coco for Best Leading Actor in a Play, Linda Lavin for Best Featured Actress in a Play, and Robert Moore for Best Direction of a Play. No wins.

The Gingerbread Lady

CREW: Robert Moore (Director), Saint Subber and Nancy Enterprises (Producers), Neil Simon (Writer), David Hays (Scenic Design), Frank Thompson (Costumes), Martin Aronstein (Lighting).

CAST: Michael Lombard (Jimmy Perry), Alex Colon (Manuel), Betsy von Furstenberg (Toby Landau), Maureen Stapleton (Evy Meara), Ayn Ruymen (Polly Meara), Charles Siebert (Lou Tanner).

SEASON: Broadway from December 13, 1970, to May 29, 1971, at the Plymouth Theatre, New York.

AWARDS: Tony Award for Maureen Stapleton for Best Actress in a Play. No other nominations.

The Prisoner of Second Avenue

CREW: Mike Nichols (Director), Saint Subber and Nancy Enterprises (Producers), Neil Simon (Writer), Richard Sylbert (Scenic Design), Anthea Sylbert (Costumes), Tharon Musser (Lighting).

CAST: Peter Falk (Mel Edison), Lee Grant (Edna Edison), Vincent Gardenia (Harry Edison), Florence Stanley (Pearl), Tresa Hughes (Jessie), Dena Dietrich (Pauline).

SEASON: Broadway from November 11, 1971, to September 29, 1973, at the Eugene O'Neill Theatre, New York.

AWARDS: Tony Awards for Vincent Gardenia for Best Featured Actor in a Play and Mike Nichols for Best Direction of a Play. Nomination for Best Play.

The Sunshine Boys

CREW: Alan Arkin (Director), Emanuel Azenberg and Eugene V. Wolsk (Producers), Neil Simon (Writer), Kert Lundell (Scenic Design), Albert Wolsky (Costumes), Tharon Musser (Lighting).

CAST: Jack Albertson (Willie Clark), Lewis J. Stadlen (Ben Silverman), Sam Levene (Al Lewis), Joe Young (Patient), John Batiste (Eddie), Lee Meredith (Sketch Nurse), Minnie Gentry (Registered Nurse).

SEASON: Broadway from December 20, 1972, to October 27, 1973, at the Broadhurst Theatre; October 30, 1973, to February 9, 1974, at the Shubert Theatre, and February 11, 1974, to April 21, 1974, at the Lunt-Fontanne Theatre, New York.

AWARDS: Tony Award nominations for Best Play, Best Actor in a Play for Jack Albertson, and Best Direction of a Play for Alan Arkin.

The Good Doctor

CREW: A.J. Antoon (Director), Emanuel Azenberg and Eugene V. Wolsk (Producers), Neil Simon (Writer, adapted and suggested by short stories by Anton Chekhov), Tony Walton (Scenic Design and Costumes), Tharon Musser (Lighting), Peter Link (Music).

CAST: Christopher Plummer, René Auberjonois, Marsha Mason, Barnard Hughes, Frances Sternhagen.

SEASON: Broadway from November 27, 1973, to May 26, 1974, at the Eugene O'Neill Theatre, New York.

AWARDS: Tony Award for Frances Sternhagen for Best Actress in a Featured Role in a Play. Nominations for Best Score for Peter Link, Best Actor in a Play for René Auberjonois, and Tharon Musser for Best Lighting Design.

God's Favorite

CREW: Michael Bennett (Director), Emanuel Azenberg and Eugene V. Wolsk (Producers), Neil Simon (Writer), William Ritman (Scenic Design), Joseph G. Aulisi (Costumes), Tharon Musser (Lighting).

CAST: Vincent Gardenia (Joe Benjamin), Lawrence John Moss (Ben Benjamin), Laura Esterman (Sara Benjamin), Marla Karnilova (Rose Benjamin), Terry Kiser (David Benjamin), Rosetta LeNoire (Mady), Nick LaTour (Morris), Charles Nelson Reilly (Sidney Lipton).

SEASON: Broadway from December 11, 1974, to March 23, 1975, at the Eugene O'Neill Theatre, New York.

AWARDS: One Tony Award nomination for William Ritman for Best Scenic Design.

California Suite

CREW: Gene Saks (Director), Emanuel Azenberg and Robert Fryer (Producers), Neil Simon (Writer), William Ritman (Scenic Design), Jane Greenwood (Costumes), Tharon Musser (Lighting).

CAST: Tammy Grimes (Hannah Warren/Diana Nichols/Gert Franklyn), George Grizzard (William Warren/Sidney Nichols/Stu Franklyn), Jack Weston (Marvin Michaels/Mort Hollender), Leslie Easterbrook (Bunny), Barbara Barrie (Millie Michaels/Beth Hollender).

SEASON: World premiere from April 23 to June 5, 1976, at the Ahmanson Theatre, Los Angeles. Broadway from June 10, 1976, to July 2, 1977, at the Eugene O'Neill Theatre, New York.

NOTE: The character of Bunny was new for the Broadway season.

Chapter Two

CREW: Herbert Ross (Director), Emanuel Azenberg (Producer), Neil Simon (Writer), William Ritman (Scenic Design), Noel Taylor (Costumes), Tharon Musser (Lighting).

CAST: Judd Hirsch (George Schneider), Anita Gillette (Jennie Malone), Cliff Gorman (Leo Schneider), Ann Wedgeworth (Faye Medwick).

SEASON: World premiere from October 4 to November 26, 1977, at the Ahmanson Theatre, Los Angeles. Broadway from December 4, 1977, to January 15, 1979, at the Imperial Theatre, New York, and January 16 to December 8, 1979, at the Eugene O'Neill Theatre, New York.

AWARDS: Ann Wedgeworth won the Tony Award for Best Featured Actress in a play. Nominations for Best Play, Anita Gillette for Best Leading Actress, and Cliff Gorman for Best Featured Actor.

They're Playing Our Song

CREW: Robert Moore (Director), Emanuel Azenberg (Producer), Neil Simon (Book), Marvin Hamlish (Music), Carole Bager Sayer (Lyrics), Larry Blank (Musical Director), Patricia Birch (Choreography), Douglas W. Schmidt (Scenic Design), Ann Roth (Costumes), Tharon Musser (Lighting).

CAST: Robert Klein (Vernon Gersch); Lucie Arnaz (Sonia Walsk); Wayne Mattson, Andy Roth and Greg Zadikov (Voices of Vernon Gersch); Helen Castillo, Celia Celnick Matthau, and Debbie Shapiro (Voices of Sonia Walsk); Phillip Cusack (Voice of Phil the Engineer).

SEASON: World premiere from December 7, 1978, to January 27, 1979, at the Ahmanson Theatre, Los Angeles. Broadway from February 11, 1979, to September 6, 1981, at the Imperial Theatre, New York.

AWARDS: Tony nominations for Best Musical, Best Book of a Musical, Best Actor in a Musical, and Best Director of a Musical. No wins.

I Ought to Be in Pictures

CREW: Herbert Ross (Director), Emanuel Azenberg (Producer), Neil Simon (Writer), David Jenkins (Scenic Design), Nancy Potts (Costumes), Tharon Musser (Lighting).

CAST: Dinah Madoff (Libby), Joyce Van Patten (Steffy), Ron Leibman (Herb).

SEASONS: World premiere from January 17 to March 2, 1980, at the Mark Taper Forum, Los Angeles. Broadway from April 3, 1980, to January 11, 1981, at the Eugene O'Neill Theatre, New York.

AWARDS: Dinah Manoff won the Tony Award for Best Featured Actress in a play. No other nominations.

Fools

CREW: Mike Nichols (Director), Emanuel Azenberg (Producer), Neil Simon (Writer), John Lee Beatty (Scenic Design), Patricia Zipprodt (Costumes), Tharon Musser (Lighting), John Rubenstein (Music).

CAST: John Rubinstein (Leon Tolchinsky), Gerald Hiken (Snetsky), Fred Stuthman (Magistrate), David Lipman (Slovitch), Joseph Leon (Mishkin), Florence Stanley (Yenchna), Harold Gould (Doctor Zubritsky), Mary Louise Wilson (Lenya Zubritsky), Pamela Reed (Sophia Zubritsky), Richard B. Shull (Gregor Yousekevitch).

SEASON: Broadway from April 6 to May 9, 1981, at the Eugene O'Neill Theatre, New York.

Little Me

CREW: Robert Drivas (Director); Ron Dante, Wayne Rogers, Steven Leber, David Krebs, J. McLaughlin, Mark Piven, Warner Theatre Productions and Emanuel Azenberg (Producers), Neil Simon (Book based on the novel by Patrick Dennis), Cy Coleman (Music), Lyrics (Carolyn Leigh), Harold Wheeler (Music Orchestrator), Donald York (Musical Director), Peter Gennaro (Choreography), Tony Walton (Scenic Design and Costumes), Beverly Emmons (Lighting).

CAST: Gibby Brand (Announcer/Attorney/Bandleader/Preacher/German Soldier/General/Yulnick), Jessica James (Belle, Today), Henry Sutton (Charlie Drake/Greensleeves/Town Spokesman/Assistant Director/Croupier), Mary Gordon Murray (Belle/Baby Belle), Mary Small (Momma), Mary C. Holton (Ramona), Gail Pennington (Cerine), Brian Quinn (Bruce/Sailor #1), Victor Garber (Noble Eggleston/Val du Val), Fred Poitrine (Noble Junior), James Coco (Flo Eggleston/Amos Pinchley/Mr. Worst/Otto Schnitzler/Prince Cherney), James Brennan (Pinchley Junior, Bernie Buchsbaum/Croupier), Maris Clement (Ms. Kepplewhite), Sean Murphy (Nurse), Don Correia (Benny Buchsbaum/Frankie Polo), Bob Freschi (Henchman/Green Captain), Bebe Neuwirth and Gail Pennington (Boom Boom Girls), Mark McGrath (Bert/Sailor #2), Stephen Berger (Henchman/Sergeant), Andrea Green (Red Cross Nurse), David Cahn (Steward), Kevin Brooks Winkler (Pharaoh I).

SEASON: Broadway from January 21 to February 21, 1982, at the Eugene O'Neill Theatre, New York.

AWARDS: Tony Award nominations for Victor Garber for Best Actor in a Musical, Mary Gordon Murray for Best Actress in a Musical, and Peter Gennaro for Best Choreography.

Actors and Actresses

CREW: Glenn Jordan (Director), Emanuel Azenberg (Producer), Neil Simon (Writer), John Falabella (Scenic Design), David Murin (Costumes), Marcia Madeira (Lighting).

CAST: Jack Warden (Nicholas Cassell), Tom Aldredge (Harmon Andrews), Steven Culp (Tom Pryor), Polly Draper (Polly Devore), Michael Learned (Cara Heywood), Garrett M. Brown (Walter), Jay O. Sanders (Vince Barbosa).

SEASON: World premiere from February 23 to March 13, 1983, at the Hartman Theater in Stamford, Connecticut.

NOTE: Tammy Grimes was initially announced to play Cara Heywood.

Brighton Beach Memoirs

CREW: Gene Saks (Director); Emanuel Azenberg, Wayne M. Rogers, and Radio City Music Hall Productions (Producers); Center Theatre Group/Ahmanson Theatre (Associate Producers); Neil Simon (Writer); David Mitchell (Scenic Design); Patricia Zipprodt (Costumes); Tharon Musser (Lighting).

CAST: Matthew Broderick (Eugene Jerome), Joyce Van Patten (Blanche Morton), Elizabeth Franz (Kate Jerome), Mandy Ingber (Laurie Morton), Jodi Thelen (Nora Morton), Željko Ivanek (Stanley Jerome), Peter Michael Goetz (Jack Jerome).

SEASON: Premiere from December 10, 1982, to January 29, 1983, at the Ahmanson Theatre, Los Angeles. Broadway from March 27, 1983, to February 24, 1985, at the Alvin Theatre and February 26, 1985, to May 11, 1986, at the 46th Street Theatre, New York.

AWARDS: Tony Awards to Matthew Broderick for Best Featured Actor in a Play and Gene Saks for Best Direction of a Play. Nominations to Željko Ivanek for Best Featured Actor in a Play, Elizabeth Franz for Best Featured Actress in a Play.

Biloxi Blues

CREW: Gene Saks (Director), Emanuel Azenberg (Producer), Center Theatre Group/Ahmanson Theatre (Associate Producer), Neil Simon (Writer), David Mitchell (Scenic Design), Ann Roth (Costumes), Tharon Musser (Lighting).

CAST: Brian Tarantina (Roy Selridge), Matt Mulhern (Joseph Wykowski), Alan Ruck (Don Carney), Matthew Broderick (Eugene Morris Jerome), Barry Miller (Arnold Epstein), Bill Sadler (Sgt. Merwin J. Toomey), Geoffrey Sharp (James Hennesey), Randall Edwards (Rowena), Penelope Ann Miller (Daisy Hannigan).

SEASON: World premiere from December 28, 1984, to February 2, 1985, at the Ahmanson Theatre, Los Angeles. Broadway from March 28, 1985, to June 28, 1986, at the Neil Simon Theatre, New York.

AWARDS: Tony Awards for Simon for Best Play, Barry Miller for Best Featured Actor in a Play, and Gene Saks for Best Direction of a Play.

The Odd Couple

CREW: Gene Saks (Director); Emanuel Azenberg, Wayne M. Rogers and The Shubert Organization (Producers); Neil Simon (Writer); David Mitchell (Scenic Design); Ann Roth (Costumes); Tharon Musser (Lighting).

CAST: Jenny O'Hara (Sylvie), Mary Louise Wilson (Mickey), Kathleen Doyle (Renee), Marilyn Cooper (Vera), Rita Moreno (Olive Madison), Sally Struthers (Florence Ungar), Lewis J. Stadlen (Manolo Costazuela), Tony Shalhoub (Jesus Costazuela).

SEASON: World premiere from April 4 to May 26, 1985, at the Ahmanson Theatre, Los Angeles. Broadway from June 11, 1985, to February 23, 1986, at the Broadhurst Theatre, New York.

Sweet Charity

CREW: Bob Fosse (Director/Choreography); Jerome Minskoff, James M. Nederlander and Arthur Rubin and Joseph Harris (Producers); Neil Simon (Book based on the screenplay by Federico Fellini, Tullio Pinelli and Ennio Flainano); Cy Coleman (Music); Dorothy Fields (Lyrics); Fred Werner (Musical Director); Ralph Burns (Musical Orchestrator); Robert Randolph (Scenic Design and Lighting); Patricia Zipprodt (Costumes).

CAST: Debbie Allen (Charity), David Warren Gibson (Dark Glasses); Quin Baird and Jan Horvath (Married Couple), Jan Horvath (Old Maid), Jeff Shade (First Young Man), Celia Tackaberry (Woman with Hat, Panhandler, Receptionist and Good Fairy), Kelly Patterson (Ice Cream Vendor), Adrian Rosario (Young Spanish Man), Tanis Michaels (A Cop/Brother Harold), Allison Williams (Helene), Bebe Neuwirth (Nickie), Mimi Quillin (Mimi), Lee Wilkof (Herman), Tom Wierney (Doorman/Waiter), Carrie Nygren (Ursala), Mark Jacoby (Vittorio Vidal), Fred C. Mann III (Manfred), Michael Rupert (Oscar), Irving Allen Lee (Daddy Johann Sebastian Brubeck), Stanley Wesley Perryman (Brother Ray), Dana Moore (Rosie).

SEASON: Broadway from April 27, 1986, to March 15, 1987, at the Minskoff Theatre, New York.

AWARDS: Tony Awards for Best Revival, Michael Rupert for Best Featured Actor in a Musical, Bebe Neuwirth for Best Featured Actress in a Musical, and Patricia Zipprodt for Best Costume Design. Nomination for Debbie Allen for Best Actress in a Musical.

Broadway Bound

CREW: Gene Saks (Director), Emanuel Azenberg (Producer), Neil Simon (Writer), David Mitchell (Scenic Design), Joseph G. Aulisi (Costumes), Tharon Musser (Lighting).

CAST: Linda Lavin (Kate); John Randolph (Ben); Jonathan Silverman (Eugene); Jason Alexander (Stanley); Phyllis Newman (Blanche); Philip Sterling (Jack); Marilyn Cooper, MacIntyre Dixon and Ed Herlihy (Radio Voices).

SEASON: World premiere from October 6, 1986, to unknown date at the Duke University's Reynolds Theater, Durham, North Carolina. Broadway from December 4, 1986, to September 25, 1988, at the Broadhurst Theatre, New York.

AWARDS: Tony Awards for Linda Lavin for Best Actress in a Play, and John Randolph for Best Featured Actor in a Play. Nominations for Best Play, Phyllis Newman for Best Featured Actress in a Play. Finalist in the 1987 Pulitzer Prize for Drama; no winner award was given that year.

Rumors

CREW: Gene Saks (Director), Emanuel Azenberg (Producer), Neil Simon (Writer), Tony Straiges (Scenic Design), Joseph G. Aulisi (Costumes), Tharon Musser (Lighting).

CAST: Christine Baranski (Chris Gorman), Mark Nelson (Ken Gorman), Jessica Walter (Claire Ganz), Ron Leibman (Lenny Ganz), Joyce Van Patten (Cookie Cusack), Andre Gregory (Ernie Cusack), Ken Howard (Glenn Cooper), Lisa Banes (Cassie Cooper), Charles Brown (Welch), Cynthia Darlow (Pudney).

SEASON: World premiere from September 22, 1988, to unknown date at the Old Globe Theatre, San Diego, California. Broadway from November 17, 1988, to December 12, 1989, at the Broadhurst Theatre and December 13, 1989, to February 24, 1990, at the Ethel Barrymore Theatre, New York.

AWARDS: Tony Award to Christine Baranksi for Best Featured Actress in a Play. No other nominations.

Lost in Yonkers

CREW: Gene Saks (Director), Emanuel Azenberg (Producer), Neil Simon (Writer), Santo Loquasto (Scenic Design and Costumes), Tharon Musser (Lighting).

CAST: Jamie Marsh (Jay), Danny Gerard (Arty), Mark Blum (Eddie), Mercedes Ruehl (Bella), Irene Worth (Grandma Kurnitz), Kevin Spacey (Louie), Lauren Klein (Gert).

SEASON: World premiere from December 31, 1990, to unknown date at the Stevens Center for the Performing Arts in Winston-Salem, North Carolina. Broadway from February 21, 1991, to January 3, 1993, at the Richard Rodgers Theatre, New York.

AWARDS: Winner of the 1991 Pulitzer Prize for Drama. Tony Awards for Best Play, Mercedes Ruehl for Best Actress in a Play, Irene Worth for Best Featured Actress in a Play, and Kevin Spacey for Best Featured Actor in a Play.

Little Me

CREW: Jeffrey B. Moss (Director), York Theatre Company (Producer), Neil Simon (Book), Cy Coleman (Music), Carolyn Leigh (Lyrics), Leo P. Carusone (Musical Director), James Morgan (Scenic Design), Michael Bottari and Ronald Case (Costumes), Stuart Duke (Lighting), Barbara Siman (Choreography).

CAST: Jo Ann Cunningham (Older Belle), Stephen Joseph (Eggleston, Nurse, Newsboy, Cop, Preacher, German Soldier, Patient, Passenger, Assistant Director, Victor, Peasant), Denise Le Donne (Momma, Ramona, Miss K., Cop, Colette Girl, Nurse, Passenger, Newsboy, Secretary, Prop Boy, Peasant), Amelia Prentice (Young Belle, Baby), Jonathan Beck Reed (Noble, Pinchley, Val, Fred, Otto, Prince, Noble Jr.), Russ Thacker (George, Kleeg, Bennie, Headwaiter, Soldier, Steward, Sailor, Royal Doctor, Judge), Ray Wills (Brucey, Bentley, Pinchley Jr., Bernie, Lawyer, Waiter, Soldier, Sergeant, General, Captain King, Yulnick, Judge).

SEASON: Off Broadway from March 20 to April 26, 1992, at the York Theatre, St. Peter's, New York.

Jake's Women

CREW: Gene Saks (Director), Emanuel Azenberg (Producer), Neil Simon (Writer), Santo Loquasto (Scenic Design and Costumes), Tharon Musser (Lighting).

CAST: Alan Alda (Jake), Helen Shaver (Maggie), Brenda Vaccaro (Karen), Genia Michaela (Molly at 12), Tracy Pollan (Molly at 21), Joyce Van Patten (Edith), Kate Burton (Julie), Talia Balsam (Sheila).

SEASON: World premiere from March 8 to April 15, 1990, at the Old Globe Theatre, San Diego, California. Broadway from March 24 to October 25, 1992, at the Neil Simon Theatre, New York.

AWARDS: Tony Award nomination for Alan Alda for Best Actor in a Play. No other nominations.

NOTES: The Old Globe production starred Peter Coyote as well as Stockard Channing, Felicity Huffman, Candice Azzara, Talia Balsam, Amelia Campbell, Sarah Michelle Gellar and Joyce Van Patten. It was directed by Jack O'Brien, who had replaced original director Ron Link a week before the show opened. Alan Alda replaced Coyote for a season from February 20 to March 8, 1992, at the Stevens Center in Winston-Salem in the North Carolina School of the Arts' Broadway Preview Series.

I Ought to Be in Pictures

CREW: Stanley Brechner (Director and Producer), Neil Simon (Writer), James Wolk (Scenic Designer), Pamela Schofield (Costumes), David Holcomb (Lighting).

CAST: Jenn Thompson (Libby Tucker), Betsy Friday (Steffy Blondell), David Bailey (Herb Tucker).

SEASON: Off Broadway from October 7 to November 25, 1990, at the American Jewish Theatre, New York.

The Goodbye Girl

CREW: Michael Kidd (Director); Graciele Daniele (Musical Staging); Office Two-One, Inc., Gladys Nederlander, Stewart F. Lane, James M. Nederlander, Richard M. Kagan and Emanuel Azenberg (Producers); Kaede Seville (Associate Producer); Neil Simon (Book); Marvin Hamlisch (Music); David Zippel (Lyrics); Jack Everly (Musical Director); Billy Byers and Torrie Zito (Musical Orchestration); Mark Hummel (Dance Arrangements); Santo Loquasto (Scenic Design and Costumes), Tharon Musser (Lighting).

CAST: Tammy Minoff (Lucy), Bernadette Peters (Paula), Scott Wise (Billy), Susann Fletcher (Donna), Cynthia Onrubia (Jenna), Erin Torpey (Cynthia), Lisa Molina (Melanie), Carol Woods (Mrs. Crosby), Martin Short (Elliot), John Christopher Jones (Mark), Darlesia Cearcy (Stage Manager), Larry Sousa (First Man at Theatre), Mary Ann Lamb (Woman at Theatre), Rick Crom (Second Man at Theatre), Barry Bernal, Jamie Beth Chandler (TV Stage Managers), Dennis Daniels, Denise Faye, Ruth Gottschall (Mark's Mother), Sean Grant, Nancy Hess, Joe Locarro, Rick Manning and Linda Talcott.

SEASON: Broadway from March 4 to August 15, 1993, at the Marquis Theatre, New York.

AWARDS: Tony Award nominations for Best Musical, Martin Short for Best Actor in a Musical, Bernadette Peters for Best Actress in a Musical, Graciela Daniele for Best Choreography, and Michael Kidd for Best Direction of a Musical.

NOTE: The original director, Gene Saks, was replaced during out-of-town tryouts in Chicago, which ran from December 29, 1992, to January 30, 1993.

Laughter on the 23rd Floor

CREW: Jerry Zaks (Director), Emanuel Azenberg and Leonard Soloway (Producers), Ginger Montel (Associate Producer), Neil Simon (Writer), Tony Walton (Scenic Design), William Ivey Long (Costumes), Tharon Musser (Lighting).

CAST: Stephen Mailer (Lucas), Lewis J. Stadlin (Milt), Mark Linn-Baker (Val), J.K. Simmons (Brian), John Slattery (Kenny), Randy Graff (Carol), Nathan Lane (Max Prince), Bitty Schram (Helen), Ron Orbach (Ira).

SEASON: World premiere at Duke University in October 1993. Broadway from November 22, 1993, to August 27, 1994, at the Richard Rodgers Theatre, New York.

London Suite

CREW: Daniel Sullivan (Director), Emanuel Azenberg and Leonard Soloway (Producers), Ginger Montel (Associate Producer), Neil Simon (Writer), John Lee Beatty (Scenic Design), Jane Greenwood (Costumes), Ken Billington (Lighting).

CAST: Carole Shelley (Mrs. Semple, Diana and Mrs. Sitgood), Paxton Whitehead (Billy, Sidney and Dr. McMerlin), Kate Burton (Lauren, Grace and Annie), Jeffrey Jones (Brian and Mark), and Brooks Ashmanskas (Bellman).

SEASON: World premiere from October 12 to November 5, 1994, at the Seattle Repertory Theatre, Seattle, Washington. Off Broadway from March 28 to September 3, 1995, at the Union Square Theater, New York.

NOTES: The cast of the Seattle production were Jeffrey Jones (Brian and Mark), Carole Shelley (Diana, Mother and Mrs. Sitgood), Amy Ryan (Lauren), Paxton Whitehead (Billy, Sidney and Dr. McMerlin), Barbara Dirickson (Grace and Annie), Sean G. Griffin (Bellman) and Rex McDowell (Bellman and Waiter).

Proposals

CREW: Joe Mantello (Director), Emanuel Azenberg (Producer), Ginger Montel (Associate Producer), Neil Simon (Writer), John Lee Beatty (Scenic Design), Jane Greenwood (Costumes), Brian MacDevitt (Lighting).

CAST: L. Scott Caldwell (Clemma Diggins), Dick Latessa (Burt Hines), Suzanne Cryer (Josie Hines), Reg Rogers (Ken Norman), Matt Letscher (Ray Dolenz), Kelly Bishop (Annie Robbins), Peter Rini (Vinnie Bavasi), Katie Finneran (Sammii) and Mel Winkler (Lewis Barnett).

SEASON: World premiere from July 16 to August 31, 1997, at the Ahmanson Theatre, Los Angeles. Broadway from November 6, 1997, to January 11, 1998, at the Broadhurst Theatre, New York.

The Sunshine Boys

CREW: John Tillinger (Director), National Actors Theatre (Producer), Neil Simon (Writer), James Noone (Scenic Design), Noel Taylor (Costumes), Kirk Bookman (Lighting).

CAST: Jack Klugman (Willie Clark), Tony Randall (Al Lewis), Matthew Arkin (Ben Silverman), Jack Aaron (Patient), Stephen Beach (Eddie), Peggy Joyce Crosby (Sketch Nurse), Ebony Jo-Ann (Registered Nurse), and Martin Rudy (Voice-TV Director).

SEASON: World premiere from October 31 to unknown date at the Coconut Grove Playhouse, Miami. Broadway from December 8, 1997, to June 28, 1998, at the Lyceum Theatre, New York.

Little Me

CREW: Rob Marshall (Director and Choreography), Cynthia Onrubia (Associate Director and Associate Choreography), Roundabout Theatre Company (Producer), Neil Simon (Book based on the novel by Patrick Dennis), Cy Coleman (Music), Carolyn Leigh (Lyrics), David Chase (Musical Director), Harold Wheeler (Music Orchestrator), David Krane (Dance Arrangements), David Gallo (Scenic Design), Ann Hould-Ward (Costumes), Kenneth Postner (Lighting).

CAST: Martin Short (Young Noble Eggleston, Old Noble Eggleston, Amos Pinchley, Benny Buchsbaum, Val du Val, Fred Poitrine, Otto Schnitzler and Prince Cherney), Faith Prince (Belle), Brooks Ashmanskas (Pinchley Jr., Assistant Director and Doctor), Peter Benson (Kleeg, Defense Lawyer, Maitre D', Preacher, General, Captain and Victor), Michael McGrath (Bruce, Bernie Buchsbaum and Yulnick), Michael Park (Lucky), Christine Pedi (Miss Keppelwhite, Christine, Secretary, Nurse and Casino Woman) and Ruth Williamson (Momma and Mrs. Eggleston).

SEASON: Broadway from November 12, 1998, to February 7, 1999, at the Criterion Center Stage Right, New York.

AWARDS: Tony Award for Martin Short for Best Actor in a Musical. Nominations for Best Revival of a Musical, Harold Wheeler for Best Orchestrations, and Rob Marshall for Best Choreography.

Hotel Suite

CREW: John Tillinger (Director), Ellen Richard and Roundabout Theatre Company (Producers), Neil Simon (Writer), James Noone (Scenic Design), Theoni V. Aldredge (Costumes), Kevin Adams (Lighting), J. Steven White (Fight Director).

CAST: Helen Carey (Diana), Leigh Lawson (Sidney), Randy Graff (Millie), Ron Orbach (Marvin), Charlie McWade (Borden/Bellhop) and Amanda Serkasevich (Grace, Mimsey and Woman in Bed).

SEASON: Off Broadway from June 15 to September 10, 2000, at the Gramercy Theatre, New York.

The Dinner Party

CREW: John Rando (Director); Emanuel Azenberg, Ira Pittelman, Eric Krebs, Scott Nederlander, ShowOnDemand.com and Center Theatre Group/Mark Taper Forum (Producers); Ginger Montel and Marcia Roberts (Associate Producers); John Lee Beatty (Scenic Design); Jane Greenwood (Costumes); Brian MacDevitt (Lighting).

CAST: John Ritter (Claude Pichon), Henry Winkler (Albert Donay), Len Cariou (Andre Bouville), Jan Maxwell (Mariette Levieux), Veanne Cox (Yvonne Fouchet), and Penny Fuller (Gabrielle Buonocelli).

SEASON: World premiere from December 2, 1999, to January 16, 2000, at the Mark

Taper Forum, Center Theatre Group, Los Angeles. Broadway from October 19, 2000, to September 1, 2001, at the Music Box Theatre, New York.

AWARDS: Tony Award nomination for Penny Fuller for Best Featured Actress in a Play.

Oscar and Felix: A New Look at The Odd Couple

CREW: Peter Bonerz (Director), Roy Christopher (Scenic Design), Christina Haatainen Jones (Costumes), Daniel Ionazzi (Lighting).

CAST: Ryan Cutrona (Speed), Samuel Lloyd, Jr. (Roy), Richard Portnow (Murray), Vinnie-Gregory Jbara (Vinnie), John Larroquette (Oscar), Joe Regalbuto (Felix), Maria Conchita Alonso (Ynes), Alex Meneses (Julia Costazuela).

SEASON: World premiere from September 2, 2001, to June 2, 2002, and a further season from June 11 to July 27, 2002, at the Gil Cates Theater, Geffen Playhouse, California.

45 Seconds from Broadway

CREW: Jerry Zaks (Director); Emanuel Azenberg, Ira Pittelman, James M. Nederlander, Scott Nederlander and Kevin McCollum (Producers); Ginger Montel (Associate Producer); Neil Simon (Writer); John Lee Beatty (Scenic Design); William Ivey Long (Costumes); Paul Gallo (Lighting).

CAST: Lewis J. Stadlen (Mickey Fox), Dennis Creaghan (Andrew Duncan), Louis Zorich (Bernie), Kevin Carroll (Solomon Mantutu), Julie Lund (Megan Woods), Alix Korey (Arleen), Judith Blazer (Cindy), Marian Seldes (Rayleen), Bill Moor (Charles W. Browning III), Rebecca Schull (Zelda), Lynda Gravatt (Bessie James) and David Margulies (Harry Fox).

SEASON: Broadway from November 11, 2001, to January 13, 2002, at the Richard Rodgers Theatre, New York.

Rose's Dilemma

CREW: Lynn Meadow (Director), Manhattan Theatre Club (Producer), Neil Simon (Writer), Thomas Lynch (Scenic Design), William Ivey Long (Costumes), Pat Collins (Lighting).

CAST: Patricia Hodges (Rose Steiner), David Aaron Baker (Gavin Clancy), Geneva Carr (Arlene Moss), and John Cullum (Walsh McLaren).

SEASON: World premiere as *Rose and Walsh* from February 5 to March 22, 2003, at the Geffen Playhouse, California. Off Broadway from December 18, 2003, to February 1, 2004, at the City Center Stage 1, Manhattan Theatre Club, New York.

NOTES: *Rose and Walsh* was directed by David Esbjornson and starred Jane Alexander as Rose, David Aaron Baker as Clancy, Marin Hinkle as Arlene, and Len Cariou as Walsh. Mary Tyler Moore began the Off Broadway run in previews from November 20, 2003, but left the show on December 3, reportedly after being criticized by Simon for not knowing her lines.

Sweet Charity

CREW: Walter Bobbie (Director); Barry and Fran Weissler and Clear Channel Entertainment (Producers); Edwin W. Schloss, Allen Spivak, Harvey Weinstein, Hazel Feldman,

Sam Feldman, Daniel M. Posener and Jay Binder (Associate Producers), Neil Simon (Book based on an original screenplay by Federico Fellini, Tullio Pinelli and Ennio Flainano), Cy Coleman (Music), Dorothy Fields (Lyrics), Donald York (Musical Director), Don Sebesky (Musical Orchestrator), Wayne Cilento (Choreography), Scott Pask (Scenic Design), William Ivey Long (Costumes), Brian MacDevitt (Lighting).

CAST: Christina Applegate (Charity Hope Valentine), Denis O'Hare (Oscar Lindquist), Janine LaManna (Nickie), Kyra Da Costa (Helene), Ernie Sabella (Herman), Paul Schoeffler (Vittorio Vidal), Shannon Lewis (Ursula) and Rhett George (Daddy Johann Sebastian Brubeck).

SEASON: Broadway from March 4 to December 31, 2005, at the Al Hirshfeld Theatre, New York.

AWARDS: Tony Award nominations for Best Revival of a Play, Christina Applegate for Best Actress in a Musical, and Wayne Cilento for Best Choreography.

The Odd Couple

CREW: Joe Mantello (Director); Ira Pittelman, Jeffrey Sine, Ben Sprecher, Max Cooper, Scott Nederlander and Emanuel Azenberg (Producers); Roy Furman and Jay Binder (Associate Producers); John Lee Beatty (Scenic Design); Ann Roth (Costumes); Kenneth Postner (Lighting); Mark Shaiman (Music).

CAST: Nathan Lane (Oscar Madison), Matthew Broderick (Felix Ungar), Rob Bartlett (Speed), Brad Garrett (Murray), Peter Frechette (Roy), Lee Wilkof (Vinnie), Olivia d'Abo (Gwendolyn Pigeon), and Jessica Stone (Cecily Pigeon).

SEASON: Broadway from October 27, 2005, to June 4, 2006, at the Brooks Atkinson Theatre, New York.

Barefoot in the Park

CREW: Scott Elliott (Director); Robyn Goodman, Roy Gabay, Walter Grossman, Geoff Rich, Danzansky Partners, Ergo Entertainment and Ruth Hendel (Producers); C.J. Entertainment, URL Productions, Paramount Pictures Corporation, Leah Frankel, Ed Frankel, Stephen Kocis and Oliver Dow (Associate Producers); Neil Simon (Writer); Derek McLane (Scenic Design); Isaac Mizrahi (Costumes); Jason Lyons (Lighting).

CAST: Amanda Peet (Corie Bratter), Patrick Wilson (Paul Bratter), Jill Clayburgh (Corie's mother, Mrs. Banks), Tony Roberts (Victor Velasco), Adam Sietz (Telephone Repairman), and Sullivan Walker (Deliveryman).

SEASON: Broadway from February 16 to May 21, 2006, at the Cort Theatre, New York.

AWARDS: None.

Brighton Beach Memoirs

CREW: David Cromer (Director), Ira Pittelman, Max Cooper, Jeffrey Sine, Scott Delman, Ruth Hendel, Roy Furman, Ben Sprecher, Wendy Federman, Scott Landis and Emanuel Azenberg (Producers); Sheila Steinberg (Associate Producer); Neil Simon (Writer); John Lee Beatty (Scenic Design); Jane Greenwood (Costumes); Brian MacDevitt (Lighting).

CAST: Laurie Metcalf (Kate Jerome), Dennis Boutsikaris (Jack Jerome), Santino Fontana (Stanley Jerome), Jessica Hecht (Blanche Morton), Gracie Bea Lawrence (Laurie Morton), Noah Robbins (Young Eugene Morris Jerome), and Alexandra Socha (Nora Morton).

SEASON: Broadway from October 25 to November 1, 2009, at the Nederlander Theatre, New York.

NOTES: This production was scheduled to run in repertory with a production of *Broadway Bound* beginning performances November 18 and opening December 10, 2009, but it closed before its first preview. It was to feature the same cast as *Brighton Beach Memoirs* with the exception of Josh Grisetti, who was to assume the role of older Eugene, and Allan Miller in the role of Ben.

Promises, Promises

CREW: Rob Ashford (Director and Choreography); Broadway Across America, Craig Zadan, Neil Meron, The Weinstein Company, Terry Allen Kramer, Candy Spelling, Pat Addiss, Michael Speyer, Bernie Abrams, Takonkiet Viravan, Scenario Thailand, Norton Herrick, Barry and Fran Weissler, TBS Service, and Laurel Oztemel (Producers); Michael McCabe, Joseph Smith, and StageVentures 2009 No. 2 Limited Partnership (Associate Producers); Neil Simon (Book based on the screenplay *The Apartment* by Billy Wilder and I.A.L. Diamond), Burt Bacharach (Music), Hal David (Lyrics), Phil Reno (Musical Director), Jonathan Tunick (Musical Orchestrator), David Chase (Dance Music Arranger), Scott Pask (Scenic Design), Bruce Pask (Costumes), Donald Holder (Lighting).

CAST: Sean Hayes (Chuck Baxter), Kristin Chenoweth (Fran Kubelik), Tony Goldwyn (J.D. Sheldrake), Katie Finneran (Marge MacDougall), Dick Latessa (Dr. Dreyfuss), Brooks Ashmanskas (Mr. Dobitch), Peter Benson (Mike Kirkeby), Sean Martin Hingston (Mr. Eichelberger) and Ken Land (Jesse Vanderhof).

SEASON: Broadway from April 25, 2010, to January 2, 2011, at the Broadway Theatre, New York.

AWARDS: Tony Award to Katy Finneran for Best Featured Actress in a Musical. Nominations for Sean Hayes for Best Actor in a Musical, Rob Ashford for Best Choreography, and Jonathan Tunick for Best Orchestrations.

Bibliography

Adler, Renata. "Screen: Sweatshirt Meets an Apron; Matthau and Lemmon Star in 'Odd Couple.'" *New York Times*, May 3, 1968. Retrieved May 23, 2013, from http://www.nytimes.com.

Anklewicz, Larry. *Guide to Jewish Films on Video.* Hoboken, NJ: KTAV, 2000.

Ballenger, Seale. *Hell's Belles: A Tribute to the Spitfires, Bad Seeds and Steel Magnolias of the New and Old South.* Berkeley, CA: Conari, 1997.

Baltake, Joe. *Jack Lemmon: His Films and Career.* New York: Citadel, 1986.

Bancroft, Anne. Interview with Dinah Shore on *Dinah!* 20th Century–Fox Television, 1975.

Barnes, Clive. "'God's Favorite' Is Simon's Job on L.I." *New York Times*, December 12, 1974. Retrieved July 22, 2013, from http://www.nytimes.com.

_____. "Stage: 'California Suite' Opens." *New York Times*, June 11, 1976. Retrieved September 30, 2013, from http://www.nytimes.com.

_____. "Stage: Creeping Paranoia and Crawling Malaise." *New York Times*, November 12, 1971. Retrieved October 21, 2013, from http://www.nytimes.com.

_____. "Stage: 'Red Hot Lovers'; Comedy by Neil Simon Opens at the O'Neill." *New York Times*, December 29, 1969. Retrieved June 11, 2013, from http://www.nytimes.com.

_____. "Stage: Simon's Chekhov; 'The Good Doctor' Pays Visit to the O'Neill." *New York Times*, November 28, 1973. Retrieved July 21, 2013, from http://www.nytimes.com.

_____. "Theater: Moriarty as Richard III; Casting Is Fascinating and Challenging." *New York Times*, October 21, 1974. Retrieved July 22, 2013, from http://www.nytimes.com.

_____. "Theater: Neil Simon Play; Miss Stapleton Stars in 'Gingerbread Lady.'" *New York Times*, December 14, 1970. Retrieved June 17, 2013, from http://www.nytimes.com.

_____. "Theater: Neil Simon's 'Sunshine Boys'; Levene and Albertson Play Vaudevillians Tone Is Bitter-Sweet at the Broadhurst." *New York Times*, December 21, 1972.

_____. "Theater: 'Plaza Suite,' Neil Simon's Laugh Machine." *New York Times*, February 15, 1968. Retrieved June 2, 2013, from http://www.nytimes.com.

_____. "Theater: Simon-Bacharach 'Promises, Promises.'" *New York Times*, December 2, 1968. Retrieved June 3, 2013, from http://www.nytimes.com. Retrieved July 13, 2013, from http://www.nytimes.com.

Barnier, Kathryn. *Broadway Legends.* Broadway Legends LLC, 2001.

Barthel, Joan. "Life for Simon—Not That Simple; Life for Simon—Not Simple." *New York Times*, February 25, 1968. Retrieved June 1, 2013, from http://www.nytimes.com.

Baxter, John. *De Niro: A Biography.* London: HarperCollins, 2013.

_____. *Hollywood in the Sixties.* The International Film Guide Series. London: Tantivy Press; New York: A.S. Barnes, 1972.

_____. *Woody Allen: A Biography.* New York: Carroll and Graf, 1999.

Benjamin, Richard. *My Favorite Year.* Brooksfilms Limited/Michael Gruskoff Productions, 1982.

Benny, Jack, and Walter Matthau. *Makeup test for the Sunshine Boys.* September 18, 1974. Viewed July 27, 2013, on YouTube.com.

Bergan, Ronald. *The United Artists Story.* London: Crown, 1988.

Bianco, Robert. "'Goodbye Girl' doesn't age well." *USA Today*, January 15, 2004. Retrieved December 10, 2013, from http://www.usatoday30.usatoday.com.

Bill, Tony. *Movie Speak: How to Talk Like You Belong on a Film Set.* New York: Workman, 2009.

Biography. *Bob Fosse: Dancing on the Edge.* A&E Network, 1999.

_____. *Neil Simon, the People's Playwright.* ABC News Productions for the A&E Network, 1998.

Bloom, Ken. *Hollywood Musicals: The 101 Greatest Song-and-Dance Movies of All Time.* New York: Black Dog and Leventhal, 2010.

Bogart, Paul. Interview. *Director's Guild of Amer-*

ica. Retrieved November 30, 2013, from http://www.dga.org.

Bogle, Donald. *Toms, Coons, Mulattoes, Mammies, and Bucks: An Interpretive History of Blacks in American Films*. New York: Continuum, 2001.

Brantley, Ben. "Theater Review: 'Barefoot in the Park.' Early Simon, Dressed by Mizrahi." *New York Times*, February 17, 2006. Retrieved November 25, 2013, from http://www.nytimes.com.

_____. "Theater Review: 'Brighton Beach Memoirs.' Neil Simon's Jeromes, at Home at the Nederlander." *New York Times*, October 26, 2009. Retrieved November 25, 2013, from http://www.nytimes.com.

_____. "Theater Review: Broken Lives and Healing at the Coffee Shop." *New York Times*, November 12, 2001. Retrieved November 22, 2013, from http://www.nytimes.com.

_____. "Theater Review: A Fine Meal: Please Pass the Vitriol." *New York Times*, October 20, 2000. Retrieved November 22, 2013, from http://www.nytimes.com.

_____. "Theater Review: A Lone Woman in the Forest? Is This a Neil Simon Play?" *New York Times*, November 7, 1997. Retrieved June 7, 2013, from http://www.nytimes.com.

_____. "Theater Review: 'Doctor, My Life's Just a Joke.' 'So Laugh.'; A Couple of Young Septuagenarians Bask in Simon 'Sunshine.'" *New York Times*, December 9, 1997. Retrieved November 22, 2013, from http://www.nytimes.com.

_____. "Theater Review: Martin Short Times Eight in 'Little Me.'" *New York Times*, November 13, 1998. Retrieved May 7, 2013, from http://www.nytimes.com.

_____. "Theatre Review: More Ghosts than Originally Planned." *New York Times*, December 19, 2003. Retrieved November 15, 2013, from http://www.nytimes.com.

_____. "Theatre Review: 'The Odd Couple.' Misery Loves a Roommate." *New York Times*, October 28, 2005. Retrieved November 15, 2013, from http://www.nytimes.com.

_____. "Theater Review: 'Promises, Promises.' Back in the '60s: Let's Tryst Again." *New York Times*, April 26, 2010. Retrieved November 25, 2013, from http://www.nytimes.com.

_____. "Theatre Review: 'Sweet Charity,' After a Rocky Road, Finally Reaches Broadway." *New York Times*, May 5, 2005. Retrieved November 25, 2013, from http://www.nytimes.com.

Bronstein, Elizabeth. *Intimate Portrait: Marsha Mason*. The Greif Company/Lifetime Productions, 1998. Video released by Unapix/a-Pix Entertainment, 2000.

Brown, Cecil. *Pryor Lives!: Kiss My Rich, Happy Black ... Ass! A Memoir*. New York: CreateSpace Independent Publishing Platform, 2013.

Browne, Ray Broadus, and Pat Browne. *The Guide to United States Popular Culture*. New York: Popular, 2001.

Buck, Jerry. "'American Masters' Looks at Life of Neil Simon." *Reading Eagle*, August 16, 1989. Re-trieved November 25, 2013, from http://www.google.com/newspapers.

Burdick Harmon, Melissa. "Bright Lights, Big City: Resplendent, Resilient New York." *Biography*, September 2002, 97–105.

_____. "Simon Says ... Playwright Neil Simon Reflects on a Lifetime of Comedy Mixed with Tears." *Biography*, September 2002, 92–95.

Burns, George. *Living It Up*. New York: Penguin, 1980.

_____. *The Most of George Burns*. New York: Galahad, 1991.

Burns, George, with David Fisher. *All My Best Friends*. New York: Perigee, 1990.

Busch, Charles. "Television: London Calling." *The Advocate*, September 17, 1996, 80–81.

Caesar, Sid. *The Sid Caesar Collection—50th Anniversary*. Creative Light Entertainment, 2000. DVD released by New Video Group, 2005.

_____. *The Sid Caesar Collection—50th Anniversary. The Buried Treasures*. Creative Light Entertainment, 2000. DVD released by New Video Group, 2004.

_____. *The Sid Caesar Collection—50th Anniversary. The Fan Favorites*. Creative Light Entertainment, 2000. DVD released by New Video Group, 2005.

Caesar, Sid, with Eddy Friedfeld. *Caesar's Hours: My Life in Comedy with Love and Laughter*. New York: PublicAffairs, 2003.

Caine, Michael. *Acting in Film: An Actor's Take on Movie Making*. New York: Hal Leonard, 2000.

_____. *The Elephant to Hollywood*. London: Hachette UK, 2010.

Calta, Louis. "'New Faces of '56' in debut tonight; Sillman's Latest Revue, at the Barrymore, Includes Artists from Abroad." *New York Times*, June 14, 1956. Retrieved October 24, 2013, from http://www.nytimes.com.

_____. "Season's Starter Is 'Catch a Star!'; Revue with Pat Carroll and David Burns Will Open Tonight at Plymouth." *New York Times*, September 6, 1955. Retrieved October 24, 2013, from http://www.nytimes.com.

Canby, Vincent. "California Suite (1978)." *New York Times*, December 21, 1978. Retrieved September 30, 2013, from http://www.nytimes.com.

_____. "The Cheap Detective (1978). Screen: Simon's 'Cheap' Detective: Everybody Revisited." *New York Times*, June 23, 1978. Retrieved September 10, 2013, from http://www.nytimes.com.

_____. "Film: Simon's 'Biloxi Blues,' Coming of Age in the Army." *New York Times*, March 25, 1988. Retrieved November 14, 2013, from http://www.nytimes.com.

_____. "The Goodbye Girl (1977)." *New York Times*, December 1, 1977. Retrieved September 2, 2013, from http://www.nytimes.com.

_____. "'Heartbreak Kid': Elaine May's 2d Effort as Director Arrives." *New York Times*, December 18, 1972. Retrieved July 14, 2013, from http://www.nytimes.com.

_____. "Matthau Back in Simon's Hollywood." *New*

York Times, March 28, 1982. Retrieved October 15, 2013, from http://www.nytimes.com.

———. "Murder by Death (1976). Simon's Breezy 'Murder by Death.'" *New York Times*, June 24, 1976. Retrieved September 15, 2013, from http://www.nytimes.com.

———. "Review/Film: Marriage as Eternal Punishment." *New York Times*, April 15, 1991. Retrieved November 24, 2013, from http://www.nytimes.com.

———. "Screen: Adaptation of Neil Simon's 'Plaza Suite.'" *New York Times*, May 14, 1971. Retrieved June 24, 2013, from http://www.nytimes.com.

———. "Screen: A Blow-Up of 'Sweet Charity.'" *New York Times*, April 2, 1969. Retrieved June 10, 2013, from http://www.nytimes.com.

———. "Simon's 'Only When I Laugh.'" *New York Times*, September 23, 1981. Retrieved November 5, 2013, from http://www.nytimes.com.

———. "The Sunshine Boys (1975)." *New York Times*, November 7, 1975. Retrieved August 19, 2013, from http://www.nytimes.com.

———. "Theatre Review: London Suite; Simon Times 4, and Off Broadway, Yet." *New York Times*, April 10, 1995. Retrieved November 17, 2013, from http://www.nytimes.com.

Cardullo, Bert. *Vittorio De Sica: Actor, Director, Auteur.* Newcastle upon Tyne: Cambridge Scholars, 2009.

Castell, David. *The Films of Robert Redford.* St. Paul, MN: BCW, 1977.

Churnin, Nancy. "Rewritten 'Jake's Women' Back on Broadway Track." *Los Angeles Times.* September 5, 1991. Retrieved November 17, 2013, from http://www.latimes.com.

Clark Bradley, Christine. *The 9th Annual Kennedy Center Mark Twain Prize for American Humor.* WETA, Washington, D.C., and Mark Krantz Productions, 2006.

Clarke, Gerald. *Capote: A Biography.* New York: Simon and Schuster, 2010.

Cooney, Tim. *Work in Movies? Are You Crazy!* Bloomington, IN: Trafford, 2009.

Crivello, Kirk. *Fallen Angels: The Lives and Untimely Deaths of 14 Hollywood Beauties.* Secaucus, NJ: Citadel, 1988.

Crowther, Bosley. "Screen: 'After the Fox.'" *New York Times*, December 24, 1966. Retrieved May 30, 2013, from http://www.nytimes.com.

———. "The Screen: 'Barefoot in the Park.'" *New York Times*, May 26, 1967. Retrieved May 13, 2013, from http://www.nytimes.com.

———. "The Screen: 'Come Blow Your Horn'; Sinatra Film Arrives at the Music Hall." *New York Times*, June 7, 1963. Retrieved May 7, 2013, from http://www.nytimes.com.

Crowther, Bruce. *Robert Redford.* Tunbridge Wells, UK: Spellmount, 1985.

Curtiz, Michael. *Casablanca.* Warner Bros./First National Picture/Hal. B. Wallis Production, 1942.

Davis, Curt. "Marsha Mason and Neil Simon: A Second Act." *People* 1.2 (1974): 47–49.

Davis, Sammy, Jr., and Gerald Early. *The Sammy Davis, Jr., Reader.* New York: Farrar, Straus and Giroux, 2001.

Dawson, Nick. *Being Hal Ashby: The Life of a Hollywood Rebel.* Lexington, KY: University of Kentucky Press, 2009.

Delamater, Jerome. *Dance in the Hollywood musical.* Ann Arbor, MI: UMI Research Press, 1988.

Denby, David. "Movies: Jewish Boys Don't." *New York Magazine*, January 19, 1987, 77–78.

———. "Movies: Skirting Trouble." *New York Magazine*, March 28, 1988, 97–98.

Denis, Christopher. *The Films of Shirley MacLaine.* New York: Citadel, 1980.

Denzin, Norman K. *Hollywood Shot by Shot: Alcoholism in American Cinema.* New York: Transaction, 1991.

Dick. Bernard F. *City of Dreams: The Making and Remaking of Universal Pictures.* Lexington: University of Kentucky Press, 1997.

———. *The Star-spangled Screen: The American World War II Film.* Lexington: University of Kentucky Press, 1996.

Dmytryk, Edward. *Murder, My Sweet.* RKO Radio Pictures, 1945.

Dougan, Andy. *Untouchable: Robert De Niro: Unauthorised.* New York: Random House, 2011.

Drucker, Mort, and Larry Siegel. "The Heartburn Kid." *Mad* 162 (1973): 4–10.

Dyson, Michael Eric. *Is Bill Cosby Right? Or Has the Black Middle Class Lost Its Mind?* New York: Basic Civitas, 2008.

Eames, John Douglas. *The Paramount Story.* London: Crown, 1985.

Eames, John Douglas, and Robert Abele. *The Paramount Story.* New York: Simon and Schuster, 2004.

Ebert, Roger. "Biloxi Blues." *Chicago Sun-Times*, March 25, 1988. Retrieved November 14, 2013, from http://www.rogerebert.com.

———. "Brighton Beach Memoirs." *Chicago Sun-Times*, December 25, 1986. Retrieved November 10, 2013, from http://www.rogerebert.com.

———. "The Chapter Two." *Chicago Sun-Times*, January 1, 1980. Retrieved October 6, 2013, from http://www.rogerebert.com.

———. "The Goodbye Girl." *Chicago Sun-Times*, January 1, 1977. Retrieved September 2, 2013, from http://www.rogerebert.com.

———. "The Heartbreak Kid." *Chicago Sun-Times*, January 1, 1972. Retrieved July 14, 2013, from http://www.rogerebert.com.

———. "Lost in Yonkers." *Chicago Sun-Times*, May 14, 1993. Retrieved November 18, 2013, from http://www.rogerebert.com.

———. "The Marrying Man." *Chicago Sun-Times*, April 5, 1991. Retrieved November 24, 2013, from http://www.rogerebert.com.

———. "Max Dugan Returns." *Chicago Sun-Times*, March 28, 1983. Retrieved October 22, 2013, from http://www.rogerebert.com.

———. "The Odd Couple." *Chicago Sun-Times*, June 17, 1968. Retrieved May 23, 2013, from http://www.rogerebert.com.

_____. "The Odd Couple II." *Chicago Sun-Times*, April 10, 1998. Retrieved November 26, 2013, from http://www.rogerebert.com.

_____. "Only When I Laugh." *Chicago Sun-Times*, January 1, 1981. Retrieved November 5, 2013, from http://www.rogerebert.com.

_____. "Seems Like Old Times." *Chicago Sun-Times*, December 24, 1980. Retrieved October 10, 2013, from http://www.rogerebert.com.

_____. "The Slugger's Wife." *Chicago Sun-Times*, March 29, 1985. Retrieved October 26, 2013, from http://www.rogerebert.com.

_____. "Star Spangled Girl." *Chicago Sun-Times*, January 5, 1972. Retrieved June 30, 2013, from http://www.rogerebert.com.

Edelman, Rob, and Audrey Kupferberg. *Matthau: A Life*. New York: Taylor, 2002.

Eder, Richard. "For Neil Simon, It's 'Chapter Two.'" *New York Times*, December 5, 1977. Retrieved October 6, 2013, from http://www.nytimes.com.

_____. "Stage: 'They're Playing Our Song' Presented." *New York Times*, February 12, 1979. Retrieved October 19, 2013, from http://www.ny times.com.

Ekland, Britt. *True Britt*. Englewood Cliffs, NJ: Berkley, 1982.

Elder, Robert K. *The Best Film You've Never Seen: 35 Directors Champion the Forgotten or Critically Savaged Movies They Love*. Chicago: Chicago Review, 2013.

Epstein, Lawrence J. *George Burns: An American Life*. Jefferson, NC: McFarland, 2011.

Erens, Patricia. *The Films of Shirley MacLaine*. New York: A.S. Barnes, 1978.

Erickson, Hal. *Military Comedy Films: A Critical Survey and Filmography of Hollywood Releases Since 1918*. Jefferson, NC: McFarland, 2012.

Erskine, Thomas, and James Welsh. *Video Versions: Film Adaptations of Plays on Video*. Westport, CT: ABC-CLIO, 2000.

Evans, Peter. *Peter Sellers: The Mask Behind the Mask*. London: Prentice-Hall, 1968.

Falk, Peter. *Just One More Thing*. New York: Da Capo, 2007.

Farrelly, Peter, and Bobby Farrelly. *The Heartbreak Kid*. Dreamworks Pictures/Radar Pictures/Davis Entertainment Company/Conundrum, 2007. DVD released by Dreamworks Video, 2007.

Feeney Cannan, Michael. *Robert Redford: The Biography*. New York: Knopf, 2011.

Fehnrenbacher Koprince, Susan. *Understanding Neil Simon*. Columbia: University of South Carolina Press, 2002.

Felini, Federico. *La notti di Cabiria*. Dino de Laurentiis/Cinematografica Les Films Marceau, 1957. DVD released by Lionsgate and Criterion, 1999.

Fishgall, Gary. *Gonna Do Great Things: The Life of Sammy Davis, Jr.* New York: Scribner, 2003.

Fonda, Jane. *My Life So Far*. New York: Random House, 2006.

Fowler, Karin J. *David Niven: A Bio-bibliography*. New York: Greenwood, 1995.

Frayn Turner, John. *Frank Sinatra*. New York: Taylor, 2004.

Freedland, Michael. *Jack Lemmon*. New York: Chivers, 1985.

Friedman, Bruce Jay. "A Change of Plan." In *Black Angels—Stories*. New York: Simon and Schuster, 1966.

Fristoe, Roger. "California Suite (1978)." *Turner Classic Movies*. Retrieved October 1, 2013, from http://www.tcm.com.

Furnish, Ben. *Nostalgia in Jewish-American Theatre and Film, 1979–2004*. New York: Peter Lang, 2005.

Garner, Joe, and James Castle. "Inside The Odd Couple." In *The Odd Couple Centennial Collection DVD*. Paramount, 2009.

Gehring, Wes D. *Parody as Film Genre: "Never Give a Saga an Even Break."* New York: Greenwood, 1999.

Geisinger, Eliott. "Urban Living: Funny and Formidable." *The Prisoner of Second Avenue* DVD featurette. Professional Films/Robbins Nest Production, 1975. DVD released by Warner Home Video, 2004.

Gerard, Jeremy. "Review: 'The Goodbye Girl.'" *Variety*, March 4, 1993. Retrieved November 17, 2013, from http://www.variety.com.

_____. "Review: 'Laughter on the 23rd Floor.'" *Variety*, November 22, 1993. Retrieved November 17, 2013, from http://www.variety.com.

_____. "Review: 'Neil Simon's Jake's Women.'" *Variety*, February 25, 1996. Retrieved December 3, 2013, from http://www.variety.com.

_____. "Review: 'Neil Simon's London Suite.'" *Variety*, September 9, 1996. Retrieved December 6, 2013, from http://www.variety.com.

Gilbert, Matthew. "'Sunshine Boys' Is Dreary as a Rainy Day." *Boston Globe*, December 26, 1997. Retrieved August 25, 2013, from http://pqasb.pqarchiver.com/boston.

Gillis, Michael. "The Cheap Detective: A Conversation with Neil Simon." Columbia/Tristar Inc., 1999.

_____. "Murder by Death: A Conversation with Neil Simon." Columbia/Tristar, 1999.

Gore, Chris. *The 50 Greatest Movies Never Made: Fifty Masterpieces from Hollywood that Never Made It to the Big Screen*. New York: St. Martin's Griffin, 1999.

Gottfried, Martin. *All His Jazz: The Life and Death of Bob Fosse*. New York: Da Capo, 2003.

_____. *George Burns and the Hundred-Year Dash*. New York: G.K. Hall, 1996.

Gow, Gordon. "Instinct." Interview with Arthur Hiller. *Films and Filming* 20.11 (1974): 12–17.

Grant, Barry Keith. *The Hollywood Film Musical*. New York: Wiley-Blackwell, 2012.

Green, Kay, and Stanley Green. *Broadway Musicals—Show by Show*. New York: Hal Leonard, 1990.

Greenspun, Roger. "Screen: Hiller 'Out of Towners.'" *New York Times*, May 29, 1970. Retrieved June 11, 2003, from http://www.nytimes.com.

_____. "Screen: 'Last of the Red Hot Lovers.'" *New York Times*, August 18, 1972. Retrieved July 2, 2013, from http://www.nytimes.com.

Grobel, Lawrence. *Conversations with Capote.* New York: Da Capo, 2000.

_____. *Endangered Species: Writers Talk About Their Craft, Their Visions, Their Lives.* New York: Da Capo, 2001.

_____. Interview with Robert De Niro. *Playboy*, January 1989. Retrieved September 8, 2013, from http://translatedby.com/you/robert-de-niro-playboy-interview-january-1989.

Grodin, Charles. *How I Got to Be Whoever It Is I Am.* New York: Grand Central, 2009.

_____. *I Like It Better When You're Funny: Working in Television and Other Precarious Adventures.* New York: Random House, 2002.

_____. *It Would Be So Nice If You Weren't Here: My Journey Through Show Business.* New York: Morrow, 1989.

Gross, Michael. "The Candidate." *New York Magazine*, November 24, 1997, 40–45, 105.

Grossbach, Robert. *Neil Simon's The Goodbye Girl.* A novelization based on the screenplay. New York: Warner, 1977.

Haddad-Garcia, George. *The Films of Jane Fonda.* New York: Citadel, 1983.

Hadley, Boze. *The Lavender Screen: The Gay and Lesbian Films: Their Stars, Makers, Characters, and Critics.* New York: Carol, 1993.

Hall, William. *Sir Michael Caine: The Biography.* New York: Whole Story Audio Books, 2009.

Harper, Valerie. "I, Rhoda." New York: Simon and Schuster, 2013.

Harris, Andrew. *Broadway Theatre.* New York: Routledge, 2013.

Hatchuel, Sarah, and Natalie Vienne-Guerin. *Shakespeare on Screen: Richard III: Proceedings of the Conference Organised at the Université de Rouen, 4–5 March 2005.* Mont-Saint-Aignan: University Rouen Havre, 2005.

Hawks, Howard. *The Big Sleep.* Warner Bros./First National Pictures/Howard Hawks Production, 1946.

Heiman, Sarah. "The Goodbye Girl (1977)." *Turner Classic Movies.* Retrieved September 2, 2013, from http://www.tcm.com.

Henry, William A., III. "Reliving a Poignant Past." *Time* 128.24 (1986): 72–78.

Hirsch, Michael. *Caesar's Writers: A Reunion of Writers from Your Show of Shows and Caesar's Hour.* Michael Hirsch Productions, 1996. DVD released by Plus8Video, 1996.

Hirschhorn, Clive. *The Columbia Story.* New York: Crown, 1989.

_____. *The Hollywood Musical.* London: Octopus, 1981.

_____. *The Universal Story.* New York: Crown, 1983.

_____. *The Warner Bros. Story: The Complete History of Hollywood's Great Studio: Every Warner Bros. Feature Film Described and Illustrated.* New York: Crown, 1987.

Hischak, Thomas S. *American Plays and Musicals on Screen: 650 Stage Productions and Their Film and Televison Adaptations.* Jefferson, NC: McFarland, 2005.

_____. *American Theatre: A Chronicle of Comedy and Drama, 1969–2000.* New York: Oxford University Press, 2001.

_____. *The Oxford Companion to the American Musical: Theatre, Film, and Television.* New York: Oxford University Press, 2008.

_____. *Through the Screen Door: What Happened to the Broadway Musical When It Went to Hollywood.* New York: Scarecrow, 2004.

Holden, Stephen. "'The Odd Couple II': When Tofu Mystery Meat Is a Metaphor for Comedy." *New York Times*, April 10, 1988. Retrieved November 26, 2013, from http://www.nytimes.com.

Holston, Kim R. *Movie Roadshows: A History and Filmography of Reserved-Seat Limited Showings, 1911–1973.* Jefferson, NC: McFarland, 2012.

Holtzman, William. *Jack Lemmon.* Pyramid Illustrated History of the Movies. New York: Pyramid, 1977.

Horvitz, Louis J. *The Kennedy Center Honors.* Kennedy Center Productions/A George Stevens, Jr., Don Mischer Presentation, 1995.

Hurt, Harry, III, and David Zanzinger. "Neil Simon. The Playwright's Malibu Beach House." *Architectural Digest*, February 1991, 178–83.

Huston, John. *The Maltese Falcon.* Warner Bros. Pictures/First National, 1941.

Inge, M. Thomas. *Truman Capote: Conversations (Literary Conversations).* Jackson: University of Mississippi Press, 1987.

Isherwood, Charles. "Review: 'Neil Simon's Hotel Suite.'" *Variety*, June 16, 2000. Retrieved November 17, 2013, from http://www.variety.com.

Jackson, Carlton. *Picking Up the Tab: The Life and Movies of Martin Ritt.* New York: Popular, 1994.

Jacobson, Lyn. "Legit Reviews: London Suite." *Variety*, October 13, 1994. Retrieved November 17, 2013, from http://www.variety.com.

Jay, Michael. *Charlie Rose Talks to Neil Simon.* November 29, 1996. Bloomberg Television. Rose Communications/WNET New York, 1996. DVD released 2006.

_____. *Charlie Rose Talks to Neil Simon.* September 28, 1999. Rose Communications/WNET New York, 1999. DVD released 2006.

Johnson, Robert K. *Neil Simon.* Boston: Twayne, 1983.

Jones, Clark. *The 1975 Tony Awards.* Bentwood Television Production, 1975.

Kael, Pauline. *5001 Nights at the Movies.* New York: Holt, Rinehart, and Winston, 1984.

_____. *Going Steady.* New York: Warner, 1970.

_____. *Reeling.* Boston, Toronto: Atlantic Monthly/Little, Brown, 1976.

_____. *Taking It All In.* New York: Holt, Rinehart and Winston, 1984.

_____. *When the Lights Go Down.* New York: Holt, Rinehart and Winston, 1980.

Kashner, Sam. "Capote's Swan Dive." *Vanity Fair*, December 2012.

Kauffmann, Stanley. "Theater: Show That Wants to Be Loved; 'Sweet Charity' Opens at Refurbished Palace." *New York Times*, January 31, 1966. Retrieved May 29, 2013, from http://www.nytimes.com.

Kelleher, Terry. "Picks and Pans Review: The Goodbye Girl." *People*, January 17, 2004. Retrieved September 6, 2013, from http://www.people.com.

Kellerman, Sally. *Read My Lips: Stories of a Hollywood Life*. New York: Weinstein, 2013.

Kelley, Kitty. *His Way: The Unauthorized Biography of Frank Sinatra*. New York: Bantam, 2010.

Kempley, Rita. "Biloxi Blues." *Washington Post*. March 25, 1988. Retrieved November 14, 2013, from http://www.washingtonpost.com.

_____. "Brighton Beach Memoirs." *Washington Post*, December 26, 1986. Retrieved November 15, 2013, from http://www.washingtonpost.com.

_____. "'Neil Simon's Lost in Yonkers.'" *Washington Post*, May 14, 1993. Retrieved November 18, 2013, from http://www.washingtonpost.com.

Kerr, Walter. "The Theater: Neil Simon's 'Star-Spangled Girl.'" *New York Times*, December 22, 1966. Retrieved June 1, 2013, from http://www.nytimes.com.

_____. "Theater: The New Neil Simon Comedy." *New York Times*, April 4, 1980. Retrieved October 15, 2013, from http://www.nytimes.com.

Kessler, Kelly. *Destabilizing the Hollywood Musical: Music, Masculinity and Mayhem*. New York: Palgrave Macmillan, 2010.

Keyser, Les. *Hollywood in the Seventies*. San Diego and New York: A.S. Barnes, 1981.

Kinberg, Judy. Dance in America. *Bob Fosse: Steam Heat*. Great Performances. WNET/Thirteen, 1990.

King, Susan. "Caesar Hails the 'Laughter' of His Old Friends." *Los Angeles Times*, June 6, 2001. Retrieved December 10, 2013, from http://www.latimes.com.

_____. "It's 'Goodbye' Again." *Los Angeles Times*, January 14, 2004. Retrieved December 10, 2013, from http://www.latimes.com.

Knight, Timothy. *Sinatra: Hollywood His Way*. New York: Running, 2010.

Koehler, Robert. "NBC Puts 'London Suite' Through a 'Seinfeld' Filter." *Los Angeles Times*, September 14, 1996. Retrieved December 10, 2013, from http://www.latimes.com.

Konas, Gary. *Neil Simon: A Casebook*. New York and London: Garland, 1997.

Koprince, Susan. *Understanding Neil Simon*. Columbia: University of South Carolina Press, 2002.

Kornbluth, Jessie. "The Kid with the Million Dollar Smile: Matthew Broderick Brightens Broadway." *New York Magazine*, March 25, 1985, 48–52.

Kubey, Robert William. *Creating Television: Conversations with the People Behind 50 Years of American TV*. New York: Taylor and Francis, 2004.

Lahr, John. "Making It Real: How Mike Nichols Recreated Comedy and Himself." *The New Yorker*, February 21 and 28, 2000, 196–214.

_____. "Master of Revels: Neil Simon's Comic Empire." *The New Yorker*, May 3, 2010, 70–76.

Lax, Eric. *Woody Allen: A Biography*. London: Vintage, 1991.

Lehmann-Haupt, Christopher. "Enter Simon, Blowing His Own Horn." Books of the Times. *New York Times*, October 24, 1986. Retrieved May 25, 2013, from http://www.nytimes.com.

Lemmon, Chris. *A Twist of Lemmon: A Tribute to My Father*. Chapel Hill, NC: Algonquin, 2006.

Lemon, Brendan. "Nathan's Peaking." *Out Magazine*, April 2001, 57–61.

Leonard, John. "Television: Intelligent Life." *New York Magazine*, March 4, 1996, 72.

_____. "Television: Not-So-Simple Simon." *New York Magazine*, March 23, 1992, 62.

Levy, Alan. "Doc Simon's Rx for Comedy." *New York Times*, March 7, 1965. Retrieved October 23, 2013, from http://www.nytimes.com.

Lewis, Roger. *The Life and Death of Peter Sellers*. New York: Applause Theatre and Cinema, 2000.

Linan, Steve. "The Sunshine Boys." *Los Angeles Times*. December 28, 1997. Retrieved August 25, 2013, from http://www.latimes.com.

Linderman, Lawrence. "Playboy Interview: Neil Simon." *Playboy* 26.2 (1979): 57–78.

Lipton, James. "Neil Simon: The Art of Theater No. 10." *Paris Review* 125 (Winter 1992). Retrieved September 8, 2013, from http://www.theparisreview.org.

Long, Robert Emmet. *Truman Capote: Enfant Terrible*. New York: Continuum, 2008.

Looney, Deborah. "Murder by Death (1976)." *Turner Classic Movies*. Retrieved September 15, 2013, from http://www.tcm.com.

MacLaine, Shirley. *My Lucky Stars: A Hollywood Memoir*. New York: Bantam, 1996.

Marshall, Bill, and Robyn Jeananne Stilwell. *Musicals: Hollywood and Beyond*. New York: Intellect, 2000.

Maslin, Janet. "Dugan Returns." *New York Times*, March 25, 1983. Retrieved October 22, 2013, from http://www.nytimes.com.

_____. "Film: Neil Simon's 'Slugger's Wife.'" *New York Times*, March 29, 1985. Retrieved October 26, 2013, from http://www.nytimes.com.

_____. "Review/Film: Simon's Serious Comedy of Contemporary Nostalgia." *New York Times*, May 14, 1993. Retrieved November 18, 2013, from http://www.nytimes.com.

_____. "Screen: Widower's Tale in Simon's 'Chapter Two': Second Time Around." *New York Times*, December 14, 1979. Retrieved October 6, 2013, from http://www.nytimes.com.

_____. "A Simon Comedy, 'Seems Like Old Times.'" *New York Times*, December 19, 1980. Retrieved October 10, 2013, from http://www.nytimes.com.

_____. "Screen: 'Brighton Beach Memoirs.'" *New York Times*, December 25, 1986. Retrieved November 10, 2013, from http://www.nytimes.com.

Mason, Marsha. *Journey: A Personal Odyssey*. New York: Simon and Schuster, 2000.

_____. "Mr. and Mrs. Neil Simon." *Architectural Digest* 37.3 (1980): 127–131.

Matthau, Charlie, and Chris Lemmon. *Audio Commentary The Odd Couple. Centennial Collection DVD*. Paramount, 2009.

McGovern, Edythe M. *Neil Simon: A Critical Study*. New York: Frederick Ungar, 1979.

McKay, James. *The Films of Victor Mature*. Jefferson, NC: McFarland, 2013.

McKay, Rick. *Broadway: The Golden Age, by the Legends Who Were There*. Second Act Productions, 2003. DVD released by RCA Victor Broadway, 2004.

McNally, Judith. "Neil Simon Discusses 'Prisoner of Second Avenue.'" *Filmmakers newsletter* 8.7 (1975): 27–32.

Medlinsky, Harvey. *Barefoot in the Park*. HBO Films, 1981. Viewed on May 11, 2013, on YouTube.com.

Meryman, Richard. "When the Funniest Writer in America Tried to Be Serious." *Life* 70.17 (1971): 60–83.

Miller, Frank. "Only When I Laugh." *Turner Classic Movies*. Retrieved November 5, 2013, from http://www.tcm.com.

_____. "Sweet Charity." *Turner Classic Movies*. Retrieved June 10, 2103, from http://www.tcm.com.

_____. "The Sunshine Boys." *Turner Classic Movies*. Retrieved August 19, 2013, from http://www.tcm.com.

Miller, Gabriel. *The Films of Martin Ritt: Fanfare for the Common Man*. Jackson: University of Mississippi Press, 2000.

_____. *Martin Ritt: Interviews (Conversations with Filmmakers Series)*. Jackson: University of Mississippi Press, 2003.

Milne, Jeff. *Six Degrees of Kevin Bacon: The Complete Guide to the Movie Trivia Game*. New York: Jeff Milne, 2009.

Morgan, Al. "A Conversation with Neil Simon." *TV Guide* 20.45 (1972): 20–24.

Morgenstern, Joseph. "These Days, Neil Simon's Art Mirrors His Life; Simon's Art and Life." *New York Times*, December 4, 1977. Retrieved October 19, 2013, from http://www.nytimes.com.

O'Brien, Daniel. *The Frank Sinatra Film Guide*. New York: B.T. Batsford, 1998.

O'Connor, Gary. *Alec Guinness: A Life*. London: Applause, 2002.

O'Connor, John J. "Review/Television: A Simon Play Fits the Small Screen." *New York Times*, March 23, 1992. Retrieved November 30, 2013, from http://www.nytimes.com.

_____. "TV: 'Cry' or Laugh with Simon." *New York Times*, November 8, 1978. Retrieved September 23, 2013, from http://www.nytimes.com.

_____. "TV Review: 5 Neil Simon Sketches Offered by N.B.C." *New York Times*, November 13, 1972. Retrieved October 3, 2013, from http://www.nytimes.com.

_____. "TV Reviews: Updated 'Plaza Suite.'" *New York Times*, December 3, 1987. Retrieved October 3, 2013, from http://www.nytimes.com.

_____. "TV Weekend: Alan Alda Returns to Neil Simon's Midlife Crisis." *New York Times*, March 1, 1996. Retrieved December 4, 2013, from http://www.nytimes.com.

Oxman, Steven. "Review: 'Neil Simon's Laughter on the 23rd Floor.'" *Variety*, May 18, 2001. Retrieved December 9, 2013, from http://www.variety.com.

Parish, James Robert. *The Hollywood Book of Breakups*. New York: John Wiley and Sons, 2010.

_____. *The Hollywood Book of Extravagance: The Totally Infamous, Mostly Disastrous, and Always Compelling Excesses of America's Film and TV Idols*. New York: John Wiley and Sons, 2011.

Parish, James Robert, and Michael R. Pitt. *The Great Hollywood Musical Pictures*. New York: Scarecrow, 1992.

Paris, Jerry. "Love and the Good Deal." *Love American Style*, November 24, 1969. CBS Paramount Television. DVD released by Paramount/CBS DVD, 2007.

Pasetta, Marty. *The American Film Institute Salute to Alfred Hitchcock*. American Film Institute, 1979.

Passafiume, Andrea. "The Big Idea: The Goodbye Girl ('77)." *Turner Classic Movies*. Retrieved July 29, 2013, from http://www.tcm.com.

_____. "Chapter Two." *Turner Classic Movies*. Retrieved October 6, 2013, from http://www.tcm.com.

_____. "The Goodbye Girl (1977)." *Turner Classic Movies*. Retrieved September 2, 2013, from http://www.tcm.com.

_____. "The Prisoner of Second Avenue." *Turner Classic Movies*. Retrieved August 6, 2013, from http://www.tcm.com.

_____. "Seems Like Old Times (1980)." *Turner Classic Movies*. Retrieved October 10, 2013, from http://www.tcm.com.

Patterson, Thom. "The Dangers of Remakes: 'Goodbye' Definitely Doesn't Mean Forever." *CNN*, January 16, 2004. Retrieved September 6, 2013, from http://edition.cnn.com.

Plimpton, George. *Truman Capote: In Which Various Friends, Enemies, Acquaintances and Detractors Recall His Turbulent Career*. New York: Anchor, 1998.

Powers, James. "Dialogue on Film: Neil Simon." *American Film* 3.5 (1978): 33–48.

Purdum, Tod S. "Happy Landing, Mr. Baldwin." *Vanity Fair*, August 2012, 74.

Read, Piers Paul. *Alec Guinness: The Authorised Biography*. New York: Simon and Schuster, 2005.

Reilly, Sue, and Kristin McMurran. "Neil Simon and Judd Hirsch Prove American Lives Can Have Second Chapters." *People* 8.25 (1977): 30–32.

Rich, Frank. "Review/Theater: How Far Two Good Sports Will Go." *New York Times*, March 5, 1993. Retrieved November 17, 2013, from http://www.nytimes.com.

_____. "Review/Theater: 'Jake's Women,' a New Chapter in the Sex Wars." *New York Times*, March 25, 1992. Retrieved November 17, 2013, from http://www.nytimes.com.

_____. "Review/Theater: Simon on Love Denied." *New York Times*, February 22, 1991. Retrieved November 15, 2013, from http://www.nytimes.com.

_____. "Review/Theater: Uncerebral Simon, Played Strictly for Laughs." *New York Times*, November 18, 1988. Retrieved November 15, 2013, from http://www.nytimes.com.

_____. "Stage: 'Bilox Blues,' Simon's New Comedy." *New York Times*, March 29, 1985. Retrieved November 10, 2013, from http://www.nytimes.com.

_____. "Stage: Neil Simon's Brighton Beach." *New York Times*, March 28, 1983. Retrieved November 6, 2013, from http://www.nytimes.com.

_____. "Stage: 'Sweet Charity,' a Bob Fosse Revival." *New York Times*, April 28, 1986. Retrieved November 11, 2013, from http://www.nytimes.com.

_____. "Theater: Coco in Simon's 'Little Me.'" *New York Times*, January 22, 1982. Retrieved May 7, 2013, from http://www.nytimes.com.

_____. "Theater: 'Fools' by Simon." *New York Times*, April 7, 1981. Retrieved October 20, 2013, from http://www.nytimes.com.

_____. "Theater: 'Odd Couple,' a Remix and Rematch." *New York Times*, June 12, 1985. Retrieved November 10, 2013, from http://www.nytimes.com.

_____. "Theater: Simon's 'Broadway Bound.'" *New York Times*, December 5, 1986. Retrieved November 11, 2013, from http://www.nytimes.com.

Riead, William C. "The Amazing Miss Cummings: An Actress at Work and Play." MGM/Warner Bros./William C. Riead Productions, 1977. *Turner Classic Movies*. Retrieved September 2, 2013, from http://www.tcm.com.

Roberts, Jerry. *Encyclopedia of Television Film Directors*. New York: Scarecrow, 2009.

_____. *The Great American Playwrights on the Screen: A Critical Guide to Film, TV, Video and DVD*. New York: Applause Theatre and Cinema, 2003.

_____. *The Hollywood Scandal Almanac: 12 Months of Sinister, Salacious and Senseless History!* New York: History Press, 2012.

Rojek, Chris. *Frank Sinatra*. New York: Polity, 2004.

Rooney, David. "Review: 'Barefoot in the Park.'" *Variety*, February 16, 2006. Retrieved November 25, 2013, from http://www.variety.com.

Rose, Charlie. *Interview with Neil Simon*. October 1, 1996. WNET New York. Rose Communications, 1996. DVD released 2006.

_____. *Interview with Neil Simon*. November 6, 1997. WNET New York. Rose Communications, 1997. DVD released 2006.

Rosenberg, Howard. "Showtime Renders Its Praises unto Comic Great Sid Caesar." *Los Angeles Times*, May 26, 2001. Retrieved December 10, 2013, from http://www.latimes.com.

Rothstein, Mervyn. "New Neil Simon Play to Close Before Reaching Broadway." *New York Times*, April 6, 1990. Retrieved November 17, 2013, from http://www.nytimes.com.

Sanders, Terry. *Words into Image: Neil Simon*. Portraits of American Screenwriters. American Film Foundation/California Institute of the Arts, 1981. DVD released by American Film Foundation, 1984.

Sarlot, Raymond, and Fred E. Basten. *Life at the Marmont: The Inside Story of Hollywood's Legendary Hotel of the Stars—Chateau Marmont*. New York: Penguin, 2013.

Schnackenberg, Robert. *Christopher Walken A to Z*. New York: Quirk, 2008.

Schoell, William, and Lawrence J. Quirk. *The Sundance Kid: A Biography of Robert Redford*. New York: Taylor, 2006.

Sennett, Ted. *Your Show of Shows*. New York: Applause Theatre and Cinema, 2002.

Sevano, Nick, and Ted Schwarz. *Sinatra: His Story from an Insider*. New York: Branden, 2013.

Sexton, Timothy. "'Bogart Slept Here': The Most Educational Comedy for Struggling Actors Never Made." December 8, 2012. Retrieved July 29, 2013, from http://movies.yahoo.com.

Shepard, Richard F. "Review/Theater: Neil Simon's Touch, in a First Effort." *New York Times*, November 18, 1990. Retrieved November 22, 2013, from http://www.nytimes.com.

Shepherd, Cybill, with Aimee Lee Ball. *Cybill Disobedience: How I Survived Beauty Pageants, Elvis, Sex, Bruce Willis, Lies, Marriage, Motherhood, Hollywood, and the Irrepressible Urge to Say What I Think*. New York: HarperCollins, 2000.

Shevey, Sandra. "Playgirl Interview: Neil Simon." *Playgirl* 3.9 (1976): 56–141.

Sikorski, Fran. "Neil Simon Explains 'There Are Two of Me.'" *The Redding Pilot*, February 24, 1983. Retrieved November 25, 2013, from http://www.google.com/newspapers.

_____. "Neil Simon Explains 'There Are Two of Me.'" Part 2. *The Wilton Bulletin*, March 2, 1983. Retrieved November 25, 2013, from http://www.wiltonbulletin.com.

Sikov, Ed. *Mr. Strangelove: A Biography of Peter Sellers*. New York: Hyperion, 2002.

Silvers, Phil. *Screen test for The Sunshine Boys*. September 30, 1974. Viewed July 27, 2013, on YouTube.com.

Simon, Neil. *The Collected Plays of Neil Simon*. Vol. 1. New York: Plume, 1971.

_____. *The Collected Plays of Neil Simon*. Vol. 2. New York: Plume, 1979.

_____. *The Collected Plays of Neil Simon*. Vol. 3. New York: Random House, 1979.

_____. *The Collected Plays of Neil Simon*. Vol. 4. New York: Simon and Schuster, 1998.

_____. Interview. *The Merv Griffin Show*, January 12, 1967. Viewed November 29, 2013, on YouTube.com.

_____. Interview with Bill Boggs. Circa December

1977. Viewed November 29, 2013, on YouTube. com.

_____. Interview with Susan Haskins and Michael Riedel. *Theater Talk*, 1997. Viewed December 1, 2013, on YouTube.com.

_____. *Neil Simon's Lost in Yonkers: The Illustrated Screenplay of the Film.* New York: Newmarket, 1993.

_____. *The Play Goes On.* New York: Touchstone, 1999.

_____. *Rewrites.* New York: Simon and Schuster, 1996.

Smith, Maggie. "Dame Maggie." Interviewed by Steve Kroft for *60 Minutes* on February 17, 2013. Retrieved September 30, 2013, from http://www.YouTube.com.

Snyder, Stephen, and Howard Curle. *Vittorio De Sica: Contemporary Perspectives.* Toronto: University of Toronto Press, 2000.

Solomon, Aubrey. *Twentieth Century–Fox: A Corporate and Financial History.* The Scarecrow Filmmakers Series. New York: Scarecrow, 1988.

Spada, James. *The Films of Robert Redford.* New York: Citadel, 1984.

Sporkin, Elizabeth. "Kim and Alec Turn Up the Heat." *People.* April 22, 1991. Retrieved November 24, 2013, from http://www.people.com.

Stapleton, Maureen, and Jane Scovell. *A Hell of a Life: An Autobiography.* New York: Simon and Schuster, 1995.

Stein, Ruthe. "Lemmon-Matthau Spark Saves 'Couple.'" *San Francisco Chronicle,* April 10, 1998. Retrieved November 26, 2013, from http://www.sfgate.com.

Steinberg, Jay. "The Cheap Detective (1978)." *Turner Classic Movies.* Retrieved September 10, 2013, from http://www.tcm.com.

Stern, Keith. *Queers in History: The Comprehensive Encyclopedia of Historical Gays, Lesbians and Bisexuals.* New York: BenBella, 2013.

Stuart, Alexander. "The Out-Of-Towners: Neil Simon and Marsha Mason on Location with Chapter Two." *Films and Filming* 26.3 (1979): 21–24.

Taraborrelli, J. Randy. *Sinatra: Behind the Legend.* New York: Carol, 1997.

Taubman, Howard. "About 'The Odd Couple'..." *New York Times,* March 21, 1965. Retrieved May 18, 2013, from http://www.nytimes.com.

_____. "Neil Simon's 'Barefoot in the Park' Opens." *New York Times,* October 24, 1963. Retrieved May 9, 2013, from http://www.nytimes.com.

_____. "Theater: Caesar and Virginia Martin in 'Little Me'; Comedian Employs His Gifts for Mimicry: Neil Simon's Musical at the Lunt-Fontanne." *New York Times,* November 19, 1962. Retrieved October 24, 2013, from http://www.nytimes.com.

_____. "Theatre: Lively Comedy; 'Come Blow Your Horn' by Neil Simon Opens." *New York Times,* February 23, 1961. Retrieved October 24, 2013, from http://www.nytimes.com.

Taylor, John Russell. *Alec Guinness: A Celebration.* London: Pavilion, 2000.

Terrance. Vincent. *Encyclopedia of Television Pilots, 1937–2012.* Jefferson, NC: McFarland, 2013.

Thames, Stephanie. "Plaza Suite." *Turner Classic Movies.* Retrieved June 24, 2013, from http://www.tcm.com.

Thomas, Marlo. *Growing Up Laughing: My Story.* New York: Hyperion, 2011.

Thomas, Tony, and Aubrey Solomon. *The Films of 20th Century–Fox: A Pictorial History.* New York: Citadel, 1985.

Thompson, Kyra. *Carol Burnett: A Woman of Character.* American Masters. Thirteen/WNET New York Production, 2007.

Travers, Peter. "Lost in Yonkers." *Rolling Stone,* February 27, 2001. Retrieved November 18, 2013, from http://www.rollingstone.com.

Tucker, Ken. "TV Review: Neil Simon's Broadway Bound." *Entertainment Weekly,* March 20, 1992. Retrieved November 30, 2013, from http://www.ew.com.

Turner, Adrian. "Neil Simon's Manhattan Melodramas." In *The Movie: The Illustrated History of the Cinema.* Chapter 96: 1,906–1,908. New York: Macmillan, 1983.

_____. "The Odder Half. Walter Matthau." In *The Movie: The Illustrated History of the Cinema.* Chapter 96: 1,909–1,911. New York: Macmillan, 1983.

_____. "The Sunshine Boys." In *The Movie: The Illustrated History of the Cinema.* Chapter 96: 1,912–1,913. New York: Macmillan, 1983.

Vallely, Jean. "Richard Dreyfuss Building Back aka Richard Dreyfuss Out of Control." *Esquire Fortnightly* 90.8 (1978): 51–62.

Weber, Bruce. "Theatre Review: Simon's Hotel Rooms, Decorated with Nostalgia." *New York Times,* June 16, 2000. Retrieved November 21, 2013, from http://www.nytimes.com.

Weiler, A.H. "Film: A New Neil Simon: 'Prisoner of Second Avenue' Opens." *New York Times,* March 15, 1975. Retrieved July 21, 2013, from http://movies.nytimes.com.

_____. "'Star Spangled Girl' on the Screen." *New York Times,* December 23, 1971. Retrieved June 30, 2013, from http://www.nytimes.com.

Werts, Tom. *Alan King: Inside the Comedy Mind of Carl Reiner.* Kings Point Productions Inc./HBO Downtown Productions, 1990. DVD released by BFS Entertainment and Multimedia Limited, 2004.

_____. *Alan King: Inside the Comedy Mind of Charles Grodin.* Kings Point Productions Inc./HBO Downtown Productions, 1991. DVD released by BFS Entertainment and Multimedia Limited, 2004.

_____. *Alan King: Inside the Comedy Mind of George Burns.* Kings Point Productions Inc./HBO Downtown Productions, 1991. DVD released by BFS Entertainment and Multimedia Limited, 2004.

_____. *Alan King: Inside the Comedy Mind of Jack Lemmon.* Kings Point Productions Inc./HBO

Downtown Productions, 1991. DVD released by BFS Entertainment and Multimedia Limited, 2004.

_____. *Alan King: Inside the Comedy Mind of Mel Brooks*. Kings Point Productions Inc./HBO Downtown Productions, 1991. DVD released by BFS Entertainment and Multimedia Limited, 2004.

_____. *Alan King: Inside the Comedy Mind of Neil Simon*. Kings Point Productions Inc./HBO Downtown Productions, 1993. DVD released by BFS Entertainment and Multimedia Limited, 2004.

Widener, Don. *Lemmon: A Biography*. San Jose, CA: IUniverse, 2001.

Williams, John A. *If I Stop I'll Die: The Comedy and Tragedy of Richard Pryor*. New York: Thunder's Mouth, 1991.

Wilmington, Michael. "Movie Reviews: Shades of Love, Pain in 'Biloxi.'" *Los Angeles Times*, March 25, 1988. Retrieved November 14, 2013, from http://articles.latimes.com.

Wilson, Earl. *The Show Business Nobody Knows*. Chicago: Cowles, 1971.

_____. *Sinatra: An Unauthorized Biography*. New York: Macmillan, 1976.

Wilson, John. *The Official Razzie Movie Guide: Enjoying the Best of Hollywood's Worst*. London: Hachette UK, 2007.

Witchel, Alex. "At Breakfast With: Alec Baldwin; A Cup of Cappuccino Named Desire." *New York Times*, May 20, 1992. Retrieved November 24, 2013, from http://www.nytimes.com.

Wood, Bret. "The Out-of-Towners." *Turner Classic Movies*. Retrieved August 7, 2012, from http://www.tcm.com.

Woolley, Renee. *Charlie Rose Interviews Neil Simon*. December 24, 1997. Rose Communications. WNET New York. DVD released 2006.

Zimmerman, Paul D. "Neil Simon: Last of the Red Hot Playwrights." *Newsweek* 75.5 (1970): 52–56.

Index

Numbers in **bold italics** indicate pages with photographs.

DATE DUE	RETURNED